BITTER HARVEST

BITTER HARVEST

A MODERN
HISTORY
OF PALESTINE

Sami Hadawi
Foreword by Dr. John H. Davis

OLIVE
BRANCH
PRESS

An Imprint of Interlink Publishing Group, Inc.

NEW YORK

This fourth revised and updated edition was first published in 1991 by

Olive Branch Press
An imprint of Interlink Publishing Group, Inc.
99 Seventh Avenue
Brooklyn, New York 11215

Originally published in 1967 by The New World Press
First impression   – July 1967
Second impression – August 1967
Third impression   – October 1967
Second edition published in 1979 by Caravan Books
First impression   – July 1979
Second impression – May 1980
Third impression   – June 1982
Fourth impression – March 1983
Third edition published in 1990 by Olive Branch Press

Library of Congress Cataloging-in-Publication Data
Hadawi, Sami.
     Bitter harvest: a modern history of Palestine / Sami Hadawi;
     foreword by John H. Davis. — 4th rev. and updated ed.
     p.   cm.
     Includes bibliographical references and index.
     ISBN 0–940793–81–4 — ISBN 0–940793–76–8 (pbk.)
     1. Jewish-Arab relations—1917–   I. Title.
DS119.7.H3   1991
956.94—dc20   91–7951
                                                                          CIP

By the same author:

Palestine: Loss of a Heritage   (1963)
The Palestine Diary 1914–1945   (1970) – co-authored
The Palestine Diary 1945–1948   (1970) – co-authored
The Village Statistics 1945   (1970) – edited
Crime and no Punishment 1939–1972 (1972)
Palestinian Rights and Losses in 1948 (1988)
The Realities of Terrorism and Retaliation (1989)

Printed and bound in the United States of America

"O Country and Home,
Never, never may I be without you,
Living the hapless life
Hard to pass through and painful,
Most pitiable of all,
Let death first lay me low, and
Death free me from this daylight,
There is no sorrow above
The loss of a native land."

Euripides
485–406 B.C.

DEDICATION

To the loving memory of those Palestinians
who fell victims of aggression in defense of
their homeland and to the future generations
of Palestinians lest they forget what they
lost and how they lost it!

Table of Contents

PART III

APPENDICES

Foreword

by *John H. Davis B.A., M.A., Ph.D.*
Former Commissioner-General of United Nations Relief and Works Agency (UNRWA) for Palestine Refugees in the Near East

I RECOMMEND this book as important reading for everyone interested in the subject of Arab-Israeli conflict; a struggle that even pre-dates the establishment of Israel as a State by more than thirty years. Mr. Hadawi is an educated Palestine Arab who as a young man distinguished himself in the service of the Mandate Government of Palestine. Then after becoming a refugee in 1948 he lived for a number of years in the United States where he travelled extensively and spoke to hundreds of American audiences. Drawing on this valuable experience Mr. Hadawi has set forth here what he believes Americans and others want to know and need to know, but what, in fact, few do know about the problem.

The fundamental issue on which Arab-Israeli conflict now centers and has centered is on the basic claims and rights of two peoples in Palestine. The author of this book has attempted to chronicle the major events of the fifty year struggle over such claims and rights in a manner that is factual, well written and well documented. In doing this, he, of course, has included an explanation as to how these events and happenings are viewed by Arab people. It is this, in fact, that enhances the value of the book, since so little has been written from this standpoint. Adding further to the merit of the publication is the objectivity with which the author views the total problem and the absence of bitterness toward the Jews as people or Judaism as a religion.

The reading of this book will add to one's depth of understanding of the subject and particularly of the thinking and feelings of tens of millions of Arab people, scattered throughout the Middle East.

Preface

WHEN MY BOOK *Palestine: Loss of a Heritage* appeared in 1963, many of my friends urged me to follow it up with a second book presenting the Arab point of view on various aspects of the Palestine problem.

They pointed out that, while many worthy books have already been written on the subject by impartial non-Arab authors, an Arab answer to Zionist and Israeli allegations and accusations would shed significant light on the thorny problem. Many objective writers had felt morally committed to disclose the injustices inflicted upon the Palestine Arabs. These recognized the dangers inherent in the foreign policy of the state of Israel: dangers that threaten the Jews living in Israel, the national interests of Jews who are citizens of other countries, the stability of the vital and strategically situated oil-rich region of the Middle East, and finally the peace of the world.

This book is no malicious attack on those who broke faith with the Arabs for independence after World War I; or on those who for either material benefits or political advantages used methods that James Forrestal, former U.S. Secretary of Defense, described as "bordering closely onto scandal;" or even on those who took advantage of human weaknesses and reached their goal no matter what the cost to other people. It is a chronicle of events that make up the Palestine tragedy.

The Palestine tragedy needs thorough investigating. People of goodwill should get to the truth of the matter; fix responsibility for the crimes committed against humanity; and adopt the long overdue measures of righting the wrong and bringing 'peace with justice' to the Holy Land — the land which has done so much to bring humanity to God.

The first edition of *Bitter Harvest* went into three printings, and was translated into Italian and German. Despite the fact that it was not possible — for obvious reasons — to place the book on the shelves of bookstores in Western countries, orders — particularly from educational institutions and students — kept coming in even after the book had gone out of print. To meet these demands, and the proddings of my friends, I agreed to issue a second edition.

More than twenty years have passed since *Bitter Harvest* first appeared, and much has happened since then. To attempt to deal with it all in chronological order, would require a second volume, which is not my intention. I therefore decided to reprint with changes in the original text by retaining what I considered essential; eliminating material that I felt had served its purpose; bringing up-to-date others; and adding topics that have since arisen.

The second edition (of 1979) went into four printings and was translated into Arabic. A third revised and updated edition was published for the first time in the U.S.A. in 1990. Once more, I am now urged to update and publish a fourth edition after copies of the previous edition became no longer available.

In the third and fourth editions, the text of the second edition has remained intact in order to serve as a historical record of events.

Part VIII updates the events surrounding the Palestine problem since the Israeli invasion of Lebanon in 1982 and the Intifada (Uprising) which began in December 1987 in the occupied territories of the West Bank and the Gaza Strip and is still going on. It also draws attention to the various peace plans that have been suggested as solutions, and discusses the Gulf crisis and the inequities of U.S. double-standard policies in the region.

Sami Hadawi
Toronto, Canada 1991

I Introduction

It is not the first time in history that partition has been resorted to as a solution to a problem. In ancient times, King Solomon ruled: If you cannot give one child to each of the two who claim to be the mother, then split the child into two and give half to one and the second half to the other.

An analogous scene was re-enacted in Palestine three thousand years later, except that the wisdom of Solomon in the judgment was lacking in this case. Like the false mother who welcomed the bisection of the child who was not hers, the Zionists accepted partition of the Holy Land because it gave them something they did not own and to which they were not entitled in justice or in equity.

Partition of countries against the will of the people is not only wrong in principle; it has been proved to be inhuman too. Wherever applied, partition has brought tragedy, destruction and suffering to millions of human beings. War came to Korea only because of the partition of the land into North and South; and the fierce battles that raged for ten years in South Vietnam with the loss of hundreds of thousands of lives and considerable destruction, came to an end only after the North and South were reunited. Although conditions of partitioned Germany appear normal at present, there is no guarantee that at some future date a leader will not arise in the country to demand the return to unity and thereby ignite another world war.

The powers that resist the will of the people of these three countries to unity and impose upon them a partition that can only be maintained by force of arms, are the same powers that have inflicted the tragedy of partition on Palestine, with one additional iniquity—they first gave equal validity to the *claim* of the Zionists to Palestine and the *right* of the Arabs to their homeland in order to justify their plan of partition, then went to a step further by encouraging the dislodgement of the Arabs from their homes and property.

After thirty years of tribulation and suffering, the world has come to recognize the error of its judgment in partitioning the Holy Land in 1947; but there is nothing that can be done to remove the evil that has been unleashed upon a peaceful people and a land held sacred by the adherents of the three great faiths. The least that can now be done is to undo the injustice by recognizing that a wrong has been committed against an innocent people and to redress it in a just manner.

There is probably no subject fraught with so many distortions and misrepresentations as the Palestine problem. It has been widely discussed, debated, lectured upon and written about in the past six decades, but still it is far from being correctly understood.

Early in this period, the Zionists succeeded in shaping world opinion into the belief that Palestine was their "Promised Land;" that it was their "historical" homeland; that it was a country without a people and the Jews were a people without a country; and that Jewish endeavor and skill would bring civilization and prosperity to the few "nomad" (bedouin) Arabs who roamed its countryside.

With unerring skill, the Zionists adapted their arguments to the special circumstances of each situation: They appealed to the Christians, using biblical language to awaken in them deep emotional undertones; to the humanitarians, urging a permanent solution of the vexatious Jewish problem; to the anti-semites, showing the way to get rid of the Jew from their midst; and to lure British politicians, an extension of imperial power was vividly portrayed through the establishment of a Jewish commonwealth in Palestine.

The thirty years that followed the vague and ambiguous promise the Zionists were able to extract from the British Government in 1917 "to view with favor the establishment in Palestine of a national home for the Jewish people," was a period of sweat and blood for the indigenous Arab inhabitants as they tried to defend their homes and homeland against an invasion the nature of which is unprecedented in the annals of modern history.

There are many, while still sympathetic to and concerned about the fate of world Jewry, who have begun to doubt the morality and justice of the Zionist claim to Palestine. The dangerous situation existing in the Middle East and its effect on world peace, has aroused deep suspicion in the minds of many as to the wisdom of continuing the hitherto unqualified moral, financial and military support of the "Jewish state."

It is now suspected that something is basically wrong; that people have been deliberately kept in the dark and given distorted facts; that the stability and peace of the vital Middle East area are at stake.

World opinion has been led to believe that the Palestine problem is a conflict between Israel and the Arab States over the sovereignty of territory that the Arab States regard as part of the Arab homeland. The Israelis, on the other hand, claim Palestine as theirs by reason of the Balfour Declaration of 1917, the United Nations Partition Resolution of 1947, subsequent military conquests and what is commonly referred to as the "Biblical Promises." In other words, it is presumed to be a territorial dispute between nations, similar in some respects to the dispute between India and Pakistan over Kashmir.

This Zionist approach is not without a motive. It is intended to confuse the issue and to obliterate the memories of the crimes committed against the Palestine Arabs—crimes which have been described by British historian Arnold Toynbee as no less heinous than the Nazi crimes against the Jews. Its purpose is also to by-pass standing United Nations resolutions calling upon the Israelis to surrender the extra territory they occupied by force of arms beyond the area assigned to the "Jewish state" under the Partition Plan of 1947; to give the refugees the choice between repatriation and compensation; and to permit the internationalization of Jerusalem. To label the conflict as a dispute between nations, divests it of its human and just elements and puts it in the same category as other world territorial issues where the parties proffer claims and counter-claims perhaps of equal strength.

The truth of the matter is that the Palestine problem must be called first and foremost a dispute between the Palestine Arabs and the Jews before it can be labelled as an Arab states-Israeli conflict. The issue is fundamentally one of individual rights and principles, as well as of territory and must be treated as a moral and political issue.

No matter what language diplomacy uses in defining the rights of the Palestine Arabs, the fact remains that the major portion of the territory now called "Israel" is legitimately owned by individual Arabs. Their rights derive from the universally accepted principle that a country belongs to its indigenous inhabitants. The fact that the Arabs fled in terror, because of real fear of a repetition of the 1948 Zionist massacres, is no reason for denying them their homes, fields and livelihoods. Civilians caught in an area of military activity generally panic. But they have always been able to return to their homes when the danger subsides. Military conquest does not abolish private rights to property; nor does it entitle the victor to confiscate the homes, property and personal belongings of the non-combatant civilian population. The seizure of Arab property by the Israelis was an outrage. It was described by many distinguished writers as "robbery."

The position of the Arab states fully supports the Palestine Arabs' demand for rights to homes and country. Any solution agreed to by the Palestine Arabs would be acceptable to the Arab states. Conversely, the Arab states cannot conclude a settlement that is unacceptable to the Palestine Arabs.

A solution of the Palestine problem, however, does not necessarily mean a settlement of the Arab states-Israeli conflict. While the former may have some influence on the latter, the Arab states-Israeli conflict arises out of the danger that Zionist ambitions for expansion poses to the territorial integrity of the Arab States. Israel's mass immigration policy and land acquisition goals constitute a serious threat to the peace and stability of the Middle East region. Israeli leaders have repeatedly declared the need for a larger land area. Actions, such as the planned invasion of Egypt in 1956 and the attempted annexation of the Sinai Peninsula and the Gaza Strip territory—which inspired David Ben Gurion to proclaim the areas as having been "freed" and "liberated"—

provide ample proof of Israeli future aspirations. This policy has been further confirmed by the June 1967 War and Israeli refusal since to withdraw from occupied territories.

It will be recalled that as early as 1948, the late UN mediator Count Folke Bernadotte—who was assassinated by the Israelis because of his recommendations for a solution of the Palestine problem not in conformity with Israeli policy—warned the Security Council: "It could not be ignored that unrestricted immigration to the Jewish area of Palestine might, over a period of years, give rise to a population pressure and to economic and political disturbances which would justify present Arab fears of ultimate Jewish expansion in the Near East." He added: "It can scarcely be ignored that Jewish immigration into the Jewish area of Palestine concerns not only the Jewish people and territory but also the neighboring Arab world."[1]

It would, indeed, be suicidal for the Arab states to relax their vigilance and allow themselves to be deceived by the Jekyll and Hyde image of the Zionist-Israel character. While the Israelis claim they want peace, they are actually preparing all the time for war. If expansion is not their ultimate aim, what is the meaning of David Ben Gurion's statement: "To maintain the *status quo* will not do. We have set up a dynamic state, bent upon expansion"?[2] This ambition he reiterated in 1952 when he said: "Israel . . . has been established in only a portion of the land of Israel. Even those who are dubious as to the restoration of the historical frontiers, as fixed and crystallized from the beginning of time, will hardly deny the anomaly of the boundaries of the new State."[3]

If these statements by the architect of the "Jewish state" can be waved aside as pure fantasy, the declaration of the leader of the *Herut* Party—the second largest in the Israeli Parliament and which claimed credit for the ousting of the British from Palestine—confirms Zionist intentions that expansion is always their goal. He said: "I deeply believe in launching preventive war against the Arab states without further hesitation. By doing so, we will achieve two targets: firstly, the annihilation of Arab power; and secondly, the expansion of our territory."[4]

This latter declaration by Menachem Begin was implemented in 1967 with the invasion and occupation of the Sinai Peninsula and the Gaza Strip, the Golan Heights and the West Bank of Jordan.

Many were the Zionist promises and declarations that sought to lull the Arabs into a false sense of security and to mislead world opinion. When the Zionists promoted settlement of the Holy Land in 1920 as a result of the Balfour Declaration, they spoke lavishly of their goodwill toward their Arab neighbors and of the many skills and advantages they would bestow upon the country. For example, at the Zionist Congress in 1921, a resolution was passed that "solemnly declared the desire of the Jewish people to live with the Arab people in relations of friendship and mutual respect and, together with the Arab people, to develop the homeland common to both into a prosperous community which would ensure the growth of the peoples."[5]

The world has seen how, thirty years later, the Arab people of Palestine benefitted from Jewish immigration by expulsions and dispossessions under the most cruel conditions. Instead of peace and tranquility, the Holy Land has been turned into a battlefield; the Middle East is now a cauldron of unrest and instability; misery, hatred and bitterness prevail where previously there was harmony and friendship between Arab and Jew.

During this period, the Zionist-Israeli propaganda machine succeeded in convincing world public opinion that the Palestine tragedy was really a territorial dispute between the neighboring Arab states and Israel, with the latter determined to "push the Jews into the sea" and "annihilate the State of Israel." At the same time, it branded the Palestine Liberation Organization as a terrorist organization that murders innocent Jews to no advantage.

In this way, the Zionists have been able to divert attention from the crimes committed against the Palestinians first as Zionists during the period of the Mandate, and then as Israelis after the establishment of the Jewish State. Furthermore, they have been able to win sympathy for Israel as a so-called peace-loving nation that is a victim of Arab aggression; and to raise funds through the United Jewish Appeal and the sale of Israeli Bonds to exploit usurped Arab homes and Arab lands.

To the Israelis, peace means recognition by the Arab states of Israeli sovereignty over existing Israeli-occupied territory; the removal of the Arab boycott; the opening of the Suez Canal to Israeli shipping; and Arab acquiescence in the diversion of the waters of the River Jordan even though it is to the detriment of Arab rights and interests. By achieving these objectives, the Israelis hope to improve their economy and provide greater man-power through new immigrants, for ultimate realization of their dream of an "empire" from the "Nile to the Euphrates." As for the Palestine Arabs whom they expelled and dispossessed, this is a matter they claim, which was the result of alleged Arab aggression against the Jewish state. Such being the case, they say, it is for the Arab governments, not Israel, to find a home for the Palestine Arabs.

Peace, in order to be real, has to be based on justice and equity. Ironically, Israel, while claiming to have a right to exist by reason of an act of the United Nations, refuses to honor her responsibilities to the organization that created it. According to a declaration by David Ben Gurion in 1953 Israel "considers the United Nations resolution of November 29, 1947, as null and void."[6] If the Israelis are permitted to discard the United Nations resolution that gave birth to their state, by the same token Arab refusal to recognize the existence of the Jewish state is fully justified.

True and durable peace can come to the area only when the Israelis agree to withdraw entirely from occupied territories, including East Jerusalem; give adequate guarantees that they will no longer pose a threat to Arab lands; and sit and negotiate with the Palestine Liberation Organization as the representative of the Palestinian people on ways and means of settling their differences.

"Only an internal revolution," wrote Israeli Nathan Chofshi from Tel Aviv, "can have the power to heal our people of their murderous sickness of baseless hatred [for the Arabs]. It is bound to bring eventual ruin upon us. Only then will the old and the young in our land realize how great was our responsibility to those miserable wronged Arab refugees in whose towns we have settled Jews who were brought from afar; whose homes we have inherited, whose fields we now sow and harvest; the fruit of whose gardens, orchards and vineyards we gather; and in whose cities that we robbed, we put up houses of education, charity and prayer, while we babble and rave about our being the 'People of the Book' and the 'Light of the Nations.'"[7]

II Historical Background

The Land and the People

The territory of Palestine covers a total area of 10,435 square miles and is about the size of Vermont or about one and one-half times the size of Wales in the United Kingdom.

The land area comprises 10,163 square miles (about 6,589,755 acres) and the water area 272 square miles. The latter includes what used to be Lake Huleh (5 square miles), Lake Tiberias or the Sea of Galilee (62 square miles) and half of the area of the Dead Sea (405 square miles). The other half was in what used to be Transjordan.

Palestine was largely an agricultural country. Generally speaking it may be divided into four distinct soil regions:

(a) *The coastal plains*—These consist of first-class fertile land with an abundance of underground water and a plentiful rainfall. The plains have always been highly developed and contained large stretches of citrus groves.

(b) *The hill region*—This region is predominantly rocky, but with proper terracing is suitable for the planting of deciduous trees. The olive is its principal crop. In winter, the large patches of land are cultivated with wheat and barley; and in summer, corn, tomatoes and other vegetables, are grown under dry-farming cultivation.

(c) *The Jordan Valley*—This region lies below sea-level where the soil is good for any kind of cultivation, including citrus and tropical fruits. But owing to lack of sufficient rainfall, cultivation must necessarily depend on irrigation from streams or pumped from the River Jordan.

(d) *The Southern Desert (Negev)*—This region comprises nearly half the lands of Palestine (3,144,246 acres). The northern portion (some 640,000 acres) consists of good soil and is suitable for irrigation. The southern portion (2,500,000 acres) running from about five miles south of Beer-sheba to its apex at the Gulf of Aqaba—except for small sporadically distributed localities totalling some 90,000 acres suitable for patch culti-vation and only in years when there is sufficient rainfall—consists of deeply eroded uplands and rift valleys.

Public opinion has been led to believe that Palestine was a neglected, desolate land without a people in need of a people without a country and that all developments and progress were the result of Zionist initiative and skill. This is not true.

The Holy Land, since the Crusades, has been renowned for its olive groves and olive oil industry; and long before large-scale Zionist immi-gration began in 1920, Palestine was known as a citrus exporting country, famous for the *Jaffa Orange*. It is unknown when the citrus industry was first developed in Palestine, but the record shows that in 1912–1913, the Arabs had exported 1,608,570 cases of oranges to Europe for a cost of $1,488,500.[1]

As regards the hill regions, the country is covered with olive or-chards, vineyards and other deciduous fruit trees; while the lands in the South were used for the cultivation of grain, and those in the Jordan Valley for the production of vegetables and fruits. Every inch of fertile soil was used to full capacity; and more and more rocky patches were being turned into orchards and groves. A visit to the village of Qalqilya, in the occupied West Bank, which lost all its citrus groves to the Israelis in 1948, will surprise the visitor how once dead or marginal land has been revived and turned into citrus groves and other plantations—all this without outside financial help and is a credit to the tenacity and skill of the Arab farmer.

Arab-Jewish Relations in History

According to Moslem doctrine, Christians and Jews are regarded as "People of the Book," believers in God, revelation and the day of judgment. As such, they are not to be persecuted or forced to become Moslems. No attempt was made to subject them to the Moslem legal code; they were left free to regulate their own communal and personal life in accordance with their own religious laws.

In general, the principles of Islam were obeyed and in consequence the Jewish community in the different Arab countries flourished throughout the centuries of medieval Arab rule. Although they pre-served much of their exclusiveness, they became Arabized in their language and culture. In the history of Jewish culture the Arabic period is among the happiest and most brilliant. In Spain, in Egypt and elsewhere, the Arabized Jews not only carried on their own life of devotion and learning, but contributed to the general Arabic civilization. In science, medicine, scholarship and speculative thought, Jews helped to enrich the literature of the Arabic tongue; and individual Jews were able to reach the highest positions in the State.

With the fall of Arab power in Spain, North Africa and the Arab Middle East became places of refuge and a haven for the persecuted Jews of Spain and elsewhere, where they could pursue their daily lives in perfect freedom and equality.

Thus, one can leaf through the pages of Middle East history and survey many eras of civilization and still find the same story of mutual respect between Arabs and Jews. In the Holy Land, as elsewhere in Arab lands, they lived together in harmony, a harmony only disrupted when the Zionists began to claim that Palestine was the "rightful" possession of the "Jewish people" to the exclusion of its Moslem and Christian inhabitants. Before the advent of Zionism, an atmosphere of goodwill prevailed on all sides in the Holy Land. No community trespassed on the rights of another and each worshipped the One God in its own way.

The first signs of unrest between Arab and Jew occurred in 1920 when Zionist designs on the Holy Land became apparent. Riots broke out in Jerusalem on Easter Sunday in April of that year, as a result of which many people on both sides, who had recently been living on the best of terms, lost their lives needlessly. This initiated the deterioration of Arab-Jewish relations. As Zionism pushed its mass immigration policy, started an extensive campaign of purchasing Arab lands and excluding Arab labor from orange groves and Jewish enterprises, relations between the two communities became more and more strained, erupting from time to time into bloody disturbances. There followed the riots of 1921, 1926; and in 1929, the most severe disturbances occurred throughout the country, resulting in much damage to property and loss of life. After that period, the Jews isolated themselves into separate areas and began to build up their underground forces to "seize" the country in due time. From then on, there was little intercourse between the two communities as each drifted its own way, one to plan how to occupy the country, the other to make a feeble effort to defend what rightfully belongs to it.

Notwithstanding what happened in Palestine, and the efforts of the Zionist/Israeli propaganda machine to disrupt the friendly relations that existed between the Arab and Jewish communities in other Arab countries, these relations have not been affected. Significant in this respect is the testimony of Gottfried Neubruger, a prominent member of the American Jewish community who visited the Arab world in 1960. One of the conclusions he drew from his visit was, "Arab anti-Zionism is about universal, yet I feel," he said, "that it is a basic fallacy and a grave error to equate this with anti-Semitism." He added, "The majority of the population of such countries as Egypt, Tunisia and Morocco, where Jew and Moslem have long lived side by side, is intuitively friendly to Jews. This does not diminish the fact that those same Arabs are strongly hostile to Israel and are deeply suspicious of Israeli future aims and activities . . ."[3]

British War Pledges of Arab Independence (1915–1916)

The World War I "war aims" of the Allies in Arab territories, as explicitly expressed from time to time in a number of official declarations and pronouncements, were: ". . . guaranteeing their liberation and the development of their civilization;" to establish, "national governments and administrations deriving their authority from the initiative and the free choice of the native population;" to recognize Arab independence as soon as "effectively established;" and "to ensure impartial and equal justice to all, to facilitate the economic development of the country . . . to foster the spread of education . . ."[4]

Point XII of President Wilson's famous address of January 8, 1918, was devoted to the Ottoman Empire. The following is pertinent to Palestine: "The Turkish portions of the present Ottoman Empire should be assured a secure sovereignty, but the other nationalities that are under Turkish rule should be assured an undoubted security of life and an absolutely unmolested opportunity of autonomous development . . ."[5]

With the outbreak of World War I, the Arabs saw their chance to rid themselves of Turkish domination and regain their political independence. Sherif Hussein of Mecca, as spokesman for the Arab cause, approached Sir Henry McMahon, British High Commissioner in Cairo, on July 14, 1915, offering Arab aid in the war against Turkey if Britain would, in return, pledge its support of Arab independence within a certain territory that he specified as ". . . bounded on the north by Mersina and Ádana up to the 37° of lattitude, on which degree fall Birijik, Urfa, Mardin, Midiat, Jezirat [Ibn'Umar], Amadia, up to the border of Persia; on the east by the borders of Persia up to the Gulf of Basra; on the south by the Indian Ocean, with the exception of the position of Aden to remain as it is; on the west by the Red sea, the Mediterranean Sea up to Mersina."[6]

A correspondence—later known as the Hussein-McMahon Correspondence—consisting of ten letters, was exchanged during the period July 1915 to March 1916, culminating in a British promise of Arab independence as follows:

> "The two districts of Mersina and Alexandretta and portions of Syria lying to the west of the districts of Damascus, Homs, Hama and Aleppo cannot be said to be purely Arab and should be excluded from the limits demanded.
> "With the above modification and without prejudice to our existing treaties with Arab chiefs, we accept those limits."

McMahon went on to say, "As for these regions lying within those frontiers wherein Great Britain is free to act without detriment to the interest of her ally France, I am empowered in the name of the Government of Great Britain to give the following assurances and make the following reply to your letter:

> "Subject to the above modifications, Great Britain is prepared to recognize and support the independence of the Arabs in all the regions within the limits demanded by the Sherif of Mecca."*

---

*The British Government later contended that Palestine was *not* included in the British pledge of Arab independence and claimed that the area cited as being *"west* of the line Damascus, Homs, Hama, and Aleppo," was excluded.

A Committee was formed in 1939 to study the *Correspondence*. Sir Michael McDonell, former Chief Justice of Palestine, expressed the opinion that "Palestine *was* included," otherwise why "speak of the districts of Damascus, Homs, Hama and Aleppo, not one of which is east of Palestine and all of which go northward in that order away from Palestine?" "Why say

The Sykes-Picot Agreement (1916)

Before the ink was dry on the British pledge of Arab independence, the British government was busy negotiating secretly with the French and Russian governments for the division among themselves of the Asiatic provinces of the Ottoman Empire after victory.

The Agreement—named after the two main negotiators—roughly provided, in the Arab areas, for:

(a) an independent Arab state or a confederation of Arab states in a part of what is now geographically known as Saudi Arabia and Yemen;

(b) France in Lebanon and Syria, and Britain in Iraq and Trans-jordan, "to establish such direct or indirect administration or control as they may desire and as they may deem fit to establish after agreement with the Arab States or Confederation of Arab States;"

(c) Parts of Palestine to be placed under "an international administration of which the form will be decided upon after consultation with Russia and after subsequent agreement with the other Allies and the representatives of the Sherif of Mecca."[8]

Analyzing the provisions of the Agreement, George Antonius, an Arab authority on the subject, said of it: "What the Sykes-Picot Agreement did was, first, to cut up the Arab rectangle in such a manner as to place artificial obstacles in the way of unity. . . . Whatever gains the Allied Powers may have hoped to derive from the partition of that territory, it showed a lack of perspicacity on their part to have imagined that it could make for peaceful or lasting settlement."

"Another peculiarity of the Agreement," said Antonius, "was that it provided for a topsy-turvy political structure in which the first were to come last and the last first. The inhabitants of Syria and Iraq," he pointed out, "were politically more developed and mature than the inhabitants of the inland regions. Yet the Agreement provided that the greater part of Syria and Iraq might be placed under a regime of direct foreign administration, while the inland regions were in any case to form independent Arab States. The absurdity of these provisions is particularly evident in the case of the regions destined to form the British sphere of influence."

"But more serious even than those errors of judgment, was the breach of faith, Antonius added. "The Agreement," he said, "had been negotiated and concluded without the knowledge of the Sherif Hussein

---

nothing," he enquired, "of the Sanjaqs of Hauran and Maan to the west of which the whole of Palestine lies? Why not," he continued, "if Palestine was to be described, speak of Lake Huleh, the River Jordan, the Lake of Tiberias and the Dead Sea as the eastern boundaries?"

Sir Michael then remarked, "To suggest that an area of the size of Palestine and of the importance of the Holy Land, if not excluded by the act that it did not lie west of the districts of Damascus, Homs, Hama and Aleppo, was intended to be excluded by a side wind by the reference to the interests of France which, at the very time, the British Government was refusing to admit, is an argument that will not hold water."

The Committee's findings were: "In the opinion of the Committee, it is, however, evident from these statements that His Majesty's Government were not free to dispose of Palestine without regard for the wishes and interests of the inhabitants of Palestine and that these statements must all be taken into account in any attempt to estimate the responsibilities which—upon any interpretation of the Correspondence—His Majesty's Government have incurred towards these inhabitants as a result of the Correspondence."[7]

and it contained provisions that were in direct conflict with the terms of Sir Henry McMahon's compact with him. Worse still, the fact of its conclusion was dishonestly concealed from him because it was realized that, were he to have been apprised of it, he would have unhesitatingly denounced his alliance with Great Britain."

Antonius described the Agreement as "a shocking document," adding, "it is not only the product of greed at its worst, that is to say, of greed allied to suspicion and so leading to stupidity; it also stands out as a startling piece of double-dealing."[9]

Others also condemned the Agreement, but naturally for different reasons. Lord Curzon said of it: "When the Sykes-Picot Agreement was drawn up, it was, no doubt, intended by its authors . . . as a sort of fancy sketch to suit a situation that had not then arisen and which it was thought extremely unlikely would ever arise; that, I suppose must be the principal explanation of the gross ignorance with which the boundary lines in that Agreement were drawn."[10]

Lloyd George, then Prime Minister, without whose approval the Agreement could not have been concluded, nevertheless described it as "'a foolish document' and thought it 'inexplicable that a man of Sir Mark Sykes' fine intelligence should ever have appended his signature to such an arrangement.'"[11]

The Balfour Declaration (1917)

Since 1897, when the Zionist movement was officially launched, Theodor Herzl and his collaborators were intent on the establishment of a Jewish state in Palestine. Herzl then declared: "Let the sovereignty be granted us over a portion of the globe large enough to satisfy the rightful requirements of a nation; the rest we shall manage for ourselves . . ."[12]

The outbreak of World War I gave the Zionists their opportunity: 1916 was a disastrous year for the Allies: Losses on the western front were three men for every two German casualties, while German submarines were taking a heavy toll of Allied shipping. The Allies' only hope was for the United States to enter the war on their side.

Into this gloomy picture walked James Malcolm, an Oxford-educated Armenian who had many contacts in high British circles. He was particularly friendly with Sir Mark Sykes of the Foreign Office. Sir Mark told him that the Cabinet was looking anxiously for U.S. Government intervention in the war. Malcolm replied: "You are going the wrong way about it. You can win sympathy of certain politically minded Jews everywhere, and especially in the United States, in one way only and that is, by offering to try and secure Palestine for them."[13]

From then things began to move. Louis Brandeis, U.S. Supreme Court Judge and a personal confidant of Woodrow Wilson, was influenced to win over the President; and in April 1917, the United States entered the war on the side of the Allies. On November 2, 1917, British Foreign Minister Arthur Balfour issued his ill-fated Declaration that now bears his name.

The part played by the Zionists in bringing the United States into the War has been referred to on many occasions. It is supported by the following admissions:

Winston Churchill—"The Balfour Declaration must, therefore, not be regarded as a promise given from sentimental motives; it was a practical measure taken in the interests of a common cause at a moment when that cause could afford to neglect no factor of material or moral assistance."[14]

Lloyd George—"There is no better proof of the value of the Balfour Declaration *as a military move* than the fact that Germany entered into negotiations with Turkey in an endeavour to provide an alternative scheme which would appeal to Zionists."[15] Appearing before the Palestine Royal (Peel) Commission in 1937, Lloyd George was more explicit as to the reasons that prompted his Government to grant the Balfour Declaration. Paragraph 16 of the Report has the following entry:

"The Zionist leaders (Mr. Lloyd George informed us) gave us a definite promise that, if the Allies committed themselves to giving facilities for the establishment of a national home for the Jews in Palestine, they would do their best to rally Jewish sentiment and support throughout the world to the Allied cause. They kept their word."[16]

The text of the Balfour Declaration, issued on November 2, 1917[17] in the form of a letter addressed to Edmond de Rothschild, may be divided into three parts:

The *first*, applicable to the Jews, provided: "His Majesty's Government view with favor the establishment in Palestine of a national home for the Jewish people and will use their best endeavors to facilitate the achievement of this object."

The *second* affecting the rights and position of the Moslem and Christian inhabitants, stipulated: "It being clearly understood that nothing shall be done which may prejudice the civil and religious rights of existing non-Jewish communities in Palestine."

The *third*, referring to the position of Jews outside Palestine, ruled: "The rights and political status enjoyed by Jews in any other country" shall not be prejudiced by "the establishment in Palestine of a national home for the Jewish people." This latter protective clause gave the Jews the homeland of another people while safeguarding their own rights in their countries of origin!

Reading through the *second* safeguarding clause, it will be observed that the Moslem and Christian inhabitants are mentioned in such a way as to give an entirely false picture of their position in the country and their indubitable right to it. Although constituting, in 1917, 92% of the population, they were referred to as "the existing non-Jewish communities of Palestine." This tended to give the erroneous impression that they were an insignificant minority occupying a position subordinate to the Jews. This clause, by purporting to protect the rights of the Arabs as "the existing non-Jewish communities," in reality aimed at robbing them in due course (as did actually happen) of their right to the country as owners and inhabitants.

But leaving aside this deception and looking at the implications of the safeguarding clause, there is only one possible inference that can be drawn from it and only one possible judgment that can be passed on it, that it was sufficient to nullify the rest of the Declaration. The British Government should have known that what the Zionists wanted would have constituted a disastrous encroachment on Arab rights in Palestine. In effect what the British Government had promised was to help the Zionists achieve their aim, provided that nothing was done to enable them to achieve it! In practice, the British Government eventually fulfilled its first obligation and neglected to protect the rights of the Arab inhabitants.

Arabs Reassured of Fulfillment of War Promises (1918)

The Arabs were unaware that the British Government, after promising to support Arab independence, had concluded two secret agreements that conflicted with Arab aspirations—The Sykes-Picot Agreement, dividing Arab territories between Britain and France; and the Balfour Declaration signing away to the Jews Arab rights in Palestine. The texts of the two instruments were disclosed by the Bolsheviks on coming to power in 1917, and widely publicized by the Turkish military commander as a sign of British betrayal of pledges to the Arabs.

The disclosure caused great anxiety in Arab circles and the Sherif Hussein requested from the British Government an explanation. The assurances given at various times did not convince the Arabs yet they continued the fight against the Turks. These were:

(1) *The Hogarth Message* of January 1918—An explicit assurance was given that "Jewish settlement in Palestine would only be allowed in so far as would be consistent with the political and economic freedom of the Arab population."[18] The phrase, "the political and economic freedom of the population" is very significant in that it represented a fundamental departure from the text of the Balfour Declaration that purported to guarantee only the "civil and religious rights" of the Arab population and, as will be readily seen, offered a guarantee of Arab independence and sovereignty, which the phrase used in the Balfour Declaration did not.

(2) *The Bassett Letter* of February 8, 1918—This was another reassurance that "His Majesty's Government and their allies remain steadfast to the policy of helping any movement which aims at setting free those nations which are oppressed . . ." The letter went on to say, "The Government of His Britannic Majesty repeats its previous promise in respect of the freedom and the emancipation of the Arab people."[19]

(3) *The British Declaration to the Seven* of June 16, 1918. This declaration confirmed previous British pledges to the Arabs in plainer language than in former public utterances. The Declaration referred to the proclamations read in Baghdad and Jerusalem on March 19 and December 9, 1917, respectively and stated that these proclamations "define the policy of His Majesty's Government towards the inhabitants . . . which is that the future government . . . should be based upon the principle of the consent of the governed. This policy will always be that of His Majesty's Government."[20]

(4) *The Anglo-French Declaration* of November 9, 1918—if there had

been any doubt in the minds of the Arabs, these were dispelled by this last Declaration: "France and Great Britain agree to further and assist in setting up indigenous governments and administrations in Syria [which then included Palestine] and Mesopotamia [Iraq]."[21]

Arab Contribution in World War I

With these assurances and affirmations, the Arab war against the Turks went on with greater vigor and determination.

The most important contribution of the Arabs in the war was the occupation on July 6, 1916 of the strategic town of Aqaba. Until then the British army had been unable to cross the Suez Canal and to advance into the Sinai Peninsula. The British High Command were unaware of the Arab attack and occupation of Aqaba until T.E. Lawrence informed them during a subsequent visit to Cairo.

And what followed was no less significant. The Arab army continued to harass enemy lines of communication and to attack on all fronts along the Hejaz railway from Medina to Damascus. The extent of the Arab contribution to allied victory was summed up by Capt. Liddell Hart, Chief Military Commentator with the Allied Forces at the time. He wrote:

"In the crucial weeks while Allenby's stroke was being prepared and during its delivery, nearly half of the Turkish forces south of Damascus were distracted by the Arab forces. . . . What the absence of these forces meant to the success of Allenby's stroke, it is easy to see. Nor did the Arab operation end when it had opened the way. For in the issue, it was the Arabs who almost entirely wiped out the Fourth Army, the still intact force that might have barred the way of final victory. The wear and tear, the bodily and mental strain on men and material applied by the Arabs . . . prepared the way that produced their [the Turks] defeat."[22]

The Arab people were unaware at the time that the result of their participation in the Allied war was not to achieve for them the much sought for independence, but to change masters from Turkish to British and French, despite the latter's promises and pledges supplemented by the declared war aims of the United States. On February 11, 1918, President Wilson declared as essential to any peace settlement, "Peoples are not to be handled about from one sovereignty to another by an international conference or an understanding between rivals and antagonists." And on July 4, 1918, he said: "The settlement of every question, whether of territory, of sovereignty, of economic arrangement, or of political relationship, [be] upon the basis of the free acceptance of that settlement by the people concerned and not upon the basis of material interest or advantage of any other nation or people which may desire a different settlement for the sake of its own exterior influence or mastery."[23]

The Feisal-Weizmann Agreement (1919)

Zionists propagandized public opinion into believing that the Arabs at first were not against a Jewish national home in Palestine. They repeatedly said—and still do—that an Agreement had been reached between Chaim Weizmann, then head of the newly formed Zionist Organization and Emir Feisal, on behalf of the Arabs, to the effect that the latter had aquiesced in the establishment of a Jewish state in Palestine.

As in the Balfour Declaration, nowhere in the Feisal-Weizmann Agreement of January 1919 is there any mention of a Jewish state in Palestine. The Agreement provided, among other things, for "cordial goodwill and understanding" between Arab and Jew and "to encourage and stimulate immigration of Jews into Palestine on a large scale and as quickly as possibly to settle Jewish immigrants upon the land through closer settlement and intensive cultivation of the soil." The Agreement included a protective clause providing, "In taking such measures, the Arab peasant and tenant farmers shall be protected in their rights and shall be assisted in forwarding their economic development."

But the English text of the Agreement also included an all-important reservation written (in Arabic) in Feisal's own handwriting that has been either ignored or grossly misinterpreted. Feisal wrote:

> "Provided the Arabs obtain their independence as demanded in my memorandum dated the 4th of January 1919 to the Foreign Office of the Government of Great Britain, I shall concur in the above articles. But if the slightest modification or departure were to be made, I shall not then be bound by a single word of the present Agreement which shall be deemed void and of no account or validity and I shall not be answerable in any way whatsoever."[24]

No doubt Weizmann was able to secure this agreement from Feisal under promises that he would use his influence toward achieving the independence of all Arab territories (including Palestine) and in return Feisal agreed to immigration of Jews into Palestine. He certainly did not agree to turn Palestine over to the Jews or to establish a "Jewish state" in Palestine. At any rate, the agreement was nullified by the very fact that Feisal did not achieve the independence he sought and the Palestine "Arab peasants and tenant farmers" were not "protected in their rights" as the agreement stipulated.

The King-Crane Commission (1919)

Following the signing of the Armistice and the failure of the appointment of the previously agreed upon Inter-Allied Commission to find out the wishes of the peoples who until then had been under Turkish domination, President Woodrow Wilson dispatched an all-American King-Crane Commission to Syria (including Lebanon and Palestine) to investigate. This Commission toured the area in June and July of 1919 and interviewed people from all sections of the population.

In its analysis of the situation, the King-Crane Commission, it said, was guided by the resolution of the *Council of Four* of January 30, 1919, and the Anglo-French Declaration of November 9, 1918. The first provided that the principle "that the well-being and development" of the peoples involved formed "a sacred trust of civilization and that securities for the performance of this trust shall be embodied in the constitution of the League of Nations" was to be applied.[25] The second document, provided in unequivocal terms for "the complete and definite freeing of the peoples so long oppressed by the Turks and the establishment of national governments and administrations deriving their authority from the initiative and the free choice of the native populations."[26]

For Palestine, the Commission recommended "serious modification of the extreme Zionist Program for Palestine of unlimited immigration of Jews, looking finally to making Palestine distinctly a Jewish state."

The Commissioners explained that they "began their study of Zionism with minds predisposed in its favor, but the actual facts in Palestine, coupled with the force of the general principles proclaimed by the Allies and accepted by the Syrians have driven them to the recommendation here made."

The Commissioners pointed out that the Balfour Declaration "favoring 'the establishment in Palestine of a national home for the Jewish people,' was not equivalent to making Palestine into a Jewish state; nor could the creation of such a state be accomplished without the gravest trespass upon the 'civil and religious rights of existing non-Jewish communities in Palestine.' This fact came out repeatedly in the Commission's conferences with Jewish representatives, that the Zionists looked forward to a practically complete dispossession of the present non-Jewish inhabitants of Palestine, by various forms of purchase."

The Commissioners then referred to President Wilson's address of July 4, 1918, which laid down the following principle as one of the four great "ends for which the associated peoples of the world were fighting:" "The settlement of every question, whether of territory, of sovereignty, of economic arrangement, or of political relationship on the basis of the free acceptance of that settlement by the people immediately concerned and not upon the basis of the material interest or advantage of any other nation or people which may desire a different settlement for the sake of its own exterior influence or mastery. The Tables show," the Commissioners went on to say, "that there was no one thing upon which the population of Palestine were more agreed than upon this. To subject a people so minded to unlimited Jewish immigration and to steady financial and social pressure to surrender the land, would be a gross violation of the principle just quoted, and of the peoples' rights, though it be kept within the forms of law."

The Commissioners then remarked that "the feeling against the Zionist program is not confined to Palestine, but shared very generally by the people throughout Syria . . ."

"There is a further consideration," the Commissioners pointed out "that cannot justly be ignored, if the world is to look forward to Palestine becoming a definitely Jewish state, however gradually that may take place, that consideration grows out of the fact that Palestine is 'the Holy Land' for Jews, Christians and Moslems alike. One effect," they said, "of urging the extreme Zionist program would be an intensification of anti-Jewish feeling both in Palestine and in all other portions of the world which look to Palestine as the Holy Land."

The Commissioners then recommended that "Jewish immigration should be definitely limited", that "the project for making Palestine a Jewish commonwealth should be given up," and that Palestine should be "included in a united Syrian state, just as other portions of the country . . ."[27]

THE EASTERN ARAB WORLD

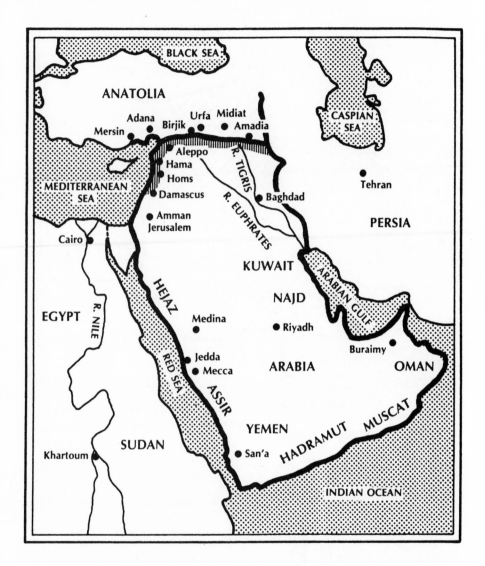

Area of Arab independence as defined by Sherif Hussein in his letter dated July 14, 1915 to Sir Henry McMahon, British High Commissioner in Egypt.

Area excluded from Arab independence as defined by Sir Henry McMahon in his letter to Sherif Hussein No. 4 dated October 24, 1915 and further explained by letter No. 6 dated December 14, 1915.

SYRIA 1916

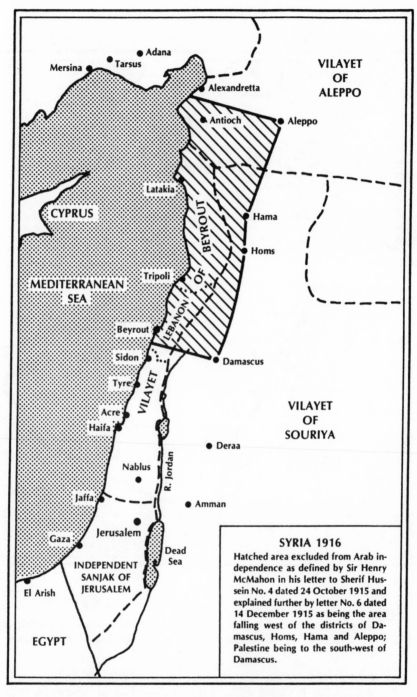

Based on map in "Palestine: The Reality" by J.M.N. Jeffries

PALESTINE
With Ottoman Administrative Divisions of Syria
(1916)

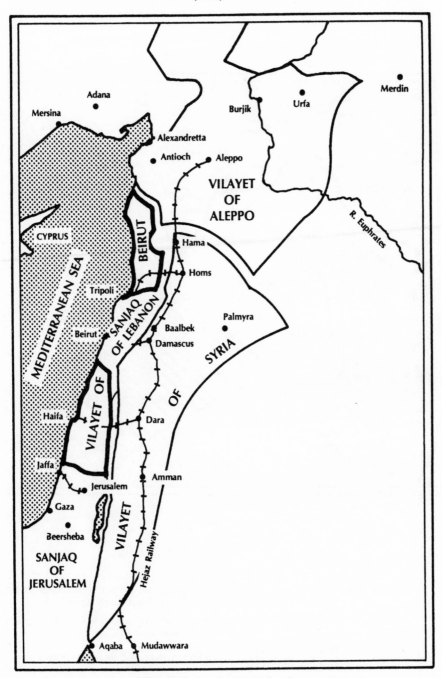

Based on map in "The Arab Awakening", by George Antonius

PARTITION OF SYRIA AND IRAQ
Under the Sykes-Picot Agreement (1916)

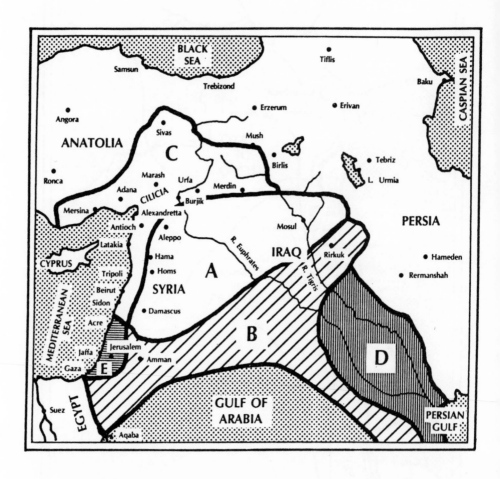

A and B - Areas in which France and Britain are prepared to recognize an
independent Area State or a Confederation of Arab States.

In Zone A, France ⎫
In Zone B, Britain ⎭   To have priority and special privileges of
                       administration and Control

In Zone C, France ⎫
In Zone D, Britain ⎭   To have direct and indirect control.

In Zone E, An international administration.

III Palestine and the Jews

The "Divine Promise"

The Zionist claim to Palestine is primarily based on ancient *Biblical Promises* of four thousand years ago that God promised Abraham that "unto thy seed have I given this land . . ." and that the words "seed of Abraham" mean only those who today are, by religion, *Jews*, whether or not they are the physical descendants of Abraham.

The supreme tragedy in the Palestine controversy is that Christianity's precepts of brotherly love, charity, human dignity and justice have all been desecrated in the face of a gross misinterpretation of the Holy Bible. Certain church leaders—some with good intentions, others out of ignorance—have fallen prey to Zionist propaganda and influence, believing that by lending their religious support to Zionist political ambitions in Palestine, they would be fulfilling the "Will of God" and bringing closer the second coming of the Messiah. They misinterpreted the Holy Scriptures and used their pulpits to sway their congregations in favor of the Zionist movement.

A number of authorities in the Old and New Testaments, both Christian and Jewish, who observed this exploitation of Holy Scriptures, felt concern over the dangers that such misinterpretation held for the basic principles of the Christian and Jewish faiths. They, therefore, took it upon themselves to provide, individually and in their own words, an accurate religious interpretation of the *Divine Promise* to show Christians and Jews the true way. Here is what these scholars and theologians had to say:

Dr. Alfred Guillaume, Professor of Old Testament Studies at the University of London and author of various works on the Old Testament, states: "The first explicit promise of Palestine to the descendants of Abraham was at Shechem (now Nablus) in Genesis 12:7—'Unto thy seed will I give this land.' Chapter 13:15, when Abraham is standing on a hill near Bethel, has the words: 'All the land which thou seest to thee will I give it and to thy seed for ever.' Chapter 15:18 is more explicit— 'Unto they seed have I given this land, from the river of Egypt unto the great river, the river Euphrates'!"

Guillaume explains that it is "generally supposed that these promises were made to the Jews and to the Jews alone. But," he points out, "that is not what the Bible says. The words 'to thy seed' inevitably include Arabs, both Muslims and Christians, who claim descent from Abraham through his son Ishmael. Ishmael was the reputed father of a large number of Arab tribes and Genesis records that Abraham became the father of many north Arabian tribes through his concubine Keturah. It cannot be argued," he adds, "that the words of Genesis 21:10–12 necessarily cancel the promise made to Abraham's seed as a whole: '(Sarah) said to Abraham, cast out this bondwoman and her son; for the son of this bondwoman shall not be heir with my son Isaac. And the thing was very grievous in Abraham's sight on account of his son. And God said unto Abraham: Let it not be grievous in thy sight because of the lad and because of thy bondwoman; in all that Sarah saith unto thee hearken unto her voice: for in Isaac shall seed be called unto thee. And also of the son of the Bondwoman will I make a nation, *because he is thy seed.*'"

It should be noted that when Abraham made a covenant with God through circumcision (Chapter 17:8) and all the land of Canaan was promised to him as "an everlasting possession," *it was Ishmael who was circumcised; Isaac had not then been born.*

Professor Guillaume goes on to remark, "It is true that henceforth among the descendants of Isaac 'the seed of Abraham' was taken to mean the Israelites; but from the beginning it was not so and *the descendants of Ishmael had every right to call and consider themselves of the seed of Abraham.*"

On the question of whether the "Promise" was not irrevocable, Guillaume explains that "there never was an unconditional promise of an everlasting possession; though a long and indefinite period was intended . . ." He added: "Had we no prophetic messages to guide us, it will be apparent that these promises of possession of the land of Canaan were not unconditional: the covenant relation between Israel and God demanded loyalty from the people, and individual and corporate righteousness. Were the people to fail in these respects, a terrible doom awaited them. The following words spoken by Moses in the 28th Chapter of Deuteronomy apply in parts so easily to the sufferings of Jewry in the past few years that many have seen in them a prophecy of our own times:

"It shall come to pass if thou wilt not harken unto the voice of the Lord thy God to observe to do all his commandments and his statutes which I command thee this day; that all those curses shall come upon thee and shall overtake thee . . . And the Lord shall scatter thee among the peoples, from the one end of the earth even unto the other end of the earth; and there thou shalt serve other gods, which thou hast not known, thou nor thy fathers, even wood and stone. And amongst these nations shalt thou find no ease and there shall be no rest for the sole of thy foot; but the Lord shall give thee there a trembling heart and failing of eyes and pining of souls; and thy life shall hang in doubt before thee . . ."

"It is clear," Guillaume concludes, "that the divine promises to the patriarchs have been annulled by the national apostasy; and when the Assyrian captivity removed the population of Samaria, and the Babylonian captivity of the people of Judah, the prophets saw in the disasters a vindication of the divine justice on a disobedient and gain-saying people. But they taught their people that a remnant would return . . . The Jews did return to Judea, they did rebuild the walls of Jerusalem and they did rebuild the temple; and after fluctuating fortunes, they did secure a brief period of political independence and expansion under the Maccabees. Thus the prophecies of the *Return* have been fulfilled, and they *cannot* be fulfilled again. Within the canonical literature of the Old Testament, there is no prophecy of a second return after the return from the Babylonian exile, because:

(i) After the Exile all the Jews who wished to do so had returned to the Holy Land, though a great many more preferred to remain where they were, and they formed the *Diaspora*, which afterwards became the backbone of the Christian Church; and

(ii) the last of the prophets died centuries before the destruction of Jerusalem in A.D. 70."[1]

Dr. William H. Stinespring, Professor of New Testament and Semitics at Duke University, North Carolina and a Minister in the Presbyterian Church, explains, "there is no basis in either Old or New Testament to support the claim of the Zionists that a modern Jewish state in Palestine is justified or demanded by the Bible or by Biblical prophecy. The 'promises' of Biblical prophecy," he said, "apply to all mankind, and not only to Jews or Zionists; that such terms as 'victory' and 'salvation,' in their true Biblical meaning, connote religious and spiritual achievements and not the conquest or degradation of political enemies; and, more specifically, that such terms as 'Israel,' 'the new Israel' or 'the Israel of God,' in the New Testament apply to the Ideal Christian Church, or to a body of true believers in the religious sense."

Dr. Stinespring goes on to point out, "the evidence is overwhelming that no true Christian, believing in the New Testament, could possibly confuse the modern Israel, brought into being by political machination and military power accompanied by ruthless deprivation of the native inhabitants, with the Israel of God of Christian faith. These two Israels contradict one another completely," Stinespring emphasized.

Dr. Stinespring concludes his study by saying, "Even without the specific statements of the New Testament with regard to the spiritual and religious nature of the promises of Israel, the Old Testament alone in its truest sense and in the hands of its truest interpreters, pointed to a *spiritual* kingdom for all mankind and not to a *political* Israel that occupies territory and homes belonging naturally to another people and reduces some of its inhabitants to second-class citizenship. Moreover, Judaism, like Christianity," he said, "has had a continuous history since Biblical times; and the best insights of this continuing tradition also lead towards an *Israel of the spirit and not of the flesh*."[2]

Dr. Ovid R. Sellers, former Professor of Old Testament and Dean of McCormick Theological Seminary and Minister in the United Presbyterian Church, is another source which disproves the Zionist claim that the establishment of the state of Israel was in fulfillment of Biblical prophecy. He states: "From its beginning the Christian Church kept the Old Testament as its sacred literature. This was because the Christians believed that their religion was not something entirely new, but a fulfillment of the old. The Ten Commandments still were in effect and the prophecies of a coming Messiah had been fulfilled in Jesus Christ. Early Christian missionaries, particularly Paul, taught that a Gentile by accepting Christ could become heir to the promises made to Israel. 'For in Christ neither circumcision availeth anything, nor uncircumcision, but a new creature. And as many as walk according to this rule, peace be on them and mercy, and upon the Israel of God' (Galatians 6:15–16). This Israel of God, according to Paul, was the community of all believers," Dr. Sellers added.

Dr. Sellers concludes, "a Christian, relying on Christian Scripture, can think of Israel not as a geographical, ethnical, or political unit, but as the body of all believers, 'the Israel of God.'"[3]

Dr. Frank Stagg, Professor of New Testament at the Southern Baptist Theological Seminary in New Orleans, arrives at the same conclusions as his colleagues and ends up by pointing out that "to identify modern Israel, the state or the Jewish people, with the 'Israel of God' is to miss the teaching of the New Testament at one of its most vital points."[4]

The Right Reverend Jonathan G. Sherman, Suffragan Bishop of the Episcopal Diocese of Long Island, New York, points out, "The history of Israel demonstrates that God is not primarily concerned with Israel's military conquests or geographical security or economic prosperity: the prophets' predictions are fulfilled when Israel is destroyed as a nation in 722 B.C. and when Judah is driven into exile in 586 B.C. What then? What God is interested in, say the prophets, is a relationship with Israel grounded in God's righteousness, justice and mercy, a relationship between God and man that involves at every point a right relationship between man and man." The Bishop concludes his study with the statement, "In the Old Covenant God promised to the children of Israel military victory over their enemies in order that they might enter into the land flowing with milk and honey on the condition of Israel's obedience to his commandments. Israel failed to keep the covenant and so forfeited the promises of God. But God promised a New Covenant, to be written not on tables of stone but in the hearts of his people (Jeremiah 31:31–33; Corinthians 3.2f). Of this New Covenant Jesus is the mediator (Hebrews 8:6–13; 9:15). In place of victory over human enemies Jesus gives us victory over sin and death (I Corinthians 15:55–57). In place of the land of Canaan, He gives us His kingdom (St. Luke 12:32). In place of milk and honey, He gives us the fruit of the Spirit—love and joy and peace and forgiveness. Verily, 'in Him all the promises of God are Yes!'" (II Corinthians 1:20).[5]

Dr. Elmer Berger, a gifted rabbi, and an author of many books on Judaism, came to the same conclusions as did his Christian counterparts. He added, "no Orthodox Jew believes the present state of Israel has come into being in a process which fulfills the injunctions of the Old Testament. There are Orthodox Jews," he said, "who actually repudiate the present Israeli sovereignty as a profanation of the Biblical texts. This attitude is most vigorously and dramatically represented in precisely that part of the state of Israel where the most traditional Judaism is observed—the Mea Shearim quarter of the City of Jerusalem. Here lives the *Neturei Karta* who regard the present state of Israel as a subversive phenomenon to their faith and who, themselves, indulge in frequent acts of defiance of the governmental authority of the state of Israel. There are less well known but equally convinced followers of the same position among the Orthodox Jews of the United States. These groups, at times, have made representations to the United Nations. They are particularly agitated over the claims of the New City of Jerusalem advanced by the state of Israel. They prefer internationalization of a Jerusalem once again uniting the old and the new cities."

"This attitude," Rabbi Berger points out, "cannot necessarily be equated with an anti-Israel position, although there are those in these groups who do oppose the present state and who agree it came about, not through fulfillment of the Word of God, but as a result of the secular-political activities of Zionism. It cannot, therefore, be a fulfillment of Old Testament prophecy; and it does not represent, for these people, the Messianic dream. They regard Israel as a secular state, devoid of Zion."

Rabbi Berger concludes by stating, "The most charitable construction which can be put upon the state of Israel therefore, in the context of considering its Biblical legitimacy, is that through methods having no sanction in the Bible at all, a political sovereignty has been established. In a majority population of Jews, a minority is still engaged in a furious, *political* battle to compel the State to adopt a character which *could* be equated with the Biblical prophecies. The equating is *not* accomplished today. The fulfillment is not even remotely near realization. Neither the process which gave birth to Israel nor the result, in the form of the state itself, can—by any theory with the integrity which is central to all genuine religions—be regarded as justified by the magnificent ethical and religious declarations of the spiritual giants whose words are immortalized in Scripture."[6]

The findings of these distinguished scholars in religion leave no doubt that the Zionist claim to Palestine is neither correct nor legitimate. Besides, one can go a step further to prove the absurdity of the Zionist claim: Nowhere is the notion found that being a Jew is synonymous with physical descent from Abraham. Many Jews in history have been converts from other stock. There were the Black Jews of Malabar, and the Falashas of Ethiopia. The current political leaders of Israel, as well as the Jewish immigrants who hail from Central Europe, Poland, Russia and the United States, are mostly of Khazar extraction, descendants of Caucasian Russians whom Byzantine Jews converted to Judaism in the mid-eighth century.[7]

Palestine may be associated with those who today profess the Jewish religion, but this association is only spiritual, not physical. Sir Edwin S. Montagu, Secretary of State for India in the Lloyd George Cabinet, which approved the Balfour Declaration in 1917, told his Christian colleagues at the time: As a Jew, "I deny that Palestine is today associated with the Jews . . . It is quite true," he said, "that Palestine plays a large part in Jewish history, but so it does in modern Mohammedan history and, after the time of the Jews, surely it plays a larger part than any other country in Christian history. The Temple," he pointed out, "may have been in Palestine, but so was the Sermon on the Mount and the Crucifixion."

Sir Edwin warned, "Zionism has always seemed to me to be a mischievous political creed, untenable by any patriotic citizen of the United Kingdom. If a Jewish Englishman," he said, "sets his eyes on the Mount of Olives and longs for the day when he will shake British soil from his shoes and go back to agricultural pursuits in Palestine, he has always seemed to me to have acknowledged aims inconsistent with British citizenship and to have admitted that he is unfit for a share in public life in Great Britain, or to be treated as an Englishman."

Montagu then asserted, with emphasis, "there is not a Jewish nation." He referred to members of his own family, whom, he said, had been in the country for generations, as having "no sort or kind of community or views or of desire with any Jewish family in any other country beyond the fact that they profess to a greater or less degree the same religion. It is no more true," he pointed out, "to say that a Jewish Englishman and a Jewish Moor are of the same nation than it is to say that a Christian Englishman and a Christian Frenchman are of the same nation."[8]

The Early Hebrews and Present-Day Jews

Significantly, in this respect, Harry L. Shapiro, Chairman of the Department of Anthropology at the American Museum of Natural History, states, in a study of the biological history of the *Jewish people*, that the Jews "are not a clan, a tribe, or in a strict sense, a nation." After briefly tracing their history, Dr. Shapiro declares: "It is odd, in the light of their past, that the Jews are often considered and much effort expended to prove them to be a distinct race . . . These [biological] comparisons . . . prove that the fundamental requirement for any claim that the Jews form a racial entity cannot be met, at least by those traditional standards of racial classification . . . The wide range of variation between Jewish populations in their physical characteristics and the diversity of the gene frequence of their blood groups, render any unified racial classification for them a contradiction in terms."[9]

Another distinguished anthropologist dispels "the myth of the Jewish race." Professor Juan Comas of the National University of Mexico, comments, "though the idea of 'racialism' evokes in most a negative response, it is curious how the idea survives, because various groups find it useful. Zionist Jews, for example, speak constantly of a 'Jewish people,' with distinct racist-like overtones, by which they mean a continuity not only of history but of blood, culture and destiny as well.

Such an approach," he points out, "is the more remarkable after the terrible treatment their co-religionists in Germany endured in the name of racialism. They do so," he presumed, "to justify their establishment of a 'homeland' in Israel, and to strengthen the ties with and the support from, Jews by religion in other countries."

Professor Comas then explains, "The anthropological fact is that Jews are racially heterogeneous and there is no foundation for the claim that there is a Jewish race. Their constant migrations through history and their relations—voluntary or otherwise—with the widest variety of nations and peoples have brought about such a degree of cross-breeding that the so-called people of Israel can produce examples of traits typical of every people. For proof, it will suffice to compare the rubicond, sturdy, heavily-built Rotterdam Jew with his co-religionist, say in Salonika with gleaming eyes in a sickly face and skinny, high-strung physique . . ."

Comas then classifies the Jews, according to origin, into the following separate groups:

(a) Descendants of Jewish emigrants from Palestine (very few);

(b) Descendants of unions between Jews of mixed Asiatic descent or between Jews and other groups, who might be called cross-crossbreeds;

(c) Jews by religion but having anthropologically no connection whatsoever with the Jews of Palestine and consisting simply of individuals of other human strains converted to the Hebrew religion.

Under the last classification, he gives as "a typical example" Bulan, King of the Khazars, converted to Judaism in A.D. 740 with many of his nobles and peoples.

In support of his argument, Professor Comas points out that in Germany, between 1921 and 1925, for every 100 Jewish marriages, there were 58 all-Jewish and 42 mixed. In Berlin, in 1926, there were 861 all-Jewish marriages and 554 mixed. He then states, "the figures speak for themselves, especially if we take into account the large number of partners who became Jews by religion although there was nothing 'Semitic' about them."

To confirm his analysis, Professor Comas solicits the views of two other authorities on the subject: R.N. Salman says, "The purity of the Jewish race is imaginary; the widest variety of ethnic types is found among Jews. More particularly, in Germany and Russia, there are Jews who do not display the smallest Semitic characteristics."

To this, M. Fishberg adds: "The percentage of light-eyed blonds and their irregular distribution in the various centers of Jewish population, is at least as great as that observable between any of the peoples of Europe. The claims of Jews to purity of descent are so vain and baseless as the allegations of a radical difference between Jews and the so-called Aryan race on which anti-Semitism is based."[10]

One further point in support of this argument is that the Jews' own definition of "who is a Jew" has always been, "a Jew is the son of a Jewish mother, or, alternately, is a person who has been accepted into Judaism through the recognized process of proselytization."[11]

But on the emergence of the Jewish state, the question of "who is a Jew today" created quite a problem for the Israelis. Jewish immigration—particularly from Poland—brought in "a high proportion of mixed marriages, i.e., marriages in which one of the couples maintained a non-Jewish identity." In most cases, it was pointed out, "the non-Jewish partner was the mother and hence the offspring, by Jewish law, was non-Jewish."[12]

It is, therefore, sheer fallacy to say that the descendants of Jews of all lands are of one blood and that they are related to the early Hebrews and, as such, "heirs according to the promise." The absurdity of the Zionist claim and the accuracy of the findings of the distinguished anthropologists—if further proof is needed—is best illustrated—to quote one example—in the case of the black actor Sammy Davis Jr. who embraced Judaism some years ago. According to Zionist logic, as legislated in the Israeli *Status Law* and *Law of the Return*, Davis is considered to be now living in "exile" in his homeland America, pining for the day to return "home" to Palestine! Ironically, while a total stranger in language, color, culture and race can acquire a right to go to Palestine by merely adopting Judaism, the Moslem and Christian inhabitants of the Holy Land—whose physical descent from Abraham can hardly be questioned—if the "Biblical" promises have any legitimacy in the 20th century at all—are denied the right to live in the country of their birth!

If Christians can, in the face of all these facts still regard the Zionist claim to Palestine as conforming to Biblical prophecies, to the exclusion of its Moslem and Christian inhabitants, then it is suggested that Christ's coming and His Supreme Sacrifice on the Cross to save humanity was in vain and Christianity has, apparently, no heavenly purpose to fulfill. It is indeed inconceivable that a Christian born and reared in Palestine, is not regarded as an "heir according to the Promise."

Zionism's "Historical" Claim

Another angle of the Zionist claim to Palestine is that the early Hebrews (or Israelites) were in previous occupation of the land.

The only real title which any people has to its country comes from *birth and long and continued possession*. It is these that give the British their right to Britain, the French their right to France and the Americans their right to America. This is a criterion that the common acceptance of humanity has set up as a universal principle. It is recognized as the basis of the integrity and security of all nations and no just international order can be established in the world today on any other foundation.

If such a formula can apply to a new country like America with its only four-hundred and fifty years of history, how much sounder in comparison is the right of the Palestine Arabs to their country, which dates back to the dawn of history? The Palestine Arabs of today—Moslems and Christians—are not, as is popularly believed, all exclusively the descendants of the Islamic desert conquerors of 1,300 years ago; they are, in fact, mainly the descendants of the original native population—Philistines, Canaanites, etc. They were there when the early Hebrews invaded the land in about 1500 B.C., survived the Israelite occupation, retained possession of a large part of the country throughout the Israelite period and remained in the country after the

Hebrew "dispersion," to be intermingled first with the Arabs in the seventh century, then with the Crusaders in the 11th Century and continued the occupation of the land in their new Arabized character until the Zionist invasion in 1948.

The historical connection of the early Hebrews (or Israelites) with Palestine is not one based on *birth* and *long possession*—as is the case with the Palestine Arabs—but upon *occupation through invasion*. The duration of this occupation is little known; a brief description is given below:

1. In the second millenium B.C., a Semite tribe invaded the east coast of the Mediterranean. Its members became known as Hebrews and later Israelites since they claimed descent from Abraham through his son Jacob, otherwise known as Israel.

2. Their tradition has it that they migrated to Egypt and eventually were led back by Moses.

3. By 1100 B.C., they had conquered most of the hill-country of Palestine and had done so with the ferocity common to all early conquerors.

4. There was much disunion among them, until the hostility of the Philistines—the original inhabitants of the country—forced them into solidarity and led them to establish a monarchy, first under David (1010—970 B.C.), then under Solomon (970—930 B.C.) who managed to enlarge his territory. But his death ushered in the Hebrews' decline.

5. Soon the kingdom was divided into two, which were sometimes at war with each other: In the North, the Kingdom of Israel centered around Samaria; in the South, the Kingdom of Judah.

6. Between 721 and 715 B.C., the northern Kingdom was incorporated into Assyria, and the southern one acknowledged Assyrian suzerainty.

7. In 585 B.C., the new Babylonian Empire under Nebuchadnezzar sacked Jerusalem and took many of its people into captivity to Babylon.

8. In 539 B.C., Cyrus occupied Babylon and freed the Jews, of whom some 40,000 returned to Palestine, the larger part choosing to remain in Babylon.

9. Under the Persians then the Ptolemies, Jewish recorded history is obscure, although modern scholars claim that the period saw the flowering of Hebrew culture.

10. When the Greeks tried to impose their gods, the Hebrews revolted and from about 150 B.C. onwards they recovered most of what Solomon had once ruled.

11. But in 63 B.C., Pompey stormed Jerusalem, and Palestine became virtually a Roman province. There were several revolts, but in A.D. 135 the Romans put an end to Jewish Palestine by destroying Jerusalem.

Such at best is the connection of the early Hebrews (or Israelites) with Palestine. It was short-lived, unstable, intermittent, long extinct, based on nothing better than the right of conquest and subject to the condition that there should have been national or racial affinity between the Hebrews of 4,000 years ago and the Russian, Polish, American and European Jews of today.

If this transitory occupation can give the Zionists a "historic right" to the country, then it may be argued that the Arabs, who occupied Spain continuously for 800 years, could claim that country today, while the Italians could claim the British Isles and the Indians demand the withdrawal from the Americas of all those who settled in the Western hemisphere and now call themselves Americans, Canadians, and Latin Americans. If all nations were to adopt this strange Zionist logic, the world would be in utter chaos.

The so-called "miracle of Israel's restoration" in 1948 was not according to God's Will as the Zionists and some misguided Christians would have the world believe, but as a very un-Christian human international crime against the Moslem and Christian inhabitants of the Holy Land.

IV The Zionist Movement

Principles and Objectives

The basic issue in the Palestine question is the uprooting and dispossession of an entire nation in order to make room for the "ingathering" in Palestine of Jews from all parts of the world. Whereas some of these Jews may have been victims of terror and injustice, nonetheless, they are being used as pawns in the political program of Jewish nationalism. The building up of a Jewish population in Palestine was not inspired purely by humanitarian considerations, but achieved principally in order to fulfill the political aspirations of a major ideological movement—Zionism.

The Zionist movement that began in the nineteenth century, took official shape in 1897 with the holding of the First Congress in Basel, Switzerland. The leader of the movement was Theodor Herzl, an Austrian lawyer, who died in 1904.

The aims of the movement, as formulated by that first Congress, were:

"Zionism strives to create for the Jewish people a home in Palestine secured by public law. The congress contemplates the following means to the attainment of this end:
1. The promotion on suitable lines of the colonization of Palestine by Jewish agricultural and industrial workers.
2. The organization and binding together of the whole of Jewry by means of appropriate institutions, local and international, in accordance with the laws of each country.
3. The strengthening and fostering of Jewish national sentiment and consciousness.
4. Preparatory steps toward obtaining Government consent where necessary to the attainment of the aim of Zionism."[1]

Zionism, as a political philosophy, preaches that the Jews are one people and one nation requiring their own land, to which all Jews must eventually return. Zionism thus spurns the concept of religious fellowship and seeks to endow them with national attributes. For those Jews who choose not to be "ingathered," Zionism attempts to thwart their civic, cultural and social integration in lands outside of Israel, in order to attach them to a common "nationhood" of Jews. It seeks the deepening of a *Jewish* national consciousness in order to strengthen the economic, political and cultural ties that bind world Jewry to the sovereign national center in Israel. Thus, while Christians and Moslems live in many nations and owe allegiance to various flags, Jews, according to Zionist dogma, are only *one* nation. Though they live in many countries, they are considered to be in the *Diaspora* (exile), and are supposed to be longing to live in *Eretz Israel* (Palestine) alone.

Zionists have always recognized that, in order to attain their primary goal of "ingathering" all Jews in their own "homeland," two campaigns will have to be successfully waged: one, the creation of a legal-political entity known as "the Jewish people;" the other, recognition of this "Jewish people" concept in international law.

Judaism versus Zionism

Many people make the simple mistake in believing that Judaism and Zionism are the same. This is not so. *Judaism* is a religion of universal values. Jews are regarded as members of a religious fellowship, who have no national or ethnic ties with their co-religionists of other lands. In the countries of their citizenship, Jews, like Christians and Moslems, have national ties with their fellow-citizens, irrespective of their religious faith. *Zionism*, on the other hand, is an international political movement which aspires to link all Jews, by means of ethnic, nationalistic bonds into a world-wide nation, a peoplehood, having as its political and cultural center the state of Israel.

Commenting in 1944 on the effect of Zionism on Jewish interests, Professor William E. Hocking, said, he believes "political Zionists are the chief enemies of the Jewish interest in the world of tomorrow." He inquires, "What can they hope to gain by extricating their brethren from the prejudices of Europe only to build a community in Palestine which has to be protected by Western force because it is cradled in an environment of sedulously cultivated distrust and fear."[2]

Recognition of Zionism

In 1917, the British Government became the first Power to recognize the Jewish people, by granting the World Zionist Organization the Balfour Declaration. To be sure, even then, British and American anti-Zionist Jews saw in the Declaration a danger to their own security, and forced the inclusion of a safeguard clause, designed to protect the "rights and political status enjoyed by Jews in any other country" (outside Palestine). And in 1924, the United States Government, by accepting the British Mandate over Palestine in a Covenant signed with

Britain, supported the incorporation of the safeguard clause in the entire Declaration.

Thus, the stage was set for Zionist exploitation of these and other formal documents. The safeguard clause was blithely disregarded, while emphasis was placed, whenever and wherever possible, on a legal-political relationship for all Jews, through the Jewish Agency for Palestine, with Zionism acting as a public body and internationally recognized as spokesman for a legal-political entity known as "the Jewish people." As time passed, the world appears to have accepted this Zionist formula, while those Jews who opposed it became fewer and weaker.

Zionist-Israeli Condominium

In 1948, the new state of Israel legislated "the Jewish people" concept into legal form. The *Law of Return* and the *Nationality Act* granted "every Jew . . . certain rights." In 1952, the Israeli Parliament enacted the *Status Law*, which defined the tasks assigned to Zionism throughout the world and inside Israel, as a quasi-govenmental agent of the state of Israel. These "tasks" were set forth in 1954 in a "Covenant" signed by the Israeli Government and the World Zionist Organization.[3] The Statute and Covenant legally directed the World Zionist Organization to do for the state of Israel, beyond its own boundaries, what the state neither can nor may do itself. These include: exertion of political pressure on governments,[4] the financing and recruiting of mass emigration to Israel, conducting and directing propaganda on behalf of Israel in times of crisis, etc.[5]

The connection between Israel and the World Zionist Organization was reiterated in 1959 by a new government coming to power and further strengthened on March 15, 1964, when a communiqué was signed. The Prime Minister explained that the purpose of the communiqué was to bolster Zionist programs that were in the "vital interest" of his Government. The purpose, he said, was the classic Zionist goal of "conquering the communities" of Jews in the areas outside Israel.

The Israeli judiciary as well advances the concept of "the Jewish people." In the Eichmann Trial Judgment, the Supreme Court stated that the state of Israel is recognized in international law as the "sovereign state of the Jewish people."

The Israeli Government persistently uses international or domestic events to deepen its claim of legal-political linkage with all Jews. For example, in 1959 and 1960, when "swastika" markings appeared in many countries, Israel took upon itself the responsibility to send formal notes to some twenty governments, including the United States, expressing concern for the safety of their citizens of the Jewish faith. The Israeli attitude was criticized in certain Jewish circles in England as "interference in the internal affairs of British Jewry." To this the late Prime Minister Mrs. Golda Meir retorted, "Israel is determined not to yield the right to speak on any Jewish subject. If there are Jews abroad who find themselves embarrassed by this attitude, let them be embarrassed."[6]

On March 15, 1964, the Israeli Cabinet and the Jewish Agency Executive held a joint session and issued a communiqué in which they expressed their joint concern for the "enhancement of the Zionist spirit in Jewish life." At this meeting, the 1954 "Covenant" was ratified which included the "Basic Principle of Government Program" approved by the Israeli Parliament on December 17, 1959.

Paragraph 59 of this "Program," entitled *Chapter VII: Ties with Jewry and the Zionist Movement*, provides, among other things, for "the fight against all signs of assimilation [of Jews in their countries of origin] and denial of Jewish peoplehood."[7]

This unique racist provision, which attempts to block the integration of the Jews of different countries in their respective gentile communities, was attacked by Dr. Elmer Berger, then Executive Vice-President of the American Council for Judaism, who said: "What is incomprehensible, illogical, and absurd, is that the state of Israel, with seeming impunity, is permitted to operate part of its government in the United States, in direct impact upon United States citizens and in support of this conflicting policy. What is further incomprehensible, illogical and absurd is that the United States Government leaves United States citizens vulnerable to exploitation by the foreign sovereignty for extracting funds and political support to operate the machine and program which is admittedly designed to persuade these Americans to support the policy of the foreign state and ultimately to expatriate themselves."[8]

Relationship of Israel to World Jewry

David Ben Gurion, the architect of the Jewish state, outlined the relationship of world Jewry to Israel as follows:

"On the world scene and in the Middle East, Israel's endeavors must be the same—military and moral—but its destiny depends wholly upon the third domain, the Jewish people in all its dispersion. The state of Israel is a part of the Middle East only in geography, which is, in the main, a static element. From the more decisive standpoints of dynamism, creation and growth, Israel is a part of world Jewry. From that Jewry it will draw all the resources and the means necessary for the upbuilding of the nation of Israel and the development of the Land; through the might of world Jewry it will be built and built again. A community of destiny and destination joins together indissolubly the state of Israel and the Jewish people. There is an indestructible bond, a bond of life and death between them."[9]

Addressing the 25th World Zionist Congress in the Israeli-occupied part of Jerusalem in January 1961, David Ben Gurion told his audience that "Since the day the Jewish state was established and the gates of Israel were flung open to every Jew who wanted to come, every religious Jew has daily violated the precepts of Judaism and the Torah of Israel by remaining in the *Diaspora*." He denounced all Jews outside of Israel as "godless."[10]

Later, speaking before the Israeli Parliament, he said: "Being an American and being a Jew are two different things. I know of only one

Zionist in America whom I would call a Zionist and I will not give his name. He does not think of himself as an American. He thinks of himself only as a Jew."[11] And on another occasion, Ben Gurion said: "When a Jew in America or South Africa speaks of 'our government' to his fellow Jews, he usually means the government of Israel, while the Jewish public in various countries view the Israeli ambassador as their own representative."[12]

Nahum Goldmann, an American citizen and President of the World Zionist Organization, was no less emphatic on the relationship between world Jewry and Israel. Speaking before the 25th Zionist Congress, he said:

> "*Diaspora* Jewry must have the courage to proclaim and defend its relationship of partnership and responsibility *vis-a-vis* Israel. It has to overcome the conscious or subconscious fear of so-called double loyalty. It has to be convinced that it is fully justified in tying up its destiny with Israel's. It has to have the courage to reject the idea that Jewish communities owe loyalty to the states where they live."[13]

In March 1961, Dr. Goldmann is quoted as having said: "To allow people many loyalties was the essence of democracy. To demand a single loyalty was Nazism."[14]

Jewish Opposition to Zionism

The American Council for Judaism, an anti-Zionist organization, protested to the U.S. government Israel's self-appointed role of speaking for the Jews of the United States. After four years of private discussion, the U.S. Department of State, in a letter dated April 20, 1964, finally made its stand clear by informing the Council that "It does not recognize a legal-political relationship based upon the religious identification of American citizens. It does not in any way discriminate among American citizens upon the basis of their religion. Accordingly, it should be clear that the Department of State does not regard the 'Jewish people' concept as a concept of international law."[15]

This statement has been interpreted as separating Zionism from the state of Israel; limiting Israel's sovereignty to its own legal citizens and nationals; shifting U.S. policy from acquiescence, or seeming acquiescence, to outright rejection of the "Jewish people" claim; stamping Zionist-Israel claims as being inconsistent with the fundamental constitutional rights of U.S. citizens; and initiating a step which might have significance in the interpretation of international law.

The statement might have had some value if it had been addressed to the Israeli Government in the form of a protest against Israeli legislation involving American citizens; also American Zionists should have been reminded by their Government that the "Covenant" they signed with the Israeli leaders was in conflict with their responsibilities as American citizens. Instead, the statement remained a "dead letter;" and Zionist activities in the United States on behalf of Israel did not diminish, even where these activities are detrimental to U.S. interests in the Middle East. On the contrary, evidence is abundant that they have been stepped up with greater participation of the White House, the Government and policy-makers.

Another opposition to the "State of Israel" concept comes from Rabbi Hirsch, a pious Orthodox Jew and leader of the *Neturei Karta* (Guardians of the City), who lives in the Mea-Shearim Quarter of Jerusalem. The number of his followers, he claims, is about 10,000 in Jerusalem, but extends to about 100,000 worldwide.

In an article published in *The Washington Post* of October 3, 1978, Rabbi Hirsch is reported to have declared: "The 12th principle of our faith, I believe, is that the Messiah will gather the Jewish exiled who re-dispersed throughout the nations of the world. Zionism is diametrically opposed to Judaism. Zionism wishes to define the Jewish people as a nationalistic entity. The Zionists say, in effect, 'Look here, God. We do not like exile. Take us back, and if you don't, we'll just roll up our sleeves and take ourselves back.'"

The Rabbi continues: "This, of course, equals heresy. The Jewish people are charged by Divine oath not to force themselves back to the Holy Land against the wishes of those residing there. So if they do, they are open to the consequences. The Talmud," he added, "says this violation will make your flesh prey to the deer of the forest. The Jewish people were given the Holy Land by God, and we sinned and we were exiled and charged not to take back the land. Therefore, a Jewish state can only expect consequences which no one would look forward to. The Holocaust was due to Zionism."

Jewish Critics of Zionism

Other critics of the Zionist philosophy who saw the dangers inherent in the establishment of a purely Jewish state in Palestine, include the following Jewish personalities:

Albert Einstein—"I should much rather see reasonable agreement with the Arabs on the basis of living together in peace than the creation of a Jewish State. Apart from practical considerations, my awareness of the essential nature of Judaism resists the idea of a Jewish State, with borders, an army, and a measure of temporal power, no matter how modest. I am afraid of the inner damage Judaism will sustain—especially from the development of a narrow nationalism within our own ranks, against which we have already had to fight strongly, even without a Jewish State. We are no longer the Jews of the Maccabee period. A return to a nation in the political sense of the word, would be equivalent to turning away from the spiritualization of our community which we owe to the genius of our prophets."[16]

Judah L. Magnes—"Will the Jews here [Palestine] in their efforts to create a political organism become devotees of brute force and militarism as were some of the late Hashmoneans? We seem to have thought of everything except the Arabs . . . If we have a just cause, so have they. If promises were made to us, so were they made to the Arabs. If we love the land and have a historical connection with it, so too the Arabs . . . If we wish to live in this living space, we must live with the Arabs, try to make peace with them . . . We stand over against the great Arab democracies as interlopers . . . We must look for an *entente cordiale*. Not upon the basis of force and power, but upon that of human solidarity and understanding . . . Is our nationality like that of all the nations, pagan, and based upon force and violence, or is it a spiritual nationality? The right of the Jew does not confer the right of political majority."[17]

Morris R. Cohen—"I am still disturbed by the concept of a Jewish State. Is a Jewish State a racial state, based on mystic ideas of 'Blood and Soil?' Will a non-Jewish inhabitant have equal rights in such a State? Will it be possible for a non-Jew to hold office? Will a Moslem, for example, find no legal obstacle to becoming President of the republic? If Jews are permitted to immigrate, will Arabs be excluded from immigration on equal terms? Certainly I could never bring myself to support efforts to establish a Jewish State which would not be in accord with the democratic principles of separation of Church and State, and equality of civil, religious and economic rights to all inhabitants, regardless of race and creed."[18]

Lessing J. Rosenwald—"I still believe that Zionism, a nationalist movement, is deleterious to Jewish citizens of the United States, and to the Jewish nationals of many other countries outside Israel. I still remain a firm adherent to the American Council of Judaism and the principles upon which it was founded and which it still maintains."[19]

Arab Rejection of Zionism

The entry of individual Jews into Palestine was never questioned by the Arabs prior to the advent of Zionism, beyond the normal investigations conducted with respect to aliens seeking to settle in any country. Jews were expected to integrate and share in the responsibilities, rights and privileges of citizenship. But when the Zionists attempted in the early part of this century to obtain possession of the country through bribery and the offer of generous advantages, this was resisted by the Ottoman Sultan on the grounds that it was detrimental to the interests of the Arab population.

The fundamental reason for Arab opposition to Zionism is based upon the fact that the Moslem and Christian inhabitants of the country could not be expected to yield to an ideology which sought to wrest—as later events proved—their homeland from them. The Arabs rejected absolutely and unanimously any attempt to destroy the Arab character of Palestine. They still do. The Arabs claim the right of a population to decide the fate of the country which they had occupied throughout history. To them it is obvious that this right of immemorial possession is inalienable; and that it could not be overruled either by the circumstances that Palestine had been governed by the Ottomans for 400 years, or that Britain had conquered the land during World War I, or that a Jewish state has been established in part of it by brute force.[20]

Zionism and Anti-Semitism

An impression existed at one time that "Zionism would diminish anti-Semitism in the world. We are witness to the opposite," declared

Dr. Judah Magnes, the late President of the Hebrew University in Jerusalem.[21]

There is a principle that has guided inquiries into crimes and disturbances from Roman times to the present day. The Romans asked *Cui bono*? For whose benefit is it? And today, detectives will start an investigation by determining who stood to benefit from a crime. We may therefore consider: Who derives the most advantage from anti-Semitism? Do the Arabs? the Jews? or the Zionists?

The Arabs have nothing to gain and much to lose from anti-Semitic practices. First, were it not for Hitler's inhuman policy of racial discrimination and persecution, the Jews of Europe would never have left their homes in significant numbers; the Palestine tragedy would not have occurred; and the present tension and instability in the Middle East would not have arisen. Second, the aims of the anti-Semites run contrary to Arab interests and security. Anti-Semitic practices mean insecurity for Jews in their countries of origin, inducing greater immigration to Palestine, thereby creating a population problem in that country and the inevitable need for territorial expansion. Such conditions can only aggravate the Arab-Israeli conflict still further; make it more difficult for the Palestine Arabs to regain their homes peacefully; and increase conflict in the Middle East.

But the Zionists have much to gain and nothing to lose from the creation of a feeling of insecurity among world Jewry. Without the constant threat of anti-Semitism there could be no Zionism; Jewish immigration to Israel would diminish if not cease altogether; Israel would lose the colossal financial aid it now receives from United States and world Jewry; and the Jewish state would cease to become the nationalist empire and fulcrum for international political influence and economic control envisaged by the Zionists.

The close relationship between Zionism and anti-Semitism was commented upon by British historian Arnold Toynbee in May 1961. Speaking at the annual meeting of the American Council for Judaism in Philadelphia, Toynbee stated: "Zionism and anti-Semitism are expressions of an identical point of view. The assumption underlying both ideologies is that it is impossible for Jews and non-Jews to grow together into a single community and that therefore a physical separation is the only practical way out. The watchword of anti-Semitism," he said "is 'Back to medieval apartheid;' the watchword of Zionism is 'Back to the medieval ghetto.' All the far-flung ghettos in the world are to be gathered into one patch of soil in Palestine to create a single consolidated ghetto there," Toynbee concluded.[22]

The Zionist smear of anti-Semitism is being used extensively and indiscriminately against all those who disagree with Zionist policy. An American citizen, in a letter to the press, complained that he was "weary of being labelled an anti-Semite for expressing views about the foreign state of Israel which are contrary to those of 'American' Zionists. Do the concepts of 'brotherhood' and 'tolerance,'" he asks, "apply only in one direction? I suspect," he said, "it is the threat of being called anti-Semitic by the very vocal Zionists which prevents American politicians from objectively debating the issues of American foreign policy *vis-à-vis* the

Middle East."[23]

"Anti-Semitism is being used by the Zionist movement as a double-edged weapon: On the one hand, it serves to silence any person who opposes Zionism and Israeli policy; on the other hand, it is used to discourage Jews from becoming assimilated into the lives of the countries of their origin.

Commenting on the first point, Professor David Riesman, of Harvard University, said: "The Zionists can muster not merely the threat of the Jewish vote and the no less important Jewish financial and organizational skills, but also the blackmail of attacking anyone who opposes their political aims for Israel as an anti-Semite."[24]

On the question of assimilation, Dr. Nahum Goldmann, President of the World Zionist Organization, in a speech he delivered on July 23, 1958 at the opening of the World Jewish Congress in Geneva, Switzerland, is reported by *The New York Times* to have warned world Jewry that "a current decline of overt anti-Semitism might constitute a new danger to Jewish survival . . . Jews nearly everywhere are equal citizens, both politically and economically," Goldmann said. "However," he asserted, "the disappearance of anti-Semitism in its classical meaning, while beneficial to the political and material situation of Jewish communities, has had a very negative effect on our internal life . . ."[25]

Another expression of the values of anti-Semitism as a deterrent to Jewish assimilation, comes from a report from the Israeli-occupied sector of Jerusalem. Speaking before the Zionist General Council held in January 1966, Rabbi Mordechai Kershblum, of New York, stressed the importance of fighting assimilation. "I always fear," the Rabbi said, "lest the anti-Semites have adopted a new method. Instead of torture and persecution, they say, 'Give them peace and they will disappear of their own accord.'"[26]

Perhaps the most important exploitation of anti-Semitism, as a device to achieve Zionist ends, was revealed in an article in *Davar*, the official organ of the Socialist Labour (*Mapai*) Party. Editor Sharun wrote: "I shall not be ashamed to confess that, if I had the power as I have the will, I would select a score of efficient young men—intelligent, decent, devoted to our ideal and burning with desire to help redeem Jews—and I would send them to the countries where Jews are absorbed in sinful self-satisfaction, plague these Jews with anti-Semitic slogans, such as 'Bloody Jew,' 'Jew go to Palestine' and similar intimacies. I can vouch that the results, in terms of considerable immigration to Israel from these countries, would be ten thousand times larger than the results brought by thousands of emissaries who have been preaching for decades to deaf ears."[27]

The aims of the Zionist movement, apart from "ingathering" the Jews of the world into the Palestine area, are to "shake-down" Jews who do not go to Israel for contributions toward its support, solicit United States and United Nations assistance to Israel and promote the idea of Israel as the representative and guardian of the rights and interests of Jews wherever they may be. The letters of protest sent by the Israeli Government to the more than twenty states where "swastikas" appeared and the Adolph Eichmann trial, indicate the role which the Jewish state has assigned to itself. Israel speaks out on behalf of world Jewry, defends the interests of all Jews, whether they seek it or not.

The pro-Zionist Kimche brothers wrote that it was the Hitlerite catastrophe that gave post-war Zionism "a moral argument to which the Gentile world could have no answer;" and that when the British Navy turned immigrant ships away from the Palestine coast in the 1940's, it gave "the Jews a great moral weapon."[28]

Commenting, author Erskine H. Childers, wrote, "one of the most massively important features of the entire Palestine struggle was that Zionism deliberately arranged that the plight of the wretched survivors of Hitlerism should be a 'moral argument' that the West had to accept. This was done by seeing to it that Western countries did not open their doors, widely and immediately, to the inmates of the DP [displaced persons] camps. It is incredible," Childers continued, "that so grave and grim a campaign has received so little attention in accounts of the Palestine struggle—it was a campaign that literally shaped all subsequent history. It was done by sabotaging specific Western schemes to admit Jewish DPs,"[29] or when President Roosevelt, during the war, was considering the feasibility of helping Jewish refugees to settle in America and elsewhere, his plan, which would have absorbed all the DPs of Europe, was scotched by Zionists, not by anti-Semites.[30]

Speaking at the Sixth Annual National Conference of the American Council for Judaism, Morris L. Ernst revealed the extent of opposition to the efforts of President Roosevelt "to give relief to the people pushed around by Hitler." Mr. Ernst disclosed that as the representative of the President, he was "thrown out of parlors of friends of mine" when he discussed with them his plan of relief for DPs, who very frankly warned him: "Morris, this is treason—you're undermining the Zionist movement," to which he replied: "Yes, maybe I am. But I'm much more interested in a haven for a half a million or a million people—oppressed throughout the world."[31]

Childers then stated: "With the West's doors thus closed, the salvation of the DPs was presented to the world solely, desperately and morally as lying in and through a Jewish state in Palestine. Creaking ships were loaded with DPs and sent to Palestine in the certain knowledge that they would be turned back; but, as the Kimches obliquely admit, the very turning-back would add a 'moral weapon' to the already prepared 'moral argument.'"

Childers went on to say: "The very basis of the post-war Palestine struggle was an appeal to the world's humanitarianism over a situation deliberately designed to canalize that humane instinct into one premise: Jewish statehood in Palestine." He added: "None of us who remember the emotional atmosphere of the time can dismiss the role this Zionist campaign played in all that followed. The evidence of the campaign, though suppressed by Zionists and conveniently forgotten by Western liberals who knew about it, is overwhelming. It is detailed in White House conversations. It was publicly acknowledged, for example, by Sulzberger of *The New York Times*, who asked in 1946, 'In God's name why should the fate of all these unhappy people be subordinated to the single cry of statehood'?"[32]

Richard Crossman, the champion of the Zionist cause on the Anglo-American Committee of Inquiry, writing in his 1946 Washington Diary, said: "The Zionists are terrific . . . their main preoccupation is not to save Jews alive out of Europe but to get Jews into Palestine and to establish a Jewish state."[33]

This discriminatory policy was again made clear in 1959, when Jews were allowed to leave Rumania. Those who signed to go to Israel were assisted in every way; those who elected to resettle in other countries, were not only refused the assistance of the United Jewish Appeal funds collected for needy Jews, but were made to refund money given for travel between Rumania and Austria.

A shocking disclosure of Zionist opposition to Jewish immigration to the U.S.A. was made in an article published in the May 1959 issue of *Unser Tzait*, a monthly publication of the Jewish Labor Bund, entitled "A Secret Document about Rumanian Jews." The document was a transcript of the minutes of a meeting held by the Presidents' Conference on February 25, 1959, at which the question of Jewish emigration from Rumania was discussed. The Presidents' Conference—an organization consisting of the heads of nineteen leading Zionist and pro-Zionist bodies in the United States, organized by the Jewish Agency for Israel to exert political pressure on the American government in favor of Israel—met to formulate opposition to measures favoring the admission of Rumanian Jews into the United States. Nothing was to obstruct their immigration to Israel. The Presidents' Conference also sought to persuade Senator Jacob K. Javits of New York not to introduce an immigration bill which would admit some Rumanian immigrants to the United States as refugees.[34]

Another exposure of Zionist methods this time concerning Arab countries appeared in an article by Ian Gilmour, who said: "Since the basis of Zionism is that Jewish assimilation in other countries is in the long run impossible and that anti-Semitism and persecution are bound to break out sooner or later, Zionism has almost a vested interest in racial discrimination. The Israelis mount 'rescue operations' to save allegedly threatened Jews in other countries . . ." He added: "In the Arab countries, Jewish difficulties and emigration to Israel were the result not of anti-Semitism but of Zionist activities and the existence of the state of Israel. Zionism aggravated the disease that it professed to cure,"[35] he remarked.

V   Palestine under Mandate (1920–1948)

The Mandate System

Fighting with the Turks was ended by the Armistice of October 30, 1918; and on January 30, 1919, the Supreme Council of the Peace Conference decided that the conquered Arab provinces, including Palestine, were not to be restored to Turkish rule. To circumvent the fulfillment of their promises of Arab independence, and to implement the secret Sykes-Picot Agreement of 1916, the Allied Powers devised what became known as the mandate system. This turned out to be disguised colonialism.

On June 28, 1919, the Treaty of Versailles and the Covenant of the newly established League of Nations were signed. Article 22 of the Covenant provided, "To those colonies and territories which as a consequence of the late war have ceased to be under the sovereignty of the States which formerly governed them and which are inhabited by peoples not yet able to stand by themselves under the strenuous conditions of the modern world, there should be applied the principle that the well-being and development of such peoples form a sacred trust of civilization and that securities for the performance of this trust be embodied in this Covenant. The best method of giving practical effect to this principle," the Covenant went on to say, "is that the tutelage of such peoples should be entrusted to advanced nations . . . and that this tutelage should be exercised by them as mandatories on behalf of the League."

In regard to "certain communities formerly belonging to the Turkish Empire, [which] have reached a stage of development . . . their existence as separate nations can be provisionally recognized subject to the rendering of administrative advice and assistance by a Mandatory until such time as they are able to stand alone. The wishes of these communities," the Covenant stressed, "must be a principal consideration in the selection of the Mandatory."[1]

A draft Mandate for Palestine was submitted by Britain to the Council of the League of Nations on July 24, 1922 and an agreed text was not confirmed by the Council until September 29, 1923 when it came formally into operation.

The Mandate included in the *Preamble* a text of the Balfour Declaration providing for the establishment of a Jewish national home with safeguards for the "non-Jewish communities" and Jews outside Palestine; in *Article 2*, responsibility "for placing the country under such political, administrative and economic conditions as will secure the establishment of the Jewish national home;" in *Article 4*, provision was made for a "Jewish Agency" to be recognized "as a public body for the purpose of advising and cooperating with the Administration of Palestine in such economic, social and other matters as may affect the establishment of the Jewish-national home"; and in *Article II*, the Administration was authorized to arrange with the Jewish Agency "to construct or operate, upon fair and equitable terms, any public works, services and utilities, and to develop any of the natural resources of the country."[2]

The Mandate failed to recognize the principles stipulated in *Article 22* of the Covenant of the League of Nations, namely, that Palestine—like Lebanon, Syria and Iraq—by reason of "the geographical situation of its territory, its economic conditions and other similar circumstances," had reached a stage of development where its existence as a nation "can be provisionally recognized subject to the rendering of administrative advice and assistance by a Mandatory until such time as [the inhabitants] are able to stand alone." Nor did the Mandate take into account the pledges of independence made previously to the Arabs by the Allies.

This failure can only be explained by the fact that, as in the case of the Balfour Declaration, the Arabs were not consulted in the preparation of the Mandate. The Mandate, which ostensibly at least, contained two sets of obligations to be undertaken by Britain—one toward the Jews and the other toward the Arabs—was drawn up jointly by the British government and the Zionists without regard to the rights of the third party. The Zionists believed that they, and they alone, have rights in Palestine and that the presence of the Moslem and Christian inhabitants was a passing phase.

The first interference by the Zionists in the administration of the country occurred in 1919 when it was still under military occupation. On his arrival in Jerusalem in July of that year, U.S. Court Judge Louis Brandeis—who was instrumental in obtaining the Balfour Declaration in return for bringing the United States into the war on the side of the Allies—visited British Military Headquarters on the Mount of Olives in Jerusalem. He is reported to have told General Louis Bols, the Chief Administrator, that "ordinances of the military authorities should be submitted first to the Zionist Commission." The General's Aide-de-Camp is purported to have replied: "For a government to do that would be to derogate its position. As a lawyer you realize this." But Brandeis proceeded to lay down the law as he saw it almost as if Palestine were under his jurisdiction. "It must be understood," he warned, "the British Government is committed to the support of the Zionist cause. Unless this is accepted as a guiding principle, I shall have to report it to the Foreign Office."[3]

Apparently this was too much for General Bols to take. In March 1920, he complained to London, "my own authority and that of every department of my Administration is claimed or impinged upon by the Zionist Commission, and I am definitely of opinion that this state of affairs cannot continue without grave danger to the public peace and to the prejudice of my Administration."

Sir Louis then warned, "It is no use saying to the Moslem and Christian elements of the population that our declaration as to the maintenance of the *status quo* on our entry into Jerusalem has been observed. Facts witness otherwise: The introduction of the Hebrew tongue as an official language; the setting-up of a Jewish judicature; the whole fabric of government of the Zionist Commission, of which they are well aware; the special traveling privileges to members of the Zionist Commission; these have firmly and absolutely convinced the non-Jewish elements of our partiality. On the other hand, the Zionist Commission accuses me and my officers of anti-Zionism. The situation is intolerable, and in justice to my officers and myself, must be fairly faced."

The Chief Administrator then pointed out, "It is manifestly impossible to please partisans who officially claim nothing more than a 'National Home' but in reality will be satisfied with nothing less than a Jewish state and all that it politically implies."[4]

Civil Administration Established

On July 1, 1920, a civil administration was established in Palestine; and the first officials to arrive in the country included British Zionist Jews who were placed in key positions. Some of these were: Herbert Samuel, one of the framers of the Balfour Declaration and a scion of the Zionist movement, High Commissioner; Norman Bentwich, Attorney General and chief legislator of Palestine laws; Albert Hyamson, Director of Immigration; and Max Nurock, Principal Assistant Secretary to the Government with access to all matters pertaining to policy in Palestine.

One of the early actions of this consortium was to enact the first Immigration Ordinance on August 26, 1920, fixing a quota of 16,500 immigrant Jews for the first year.

Other legislation followed—all designed to further the "Jewish national home" policy, as if the British Government had no obligations to the Arab section of the community. Significant among these, next to the Immigration Law, were laws affecting land disposition, registration and settlement, to hasten Jewish acquisition of Arab land. One of these laws—disguised as a law to protect cultivators against eviction by their landlords—had the opposite effect, ostensibly because almost all of the large tracts of land were owned by absentee land-owners living in Lebanon and Syria. Whereas relations between landlord and tenant had until then been on the best of terms, the new law gave the tenant the

MANDATE PALESTINE 1920–1948
Area: 10,435 sq. miles

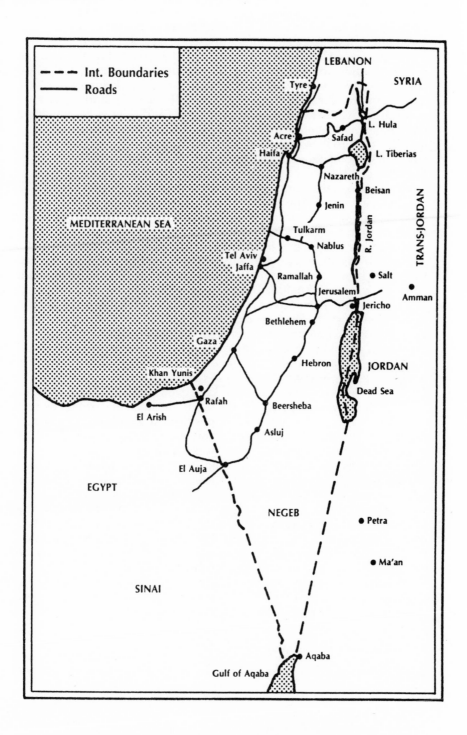

impression (and this was encouraged by Jewish land brokers) that he no longer needed to pay his rentals since the law gave him certain "tenancy rights" and protected him against eviction. Even squatters were soon able to establish "tenancy rights" under certain ambiguously worded provisions of the law. The landlord, placed in the unenviable position of owning land but getting hardly anything out of it, and burdened with taxation beyond his means, found himself in a critical situation. Here is where the Jewish land broker stepped in and offered to buy the land and rid the landlord of his problems. In one instance, over 40,000 acres, comprising 18 villages were sold, resulting in the eviction of 688 Arab agricultural families. Of these 309 families joined the landless classes, while the remainder drifted either into towns and cities or became hired ploughmen and laborers in other villages. Although eviction took place in 1922, the problem remained with the Palestine government to find land for some of these displaced persons until the termination of the Mandate in 1948.

Other measures favoring Jews were the granting to Jewish companies of concessions over state lands and the natural resources of the country, such as irrigation, electricity and the extraction of potash and other minerals from the Dead Sea.

Faced with its dual and incompatible obligations under the Mandate, and with Arab insistence that the establishment of a Jewish national home was itself an infringement of their rights, the British Government adopted two lines of policy: The *first* was to try to interpret the concept of a national home in such a way as to reassure the Arabs that it did not imply a Jewish state. The Government denied that it was the intention of His Majesty's Government to help in the establishment of anything more than a national home as a center in which the Jews of the world could take an interest and a pride. Yet all the signs indicated that a Jewish state was envisaged as soon as the Jews became a majority, or at least a sizable minority capable of taking over. The *second* line of policy was that the Government lived from 1922 in the hope that sooner or later the Arabs would give up their opposition to Zionism and become reconciled with the Jewish national home policy. Although the development of self-governing institutions was enjoined in the Mandate, in practice it was deliberately postponed because the Arab majority was known to be opposed to the other provisions of the Mandate. If genuine self-government was established immediately while the Arab majority was inflexibly opposed to Zionism, that would make impossible the fulfilment of British obligations to the Zionists. If, however, its establishment were postponed for some time, then the Arabs might be reconciled to Zionist settlement and representative institutions could thus be established without any danger of a conflict.

In fact, the majority was to be denied the right of controlling its political destiny until it should change its policy in deference to the will of the minority, or until the minority had itself become a majority.

Population and Land Ownership

At the close of World War I in 1918, Palestine was an Arab country similar to other parts of the Arab world. It had a population of about 700,000 persons, of whom 574,000 were Moslems, 70,000 were Christians, and 56,000 were Jews. The latter were mostly Arabs of the Jewish faith. About 12,000 of these Jews lived on the land as farmers, the rest carried on business in the principal towns—mainly Jerusalem.

Reliable data on the whole population of Palestine was collected twice during the thirty years of British Administration. The first census of population was taken on October 23, 1922, and the second (and last) on November 18, 1931. The second census was a very detailed one conducted along scientific lines and gave a complete picture of the demography of the country.

After the census of 1931, regular quarterly and annual estimates of the population, classified by religion, were kept by the Palestine Government Department of Statistics. These estimates were obtained by adding to the figures of 1931 the natural increase and the net migratory increases in the period between the census of 1931 and the year for which the estimate was prepared.

The census of 1931 enumerated all the persons present in Palestine at midnight of November 18, 1931, irrespective of whether they were residents of the country or not. Residents of the country who happened not to be present in Palestine were excluded. This same principle was adopted in the estimates for the years 1932 to 1946.

The population of Palestine rose from an estimate of 700,000 persons in 1918 to the figures shown below:

By Religion	1922 Census	1931 Census	1944 Estimates
Moslems	589,177	759,700	1,061,277
Jews	83,790	174,606	528,702
Christians	71,464	88,907	135,547
Others	77,617	10,101	14,098
Totals:	752,048	1,033,314	1,739,624[5]

By Race (Estimates)	1944	1946	1948
Arabs (Moslems and Christians)	1,179,000	1,293,000	1,380,000
Jews (non-Arab)	554,000	608,000	700,000*
Others	32,000	35,000	35,000
Totals:	1,765,000[6]	1,936,000[7]	2,115,000[8]

*The size of the Jewish community is in line with the size as on November 8, 1948, when it was reported to have reached 716,000 because of large-scale immigration after the creation of the state (For last figure, see Israel Government Yearbook 1950, p. 359).

According to these figures, the proportion of Jews to the total population rose from 8% in 1918 to about 12% in 1922, to about 17% in 1931, to about 31% in 1944 and in mid-May 1948. The pace of this increase in the size of the Jewish community is all the more startling considering the fact that the rate of net natural increase among the Palestinian Arabs was about 50% higher than that among Palestinian Jews (3.2% and 2.2% respectively). It was large-scale immigration that accounted for the fast rise in the ratio of Jews to the total population.

In 1918, the Jews owned only 2% (162,500 acres) out of a total land area of 6,580,755 acres.[9]

During the ensuing thirty years, the Jews purchased additional land, bringing their total holdings on the date of the termination of the Mandate in May 1948, to 372,925 acres, or 5.67% of the total land area of Palestine.[10] However, the Palestine Government estimated in 1946 that "the Jews held over 15% of the cultivable area of Palestine."[11]

Resistance to sale of land to Jews persisted throughout the period of the Mandate; and the extra area of 210,425 acres acquired between 1918 and 1948, was mostly land purchased from Lebanese and Syrian absentee landowners living outside Palestine. The area sold by Palestinians during the Mandate was about 100,000 acres only, in spite of the high prices offered and the legislation enacted that was designed to facilitate transfer of land to Jews.

Zionist land policy was incorporated in the Constitution of the Jewish Agency for Palestine, signed in Zurich, Switerland, on August 14, 1929, which in turn reflected itself in the lease contracts of the Keren Kayemeth (Jewish National Fund) and the Keren Hayesod (Palestine Foundation Fund). Sections (d) and (e) of Article 3 provided that "land is to be acquired as Jewish property and . . . the title to the lands acquired is to be taken in the name of the Jewish National Fund, to the end that the same shall be held as the inalienable property of the Jewish people." The provision goes on to stipulate that "the Agency shall promote agricultural colonization based on Jewish labor, and in all works or undertakings carried out or furthered by the Agency, it shall be deemed to be a matter of principle that Jewish labor shall be employed."[12]

The effect of this Zionist colonization policy on the Arabs was that land acquired by Jews became extra-territorialized. It ceased to be land from which the Arabs could ever hope to gain any advantage. The stringent provisions of the lease contracts entered into with the Jewish settlers made the latter undertake, under penalty of a fine and subsequent foreclosure, not to hire or employ 'non-Jewish labor;* also, if the holder died leaving as his heir a non-Jew, the Fund was to obtain the right of restitution. Nor could anyone help the Arab by purchasing the land and restoring it to common use: it was mortmain and inalienable.

Sir John Hope-Simpson, who visited Palestine in 1930 to look into Arab grievances, described both provisions as "not only contrary to Article 6 of the Mandate, but it is in addition a constant and increasing

---

*Prior to the advent of Zionism, relations between the Arab and Jewish farmers were on the best of terms, so much so, that Arab laborers working in Jewish colonies handed down their jobs from father to son, and in some cases the children were referred to by their first Arab names followed by the family names of their Jewish employers.

source of danger to the country."[13]

This racist, discriminating policy, which characterized the treatment by Israel of its post-1948 Arab minority, has its roots in the exclusiveness clauses referred to above.

Arabs Opposition to the Mandate

Arab opposition to the Mandate and the policy of the Balfour Declaration remained obstinate and unrelenting throughout the period of the Mandate.

When appeals, protests, arguments, demonstrations and strikes failed to move the British Government to fulfill its pledges to the Arabs and follow a policy of justice and equity, the Palestine Arabs resorted from time to time to violence. The first violent expression of Arab feeling occurred on Easter Sunday in April 1920; the second in May 1921; the third in August 1929; and between 1936 and 1939, an all-out rebellion broke out that was preceded by an unprecedented six-month strike.

Four principal commissions of inquiry were appointed directly as a result of the riots.[14] Their findings were invariably the same, namely,

(a) Arab disappointment at the non-fulfillment of the promises of independence that had been given to them during the First World War; and

(b) Arab belief that the Balfour Declaration implied a denial of the right of self-determination and their fear that the establishment of "a national home for the Jews" in Palestine will lead to their ultimate dispossession of their homes and homeland.

The Zionists made no secret of their intentions, for as early as 1921, Dr. Eder, a member of the Zionist Commission, "boldly told the Court of Inquiry," "there can be only one National Home in Palestine, and that a Jewish one, and no equality in the partnership between Jews and Arabs, but a Jewish preponderance as soon as the numbers of the race are sufficiently increased."[15] He then asked that only Jews should be allowed to bear arms.

British "Statements of Policy"

The Commissions of Inquiry that were appointed to establish the causes for the riots were each followed by the issue of a "Statement of Policy," each attempting to interpret the meaning of "a national home."

On June 3, 1922, the British Government issued what became known as "The Churchill Memorandum" stating that "Phrases have been used such as that 'Palestine is to become as Jewish as England is English.'" The statement went on to point out that "His Majesty's Government regard any such expectation as impracticable and have no such aim in view. Nor have they at any time contemplated . . . the disappearance or the subordination of the Arabic population, language or culture in Palestine. They would draw attention to the fact that the terms of the [Balfour] Declaration referred to do not contemplate that Palestine as a whole should be converted into a Jewish National Home, but that such a Home should be founded in Palestine."[16]

Although the "White Paper" repudiated the idea of Jewish domination over the Arabs, it established a principle for the regulation of immigration that would in time make such domination possible if not inevitable. Moreover, it was no more than a statement of formal principles and did not take into account one of the essential facts of the situation: that although the British Government might lay down a general policy, which respected the idea of a dual obligation, the Zionists were so much better organized than the Arabs and had so many more ways of putting pressure upon the Government both from within Palestine and through outside governments and organizations through the privileged status of the Jewish Agency, and in other ways, that they could always tilt the balance in their favor. While the Arabs were not reassured by statements of principle which failed to face the implications of incessant immigration and of Zionist influence, yet they still hoped that a change of British policy to ensure justice for their Arab wards would in time take place.

The riots of 1929 were followed by yet another pronouncement. This took the form of a "White Paper" that became known as "The Passfield Memorandum." In view of the importance of this second "Statement," it is reproduced at greater length:

> "Many of the misunderstandings which have unhappily arisen on both sides appear to be the result of a failure to appreciate the nature of the duty imposed upon His Majesty's Government by the terms of the Mandate. The next point therefore which His Majesty's Government feel it necessary to emphasize, in the strongest manner possible, is that in the words of the Prime Minister's statement in the House of Commons on the 3rd April last, 'a double undertaking is involved, to the Jewish people on the one hand and to the non-Jewish population on the other.'"

And again:

> "These points are emphasized because claims have been made on behalf of the Jewish Agency to a position in regard to the general administration of the country which His Majesty's Government cannot but regard as going far beyond the clear intention of the Mandate. Moreover, attempts have been made to argue, in support of Zionist claims, that the principal feature of the Mandate is the passages regarding the Jewish national home, and that the passages designed to safeguard the rights of the non-Jewish community are merely secondary considerations, qualifying, to some extent, what is claimed to be the primary object for which the Mandate has been framed.
>
> This is a conception which H.M.G. have always regarded as totally erroneous. However difficult the task may be, it would, in their view, be impossible, consistently with the plain intention of the Mandate, to attempt to solve the problem by subordinating one of these obligations to the other. The British accredited representative, when appearing before the Permanent Mandates Commission on the 9th June last, endeavoured to make clear the attitude of H.M.G. towards the difficulties inherent in the Mandate. In commenting on his state-

ments in their report to the Council, the Permanent Mandates Commission made the following important pronouncement:

"From all these statements, two assertions emerge, which should be emphasized:

(1) That the obligations laid down by the Mandate in regard to the two sections of the population are of equal weight;

(2) That the two obligations imposed on the Mandatory are in no sense irreconcilable.

The Mandate Commission has no objection to rise to these two assertions which, in its view, accurately express what it conceives to be the essence of the Mandate for Palestine and ensure its future."[17]

The Arabs, who had never recognized the legality of the Mandate imposed upon them without their consent, could not subscribe to the thesis that the two obligations contained in it were of equal weight. The Zionists proferred a *claim* to Palestine based on questionable ancient biblical and historical theories which the Arabs resisted and continue to resist; the Arabs, on the other hand, have a *right* to Palestine based on *birth* and *uninterrupted possession*.

As a result of the 1936–1939 Arab rebellion, the British Government, on May 17, 1939, issued yet another but final "Statement of Policy" that became known as "The MacDonald White Paper." After referring to the terms of the Mandate, the "Statement" pointed out, "the Royal Commission and previous Commissions of Enquiry have drawn attention to the ambiguity of certain expressions in the Mandate, such as the expression 'a national home for the Jewish people,' and they have found in this ambiguity and the resulting uncertainty as to the objectives of policy a fundamental cause of unrest and hostility between Arabs and Jews." The Government was convinced that, in the interests of peace and well-being of the whole people of Palestine, a clear definition of policy and objectives was essential. Consequently, the British Government declared that neither their undertakings to the Jews nor the national interests of Britain warranted that they should continue to develop the Jewish national home beyond the point already reached. The Government therefore decided:

1. That the Jewish National Home as envisaged in the Balfour Declaration and in previous statements of British policy had been established;

2. That to develop it further against Arab wishes would be a violation of Britain's undertakings to the Arabs, and that such a policy could only be carried out by the use of unjustifiable force;

3. That, therefore, after the admission of a final quota of 75,000 more Jewish immigrants over a period of five years, Jewish immigration should stop;

4. That during this period of five years, a restriction should be placed on the acquisition of further land in Palestine by the Jews; and

5. That at the end of the period of five years, self-governing institutions should be set up in the country.[18]

Arab and Jewish Reaction to 1939 "White Paper"

Arab reaction to the new policy of the 1939 White Paper was mixed. A certain section of the population was willing to accept it but doubted the sincerity of the British Government; the other decided to reject it as not meeting fully the aspirations of the Palestine Arabs, which was the abrogation of the Balfour Declaration and the Mandate and the granting of independence to the country.

Zionist reaction, on the other hand, was one of unanimous rejection and condemnation. A general strike was called for the day following its announcement, when violent and inflammatory speeches were made by Zionist leaders. In Jerusalem Arab shops were looted, the police stoned when they tried to maintain order, and a British constable was shot.[19]

But on the outbreak of World War II, both parties decided not to embarrass the British Government and to cease all acts of violence. As attested by the Palestine Government, "The Arabs of Palestine demonstrated their support of democracy at the outbreak of war, and there were spontaneous appeals in the Arab press to Arabs to rally to the side of Great Britain and set aside local issues; acts of terrorism were roundly condemned,"[20] while Arab notables called on the High Commissioner to assure him of their loyalty.[21] It was later admitted that the British Government was thus "able to build up the comprehensive military organization based in Cairo which was to serve them so well."[22]

The Jews in Palestine also unanimously agreed to put aside their opposition to British policy in Palestine. Jewish terrorist acts ceased, and the illegal broadcasting station closed down. The Jewish Agency issued an appeal calling on all Jews in Palestine to close their ranks and offer their assistance to Britain. But all this proved to be for a purpose.

While acts of violence against the British Administration did in fact cease, Jewish Agency operations in the field of illegal immigration continued and was intensified. More and more "illegals" began to arrive in ships that were not sea-worthy. At first, the Palestine Government turned these back; later, they were directed by the British Navy to Cyprus where the inmates were interned. This infuriated the Jewish community in Palestine, and violence against the British once again broke out.

On March 6, 1940, David Ben Gurion, representing the Jewish Agency, informed the General Officer Commanding that he was not prepared to take active steps to put an end to the disturbances protesting against the "White Paper" under which the Jewish immigrants were being refused entry into the country.

Sinking of the ships "Patria" and "Struma"

On November 25, 1940, the ship *Patria* was scuttled at her moorings in Haifa harbor by an explosion and sank in a quarter of an hour with the loss of life to 252 illegal Jewish immigrants and British police personnel. The Commission of Inquiry appointed to inquire into the circumstances found that the damage to the *Patria* had been committed by Jewish sympathizers ashore, with the cooperation of at least one person on board the ship.

At first, the British Mandatory was blamed, but eighteen years later, the story of how the massacre was arranged was disclosed by one of the participants. Dr. Herzl Rosenblum, editor of a large Zionist Tel Aviv daily, *Yedios Achronos*, related that: "This was in 1940, shortly before the affair *Patria*. A session of the small Actions Committee, of which I was a member, met in Jerusalem. At the table opposite me sat the commander of the *Patria* project, A. Golomb. When my turn came to speak, I rose and told the meeting openly everything I thought about this act, namely, that this was not a fight against England, but an irresponsible, aimless mass-murder of Jews who had been saved from the European catastrophe. I added that if any one of us believed that we had to fight the British by committing *hara-kiri*, let him commit *hara-kiri* himself; for *hara-kiri* is suicide and not an act of murder. I stated plainly that this road was open to Mr. Golomb but that he couldn't sacrifice other Jews for his 'policy' without first asking them, and particularly the children among them—a crime against which I openly protested. At this point, Mr. Golomb jumped up and attacked me with his fists. Mr. Golomb's fists did not provoke me as much as the servility of all the committee members, none of whom supported me. When I left the meeting, everything in me was an uproar. I could not control my feelings. I thought of the Russian terrorists who refused to throw a bomb at the Czar because he was in the company of a child and woman, although this child or woman did not belong to the Revolutionists, but to the hated enemy—the Czar. But we murdered with our bare hands our own children, their mothers, sisters and dear ones, and yet everything is in order. Rejoice our people!" he concluded.

Moshe Sharett, who heard this criticism, replied in his memorial oration: "It is sometimes necessary to sacrifice a few in order to save the many." But David Flinker, the Israeli correspondent of the Zionist *Tog-Journal*, commented: "Yes, it is true that a commander occasionally must send to death some soldiers in order to save his city or country. The question, however, is whether this was true in the case of the *Patria*, and whether it was permissible to follow this principle . . . This [blowing up of the ship] was a political demonstration against the British, carried out at the cost of 250 innocent Jews—men, women and children."*[23]

On February 24, 1942, the ship *Struma*, carrying illegal immigrants to Palestine sank in the Black Sea as a result of an explosion in which 760 Jewish lives were lost. As in the case of the *Patria*, the British Government was blamed; and, as in the case of the *Patria*, some day the truth might become known how the *Struma* was sunk.

---

*In later years, it was admitted that the Hagana general staff had the ship blown up in order to lay this charge at the door of the Mandatory Government. This was disclosed in the *New York Morning Freiheit* of November 27, 1950 in which the Israeli correspondent, wrote of the Hagana decision: "The English must be given to understand that Jews would not be driven away from their own country. The *Patria* must be blown up. The decision was conveyed to Hagana members on the *Patria*, and in the hush of night, preparations had begun for the execution of the tragic act."

Zionists Resume Political Activity

The first three years of the war were however profitably used by the Zionists in their plans for Palestine. They employed all means to procure arms; bring in illegal immigrants; recruit and train them for their own fight after the war. In the political field, great activity was observed. In May 1942, a conference of American, European and Palestinian Zionists was held at the Biltmore Hotel in New York under the sponsorship of an Emergency Committee on Zionist affairs. The "Platform" included an affirmation by the conference of "its unalterable rejection of the White Paper of May 1939, and denies its moral or legal validity. The White Paper," it said, "seeks to limit, and in fact to nullify Jewish rights to immigration and settlement in its denial of sanctuary to Jews fleeing from Nazi persecution . . ."

The conference then demanded, "In the struggle against the forces of aggression and tyranny, of which Jews were the earliest victims, and which now menace the Jewish National Home, recognition must be given to the right of the Jews of Palestine to play their full part in the war effort and in the defence of their country, through a Jewish military force fighting under its own flag and under the high command of the United Nations." It urged "that the gates of Palestine be opened; that the Jewish Agency be vested with control of immigration into Palestine and with the necessary authority for upbuilding the country, including the development of its unoccupied and uncultivated lands; and that Palestine be established as a Jewish commonwealth integrated in the structure of the new democratic world."[24]

On the basis of this "Program," the Jewish Agency presented the British Government on May 22, 1945—a fortnight after VE Day—with the following demands:

1. That an immediate decision be announced to establish Palestine "undivided and undiminished" as a Jewish state;

2. That the Jewish Agency be invested with the control of Jewish immigration into Palestine;

3. That an international loan be raised to finance the immigration of the "first million" Jews to Palestine;

4. That reparations in kind from Germany be granted to the Jewish people for the "rebuilding" of Palestine; and—as a first installment—that all German property in Palestine be used for the resettlement of Jews from Europe;

5. That free international facilities be provided for the exit and transit of all Jews who wish to settle in Palestine.[25]

Zionists Acts of Violence

Responsibility for the acts of violence in Palestine between 1943 and 1948 rested entirely with the *Hagana* (meaning "Defence") and its two splinter groups, the *Irgun Zvei Leumi* (meaning "National Military Organization") and the *Stern Gang* (self-styled "Freedom Fighters of Israel"). The Irgun split from the "mother" organization—Hagana—in 1935, and the Stern Gang in turn split from the Irgun in 1939.

Whereas the Hagana adhered to a socialist philosophy and obeyed the orders of the Jewish Agency for Palestine, the Irgun Zvei Leumi owed political allegiance to the Revisionists, the extreme nationalist wing of the Zionist movement.

All three groups cooperated when they found this more profitable, but each in its own way. Their objective, however, was the same, namely, the establishment of a "Jewish state," but they differed in method of achieving this objective. The Hagana at first showed restraint because of its relationship to the Jewish Agency. The Irgun Zvei Leumi, on the other hand, had no need for caution and could therefore afford to be more ruthless. From the beginning it was organized on the strictly conspiratorial lines of a terrorist underground movement; and its recruits were mostly from among the Yemenite and Sephardic Jews who were taught Polish underground tactics. In this manner, the Jewish Agency could—as it always did—disclaim responsibility for any action that shocked the world by reason of its brutality.

The origin of the Hagana—the illegal military arm of the Zionist movement, established and maintained by the officially-recognized Jewish Agency—goes back to the 1870's when the first Jewish agricultural colonies were established in Palestine as the forerunners of the envisaged "Jewish state." At first, the duties of these *Hashomer* (Watchmen), as they were then named, were to provide protection against possible stealing. There was then no other reason because the aims of these early settlers were generally still unknown to the Arab inhabitants.

The transformation of the *Hagana* into a fighting force began only after World War I when mass immigration started in earnest and the political Zionist movement had received the recognition of the Allied powers. Eliahu Colomb, one of the first "Watchmen," became the Commander of the Hagana and its new role as a para-military organization was to recruit, train and equip all able-bodied young men and women for the day when it would be possible to seize the country by force and establish the Jewish State.

The disturbances of the 1920s enabled Jewish settlements to obtain a limited quantity of arms from the Government for self-protection. These were placed in sealed armories in charge of the village *Mukhtar* (headman) to be opened only in case of a serious emergency. But it gave the Hagana—whose existence was supposedly unknown to Government— the opportunity to augment its Government issues with illicit arms and ammunition and to start training in attack as in defence.

By 1946, the Hagana had become a strong military establishment. A "White Paper," published by the Mandatory Government that year, described the Hagana as an illegal and well-armed military organization, organized under a central command with subsidiary territorial commands, in three branches, each of which includes women, viz:

a static force composed of settlers and townsfolk,
    with an estimated strength of 40,000;
a field army, based on the Jewish Settlement Police and
    trained in more mobile operations, with an
    estimated strength of 16,000;
a full-time force (Palmach), permanently mobilized and
    provided with transport, with an estimated peace

establishment of 2,000 and war establishment of
some 6,000

The "White Paper" added that something in the nature of conscrip-
tion is in force; a year's service being obligatory for senior school
children, male and female, between the ages of 17 and 18. The Jewish
publication, *Haboker*, stated that prior to November 11, 1945, "every
Movement must submit to the Jewish Agency's Recruiting Department
in Tel Aviv a roster of its members, male and female, who must enlist."

The same "White Paper" added that the Irgun had a strength estimated at between 3,000 and 5,000; while the Stern Gang had between
200 and 300 dangerous fanatics.*[26]

The first signs of Zionist acquisition of illicit arms came to light in
October 1935 when "a large quantity of arms and ammunition smuggled
in a consignment of cement from Belgium was discovered at Jaffa port
and led to rumors among Arabs that the Jews were extensively arming
themselves."[27]

With the increase in the Jewish population as a result of mass
immigration and the entry of elements brought into the country with the
sole purpose of creating a Jewish majority and establishing a "Jewish
state," the ranks of those for whom arms and training had to be found
obviously swelled. The second World War brought about just that
opportunity. While the British Government was engaged with the war
against Germany, the Zionist Organization was busy acquiring arms
and training its underground forces.

As early in the War as October 5, 1939, forty-three Jews, wearing
uniforms, were arrested while engaged in military maneuvers and
carrying rifles and bombs; on November 18 of the same year, thirty-eight
Revisionist Jews, engaged in maneuvers and carrying arms, bombs,
gelignite, etc., were arrested; and on January 22, 1940, a search of the
Jewish settlement of Ben Shemen revealed a hoard of arms and ammunition.[28]

According to the Palestine Government: "During March 1943, there
was a notable increase in the number and magnitude of thefts of arms
and explosives from military establishments, and shortly afterwards
there was revealed the existence of a large scale stealing racket connected with the *Hagana* and with ramifications throughout the Middle
East. Jewish feeling against action by Government and the military
authorities to stop this traffic was roused by the trial by military court of
two Jews who had taken part in the traffic. The 'arms trial,' as it came to
be known, was preceded by the trial of two British military deserters
(Privates Harris and Stoner) who were sentenced each to fifteen years
imprisonment for complicity in the thefts . . ."

"In passing sentence the President of the court stated that the trial
had shown 'that there is in existence in Palestine a dangerous and
widespread conspiracy for obtaining arms and ammunition from His
Majesty's Forces' and that the organization behind the activities of the

---

*Zionist terrorism was not confined to British targets, but included individual Palestinians. See
Begin and Co.: As they Really Are, an Anthology by Prof. Israel Shahak, 2 Bartenura Street,
Jerusalem, September 1977.

two accused 'seems to have had considerable funds at its disposal and to possess wide knowledge of military matters, including military organization.'

"The trial caused considerable bitterness on the part of the Jewish community against Government who, they thought, should recognize that the Jews had a moral right to arm; feeling was aggravated by the fact that the trial was held in public and that the Jewish official bodies had been mentioned in the course of the proceedings."[29]

With signs that the Nazi menace to Palestine was over and that the Allies would finally be winning the war, the Zionist campaign of terror began in earnest at the end of January 1944 and continued until the end of the Mandate in 1948. These acts of violence and sabotage coming as they did at a time when England's hands were still full with the war against Germany and therefore least able to maintain law and order, harassed the Government. Consequently, on October 10, 1944, the Officer Administering the Government and the Commander-in-Chief, Middle East, issued a joint official communiqué in which it was clearly stated that the terrorists and "their active and passive sympathizers are directly impeding the war effort of Great Britain" and "assisting the enemy." The communiqué called upon "the Jewish community as a whole to do their utmost to assist the forces of law and order in eradicating this evil thing within their midst;" it added that "verbal condemnation of outrages on the platform and in the press may have its effect but is not in itself enough; what is required is actual collaboration with the forces of law and order, especially the giving of information leading to the apprehension of the assassins and their accomplices." The communiqué then demanded "of the Jewish community in Palestine, their leaders and representative bodies to recognize and discharge their responsibilities and not to allow the good name of the *Yishuv* to be prejudiced by acts which can only bring shame and dishonor on the Jewish people as a whole."[30]

The situation did not alter. Government buildings continued to be blown up, railway tracks and telephone lines were cut, British personnel assassinated; but the most outstanding acts of terror were:

(1) On November 6, 1944, two Zionist gunmen of the Stern Gang murdered Secretary of State Lord Moyne in Cairo. It is generally held that the assassination was an act of revenge for the anti-Zionist policy he was believed to have advocated.[31] A Zionist writer had listed the charge: he had been 'busy rigging up' the Arab League as a counterforce to Zionism; as Colonial Secretary in 1941 and 1942, he 'vehemently' opposed Jewish immigration; he had made a declaration in the House of Lords on June 9, 1942 that the Jews were not the descendants of the ancient Hebrews and had no 'legitimate claim' to the Holy Land; and he was 'an implacable enemy of Hebrew independence.'[32]*

---

*According to the *Evening Star* of Auckland, New Zealand of July 2, 1975, "the bodies of Eliahu Hakim and Eliahu Beit-Zouri, executed for the 1944 slaying of Lord Moyne," were exchanged for "20 Arab prisoners." The bodies on being taken over, "lay in Jerusalem's Hall of Heroism and were then given a military burial on Mt. Herzl."

On November 17, Sir Winston Churchill, then Prime Minister and an ardent Zionist, made a revealing statement in the House of Commons regarding the assassination: "If our dreams for Zionism," he said, "are to end in the smoke of assassins' pistols and our labors for its future are to produce a new set of gangsters worthy of Nazi Germany, many like myself will have to reconsider the position we have maintained so consistently and so long in the past. If there is to be any hope of a peaceful and successful future for Zionism, these wicked activities must cease; and those responsible for them must be destroyed, root and branch."[33]

(2) On July 22, 1946, a wing of the King David Hotel in which the Government Secretariat and part of the military headquarters were housed, was blown up causing the death of about 100 Government officials—British, Arab and Jewish.*[34]

Indignant at the cowardly act, the General Officer Commanding in Palestine, circulated a letter on July 26 to his troops in which he stated, "The Jewish community of Palestine cannot be absolved from responsibility for the long series of outrages culminating in the blowing up of a large part of the Government Offices in the King David Hotel causing grievous loss of life. Without the support, active and passive, of the general public," he said, "the terrorist gangs who actually carry out these criminal acts would soon be unearthed, and in this measure the Jews in this country are accomplices and bear a share in the guilt."

The General then decided "to put out of bounds to all ranks all Jewish places of entertainment, cafés, restaurants, shops and private dwellings. No soldier," he ordered, "is to have any intercourse with any Jew; and intercourse in the way of duty should be as brief as possible and kept strictly to the business in hand."[35]

(3) On December 29, a British army major and three British non-commissioned officers were abducted and flogged as a reprisal for the execution of a sentence of 18 strokes imposed by a military court on a Jewish terrorist.[36]

(4) On July 30, 1947, two British sergeants (Martin and Paice), spending the afternoon innocently on the beach in the Jewish town of Natanya, were dragged away and hanged in an eucalyptus grove on the outskirts of the town and their bodies made into

(continued from page 59)

"In London, the British Government expressed its regret that Israel saw fit to honor a terrorist act in its public ceremonies. Two British members of Parliament called the ceremony the 'honoring of assassins' and said it conflicted with Israeli complaints of Palestinian terrorism." Labor MP David Watkins said "it was sad that 'cold-blooded murderers' should be represented as heroes." MP John Stokes said: "It makes the British people sick."

*By a stroke of luck, the author was late for his usual weekly meeting at the King David Hotel, to consider a revision of "the Collection of Taxes Ordinance." He was on his way up the hill when the first explosion occurred, took cover, and when he started to walk again, the big explosion occurred. His four colleagues on the Committee, who were then apparently meeting, were killed.

"booby traps," said to be in reprisal for the execution of two
Jewish terrorists. A notice reading "This is the sentence of Irgun's
High Command" was attached to the bodies.[37]

Jewish Agency Directs Violence

On July 24, 1946, the Mandatory Government issued a "Statement of
Information relating to Acts of Violence" in which it declared that the
information that was in the possession of His Majesty's Government has
led them to the conclusion that "the Hagana and its associated force the
Palmach (working under the political control of prominent members of
the Jewish Agency), have been engaging in carefully planned movements of sabotage and violence under the guise of 'the Jewish Resistance
Movement;' that the Irgun Zvei Leumi and the Stern Gang have worked
since last Autumn in co-operation with the Hagana High Command on
certain of these operations; and that the broadcasting station 'Kol Israel,'
which claims to be 'the Voice of the Resistance Movement' and which
was working under the general direction of the Jewish Agency, has been
supporting these organizations."[38]

The revelation that the Jewish Agency was not only in touch with
Hagana, Irgun and the Stern Gang but actually coordinated and directed
their activities of murder, destruction and sabotage, did not come as a
surprise. The Jewish Agency challenged the British Government, alleging that the information in the possession of His Majesty's Government
was not authentic. In answer to a complaint on the subject made to the
United Nations Special Committee that visited Palestine in 1947 to
consider the "future government of Palestine," the Government described Hagana as "not a purely 'defensive' organization." It said, "In
its attack on Givat Olga, the sabotage of the railways, the ambushing of
the police during the attack on Athlit camp, and the attacks on the radar
stations on Mount Carmel and at Sarona, the Hagana was used for
coercive 'terrorist' purposes. Its difference from the dissident Irgun Zvei
Leumi and Stern Groups was not in any principle, but only in regard to
choice of strategic moments to apply force."[39]

The authenticity and accuracy of the documents in the hands of the
Government were later confirmed by Menachem Begin, then leader of
the *Irgun Zvei Leumi* and after 1977 Prime Minister of Israel. Commenting on Cmd. 6873 of July 24, 1946, in regard to the secret telegrams
exchanged between the various Zionist para-military organizations and
the Jewish Agency, said: "These telegrams mysteriously found their
way to the British Intelligence, and were seized and decoded by its
agents. They were published in a special White Paper by the British
Government. I must record that this particular White Paper on 'Violence
in Palestine' was one of the few British documents on Palestine that I
have read in which there were scarcely any distortions . . . Thus, for
example, it quotes a broadcast of *Kol Israel* and adds that this broadcast is
of particular importance in view of its having been approved by the
Head of the Political Department of the Jewish Agency, Mr. Moshe
Shertok."[40]

In a report to the Secretary of State, the High Commissioner described the situation in Palestine in May 1947 in the following terms:

"The first and most important element in the situation is that, because of political differences with the mandatory administration on account of the inability of His Majesty's Government to accede to Jewish demands, the Jewish community, whose dissident members are responsible for these outrages, have declined and still decline to give any assistance to the police and military forces in the maintenance of law and order. These forces are thus working in and among a population of over 600,000 whose leaders have refused to call for cooperation with the police against the extremists and have thus, however much they themselves may not have wished it, in effect encouraged the terrorist groups to further lawlessness and wanton assaults by all available means upon constituted authority in almost any form.[41]

In July 1947, the Palestine Government, in a supplementary memorandum to the UN. Special Committee, said: "When the war against Germany and Japan was seen to be approaching a successful conclusion, the Jews brought into action their weapons of lawlessness and terrorism in support of their own political aims and ambitions." The memorandum pointed out, "The right of any community to use force as a means of gaining its political ends is not admitted in the British Commonwealth. Since the beginning of 1945, the Jews have implicitly claimed this right and have supported, by an organized campaign of lawlessness, murder and sabotage, their contention that, whatever other interests might be concerned, nothing should be allowed to stand in the way of a Jewish state and free Jewish immigration into Palestine."[42]

Sympathy and support for the Jewish terrorists was not confined to the Jewish community in Palestine. The terrorists had many sympathizers and supporters in the United States without whose contributions terrorism and sabotage would not have been possible. At the time when Zionist terrorism was at its highest, Ben Hecht, a rich and influential Jewish Hollywood screen writer, published an encouraging "Letter to the Terrorists of Palestine" in the *New York Herald Tribune* of May 15, 1947, He said "The Jews of America are for you. You are their champions. You are the grin they wear. You are the feather in their hats."

"In the past fifteen hundreds years," he added, "every nation of Europe has taken a crack at the Jews. This time the British are at bat. You are the first answer that makes sense—to the New World."

"Every time you blow up a British arsenal, or wreck a British jail, or send a British railroad-train sky high, or rob a British bank, or let go with your guns and bombs at the British betrayers and invaders of your homeland," he gloated' "the Jews of America make a little holiday in their hearts." He concluded by assuring his "brave friends, we are working to help you. We are raising funds for you . . ."[43]

Termination of Mandate

In 1947, at the height of Zionist acts of terrorism and sabotage, the Mandatory Government made one last attempt to settle the Palestine problem by suggesting to both Arabs and Jews that British trusteeship over Palestine should continue for another five years with the declared object of preparing the country as a whole for independence.[44]

The Arabs presented their own proposals for independence with guarantees for Jewish minority rights that were unacceptable to the British Government; the Jewish Agency, on the other hand, rejected the Government's proposals out-right and intensified its terrorist and sabotage activities.

On February 18, 1947, the British Foreign Secretary announced in the House of Commons that His Majesty's Government had found, "the Mandate has proved to be unworkable in practice, that the obligations undertaken to the two communities had been shown to be irreconcilable,[45] and therefore announced its intention of giving it up.

VI The Palestine Problem before the United Nations (1947– 1948)

General Assembly Seized with The Problem

On April 2, 1947, the United Kingdom delegation to the United Nations addressed a letter to the Secretary-General of the United Nations requesting that the question of Palestine be placed on the agenda of the next regular session of the General Assembly, and, further, that a special session of the General Assembly be summoned as soon as possible for the purpose of constituting and instructing a special committee to prepare for the consideration of the question by the Assembly at its next regular session.[1]

On April 21 and 22, 1947, five Member States (Egypt, Iraq, Syria, Lebanon and Saudi Arabia) communicated to the Secretary General the request that the following additional item be placed on the agenda of the special session:

"The termination of the Mandate over Palestine and the declaration of its independence."[2]

On April 29, 1947, the General Committee of the Assembly recommended the inclusion in the agenda of the item submitted by the United Kingdom;[3] and on April 30, 1947, decided by a vote of eight to one, with five abstentions, not to recommend the inclusion in the agenda of the item demanded by the Arab States.[4]

Notwithstanding this rejection, the item was still included for discussion by the General Assembly under the special terms of rule 18. At its 70th meeting on May 1, 1947, the General Assembly approved the inclusion in the agenda of the item submitted by the United Kingdom Government;[5] and at its 71st meeting of the same date, rejected by a vote of 24 to 15 with 10 abstentions the inclusion of the item proposed by the Arab states.[6]

Thus, the sole item on the agenda of the special session was that submitted by the United Kingdom Government, viz: "Constituting and instructing a special committee to prepare for the consideration of the question of Palestine at the second regular session." The item was then referred to the First Committee of the General Assembly for its consideration.

The manner in which the British Government had referred the Palestine problem to the United Nations, and the action taken by the latter as described above, left much to be desired from the point of view of the Arab states and the Arabs of Palestine. The Arabs felt that both the British action and that of the United Nations were not in conformity with the provisions on self-determination prescribed in the United Nations Charter.

On May 5, 1947, the General Assembly decided that the First Committee should grant a hearing to the Jewish Agency;[7] and on May 7, 1947, a similar decision was adopted with regard to the Arab Higher Committee for Palestine.[8]

At the meeting of the General Assembly held on May 15, 1947, the representative of the United Kingdom declared: "We have tried for years to solve the problem of Palestine. Having failed so far, we now bring it to the United Nations in the hope that it can succeed where we have not. All we say," he added, "is that we should not have the sole responsibility for enforcing a solution which is not accepted by both parties and which we cannot reconcile with our conscience."[9]

It took the British Government thirty years to find out that the Mandate for Palestine was "unworkable" and Britain's obligations there "irreconcilable."

The First Committee devoted twelve meetings to the consideration of the question of constituting and instructing a special committee on Palestine. At its 57th meeting on May 13, 1947, the First Committee, by a vote of 13 to 11, with 29 abstentions,[10] recommended the following composition of the Special Committee which was subsequently approved in the General Assembly by a vote of 39 to 3, with 10 abstentions:

Australia, Canada, Czechoslovakia, Guatemala, India, Iran, Netherlands, Peru, Sweden, Uruguay, Yugoslavia.

The Assembly adopted the recommendations of the First Committee at the 79th meeting on May 15, 1947, by a final vote of 45 to 7 with 1 abstention.[11]

The Palestine Arabs strongly objected to the whole idea of forming yet another committee of enquiry into the Palestine problem. The Arab states all voted against the Assembly resolution and were supported by the Moslem states of Afghanistan and Turkey, with Thailand abstaining.

The Problem Before Special Committee (UNSCOP)

The members of the Special Committee arrived in Palestine on June 14 and 15, 1947, and during their stay in the Middle East, held 36 meetings. It was evident to the Palestine Arabs that the majority of the members of the Special Committee had arrived in Palestine predisposed to accepting a Zionist "solution" of the Palestine problem based on partition of the Holy Land. Consequently, the Arab Higher Committee, as the spokesman of the Palestine Arabs, cabled the Secretary-General of the United Nations informing him that after a thorough study of the deliberations and circumstances under which the Palestine fact-finding committee had been formed and the discussions leading up to its terms of reference, the Palestine Arabs had decided to abstain from collaboration with the Special Committee and to desist from appearing before it for the following reasons:

Firstly, United Nations' refusal to adopt the natural course of inserting the termination of the Mandate and the declaration of independence of Palestine in the agenda of the special session of the General Assembly and in the terms of reference of the Special Committee;

Secondly, United Nations' failure to detach the Jewish world refugee question from the Palestine problem;

Thirdly, the transgression of the interests of the Palestine inhabitants in the name of world religious interests although these latter were not the subject of contention.

The Arab Higher Committee then pointed out that the Palestine Arabs' natural rights to their country were self-evident and could not continue to be subject to investigation but deserved to be recognized on the basis of the principles of the United Nations Charter.[12]

After completing its investigations in Palestine, the Special Committee retired to Geneva to start its deliberations and prepare its report. But before doing so, it formed a sub-committee—in spite of Arab protests—to visit displaced persons camps in Germany and Austria to look into the situation of the inmates of certain assembly centers. Among their observations was one in regard to the propaganda to which the Jewish refugees had been subjected. They reported that "some actual evidence was seen in the form of posters and written material at some of the centers. In particular, at one center," the sub-committee pointed out, "a poster was noted with the inscription 'Palestine—a Jewish State for the Jewish People' and also a large pictorial design showing Jews from eastern Europe on the march toward Palestine shown as a much larger area than the present geographical limits."

The sub-committee went on to say, "our inquiries, so far as they went, indicated that in the schools in the various centers children are being taught Hebrew and given an intimate historical and geographical knowledge of Palestine."

The sub-committee then commented: "Naturally, also, the continual presence in the centers of representatives of such bodies as the Central Committee of Liberated Jews, the Jewish Agency, the American Joint Distribution Committee, and other voluntary organizations gives every opportunity for general indoctrination of the idea of settlement in Palestine . . ."[13]

On August 31, 1947, the Special Committee completed its report[14] and submitted it to the General Assembly. This embodied twelve general recommendations. Eleven of these were approved unanimously, and the twelfth (with two members dissenting and one recording no opinion) provided that "In the appraisal of the Palestine question, it be accepted as incontrovertible that any solution for Palestine cannot be considered as a solution of the Jewish problem in general."

The eleven recommendations approved unanimously, provided for the termination of the Mandate, independence for Palestine after a transitional period during which administration of the country would be the responsibility of the United Nations, and for the preservation of the Holy places. The General Assembly was to undertake immediately the initiation and execution of an international arrangement whereby the problem of the distressed European Jews, of whom approximately 250,000 were in assembly centers, should be dealt with as a matter of extreme urgency for the alleviation of their plight and of the Palestine problem. Minority rights were to be protected, peaceful relations were to be a prerequisite to independence, provision was to be made for economic unity, and the abolition of the capitulations, and lastly, an appeal was to be made to both parties to end acts of violence.

The Committee then presented two alternatives:

(1) *A Plan of Partition with Economic Union* supported by seven members of the Committee: Canada, Czechoslovakia, Guatemala, Netherlands, Peru, Sweden and Uruguay. This plan, which became known as the *Majority Plan*, divided Palestine into an Arab State, a Jewish State, and an international zone of Jerusalem and its environs under United Nations jurisdiction. In area, the Arab state was to comprise 4,476 square miles or 42.88% of the total; the Jewish State 5,893 square miles or 56.47%; and the Jerusalem International Zone 68 square miles or 0.65%. As regards population, the Jewish State was to contain 498,000 Jews and 497,000 Arabs, and the Jerusalem International Zone 105,000 Arabs and 100,000 Jews. At the time, Jewish land ownership within the frontiers of the proposed Jewish State was less than 10% and less than 6% in the whole of Palestine.

(2) *A Federal State Plan* supported by three members: India, Iran and Yugoslavia. This plan, which became known as the *Minority Plan*, provided, *inter alia*, that an independent state of Palestine would be established which would comprise an Arab State and a Jewish State. Jerusalem would be its capital. The federal state would comprise a federal government and governments of the Arab and Jewish states respectively. The federal government would exercise full powers over such matters as national defence, foreign relations, immigration, currency, inter-state waterways, transport and communications. The Arab and Jewish states would enjoy full power over local self-government in its various aspects. There was to be a single Palestinian nationality and citizenship, with guaranteed equal rights for all minorities and fundamental human rights and freedoms, as well as free access to the Holy places.

The Zionists received the *Majority Plan* with keenness and enthusiasm since it fully accorded with their aspirations for a Jewish state. To the Arabs, both plans were totally unacceptable for obvious reasons: The *Majority Plan*, because it blatantly destroyed the territorial integrity of their homeland; made a 50% Arab population in the proposed Jewish state officially and permanently subservient to the other 50% comprising the Jewish population; and gave the latter control over Arab lands. The *Minority plan* was equally rejected primarily because of its implicitly partitionist content.

Report of UNSCOP Before Ad Hoc Committee

On September 23, 1947, the General Assembly established an *Ad Hoc* Committee to consider the report of UNSCOP.

On September 25, 1947, the *Ad Hoc* Committee began its deliberations, and on September 29, 1947, the Representative of the Arab Higher Committee was invited to address the Committee. He began by stating that it was the sacred duty of the Arabs of Palestine to defend their country against all aggression, including the aggressive campaign being waged by the Zionists with the object of securing by force a country—Palestine—which was not theirs by right. The *raison d'être* of the United Nations was, he said, to assist self-defence against aggression.

The rights and patrimony of the Arabs of Palestine had been the subject of no fewer than eighteen investigations within 25 years, and all to no purpose. Commissions of inquiry had either reduced the national and legal rights of the Palestine Arabs or had glossed over them. The few recommendations, he said, favorable to the Arabs had been ignored by the Mandatory Power. For these and for other reasons already communicated to the United Nations, it was not surprising that the Arab Higher Committee should have abstained from the nineteenth investigation (i.e., UNSCOP's) and refused to appear before it.

The representative of the Arab Higher Committee then pointed out that the struggle of the Arabs of Palestine against Zionism had nothing in common with anti-Semitism. The Arab world, he said, had for centuries been one of the rare havens of refuge for the Jews of the world until the atmosphere of neighborliness had been poisoned by the Balfour Declaration and by the aggressive spirit the latter had engendered in the Jewish community.

He disputed the claims of world Zionism to Palestine as having no legal or moral basis. The religious connection of the Jews with Palestine, which he noted was shared by Moslems and Christians, gave them no secular claim to the country. As for the Balfour Declaration, the British Government had no right to dispose of Palestine, which it had occupied in the name of the Allies as a liberator and not as a conqueror. The Declaration was in contradiction to the Covenant of the League of Nations and was an immoral, unjust and illegal promise.

The Palestine spokesman then said that no people would be more pleased than the Arabs to see the distressed Jews of Europe given permanent relief. But Palestine, he pointed out, had already absorbed far more Jews than its just share, and the Jews could not impose their will on other nations by choosing the place and the manner of their relief, particularly if that choice was inconsistent with the principles of international law and justice, and prejudicial to the interests of the nation directly concerned.

He noted that the solution of the Palestine problem was simple. It lay in the Charter of the United Nations in accordance with which the Arabs of Palestine, constituting the majority of the population, were entitled to a free and independent state. The United Nations, he pointed out, was not legally competent to decide or impose Palestine's constitutional organization, and he went on to outline the following principles as the basis for the future constitutional organization of the Holy Land:

1. That an Arab State in the whole of Palestine be established on democratic lines.

2. That the Arab State of Palestine respect human rights, fundamental freedoms and equality of all persons before the law.

3. That the Arab State of Palestine protect the legitimate rights and interests of all minorities.

4. That freedom of worship and access to the Holy Places be guaranteed to all.

He then explained that the following steps would have to be taken to give effect to the above-mentioned four principles:

(a) A Constituent Assembly should be elected at the earliest possible time. All genuine and law-abiding nationals of Palestine would be entitled to participate in the elections of the Constituent Assembly.

(b) The Constituent Assembly would, within a fixed time, formulate and enact a Constitution for the Arab State of Palestine, which should be of a democratic nature and should embody the above-mentioned four principles.

(c) A Government should be formed within a fixed time, in accordance with the terms of the Constitution, to take over the administration of Palestine from the Mandatory Power.

Such a program, he stressed, was the only one which the Arabs of Palestine were prepared to accept. The only item on the Committee's agenda with which the Arab Higher Committee would associate itself was item 3, namely, "The termination of the Mandate over Palestine and the recognition of its independence as one State."[15]

On October 22, 1947, the *Ad Hoc* Committee appointed two Sub-Committees to examine and report on the findings of UNSCOP:

Sub-Committee 1,[16] (comprising Canada, Czechoslovakia Guatemala, Poland, South Africa, the Unites States of America, Uruguay, the U.S.S.R. and Venezuela) recommended the adoption of the *Majority Plan* after slight modifications.

Sub-Committee 2,[17] (comprising Afghanistan, Colombia, Egypt, Iraq, Lebanon, Pakistan, Saudi Arabia, Syria and Yemen), at its first meeting on October 23, 1947, felt that it was somewhat unfortunate that both Sub-Committee 1 and Sub-Committee 2 were so constituted as to include in each of them representatives of only one school of thought, respectively, and that there was insufficient representation of neutral countries. Accordingly, it was proposed that the Chairman of the *Ad Hoc* Committee should be requested to reconstitute Sub-Committee 2 (irrespective of what might be done with regard to Sub-Committee 1) by replacing two of the Arab States on the Sub-Committee (which were prepared to withdraw) by neutrals or countries that had not definitely committed themselves to any particular solution of the Palestine question. The Chairman of the *Ad Hoc* Committee, being approached in this connection, explained to the Sub-Committee that he could not see his way to accepting the recommendation.

To the Arabs, the composition of the membership of the Sub-Committees and the attitude of the Chairman of the *Ad Hoc* Committee, represented one thing, namely, that the partition of Palestine had already been agreed upon by the Great Powers to fit Zionist aspirations and that what was taking place in the United Nations was merely to give the semblance of legality to an illegal operation.

Nevertheless, Sub-Committee 2 proceeded with its investigation and formed three Working Groups:

1. *Legal problems*—Pakistan, Syria and Saudi Arabia
2. *Refugee problem*—Afghanistan, Colombia and Lebanon
3. *Constitutional proposals*—Egypt, Iraq and Yemen.

After considering the reports of the three Working Groups, the Sub-Committee presented its recommendations to the *Ad Hoc* Committee in the form of three draft resolutions. According to the first, the General Assembly, before recommending a solution of the Palestine problem, would request the International Court of Justice for an advisory opinion on certain legal questions connected with or arising from that problem, including questions concerning the competence of the United Nations to recommend or enforce any solution contrary to the wishes of the majority of the people of Palestine. The second resolution recommended an international settlement of the problem of Jewish refugees and displaced persons, and stated principles and proposed machinery for the cooperation of Member States in such a settlement. The third resolution provided for the creation of a provisional government of the people of Palestine to which the authority of the Mandatory Power would be transferred, as a preparatory step to the setting up of an elected Constituent Assembly. The Constitution framed by the latter would, *inter alia*, contain guarantees as regards the Holy places, human rights and fundamental freedoms. Such guarantees were enumerated in the draft resolution.[18]

On November 19, 1947, the *Ad Hoc* Committee met to consider the reports of its two Sub-Committees. The representative of the Arab Higher Committee was again invited to present the views of the Palestine Arabs. Commenting on the Zionist-inspired *Majority Plan* proposing the partition of the country, he said: "The two great champions of freedom—the U.S.S.R. and the United States—have joined hands, prompted, they said, by humanitarian motives, to support the monstrous perversion of the self-determination in Palestine. They had agreed on only one thing, namely, the partition of Palestine. They had prepared," he said, "for that destructive policy for divergent motives: the one to please Jewish voters in the United States; the other to permit tens of thousands of immigrants to inundate Palestine in order to propagate its theories and political aims . . ."

The Palestine Arab spokesman reiterated that the United Nations should "participate in establishing a democratic state as proposed by the Arabs. Nothing," he said, "would come of it but prosperity and peace for all." He referred to the treatment of Jews by Arabs in Arab Spain and in Palestine before the Balfour Declaration as examples of the spirit that could exist in Palestine if such a state were established.[19]

Voting on the recommendations of the two Sub-Committees began on November 24. First to be put to the vote were the three draft resolutions submitted by Sub-Committee 2:

Draft Resolution No. 1, was voted upon in two parts: The first part providing for the reference to the International Court of Justice for an advisory opinion concerning legal questions, was rejected by a vote of 25 to 18 with 11 abstentions. The second part, comprising the question of the competence of the United Nations to enforce any plan of partition of Palestine contrary to the wishes, or adopted without the consent of, the inhabitants of Palestine, was rejected by a bare vote of 21 to 20 with 13 abstentions.[20]

Draft Resolution No. II, dealing with Jewish refugees and displaced persons, received 16 votes in favor, 16 against, with 26 abstentions.[21]

Draft Resolution III, dealing with the establishment of an independent unitary State of Palestine, was rejected by a vote of 29 to 12 with 14 abstentions.[22] Here the United Nations dealt a severe blow to the principle of self-determination which formed the basis of the United Nations Charter.

The *Ad Hoc* Committee, having disposed of a recommendation that rested on the principles in Article 22 of the Covenant of the League of Nations and the United Nations Charter on self-determination in an obviously perfunctory manner, then turned its attention to the recommendations of Sub-Committee 1, which dealt with the Plan of Partition with Economic Union. The report of this Sub-Committee was approved by a vote of 25 to 13 with 17 abstentions.*[23]

The delegations of Syria, Iraq and Egypt protested against the partition resolution as being unjust, impractical, against the Charter and a threat to peace. The representative of Egypt reserved the right of his Government to consider the resolution as null and void.

The Report of The Ad Hoc Committee Before the General Assembly.

Consideration of the report[24] of the *Ad Hoc* Committee by the General Assembly began on November 26, 1947. The general trend appeared to be moving steadily toward the adoption of the *Majority Plan* of partition with economic union. Representatives of Member States who were not influenced by outside pressures warned against the dangers of partition. The representative of the Philippines expressed his delegation's "profound misgivings" in the wisdom of partition and said: "With interest we have followed the course of the debate since the special session of the General Assembly last April. We have carefully studied the report of the Special Committee on Palestine[25] and pondered the various proposals that have been submitted. As a result of these studies, the Philippines Government has come to the conclusion that it cannot give its support to any proposal for the political disunion and the territorial dismemberment of Palestine . . . We hold that the issue is primarily moral. The issue is whether the United Nations should accept responsibility for the enforcement of a policy which, not being mandatory under

---

*Voting *against*: Afghanistan, Cuba, Egypt, India, Iran, Iraq, Lebanon, Pakistan, Saudi Arabia, Siam, Syria, Turkey and Yemen.
Abstaining: Argentina, Belgium, China, Colombia El-Salvador, Ethiopia, France, Greece, Haiti, Honduras, Liberia, Luxemburg, Mexico, Netherlands, New Zealand, United Kingdom, Yugoslavia.

any specific provision of the Charter, nor in accordance with its fundamental principles, is clearly repugnant to the valid nationalist aspirations of the people of Palestine. The Philippines Government believes that the United Nations ought not to accept any such responsibility."*[26]

Similar misgivings felt by other Member States which later voted for partition are perhaps best expressed in the words of their delegates: The Swedish delegate admitted that the plan "has its weak sides and some dangerous omissions;"[27] the delegate from Canada said "We support the plan with heavy hearts and many misgivings;"[28] New Zealand's representative talked of the "grave inadequacies of the present proposals;"[29] while Belgium's Foreign Minister Van Langenhove said of it: "We are not certain that it is completely just; we doubt whether it is practical; and we are afraid that it involves great risks . . ."[30]

Sir Zufrallah Khan, representative of Pakistan, warned the western powers, which took it upon themselves to push through the partition resolution, "to remember that you may need friends tomorrow, that you may need allies in the Middle East. I beg of you," he pleaded, "not to ruin and blast your credit in these lands." He questioned the viability of the proposed Jewish state and the sincerity of the United States and the western powers. "They who paid lip-service to humanitarian principles," he said, "closed their own doors to the 'homeless Jews,' but voted Arab Palestine to be not only a shelter, a refuge, but also a state so that he [the homeless Jew] should rule over the Arab."[31]

On the eve of the final vote, the representative of Lebanon made the following statement: "To judge by the press reports which reach us regularly every two or three days, I can well imagine to what pressure, to what manoeuvres your sense of justice, equity and democracy has been exposed during the last thirty-six hours. I can also imagine how you have resisted all these attempts in order to preserve what we hold dearest and most sacred in the United Nations, to keep intact the principles of the Charter, and to safeguard democracy and the democratic methods of our organization. My friends, think of these democratic methods, of the freedom in voting which is sacred to each of our delegations. If we were to abandon this for the tyrannical system of tackling each delegation in hotel rooms, in bed, in corridors and anterooms, to threaten them with economic sanctions or to bribe them with promises in order to compel them to vote one way or another, think of what our organization would become in the future."[32]

Notwithstanding the hesitations of some, the misgivings of others, and the warnings of the Arab and other states, the General Assembly, on November 29, 1947, adopted the *Majority Plan* providing for the partition of Palestine by a vote of 33 in favor, 13 against, with 10 abstentions.**[33]

---

*On the orders of his Government, Mr. Romulo was on the s.s. *Queen Elizabeth* bound for Europe within hours after delivering his speech against partition. The Philippines then voted for partition.

**The voting was:

(33) *In favor*—Australia, Belgium, Bolivia, Brazil, Byelorussian SSR, Canada, Costa Rica, Czechoslovakia, Denmark, Dominican Republic, Ecuador, France, Guatemala, Haiti, Iceland, Liberia, Luxemburg, Netherlands, New Zealand, Nicaragua, Norway, Panama, Paraguay,

The Partition Plan divided Palestine into six principal parts. Three were allotted to the *Jewish state*, and three, with the enclave of Jaffa, to the *Arab state*. The purpose behind this extraordinary and unnatural division was to include within the *Jewish state* all areas owned and inhabited by Jews, even though this meant the inclusion of large areas owned and inhabited by Arabs. The *Arab state*, on the other hand, was to include the least possible number of Jews and the smallest amount of Jewish property. The City of Jerusalem and the area around it, including Bethlehem, were set aside as an *international zone* to be placed under United Nations jurisdiction.

The Partition Resolution guaranteed the civil, political, economic religious and property rights of the Arabs. It provided that the stipulations contained in the Declaration on those rights were to be recognized as fundamental laws of the state; and no law, regulation, or official action was to conflict or interfere with these stipulations or take precedence. It also stipulated that "no discrimination of any kind shall be made between the inhabitants on the grounds of race, religion, language or sex;" that "no expropriation of land owned by an Arab in the *Jewish state* shall be allowed except for public purposes;" and that "in all cases of expropriation, full compensation as fixed by the Supreme Court shall be paid previous to dispossession."

The Partition Resolution further stipulated that the Jewish and Arab states were to come into being two months after the date of termination of the Mandate, which the British Government had scheduled for May 15, 1948. In addition, the Resolution provided for the establishment of a Palestine Commission that would progressively take over the administration of the country, for ultimate transfer of responsibility to the envisaged Arab and Jewish governments.

Delegates who voted for partition did so with little or no enthusiasm. Were it not for the extreme pressures to which they and their Governments had been subjected, they would have given the matter more serious consideration and no doubt some would have come out with a different resolution. Sir Zufrallah Khan, representative of Pakistan, summed up the position of these and other delegates when he explained his own negative vote. Because of the wisdom of his words, and their applicability to the situation in the Middle East after the lapse of many years, Sir Zufrallah Khan's statement is reproduced in full:

"A fateful decision has been taken. The die has been cast. In the words of the greatest American: 'We have striven to do the right as God gives us to see the right.' We did succeed in persuading a sufficient number of our fellow representatives to see the right as we saw it, but they were not permitted to stand by the right as they saw

---

Peru, Philippines, Poland, Sweden, Ukrainian SSR, Union of South Africa, U.S.S.R., U.S.A., Uruguay, Venezuela.
   (13) *Against*—Afghanistan, Cuba, Egypt, Greece, India, Iran, Iraq, Lebanon, Pakistan, Saudi Arabia, Syria, Turkey, Yemen.
   (10) *Abstained*—Argentina, Chile, China, Colombia, El Salvador, Ethiopia, Honduras, Mexico, United Kingdom, Yugoslavia.

it. Our hearts are sad but our conscience is easy. We would not have it the other way round. "Empires rise and fall. History tells us of the empires of the Babylonians, the Egyptians, the Greeks and the Romans, the Arabs, the Persians and the Spaniards. Today, most of the talk is about the Americans and the Russians. The Holy Koran says: 'We shall see the periods of rise and fall as between nations, and that cycle draws attention to the universal law. What endures on earth is that which is beneficent for God's creatures.'

"No man can today predict whether the proposal which these two great countries have sponsored and supported will prove beneficent or the contrary in its actual working.

"We much fear that the beneficence, if any, to which partition may lead will be small in comparison to the mischief which it might inaugurate. It totally lacks legal validity. We entertain no sense of grievance against those of our friends and fellow representatives who have been compelled, under heavy pressure, to change sides and to cast their votes in support of a proposal the justice and fairness of which do not commend themselves to them. Our feeling for them is one of sympathy that they should have been placed in a position of such embarrassment between their judgment and conscience, on the one side, and the pressure to which they and their Governments were being subjected, on the other."[34]

A pertinent criticism of the manner in which the Partition Resolution was obtained came from author Alfred Lilienthal. He wrote: "The United Nations dealt a severe blow to the prestige of international law and organization by its hasty, frivolous, and arrogant treatment of the Palestine question. The General Assembly turned down the only reasonable suggestions—a referendum in Palestine and submission of the legal problems to the International Court of Justice. The Displaced Persons Problem was handled with outrageous thoughtlessness," Lilienthal pointed out. "For persons displaced by World War II, whatever, their faith, were surely a responsibility of international welfare organizations—not pawns in a whimsical power play of Jewish nationalists," Lilienthal concluded.[35]

Zionist Pressures Inside and Outside United Nations

During the period when the future of the Holy Land was in the balance, Zionist pressures inside and outside the United Nations increased. To the American public, the Zionist approach was through the Bible and the sufferings of European Jewry. To those who frowned on Zionist acts of terror and sabotage in Palestine, the Zionists made believe that their underground movement was engaged in the same kind of struggle that the American Revolutionists had waged against the very same British imperialist power, and that the establishment of a Jewish state would be one of the loftiest acts of humanitarianism.[36]

To the United States policy-maker, the Zionists waved the Jewish vote. This is confirmed by a conversation between then Secretary of Defense James Forrestal and Senator Howard J. McGrath, from Rhode Island and Democratic chairman. Forrestal argued, "No group in this country should be permitted to influence our policy to the point where it could endanger our national security." To this McGrath replied, "There were two or three pivotal states which could not be carried without the support of people who were deeply interested in the Palestine question."[37] On another occasion, McGrath stressed the fact that a substantial part of the contributions to the Democratic National Committee were made "with a distinct idea on the part of the givers that they will have an opportunity to express their views and have them seriously considered on such questions as the present Palestine question."[38]

On the other hand, those United Nations Member States, and others, who were opposed to partition, were threatened, intimidated or blackmailed. For example, the Liberian delegate to the United Nations when approached to support partition replied that he considered the method of approach as "attempted intimidation" and so reported to the State Department.[39] But when the vote came, Liberia—like Haiti and the Philippines, which also had opposed partition in the first instance—changed its vote to yes.

Arthur Hayes Sulzberger, publisher of The New York Times, describing the situation, said publicly: "I dislike the coercive methods of Zionists who in this country have not hesitated to use economic means to silence persons who have different views. I object to the attempts at character assassination of those who do not agree with them."[40]

A leading Zionist, summing up Zionist activities at the time, admitted that "Every clue was meticulously checked and pursued. Not the smallest or the remotest of nations, but was contacted and wooed. Nothing was left to chance."[41]

The part played by the United States—government and people—in bringing about a majority vote in the General Assembly, can best be illustrated by quoting from American sources:

1. The Hon. Lawrence H. Smith, declared in Congress, "Let's take a look at the record, Mr. Speaker, and see what happened in the United Nations Assembly meeting prior to the vote on partition. A two-thirds vote was required to pass the resolution. On two occasions the Assembly was to vote and twice it was postponed. It was obvious that the delay was necessary because the proponents (the U.S.A. and the U.S.S.R.), did not have the necessary votes. In the meantime, it is reliably reported that intense pressure was applied to the delegates of three small nations by the United States member and by officials 'at the highest levels in Washington.' Now that is a serious charge. When the matter was finally considered on the 29th, what happened? The decisive votes for partition were cast by Haiti, Liberia and the Philippines. These votes were sufficient to make the two-thirds majority. Previously, these countries opposed the move . . . The pressure by our delegates, by our officials, and by the private citizens of the United States constitutes reprehensible conduct against them and against us."[42]

2. Journalist Drew Pearson explained in his Merry-Go-Round column that in the end, "a lot of people used their influence to whip voters into line. Harvey Firestone, who owns rubber plantations in Liberia, got busy with the Liberian Government; Adolphe Berle, advisor to the President of Haiti, swung that vote . . . China's Ambassador Wellington

Koo warned his Government . . . The French Ambassador pleaded with his crisis-laden Government for partition."

"Few knew it," he wrote after the partition, "but President Truman cracked down harder on his State Department than ever before to swing the United Nations vote for the partition of Palestine. Truman called Acting Secretary Lovett over to the White House on Wednesday and again on Friday warning him he would demand a full explanation if nations which usually line up with the United States failed to do so on Palestine . . ."[43]

3. *Sumner Welles* affirmed, "By direct order of the White House, every form of pressure, direct or indirect, was brought to bear by American officials upon those countries outside the Moslem world that were known to be either uncertain or opposed to partition. Representatives or intermediaries were employed by the White House to make sure that the necessary majority would at least be secured."[44]

4. *James Forrestal*, then Secretary of Defense, described "The methods that had been used . . . to bring coercion and duress on other nations in the General Assembly bordered closely onto scandal."[45]

Arab Rejection of the Partition

The Arabs rejected the partition on the grounds that it violated the provisions of the UN Charter, the principles on which the Universal Declaration of Human Rights were later based, international law and practice, and the right of a people to decide its own destiny.

Arab rejection was also based on the fact that, while the population of the *Jewish state* was to be 497,000 Arabs* and 498,000 Jewish, with the Jews owning less than 10% of the *Jewish state* land area, the Jews were to be established as the ruling body—a settlement which no self-respecting people would accept without protest, to say the least.

Contrary to what public opinion has been led to believe, the General Assembly of the United Nations is not a legislative or a judicial body, and therefore its resolution on the partition of Palestine was no more than a *recommendation*. It did not have the force of a decision and it could not be binding on the majority of the people of Palestine who had opposed it and continue to do so. Besides, the action of the United Nations conflicted with the basic principles for which the world organization was established, namely, to uphold the right of all peoples to self-determination. By denying the Palestine Arabs, who formed the two-thirds majority of the country, the right to decide for themselves, the United Nations had violated its own Charter.

The Partition Resolution was also in violation of the principles enun-

---

*As a result of the Armistice signed in 1949, the Israelis now occupy an additional 220 Arab towns and villages beyond the territory assigned to the *Jewish state* under the Partition Plan . The inhabitants of these towns and villages numbered, in 1945, about 400,000. (Calculated on the basis of the figures in the *Village Statistics*, published by the Palestine Government in 1945 and the maps showing the 1947 partition and the 1949 armistice demarcation line). Added to the figure of 497,000 Arabs estimated to be in the *Jewish state* area, the Arabs affected by the Israeli occupation were, in 1948, about 897,000 persons as compared with the UN estimate of the Jewish population of 498,000 for the *Jewish state*.

ciated in the Joint Declaration of President Roosevelt and Prime Minister Winston Churchill of August 12, 1941—which became known as the Atlantic Charter—namely:

"First, their countries seek no aggrandizement, territorial or other:
"Second, they desire to see no territorial changes that do not accord with the freely expressed wishes of the peoples concerned; and
"Third, they respect the right of all peoples to choose the form of government under which they will live; and they wish to see sovereign rights and self-government restored to those who have been forcibly deprived of them . . ."

In the light of this joint undertaking, the obvious was to carry out a referendum in Palestine before a vote was taken on partition by the General Assembly. But this proposal was blocked in the United Nations by the big powers for vested interests. Even the request to refer the matter to the International Court of Justice for an expression of opinion as to whether the General Assembly was within its rights under the Charter to partition countries, was rejected.

Zionist Acceptance of the Partition

The Zionists, on their part, had no reason to reject the Partition Plan, which gave them sovereignty over Arab territory and the power to expel and disposses—as they later did—the Arab inhabitants. The Balfour Declaration gave the Zionists a foothold in Palestine, and the Partition Resolution helped them reach their goal of a *Jewish state*. Those who saw the dangers in the establishment of a Jewish state were the anti-Zionists, but their number was not sufficient to tip the scale.

In his book *The Decadence of Judaism in Our Times*, Moshe Menuhin, who became "disenchanted with the developments of political Zionism" and left Palestine because he believed "they implied wars of injustice and the degeneration of Judaism,"[46] explains why the Zionists had accepted the Partition Plan. He said: "The fanatical Jewish political nationalists, of course, accepted partition with alacrity, for the Partition Plan was merely a foothold for the full realization of *Eretz Israel* as predatory Ben Gurion and Menachem Begin had envisioned it all along, openly and unashamedly, quoting the Bible and preparing for the bloody 'redeeming' and 'ingathering'." Menuhin went on to point out, "On October 2, 1947, Ben Gurion had stated before the Elected Assembly in Jerusalem: 'I do not minimize the virtue of statehood even within something less than all the territory of the land of Israel on either bank of the Jordan.' And a little earlier, in 1946, before the Anglo-American Commission of Inquiry, he said: 'Our aim is not a majority. A majority will not solve our problem. The majority is only a stage, not a final one. You need it to estabish the commonwealth. We still have to build a national home'."[47]

Mr. Menuhin considers that Menachem Begin had been more "honest and frank" when he put it plainly: "The Jewish homeland, the area which covers both sides of the Jordan, is a complete historic and geographic entity. Dissection of the homeland is an unlawful act; agreement to dissection is also unlawful, and is not binding on the Jewish people. It is the duty of this generation to return Jewish sovereignty to these parts of the homeland which were torn from it and given to foreign rule."*48

Failure of the United Nations

Recognizing the anomaly and uniqueness of its action, the United Nations tried to protect, but only on paper, the Arabs of the propsed *Jewish state* by providing that their civil, political, economic, religious and property rights were in no way to be prejudiced by the partition. When these rights were encroached upon, the United Nations failed to fulfill its guarantees.

The League of Nations had failed to keep the peace in the world because certain nations refused to honor their obligations to the principles and rules affirmed by the League, whenever these principles conflicted with unilateral interest.

When the United Nations was created in 1945, it was hoped that the impotence of the defunct League would not return, and that nations granted membership would *unreservedly* adhere to the principles and rules of the new Organization. The fact that China, while not a member of the United Nations, had, in the opinion of the United States Government, violated the principles of the United Nations Charter to which it was not a party, by her action in Korea, barred her from membership in the world organization until 1971. Yet we find that the state of Israel, which has violated the very resolution that created the *Jewish state* in the first instance, and the obligations it "unreservedly" accepted when it was admitted into membership of the United Nations, as well as its utter disregard for its international obligations and for subsequent resolutions calling upon Israel to do certain things, continues to enjoy membership in the world body.

A Jewish State Is Born

The general impression is that the state of Israel came into being as a result of, and in conformity with, a recommendation of the United Nations General Assembly. Actually this was only part of the story. The Partition Resolution of November 29, 1947, had recommended the creation of a *Jewish state* on 56% of the territory of *Palestine*; an *Arab state* on 42% and an *International Zone of Jerusalem and Environs* on the remaining 2%. The resolution decreed that Arabs living in the area set aside for the Jewish state were to continue to reside there and to enjoy their fundamental rights and basic human liberties under the guarantees of the United Nations. The resolution further stipulated that the Jewish and Arab states were to come into being two months after British withdrawal on May 15, 1948.49

---

*The statement "these parts of the homeland which were torn from it and given to foreign rule," refers to Jordan, which the Zionists claim is part of *Eretz Israel*; and by "foreign rule," they mean the Jordan government.

However, instead of waiting until the United Nations Palestine Commission prescribed in the Partition Resolution took over authority from the British Mandatory, and in turn handed over such authority progressively to the leaders of the Arab and Jewish states, the Zionists proclaimed the state of Israel on May 14, 1948 and faced the world with a *fait accompli*. By this date they had already seized territory beyond that assigned to the Jewish state. Instead of having jurisdiction over 56% of the territory of Palestine, the Israelis occupied 77%; instead of Jerusalem being internationalized, the greater part of the Holy City was Israelized and declared the capital of the Jewish state; instead of Arabs being permitted to remain in their homes and country to lead a normal life, nearly one million men, women and children—Moslems and Christians—were forcibly expelled and dispossessed.

In fact, what actually emerged as the *Jewish state* on May 14, 1948 was anything but the state planned for under the Partition Plan. The new state of Israel was the product of brute force, created in violation of the principles of the United Nations Charter, the Universal Declaration of Human Rights, and the very resolution under which the Israelis now claim sovereignty.

PALESTINE—MAP OF PARTITION
UN Resolution 181(11) of November 29, 1947

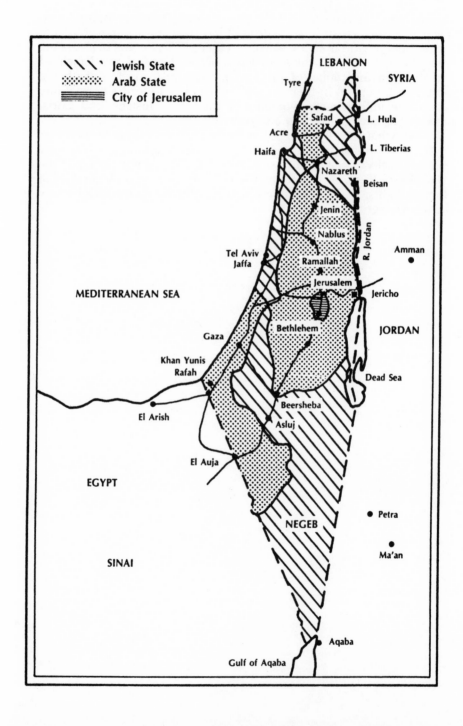

JERUSALEM INTERNATIONAL ZONE
As Resolved by General Assembly Resolution No. 181(11) of November 29,
1947

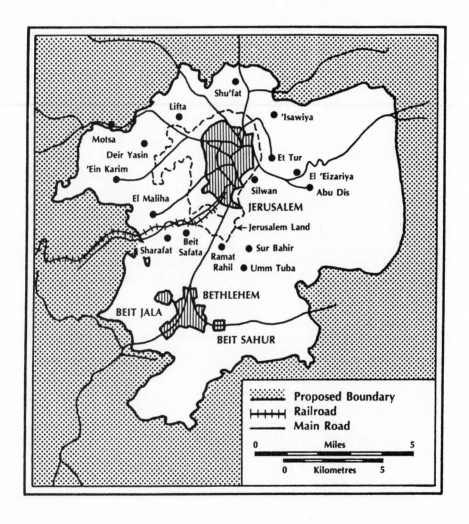

VII   Strife, War, Truce (1947–1948)

British Hands Over Authority to Zionists

The British representative at the United Nations informed the Security Council in 1948 that his government would continue to be responsible for the administration of Palestine and the maintenance of law and order for the duration of the Mandate.

At the same time, the British government issued a warning that any outside interference in the affairs of Palestine would be met with force of arms. This warning was intended, as later events proved, to keep the Arab states from coming to the aid of the Palestine Arabs who were being subjected to all kinds of attacks.

On the other hand, the Partition Resolution provided that "the administration of Palestine shall, as the Mandatory Power withdraws its armed forces, be progressively turned over to the Palestine Commission . . ."[1] This Commission, established especially by the United Nations to take steps preparatory to independence, was not permitted by the Mandatory Power to come into effective being on the grounds that there could not be two governing authorities in one country at the same time. Theoretically, the Commission existed, but it exercised no functions. It was, however, relieved "from the exercise of its responsibilities under resolution 181 (II) of November 29, 1947" on May 14, 1948, the very same day the state of Israel was proclaimed.[2] The Commission's duties were then taken over by UN Mediator Count Folke Bernadotte, but the damage to Arab rights and interests had already begun.

The British Mandatory would not hand over authority to a properly established organ of the United Nations; but no sooner was the Partition Resolution adopted when the government announced its withdrawal from Tel Aviv and environs and handed over administration and security to the local Jewish authorities. This freed the hands of the Zionists within a significant Jewish area of Palestine and arms and fighting men began to arrive through the port of Tel Aviv to augment the Zionist underground forces.

This was confirmed by Menachem Begin who declared that at the end of March 1948, the first shipload of arms and ammunition from Czechoslovakia arrived in Palestine, which proved to be a vital factor in the turning of the tide. From then on, militarily, the Zionists never looked back. Tiberias fell on April 18; on the 21st Hagana forces began to attack Haifa. On May 10 Safad fell after more than a week of heavy fighting. At the end of April, Hagana occupied the Katamon Quarter of Jerusalem; and in co-operation with Hagana, the surrender of Jaffa took place on May 13, 1948.[3]

While more and more Jewish areas were evacuated and handed over to the Zionists as the day of British withdrawal approached, British forces remained in Arab areas impeding any preparations of defense that the Arab inhabitants might have had in mind. With each new day, Zionist assaults on Arab areas increased with no British interference whatsoever. Arab appeals for British help were rejected on the grounds that there were not sufficient security forces available because of the withdrawal. Even in Jerusalem—a territory set aside to be administered by the United Nations—the British military authorities not only refused to come to the aid of the inhabitants of Katamon Quarter, but prevented the Arab Legion guarding the Iraq Consulate in the area from interfering.

The Arab inhabitants, forsaken by the government that undertook to maintain law and order and not permitted by their so-called protectors to seek outside aid, had no alternative but to flee before the advancing Zionists—an exodus, which the Zionists had planned and organized so well, that was now assisted by those who originally undertook to ensure the establishment of a Jewish national home in Palestine.

British behaviour towards Arabs and Jews during this critical period, could only be explained by the fact that the British government was determined to the last moment to fulfill its obligations to the Jews in helping them to transfer the national home into a state before they pulled out of the country.

Thus, on the date of the expiration of the mandate, the Zionist forces were already in occupation of strategic positions well within the territory assigned to the Arab state. Even Jerusalem—reserved as an international city—was not spared. Glubb Pasha, the Commanding Officer of the Arab Legion in 1948, noted, "The Jews were already in the Arab area when the Arab Legion arrived."[4]

United Nations Concern Over Violence

The United Nations became alarmed at the violence to which its Partition Resolution had unwittingly given birth. On March 19, the Security Council met, and the United States delegation stated that since it had become clear that the Partition Resolution could not be implemented by peaceful means and that the Security Council was not prepared to implement it, presumably by force, the Council should recommend a temporary trusteeship for Palestine.*

The Jewish Agency replied by rejecting a trusteeship, and declared that it was the most terrible sell-out since Munich. To thwart any attempt to nullify the Partition, the Zionists stepped up their attacks against Arab towns and villages in order to face the United Nations on May 15, 1948 with *a fait accompli*.

While the United States representative was arguing at the United Nations for a shift from partition to trusteeship, former President Harry Truman suddenly recognized the new state of Israel. He did so exactly eleven minutes after Israel had been proclaimed as a state to the utter amazement of the Zionists themselves. This hasty recognition—unprecedented in history—came as a complete surprise to the United States mission to the United Nations, which was first informed of it by the Soviet representative.

Zionist Aggression Before Termination of Mandate

The Israelis have always claimed that the Palestine war was started with the entry of the Arab armies into Palestine after British withdrawal from the country on May 14, 1948. If this is to be accepted as true, then by the same token Britain and France must be held responsible for the start of the Second World War since it was they who had officially declared war on Nazi Germany in 1939. In the case of Palestine, as in that of World War II, it is what took place *before* the two opposing armies met on the battlefield that must fix responsibility.

The war in Palestine, to be understood correctly, must be divided into three distinct phases:

The first, the period prior to the Partition Resolution of November 29, 1947 when the Zionists were planning, organizing and carrying out terror and sabotage activities with a view to expelling first the British Mandatory authorities and then the Moslem and Christian inhabitants;

The second, the six-month period between November 29, 1947 (the date of the Partition Resolution) and May 14, 1948 (the date of British withdrawal); and

The third, the period subsequent to May 14, 1948 during which the armies of the Arab states entered Palestine.

---

*On April 25, 1963, David Ben Gurion recalled: "I was then at Haganah Headquarters at Tel Aviv and could not consult my colleagues on the Zionist Executive, who were in Jerusalem. I saw it my duty immediately to state: 'This stand of the United States in no way alters fundamentally the situation in the situation in the country, nor does it undermine the establishment of the Jewish state. Establishment of the State was not, in effect, given in the United Nations resolution of last November 29—although the resolution was of great moral and political value—but by our ability to bring about a decision in the country by force. Through our own strength—if we will it and succeed in mobilizing it fully—the State will be established even now."

Ben Gurion added: "And the State came into being—and we were forced to fight for its existence. We won and I have no doubt that this was one of the greatest achievements in our history as a nation." He went on to say, "The War of Independence which lasted from May 15, 1948 to July 1, 1948, gave us a state larger and more complete than the one delineated by the United Nations General Assembly resolution of 1947. It gave us", he said, nearly all of Jerusalem, Western Galilee, the entire corridor from Jaffa to Jerusalem and all of the Negev with the exception of the Gaza Strip."[5]

The first phase has already been dealt with in Chapter V. It was the second phase, not the third, that really determined responsibility, and knowledge of it should dispel the myth that it was the Arab states that started the Palestine war.

There is ample evidence to show that the Zionists, having achieved British withdrawal following the resolution of partition, were now ready to switch their campaign of terror from the Mandatory Government to the unarmed Arab population. They aimed at two major objectives; first, to confirm Jewish dominance over the 50% Arab inhabitants living within the limits of the proposed Jewish state; and secondly, to expand those limits so as to include the greatest possible area—if not all Palestine—before Britain withdrew from the country on May 14, 1948.

The Zionist plan of *intention* was disclosed during a conversation in December 1947 between a British officer of the Jordan Arab Legion and a Palestine Government Jewish official. The former is reported to have asked the latter "whether the new Jewish state would not have many internal troubles in view of the fact that the Arab inhabitants of the Jewish state would be equal in number to the Jews." The Jewish official is reported to have replied: "Oh no! That will be fixed. A few calculated massacres will soon get rid of them."[6]

This plan was immediately put into effect. The methods used, however, varied. Some of the inhabitants "were driven out by force of arms; others were made to leave by deceit, lying and false promises."[7] Others still were "encouraged to move on by blows or by indecent acts."[8]

The Deir Yasin Massacre

The most outstanding incident which shocked the world and accelerated the panic flight of the Arab inhabitants was the massacre of over 250 men, women and children in the village of Deir Yasin on April 9, 1948. Jon Kimche, author and correspondent who was in Jerusalem at the time, described the attack as "the darkest stain on the Jewish record." He added: "It is historically important because it was to become the beginning of a second legend with which the terrorists sought to serve their cause and justify their deeds. Just as they claimed credit for the British decision to leave Palestine as being the result of the terrorists' attacks on British troops, so later they justified the massacre of Deir Yasin because it led to the panic flight of the remaining Arabs in the Jewish state and so lessened the Jewish casualties."[9]

Dov Joseph, one-time Governor of the Israeli sector of Jerusalem and later Minister of Justice, called the Deir Yasin massacre a "deliberate and unprovoked attack;"[10] while British historian Arnold Toynbee described it as "comparable to crimes committed against the Jews by the Nazis."[11] But Menachem Begin, the leader of the attack on Deir Yasin, said, "The massacre was not only justified, but there would not have been a state of Israel without the victory at Deir Yasin."*[12]

---

*The quote came from the *Jewish Newsletter* of October 3, 1960, and read, "In 1951, the leader of the Irgun, Menachem Begin, declared in his book, *The Revolt* (Henry Shuman, N.Y.), that the massacre was not only justified but that there would not have been a State of Israel without the

Unashamed of their deed and unaffected by world condemnation, the Zionist underground forces, using loudspeakers, roamed the streets of cities warning the Arab inhabitants: "The Jericho road is still open," they told the Jerusalem Arabs, "fly from Jerusalem before you are killed."[13]

Another testimony comes from British Army Major Edgar O'Ballance, a competent and objective observer, who wrote: "Many Israeli sympathizers were appalled at the ruthless way in which the Arab inhabitants were ousted from their homes and driven before advancing armies, and this caused many twinges of conscience in the Western world. The Israelis made no excuse for it, as *it was part of* their plan for the reconquest of their *Promised Land*, in which there was no room for large, hostile, alien groups."[14]

The late William Zukerman, editor of the *Jewish Newsletter* (New York), summing up the situation in Palestine wrote: " . . . the flight of the Palestine Arabs, which created the Arab refugee problem, was not a spontaneous act, nor due entirely to the propaganda call of the Arab leaders as the Zionists have claimed all along. It was a coldly calculated plan executed by the Irgun but with the knowledge of the Hagana and the Jewish Agency of the time."[15]

On the 24th anniversary of the massacre of Deir Yasin, the Israeli Hebrew newspaper *Yediot Aharonot*, published in its issue of April 4, 1972 a report written 24 years before by a young Palmach fighter called Meir Philipski, who is today known as Colonel Meir Pa'el.

The Deir Yasin massacre has had wide publicity during the years, and the later disclosure should throw much light on how and why the massacre occurred. For that reason, the report will be reproduced *in extenso*.

According to Yediot Aharonot, Pa'el "is probably the only eyewitness outside the ranks of ETZEL (Irgun Zvei Leumi) and LEHI (The Stern Gang) who investigated the secret operation at Deir Yasin on April 9, 1948, and set down what he saw with his own eyes and what he heard with his own ears in the report which he sent at the time to Israel Galili, the head of the Hagana Command."

Yediot Aharonot went on to say: "For 24 years, Pa'el has kept to himself the scenes that took place on 'the ugliest day in my life,' and a few months ago, when he was released from continuous service . . . he hesitated for a long time before allowing the report he wrote at that time to see the light of day."

The following are extracts from Pa'el's report which confirm what others have related occurred at Deir Yasin, and the vicious character of those who took part in the massacre:

"An ETZEL force went out from Beth Hakerim Quarter and attacked Deir Yasin from the southeast, while a LEHI force attacked it from the

---

(*continued from page 85*)
'victory' at Deir Yassin."

Because the quote did not include a page reference to *The Revolt*, and I could not find it in my copy of the book, I visited the editor of the *Jewish Newsletter*, William Zukerman, shortly before his death, to enquire. He replied that he replies in his writings on information he receives from Israel.

northeast. At dawn, the two forces reached the outskirts of the village.

"The people of the village discovered that members of the secret movements had entered Deir Yasin before the attackers fired their first shot, so that it was the inhabitants of the village who fired first. The attackers burst into the village and met with violent opposition. Most of the male inhabitants fled from the village with their arms, a small number of men and a large number of women and children remaining in the houses. In a short time, the raiders had obtained control of most of the village, except for the western part.

"It was noon when the battle ended, and the shooting stopped. Things had become quiet, but the village had not surrendered. The ETZEL and LEHI irregulars left the places in which they had been hiding and started carrying out cleaning up operations in the houses. They fired with all the arms they had, and threw explosives into the houses. They also shot everyone they saw in the houses, including women and children—indeed commanders made no attempt to check the disgraceful acts of slaughter.

"I myself and a number of inhabitants of Jerusalem begged the commanders to give orders to their men to stop shooting, but our efforts were unsuccessful. In the meantime, some 25 men had been brought out of the houses; they were loaded onto a freight truck and led in a victory parade, like a Roman triumph, through the Mahneh Yahuda and Zikhron Yosef Quarters [in Jerusalem]. At the end of the parade, they were taken to a stone quarry between Giv'at Sha'ul and Deir Yasin and shot in cold blood. The fighters then put the women and children who were still alive on a truck and took them to the Mandelbaum Gate."

In *Yediot Aharonot* of April 29, 1972, Meir Pa'el once again wrote on the Deir Yasin massacre, adding these new details:

"After the Palmach men left the village, the men of ETZEL and LEHI started a shameful massacre of the inhabitants—men, women, old people and children, without distinction, standing the inhabitants against walls and in corners in the houses. There is photographic evidence of this. It is true that most of the people were killed with firearms; it is true that the killing took place spontaneously immediately after the end of the battle, and it is true that the officers were not controlling their men, and showed no inclination to do so. But it was killing, even if it was carried out in hot blood.

"The ETZEL commander in Jerusalem can protest a thousand times that the victory parade in Jerusalem was a criminally concocted charge, but I, as an eye-witness, regret to have to state that this is what really happened. The Arab men were killed (in cold blood, this time) in the stone quarry between Deir Yasin and Giv'at Sha'ul, and there is photographic evidence of this too. It was thus a criminal act, not a criminally concocted charge."

Meir Pa'el goes on: Historian "Arieh Yitzhaqi tells his readers that many irregular actions took place during the War of Independence, but no action in the whole War of Independence was as atrocious as the Deir Yasin massacre, for the following reasons:

"The irregular action in Deir Yasin was carried out after the battle, when the village was in Jewish hands, and without the inhabitants having taken any provocative action that could have justified the shooting. It was not a question of cleaning up houses, but of entering them to kill and plunder. The number of Arabs killed was much greater than in all the examples cited by Mr. Yitzhaqi, including the irregular action at Lydda."

The second reason given by Pa'el is that ETZEL leaders still-refuse to criticize themselves for the Deir Yasin massacre. On the contrary, they regard it as an important event and the "principal act that made the Arabs frightened of Jewish atrocities and led them to flee. Some of them have gone so far as to assert that the Deir Yasin affair was the most important turning point in the War of Independence."[16]

Other Massacres

Other unpublished massacres, similar to the massacre at Deir Yasin, later came to light through an article written by Arieh Yitzhaqi, historian and researcher, published by Yediot Aharonot in its issue of April 14, 1972, in which the writer accuses Palmach of similar operations that he states were not restricted to ETZEL and LEHI.

"If we assemble the facts," writes Yitzhaqi, "we realize that, to a great extent, the battle followed the familiar pattern of the occupation of an Arab village in 1948. In the first months of the War of Independence, Hagana and Palmach troops carried out dozens of operations of this [Deir Yasin] kind, the method adopted being to raid an enemy village and blow up as many houses as possible in it. In the course of these operations, many old people, women and children were killed wherever there was resistance."

Yitzhaqi then lists the Arab villages raided and the number of Arabs killed as follows:

1. The village of Balad Esh-Sheikh was attacked. "In this operation, more than sixty of the enemy, most of them non-combatants, were killed in their houses."

2. The village of Sa'sa' was attacked. "In this operation, which was for many years to be regarded as a model raid because of the high standard of its execution, 20 houses were blown up over their inhabitants, and some 60 Arabs were killed, most of them women and children."

3. In the battle for the Katamon Quarter of Jerusalem, "Arab women working in the St. Simon Monastery as servants were killed."*

4. In Lydda town, the Palmach claim that "the local Arab population rose in revolt, and to suppress the revolt, orders were given to fire on anyone seen in the streets. Yeftah troops opened heavy fire on all passers-by and suppressed the revolt mercilessly in a few hours, going from house to house and firing at every moving target. According to the commander's report, 250 Arabs were killed in the fighting."

---

*The author's home is in the Katamon Quarter of Jerusalem, and on the afternoon of the day the Quarter was attacked on April 29, 1948, he was at home covering up the furniture—which was later plundered—and locking up. The only people who stayed on in the area were the inmates of the St. Simon Monastery who believed that they would be safe.

Arieh Yitzhaqi concludes stating that "There were also the indiscriminate reprisal attacks on Arab civilian communications, in which many innocent citizens were killed."[17]

Another massacre of Arab civilians occurred in October 1948 in the Lebanese village of Hula, and only recently came to light as a result of the appointment of Shmuel Lahis as the new Secretary-General of the Jewish Agency who had been convicted for his part in the crime.

According to a report by Dov Yirimiya, "there had been no resistance in the village, that there was no enemy activity in the area, and that about a hundred people were in the village. They had surrendered and had requested to be allowed to stay."

The men—some fifty of them ranging between the ages of 15–60 years—were kept in one house. When asked by the troop commander if he should send them away to follow the rest of the villagers, Yarimiya states that he ordered Lahis to keep them and make sure that they had whatever they needed until he had asked the brigade what to do with them.

Yarimiya goes on to say that "when I returned to the village the following morning with an order to send the villagers away, I found that *while I was away, two of the troops' officers had killed all the captives who were in the house with a sub-machine gun, and had then blown up the house on top of them to be their grave*. The women and children were sent west." (Emphasis by Yarimiya.).[18]

Another unpublicized massacre of which the author personally became aware of in 1951 in the course of his official duties with the Jordan government, occurred in the village of Ed-Dawayimeh, in the Hebron Sub-District. There, about 200 persons—mostly aged inhabitants who could not run away—took refuge in the village mosque, and when the Israelis entered the village, they massacred the entire crowd.

Many of the reports that the author inspected at the police station in Hebron gave the ages of the victims as between 70 and 90 years. The reasons given to the author by the desk clerk why the massacre was never reported to either the International Red Cross or to the United Nations Representative was that at the time of the event there were Egyptian and Jordanian troops in the area, neither of which knew which of them was responsible, and so the local police merely filed complaints when they were made.

One wonders why did these and other similar massacres take place. In this first instance, Dov Yirmiya states "When I asked him why he had done this, the officer answered that this was 'his revenge for the murder of his best friends in the [Haifa] refineries' (which took place in December 30, 1947, about ten months previously)."[19]

In both and similar instances, the massacres were inhuman, unjustified, and uncivilized; and the question may be asked why did they occur? In a recent publication, Professor Israel Shahak draws attention to an I.D.F. (Israel Defence Force) booklet in which "An Army Rabbi Calls for the Killing of Civilians." The call is phrased in the bluntest of terms, as follows:

"When our forces encounter the civilians during the war or in the course of pursuit or a raid, the encountered civilians may, and by

Halachic standards even must, be killed, whenever it cannot be ascertained that they are incapable of hitting us back. Under no circumstances should an Arab be trusted, even if he gives the impression of being civilized."

The Rabbi in question is Lt-Col. Rabbi Abraham Avidan (Zemel), Chief Rabbi of the Central Command; and he states his reasons for the call, as follows:

" . . . in the opinion of the Tosafot (a body of interpretation and a supplement to the Babylonian Talmud, in Jewish orthodox tradition enjoying authority almost equal to the latter—tr.) that in time of war, when Israeli troops assault the enemy, they may, and by Halachic standards even must, kill conforming civilians, or in other words, civilians whose conduct is proper. In such a case, it has been said 'Kill the best of the Gentiles' and no trust should be accorded a Gentile who will not bring harm to our troops, for the suspicion remains that in some phase of the fighting, he may cause harm nevertheless, either by supplying resources or by providing information to the enemy. It occurred, for instance, in the mishap engineered for the Jews by those in Egypt who feared the Lord. Or the famous story of the 35 in the War of Independence who, while on their way to the Etzion Block, met an old Arab who aroused their compassion and who then passed on information to the enemy.—An act which ultimately resulted in the murder of the 35 in the hands of the enemy."

Rabbi Avidan then sums up as follows: "Our sources clearly indicate that a Gentile, no matter how progressive or civilized, is not to be trusted. And besides, one must always beware lest the same Gentile who on the surface seems to be a good Gentile, abets with the enemy. Therefore, it emerges unequivocally, that those who abet must be dealt with as if they were the enemy himself. In other words, it is the very fact of abetting which turns them into a target of enmity and which defines them as an enemy who may be killed.[20]

Arabs and Jews Clash (December 1947—May 1948)

Menachem Begin, then leader of the *Irgun*, tells how "in Jerusalem, as elsewhere, we were the first to pass from the defensive to the offensive . . . Arabs began to flee in terror . . . Hagana was carrying out successful attacks on other fronts, while all the Jewish forces proceeded to advance through Haifa like a knife through butter. The Arabs began fleeing shouting 'Deir Yasin'." Begin added: "In the months preceding the Arab invasion, and while the five Arab states were conducting preparations, we continued to make sallies into Arab territory. The conquest of Jaffa stands out as an event of first-rate importance in the struggle for Hebrew independence early in May, on the eve of the invasion by the five Arab states."[21]

Another description of the fighting of that six-month period came from Major Edgar O'Ballance. He said:

"It was the Jewish policy to encourage the Arabs to quit their homes, and they used psychological warfare extensively in urging them to do so. Later, as the war went on, they ejected those Arabs who clung to their villages. This policy, which had such amazing success, had two distinct advantages: first, it gave the Arab countries a vast refugee problem to cope with which their elementary economy and administrative machinery were in no way capable of attacking; and secondly, it ensured that the Jews had no fifth column in their midst."[22]

That the Zionists started war on the Palestine Arabs before the creation of the state of Israel is confirmed by David Ben Gurion himself. He said: "As April [1948] began, our War of Independence swung decisively from defence to attack. Operation Nachshon . . . was launched with the capture of Arab Khulda near where we stand today and of Deir Muheisin, and culminated in the storming of Qastal, the great hill-fortress near Jerusalem."*[23]

On another occasion, Ben Gurion said: "The primary task of the Hagana was to safeguard our settlements and lines of communications, but here the best defense is attack. Field troops and Palmach in particular were thus deployed and quickly showed the mettle that was soon to animate our army and bring it victory. In operation Nachshon the road to Jerusalem was cleared at the beginning of April, almost all of New Jerusalem occupied, and the guerillas were expelled from Haifa, Jaffa, Tiberias, Safad while still the mandatory was present. It needed sagacity and self-control not to fall foul of the British army. The Hagana did its job; until a day or two before the Arab invasion not a settlement was lost, no road cut, although movement was seriously dislocated, despite express assurances of the British to keep the roads safe so long as they remained. Arabs started fleeing from the cities almost as soon as disturbances began in the early days of December [1947]. As fighting spread, the exodus was joined by Bedouin and fellahin, but not the remotest Jewish homestead was abandoned and nothing a tottering administration [meaning the British Mandatory] could unkindly do stopped us from reaching our goal on May 14, 1948, in a state made larger and Jewish by the Hagana."**[24]

The following is a list of the major attacks, occupations and expulsions which took place *before* the British left on May 14, 1948, *before* a single soldier from any Arab state entered Palestine and *two months before* Israel could legally be proclaimed according to the Partition Resolution:

  (a) *In the territory reserved for the Arab state*
The village of Qazaza was attacked and occupied as early as December

---

*The three villages named are part of the territory which was allotted to the 'Arab State' under the Partition Resolution.

**On March 9, 1964, *The New York Times* reported that "former Premier David Ben-Gurion and two generals who helped forge the state of Israel in 1948 argued publicly this weekend over who was responsible for this 8,000-square-mile country being so small."

In an interview with *Haboker*, a Tel Aviv daily, Ben-Gurion is reported to have said that "Israeli territory might have been greater if Gen. Moshe Dayan had been chief of staff during the war of 1948 against the Arabs of Palestine."

This belated admission removes any doubt that the Zionists had planned to occupy the whole of Palestine before the British left and before the Arab armies entered Palestine soil. It is further admission that the war was waged against the Palestine Arabs before the Arab armies came to the rescue.

1947; Salameh in March; Saris, Qastal, Biyar' Adas and the town of Jaffa, in April; and the town of Acre in May 1948, together with many other villages;

(b) *In the territory assigned to the Jewish state*

The towns of Tiberias and Haifa in April; Safad and Beisan in May 1948, besides hundreds of Arab villages;

(c) *Within the area reserved for Jerusalem International Zone*

The village of Deir Yasin was attacked where the massacre of 250 men, women and children took place on April 9, 1948; and the Arab quarter of Katamon in Jerusalem City on April 29.

During this six-months period over 300,000 Arabs were driven out of their homes and became refugees—contrary to the expressed intentions of the United Nations.

It is, however, worth noting that Chaim Weizmann, who became first President of the state of Israel in 1948, in an effort to impress the members of the United Nations Special Committee who visited Palestine in 1947, decried the dastardly crimes that were being perpetrated by his followers against the Arab and British Mandatory, which made it possible for the Jews to go to Palestine. "In all humbleness," he declared before the Committee, "*Thou shalt not kill* has been ingrained in us since Mount Sinai. It was inconceivable ten years ago that the Jews should break this commandment. Unfortunately, they are breaking it today, and nobody deplores it more than the vast majority of the Jews. I hang my head in shame when I have to speak of this fact before you."[25]

No doubt the members of the Committee were very much touched at the time by this display of false emotion. But when his forces subsequently massacred innocent people and expelled the Moslem and Christian inhabitants of the country, Dr. Weizmann's so-called shame vanished and his quotation of the commandment "Thou shalt not kill" was suddenly transformed into a declaration of "It was a miraculous clearing of the land, the miraculous simplification of Israel's task."[26]

The Arab States—Israeli War (1948)

It has already established that the Arab states were prevented from coming to the aid of the Palestine Arabs before British withdrawal on May 14, 1948. It has also been established that the Zionist underground forces had, prior to May 14, 1948, crossed over and encroached on the territory reserved for the Arab state and the Jerusalem international zone.

The Israelis now allege that the Palestine war began with the entry of the Arab armies into Palestine after May 15, 1948. But that was the second phase of the war; they overlook the massacres, expulsions and dispossessions which took place prior to that date and which necessitated Arab states' intervention.

However, before the Arab states' armies entered Palestine, the Secretary-General of the Arab League called the Secretary-General of the United Nations on May 14 informing him that the Arab states "were compelled to intervene for the sole purpose of restoring peace and security and of establishing law and order in Palestine . . ." Their intervention was also "to prevent the spread of disorder and lawlessness into the neighboring Arab lands; and to fill the vacuum created by the termination of the Mandate."[27]

Had the British government fulfilled its obligations in Palestine "to maintain law and order" up to the date of the termination of its Mandate; and had the United Nations from then on undertaken its responsibilities of ensuring peace and security for the Arab inhabitants, Arab states' intervention would have been unnecessary.

It should also be noted thath the armies of the Arab states were at no time inside the area set aside for the Jewish state under the Partition Resolution. Had the Arab states not intervened during the crucial period when the British Administration withdrew, the whole country would have been over-run by the Zionist forces.

The intentions of the Arab states, apart from having been adequately expressed in the telegram to the Secretary-General of the United Nations on May 15, 1948, were attested to by Glubb Pasha in these words: "In 1948, Trans-Jordan became involved in hostilities with Israel. She did not want to do this. She intended only to occupy that part of Palestine awarded to the Arabs . . ."[28]

Security Council Orders Truce

On May 22, the Security Council adopted a resolution calling upon "all governments and authorities, without prejudice to the rights, claims or positions of the parties concerned, to abstain from any hostile military action in Palestine, and to that end to issue a cease-fire order to their military and para-military forces."[29]

On May 29, a second directive was issued, this time calling on the parties "to undertake that they will not introduce fighting personnel" into the area "during the cease-fire." The parties were also ordered "to refrain from importing or exporting war material" into the area "during the cease-fire."[30]

The Israelis defied every provision of the cease-fire orders during the four-week interval and emerged from the truce stronger and better equipped to resume the hostilities. This is evident from the reports of the UN Mediator, as well as from his memoirs, *To Jerusalem.*

Israeli defiance of the terms of the truce manifested itself in:

(a) the release from British custody and the bringing into Palestine of thousands of illegal immigrants who had been detained in Cyprus;

(b) the training and arming of these released detainees;

(c) the smuggling into the area of large quantities of arms, ammunition, and military aircraft, mainly from communist Czechoslovakia Journalist Jon Kimche wrote in his *Seven Fallen Pillars:* "Israeli emissaries scoured the whole of Europe and America for possible supplies. American Jews were contributing generous supplies of dollars and the arms merchants were prepared to deal for dollars. The Czech were most helpful. A regular airlift began to operate from Prague to 'Aqir in southern Palestine. Rifles, ammunition and guns were now arriving. So were the first bombers—Flying Fortresses smuggled from the United States, and the Beaufort Fighter-bombers trickled out of England . . .

When the truce ended, a coherent Jewish army with a tiny but effective air force and a small and daring navy was ready to give battle."[31]

It can thus be seen that the Israeli acceptance of the truce was not accompanied by a sincere desire to implement the provisions of the order of the Security Council, but merely to gain time. This is evident from the statement of David Ben Gurion on June 10, 1948, of his government's acceptance of the cease-fire: " . . . Our bounds are set wider, our forces multiply, we are administering public services, and daily new multitudes arrive . . . All that we have taken we shall hold. During the cease-fire, we shall organize administration with fiercer energy, strengthen our footing in town and country, speed up colonization and *Aliyah* [immigration], and look to the army."[32]

Arab Expulsions

The Israelis later claimed that they urged the Arab inhabitants to stay; that they were not driven from their homes; and that they fled of their own free will or at the instigation of their leaders who promised them swift victory. In support of their argument, the Israelis quoted an appeal made to the Arabs of Haifa.

Admittedly one such appeal was made to the inhabitants of Haifa, not by the Zionist authorities responsible for Jewish affairs, but the Jewish mayor of the city on his own initiative. In no other town or area in Palestine did any member of the Jewish community urge the Arab inhabitants to stay. "Later on, when the problem of the Arab refugees became a tragedy which drew the attention of the world, Jewish apologists claimed that the Arabs had voluntarily become refugees, and that they had not been driven out."[33]

If the Haifa appeal had indeed reflected general Zionist policy toward the Arabs, the call would have emanated from the Jewish Agency as the official body of Palestine Jewry. The Agency had three opportunities to prove its good faith: the first, before the British left, which the Israelis now allege they did; the second when the state of Israel was established and the problem had become a tragedy calling for humane action; and third since 1948, to answer the call of conscience to allow the refugees to return. Instead, more and more Palestine Arabs were expelled to join the ranks of those who went before them.

The truth of the matter is that it was the concerted policy of the Zionist movement to oust the Palestine Arabs from their homes and country, because they needed Palestine free from Arabs to make room for their planned mass immigration. Without Arab lands and property it is not clear how the Zionists could establish a Jewish state.

What actually happened in Palestine was truthfully disclosed by Nathan Chofshi, a Jewish immigrant from Russia who arrived in Palestine in 1908 in the same group with David Ben Gurion. He wrote in a rebuttal of an American Zionist rabbi's assertion: "If Rabbi Kaplan really wanted to know what happened, we old Jewish settlers in Palestine who witnessed the flight could tell him how and in what manner we, Jews, forced the Arabs to leave cities and villages . . . Here was a people who lived on its own land for 1,300 years. We came and turned the native

Arabs into tragic refugees. And still we dare to slander and malign them, to besmirch their name. Instead of being deeply ashamed of what we did and of trying to undo some of the evil we committed by helping these unfortunate refugees, we justify our terrible acts and even attempt to glorify them."[34]

Professor Erich Fromm, a noted Jewish writer and thinker, had this to say on the Zionist argument that the Arab refugees left of their own accord:

> "It is often said that the Arabs fled, that they left the country voluntarily, and that they therefore bear the responsibility for losing their property and their land. It is true that in history there are some instances—in Rome and in France during the Revolutions—when enemies of the state were proscribed and their property confiscated. But in general international law, the principle holds true that no citizen loses his property or his rights of citizenship; and the citizenship right is *de facto* a right to which the Arabs in Israel have much more legitimacy than the Jews. Just because the Arabs fled? Since when is that punishable by confiscation of property and by being barred from returning to the land on which a people's forefathers have lived for generations? Thus, the claim of the Jews to the land of Israel cannot be a realistic political claim. If all nations would suddenly claim territories in which their forefathers had lived two thousand years ago, this world would be a madhouse."

Dr. Fromm goes on to say:

> "I believe that, politically speaking, there is only one solution for Israel, namely, the unilateral acknowledgement of the obligation of the state toward the Arabs—not to use it as a bargaining point, but to acknowledge the complete moral obligation of the Israeli state to its former inhabitants of Palestine."[35]

Further proof of forced Arab expulsion—if further proof is required in the face of the preceding outright disclosure—comes from Glubb Pasha, who, as commanding officer of the Arab Legion, was on the spot at the time and therefore in a position to know what was going on. He said: "The story which Jewish publicity at first persuaded the world to accept, that the Arab refugees left voluntarily, is not true. Voluntary emigrants," he pointed out, "do not leave their homes with only the clothes they stand in. People," he said, "who have decided to move house do not do so in such a hurry that they lose other members of their family—husband losing sight of his wife, or parents of their children. The fact is that the majority left in panic flight, to escape massacre. They were in fact helped on their way by the occasional massacres—not of very many at a time, but just enough to keep them running."[36]

Notwithstanding, the Israelis have not ceased to use the argument that the Arabs had not been driven out, but they have never been able to produce documentary evidence to prove their contention. Erskine B. Childers, a British writer much interested in the subject, took the trouble to investigate the situation. This is what he came up with:

"Examining every official Israeli statement about the Arab exodus, I was struck by the fact that no primary evidence of evacuation orders was ever produced. The charge, Israel claimed, was documented; but where were the documents? There had allegedly been Arab radio broadcasts ordering the evacuation; but no dates, names of station, or texts of messages were ever cited. In Israel in 1958, as a guest of the Foreign Office and therefore doubly hopeful of serious assistance, I asked to be shown the proofs. I was assured they existed, and was promised them. None had been offered when I left, but I was assured again. I asked to have the material sent to me. I am still waiting."*

Childers continues; "I next decided to test the undocumented charge that the Arab evacuation orders were broadcast by Arab radio—which could be done thoroughly because the BBC monitored all Middle Eastern broadcasts throughout 1948. The records, and companion ones by a United States monitoring unit, can be seen at the British Museum." He explained: "There was not a single order or appeal, or suggestion about evacuation from Palestine, from any Arab radio station, inside or outside Palestine, in 1948. There is repeated monitored record of Arab appeals, even flat orders, to the civilians of Palestine to stay put. To select only two examples: On April 4, as the first great wave of flight began, Damascus Radio broadcast an appeal to everyone to stay at their homes and jobs. On April 24, with the exodus now a flood, Palestine Arab leaders warned that:

'Certain elements and Jewish agents are spreading defeatist news to create chaos and panic among the peaceful population. Some cowards are deserting their houses, villages or cities . . . Zionist agents and corrupt cowards will be severely punished (Al-Inqaz—the Arab Liberation Radio—at 1200 hours)'."

"Even Jewish broadcasts (in Hebrew)," Erskine Childers continues, "mentioned such Arab appeals to stay put. Zionist newspapers in Palestine reported the same; none so much as hinted at any Arab evacuation orders."[37]

---

*For further evidence that such "calls" never existed and that the contrary was the case, see Appendix A whereby the Arab Higher Committee of the time requested the Arab governments to close their borders to Palestinians fleeing their homes in Palestine and to arrange for those who had already left to return. This request was made on March 8, 1948—before British withdrawal and before the state of Israel was established.

VIII   The Armistice (1949)

Fighting Resumed

Open hostilities between the Arab states and the Israelis began after the withdrawal of the British Administration from Palestine on May 14, 1948.

On May 22, 1948, after one week of inconclusive fighting, the Security Council adopted a resolution calling upon "all governments and authorities, without prejudice to the rights, claims or positions of the parties concerned, to abstain from any hostile military action in Palestine, and to that end to issue a cease-fire order to their military and para-military forces."[1]

On May 29, a second directive was issued, this time calling on the parties "to undertake that they will not introduce fighting personnel" into the area "during the cease-fire."[2] Later events proved that the Arab states complied with the cease-fire orders of the Security Council, but the Israelis did not.

Fighting was resumed on July 9, 1948, for nine days. A resolution by the Security Council appealing to the parties to prolong the truce was issued on July 7[3] and on July 15, the Security Council issued a further cease-fire resolution which, among other things, ordered "the governments and authorities concerned, pursuant to Article 40 of the Charter, to desist from further military action and, to this end, to issue cease-fire orders to their military and para-military forces, to take effect at a time to be determined by the mediator, but in any event not later than three days from the date of the adoption of this resolution."[4]

Notwithstanding the Security Council directives, on October 14, 1948, the Israelis attacked and occupied the town of Beersheba and the El-Auja area—both of which had been assigned to the Arab State under the Partition Resolution of 1947.

On October 19, the Security Council called for "the withdrawal of both parties from any positions not occupied at the time of the outbreak;"[5] and on November 4, the Council once again called upon the parties "to withdraw those of their forces which have advanced beyond the positions held on October 14."[6] This was a clear-cut order that Israeli presence in territory not held on October 14 and assigned to the Arab State under the Partition Plan was illegal and in violation of the truce order of July 15.

General Armistice Agreements

On November 16, the Security Council, after "taking note that the General Assembly is continuing its consideration of the future government of Palestine in response to the request of the Security Council of April 1, 1948 (S/714)," decided that, "in order to eliminate the threat to the peace in Palestine and to facilitate the transition from the present truce to permanent peace in Palestine, an armistice shall be established in all sectors of Palestine." The Council then called upon "the parties directly involved in the conflict in Palestine, as a further provisional measure under Article 40 of the Charter, to seek agreement forthwith, by negotiations conducted either directly or through the Acting Mediator on Palestine, with a view to the immediate establishment of the armistice, including:

(a) The delineation of permanent armistice demarcation lines beyond which the armed forces of the respective parties shall not move;

(b) Such withdrawal and reduction of their armed forces as will ensure the maintenance of the armistice during the transition to permanent peace in Palestine."[7]

Armistice agreements were accordingly concluded between Israel and Egypt on February 24; Israel and Lebanon on March 25; Israel and Jordan on April 3; and Israel and Syria on July 20, 1949.[8]

As a result of these agreements, Israel came into control of about 8,000 square miles of Palestine territory out of a total of 10,435 square miles, or 77.4% instead of the 56.47% allotted to the Jewish State under the Partition Plan. Jewish land-holdings in the whole territory under Israel control were only 360,941 acres, or 7.23%, out of a total of 5,104,505 acres.

The Armistice agreement with Egypt, signed on February 24, 1949, permitted the Israelis to hold on to what territory they acquired on October 14, 1948 in violation of the truce directive of July 15, 1948. But in the direction of the Gulf of Aqaba, the Israelis were limited to within half of the distance between the Gulf's shoreline and the area they then actually held. This is quite explicit from the provisions of Annex II(b) to the General Armistice Agreement, which prescribes that the armistice demarcation line in the south shall run "from point 402 down to the southermost tip of Palestine, by a straight line marking half the distance between Egypt-Palestine and Transjordan-Palestine frontiers."[9] The Israelis were thereby excluded from access to the Gulf of Aqaba. But on March 10, 1949—thirteen days after they had signed the Armistice Agreement—the Israelis launched an attack on the southern Negev area which brought their forces up to the Gulf shoreline.

The United Nations took no steps to dislodge the Israelis. Notwithstanding, their presence there was illegal. The Arab village of Umm
Rashrash located on the Gulf was occupied, the Arab villagers were
expelled and dispossessed, and Eilat was established on Arab-owned
land. To lend permanence to their newly acquired so-called right and
face the world with an accomplished fact, the Israelis immediately
embarked on the construction of port facilities and a new Jewish city.

The Israelis then argued that, with the signing of the Armistice
agreements, the Arab states could no longer claim the right of belligerency, hoping in this way to force the Arab states to a permanent peace
on the basis of the *fait accompli*. The Arab states, on the other hand,
maintained that a state of war existed between the Israelis and the Arab
states, basing their attitude on the fact that, according to international
law, "armistices or truces in the wider sense of the term, are all agreements between belligerent forces for a temporary cessation of hostilities.
They are in no way to be compared with peace and ought not to be
called temporary peace, because the condition of war remains between
belligerents and neutrals, on all points beyond the mere cessation of
hostilities."[10]

The more important provisions of the agreements were:

1. The armistice was intended to facilitate the transition from the
present truce to permanent peace in Palestine;

2. The basis on which permanent peace could be established, including primarily the question of the future government of Palestine, was
still the subject of consideration by the General Assembly "in response
to the request of the Security Council of April 1, 1948,"[11] and were not
therefore to be defined by the Armistice agreements themselves;

3. The Armistice agreements were designed merely to: (a) delineate
armistice demarcation lines; and (b) agree on "withdrawal and reduction
of armed forces" to "ensure the maintenance of the armistice."

Each agreement also included the proviso: "It is also recognized that
no provision of this agreement shall in any way prejudice the rights,
claims and positions of either party hereto in the ultimate settlement of
the Palestine question; the provisions of this agreement being dictated
exclusively by military, and not by political consideration."

The Arab states accepted their obligations under the General Armistice Agreements with every goodwill, in the belief that the agreements
were a temporary measure to give the General Assembly the opportunity to review its hasty recommendation of partition and to find an
equitable solution "for the future government of Palestine" compatible
with the principles of self-determination embodied in the United Nations Charter.

But subsequent events showed that the Israeli signature was with
certain covert aims in view. They needed time to consolidate their
military gains in Palestine and the General Armistice Agreements gave
them just that. Once their objective was achieved, they had little use for
the Armistice agreements except where they could be manipulated to
their further advantage. The following pages give a brief history of
conditions on the armistice demarcation line since the General Armistice
Agreements were concluded in 1949:

Demilitarized Zones

The Armistice Agreements with Egypt and Syria provided for four demilitarized zones—three in the north on the borders of Syria, and the El-Auja area in the south on the borders of the Sinai Peninsula.

The agreement with Jordan provided for four No-Mans Land areas—one on Jabal El-Mukabbir in Jerusalem, comprising what used to be the residence of the British High Commissioner and later occupied by the United Nations Truce Supervision Organization (UNTSO) and the Arab College area; the second, the Hadassah Hospital-Hebrew University area on Mount Scopus and the Augusta Victoria Compound on Mount of Olives in Jerusalem; the third, a strip of land in Jerusalem separating the Israeli from the Jordan sector of the City; and the fourth, an area of some 15,000 acres of agricultural land in the Latrun region on the Jaffa-Jerusalem road.

From the point of view of international law, demilitarization is a security measure of limited scope, established by treaty between two or more states, its purpose usually being—according to Oppenheim—"to prevent war by removing the opportunity of conflict as a result of frontier incidents, or to gain security by prohibiting the concentration of troops on a frontier."[12]

The agreements assigned two roles to the demilitarized zones: one was the separation of the armed forces of the two parties "in such a manner as to minimize the possibility of friction and incident," and the second provision for "the gradual restoration of normal civilian life in the area of the demilitarized zone, without prejudice to the ultimate settlement."[13]

The principal aspect of the Armistice agreements—namely, that they are not political documents but military instruments designed to remove friction between belligerents—is of major significance. The agreements do not establish peace, though they are meant to facilitate the transition to peace. Nor do they legalize Israel's territorial occupation of 1948, since they merely delineate armistice demarcation lines. Arab strict respect for these agreements and insistence that they still constitute the operative legal instruments defining relations between the signatories, is a fact that ought to be remembered, despite the June 1967 War.

In contrast, in many small ways, and on several major occasions (including the campaigns of 1956 and 1967), the Israelis have not only violated the agreements, but have unilaterally even declared them inoperative and dead.[14] Having in 1948 expanded illegally beyond what the Partition Plan had given the Jewish State in 1947, and having since the signature of the agreements expanded beyond the demarcation lines, the Israelis have good reason to ignore the Partition Plan and the agreements alike, and try to make the world forget them, since these documents reveal Israel's expansionism. What is therefore surprising is the lack of concern by many of the members of the United Nations in the face of Israel's arrogant disrespect for United Nations resolutions, and disrespect for her own signature affixed to the agreements.

The following incidents are samples of the Israeli violations in the demilitarized zones:

1. *Demilitarized Zones on Syrian Border*—On the cessation of hostilites, the Syrian army was still in occupation of the territories that later formed the demilitarized zones. No sooner did it withdraw when the Israelis stepped in and began to take measures to expel the Arab inhabitants. The Syrian government complained that the Israeli authorities were contravening their undertakings under Article V of the Armistice Agreement by not only refusing to allow the return of those who had left their homes, but was banishing into the interior those Arabs who had remained behind.*[15] The Israelis replied that the demilitarized zones were in Israeli territory and as such were not subject for discussion with the Syrian government.

The Chief of Staff reported the matter to the Security Council in a memorandum dated March 7, 1951, and at the same time gave his own interpretation of the provisions of the Armistice Agreement to the effect that "it follows that neither party to the Armistice Agreement enjoys rights of sovereignty within the zone."[16]

The Security Council considered the Syrian complaint and decided, among other things, to give effect to the following which, it pointed out, had already been agreed to by the parties at the conference held on July 3, 1949, at which the articles of the draft armistice agreement were being considered, as being "an authoritative comment on Article V of the Syrain-Israeli Armistice Agreement:"

"The question of civil administration in villages and settlements in the demilitarized zone is provided for, within the framework of an armistice agreement, in sub-paragraphs 5(b) and 5(f) of the draft article. Such civil administration, including policing, will be on a local basis, without raising general questions of administration, jurisdiction, citizenship and sovereignty.

"Where Israel civilians return to or remain in an Israel village or settlement, the civil administration and policing of the village or settlement will be Israelis. Similarly, where Arab civilians return to or remain in an Arab village, a local Arab administration and police unit will be authorized.

"As civilian life is gradually restored, administration will take shape on a local basis under the general supervision of the Chairman of the Mixed Armistice Commission.

"The Chairman of the Mixed Armistice Commission, in consultation and cooperation with the local communities, will be in a position to authorize all necessary arrangements for restoration and protection of civilian life. He will not assume responsibility for direct administration of the zone."[17]

With regard to the evacuation of the Arab residents from the demilitarized zone, the Security Council decided that "Arab civilians who have been removed from the demilitarized zone by the government of Israel should be permitted to return to their homes and that the Mixed

*General Vagn Bennike, then Chief of Staff, stated before the Security Council on November 9, 1953: "785 Arabs were removed from their homes" on the night of March 30/31, 1951.

Armistice Commission should supervise their return and rehabilitation in a manner to be determined by the commission." The council further held that "no action involving the transfer of persons across international frontiers, armistice lines or within the demilitarized zone should be undertaken without prior decision of the Chairman of the Mixed Armistice Commission."[18]

On January 6, 1955, the then Chief of Staff reported to the Security Council that "police from the state of Israel, acting under orders from police headquarters outside the demilitarized zone, dominated the zone;" adding that "the Chairman of the Mixed Armistice Commission was unable to implement the provision of the General Armistice Agreement requiring the employment of locally recruited civilian police in the zone. Repeated requests "to remove the non-local police from the demilitarized zone were rejected."[19] In May 1956, the Chief of Staff drew the attention of the Secretary General of the United Nations to the effect that "the position had not changed in any essential since his last report."[20]

In January 1958, General Carl Von Horn, of Sweden, replaced General Burns, of Canada, as fourth Chief of Staff of the United Nations Truce Supervision Organization for Palestine. During his first courtesy visit to the Israeli Foreign Office, writes Von Horn, "he was left in no doubt that the United Nations had failed regrettably to cooperate with Israel's sincere desire for a peaceful settlement, had entirely neglected in fact to show the understanding and sympathetic tolerance for a small, oppressed State which would have been in keeping with its role as a world force dedicated to peace." The General concluded that "the gist of the advice 'to assist me in my task' was that I should refrain from sticking to the rules of the Armistice Agreement."[21]

On another occasion, General Von Horn reported that, sitting in his temporary office in UN Headquarters in New York, he received a visit from Israeli Ambassador Comay. The conversation went like this: "It would be best," Ambassador Comay advised, "to forget all about that out-dated United Nations idea of running a patrol boat on Lake Tiberias; the idea was still-born and ought to be abandoned, because the Lake was essentially Israeli sovereign territory." He then pointed out that "he understood that this had already been made clear in Jerusalem. After all," he said, "why did I waste my time insisting on so many things which I knew the Israelis were opposed to?" Comay concluded: "It would be wise to listen to his advice—otherwise my life was bound to become a great deal more uncomfortable."[22]

General Von Horn replied that he "appreciated his thinly veiled threat," and pointed out, "it was really a waste of breath to attempt to intimidate the Chief of Staff of UNTSO—especially on United Nations territory." General Von Horn then borrowed a phrase of Meir's,*[23] and told him: "I did not want to be pushed around."[24]

2. *Demilitarized Zone on Egyptian Border*—The Armistice with Egypt

---

*At a meeting with Meir in Jerusalem to protest the barring of the General's path by Jewish guards on Mount Scopus from entering the demilitarized zone, Meir is reported to have retorted: "We Jews do not like to be pushed around."

provided in Article VIII, paragraph 1: "The area comprising the village of El-Auja and vicinity shall be demilitarized, and both Egyptian and Israeli armed forces shall be totally excluded therefrom." The area was to serve as the headquarters of the Mixed Armistice Commission.

On March 20, 1950, the Mixed Armistice Commission decided that the occupation by the Israeli forces of Bir Qattar within the demilitarized zone was a violation of the Armistice Agreement, and the matter was dealt with by the Security Council.[25]

On September 18, 1950, the Chief of Staff reported: "On September 2, 1950, Israeli military rounded up some 4,000 bedouins who have been living in the Negev in and around the demilitarized zone of El-Auja and drove them out of Israeli-controlled territory across the Egyptian international boundary into Egyptian territory . . . An investigation of the above incident by the Chairman of the Egyptian-Israeli Mixed Armistice Commission on September 6 revealed that refugee Arabs, representing five bedouin tribes concur in statements: (a) that they had lived in the Beersheba area under the British Mandate but had moved to El-Auja about two years ago because of Israeli pressure; (b) that since August 20, Israelis had conducted operations to clear the Bedouins, employing army troops with armored cars and guided by reconnaisance aircraft; (c) that after driving the Bedouins across the border, the Israelis burnt tents, crops and possessions; and (d) that thirteen Bedouins were killed by Israelis during these operations."[26]

On November 9, 1953, the Chief of Staff drew the attention of the Security Council to a letter dated September 21 which the Chairman of the Mixed Armistice Commission had received from the Senior Israeli Delegate. The letter had stated, *inter alia*: "The demilitarized zone being an integral part of Israel, the Palestinian Bedouin does not exist." He went on to point out: "Any Israeli activity in the demilitarized zone (beside the penetration of military forces), is an internal Israel affair and of no concern of anybody, including Egypt."[27]

On September 21, 1955, the Chief of Staff reported to the Security Council that the Israeli army had re-occupied the demilitarized zone;[28] and on August 21, 1956, he reported: "Israel opposes any meeting of the Mixed Armistice Commission at its headquarters at El-Auja situated in the demilitarized zone, which is now occupied by Israel troops;"[29] and on September 5, 1956, the Chief of Staff reaffirmed his previous reports to the effect that "the Israeli army continues to occupy the El-Auja demilitarized zone." He stressed: "El-Auja is not only the center of the demilitarized zone . . . it is also, under Article X, paragraph 2, the headquarters of the Mixed Armistice Commission. Because of her military occupation of the demilitarized zone, Israel refuses access to El-Auja to the Egyptian members of the Mixed Armistice Commission." He went on to report that on September 3, "Mr. Ben Gurion repeated his refusal to allow meetings of the Mixed Armistice Commission at El-Auja."[30]

In this way, not only the Arab inhabitants were expelled from the demilitarized zone but also the United Nations personnel and organization responsible for the implementation of the provisions of the Armistice Agreement. Had the United Nations exerted its authority within the demilitarized zone and insisted upon the withdrawal of Israeli troops and the non-encroachment on Arab rights and property within the zone, the invasion of Egypt in October 1956 might have taken a different turn.

Other areas subject to the Armistice Agreement are on the armistice demarcation line with Jordan. These are:

Mount Scopus Demilitarized zone—This area runs along the crest of a hill to the north of Jerusalem. It commands a general view of the city and dominates its east and north approaches. The entire hill is inside Jordan territory and its strategic importance is recognized.

The zone comprises the Hebrew University and Hadassah Hospital compound, as well as the Augusta Victoria building, which was being used as a hospital for the Palestine Arab refugees.

Under an agreement signed on July 7, 1948 between the Jordan and Israeli Military Commanders of Jerusalem—to which the United Nations was a third party—the area was demilitarized and officially designated to be under "United Nations protection until hostilities cease or a new agreement is entered upon."

The agreement provided for UN check-posts to be established by the UN Commander; for Arab and Jewish civilian police to be placed on duty under the UN Commander; the UN flag to fly on the main buildings; all military personnel to be withdrawn together with such of their equipment and other supplies as are not required by the UN Commander; the UN to arrange that both parties receive adequate supplies of food and water, and replacement of necessary personnel in residence on Mount Scopus. Under an annex to the agreement of the same date, it was agreed that the UN Observers would be responsible to arrange for the relief of the Jewish personnel on Mount Scopus during the first and third weeks of each month.

The General Armistice Agreement signed between the Jordan government and the Israeli authorities that followed on April 3, 1949, did not supersede the 1948 agreement; and the map of Jerusalem attached to the Armistice Agreement shows the demilitarized zone to be on the Jordan side of the armistice demarcation line and therefore outside Israeli jurisdiction.

The UN flag was hoisted over the Hebrew University and Hadassah Hospital buildings, while Jewish policemen were allowed to guard Jewish owned property within the zone. Similarly, the UN flag flew over the Augusta Victoria building and only Arab policemen were allowed into the area.

The intent and spirit of the two agreements were obvious. The demilitarized zone was supposed to be under the direct control of the Chief of Staff of UNTSO and that the civilian policemen (Arab and Jewish) who were to guard Arab and Jewish properties respectively in the zone, were supposed to obey his orders.

But in actual practice, this was not the case in the Jewish section since the agreement of July 7, 1948 was signed. Although the UN flag flew over the buildings, UN personnel were not permitted to come anywhere close to the area which the Israelis defined as an enclave of Israel; Arab farmers tending their fields in the vicinity were periodically fired upon with impunity; pedestrians crossing Arab lands on the western fringes of the zone to the village of Isawiya beyond were molested; and the United Nations did nothing to assert its authority in a territory over which its own flag flew.

With conditions being what they were, it soon became apparent to the Jordan Government that, apart from violating their obligations under the Military Agreement of 1948, the Israelis were using the convoys authorized under the annex agreement to reinforce the supposedly Jewish police guards on Mount Scopus and to militarize the zone. Jordan's suspicions were confirmed with the disclosure of two incidents. The first became known as "The Barrel Incident." U.S. Commander Elmo Hutchison, who served with the United Nations Truce Supervision Organization in Palestine from 1951 to 1955 first as observer and later as Chairman of the Israel-Jordan Mixed Armistice Commission, reported that on June 4, 1952, while the fortnightly convoy to Mount Scopus was being checked before entering Jordan territory, the United Nations guard observed that his test rod struck a metal object in the center of one of the drums. He ordered the drum taken off the truck; and while he sent for the tools to have the drum opened, the Israelis pushed the truck carrying the rest of the drums towards the Israeli checkpost outside the reach of the United Nations observers to escape further detection.

Commander Hutchison added: "Before the cutting tools could be obtained, the Israelis, in direct violation of the Armistice Agreement, moved soldiers into no-man's land and demanded the return of the remaining barrel." But the barrel was removed into the close-by office of the Mixed Armistice Commission to be held until a decision on its future could be obtained from the Chief of Staff, General William Riley, who was then in New York.

The Israelis, continued Commander Hutchison, demanded the return of the barrel without further inspection. The Jordanians, in the meantime, claimed that it was the duty of the UNTSO to check it thoroughly before it went on to Mount Scopus or was returned to Israel. All members of the mission who were present agreed, he said, that the barrel should be opened. General Riley was contacted, and after a few days he sent a message granting permission to open the barrel. The opening was set for 12:30 hours local time on June 20.

At 12:00 on the day scheduled, the door of the Mixed Armistice Commission office burst open and three Israeli officers, with pistols drawn and escorted by two enlisted men who were holding Thompson sub-machine guns at the ready, marched into the room and stationed themselves outside the barrel-room door. The Jordan military delegate, who arrived soon after appraised the situation and enquired how much of this the United Nations would tolerate. He then left in protest stating that no further MAC meetings would be held in that building.

Attempts were made by the United Nations observers at the appointed time to open the door but they were prevented by the Israeli soldiers. The Israeli authorities refused to recognize the inviolability of the United Nations office; took over the offices; placed another lock on the barrel-room door and took away the key to the MAC building in the possession of the United Nations. What transpired in the interval to tamper with the contents of the barrel is a matter of conjecture.

However, on his return from New York, General Riley condemned the Israeli action of allowing their soldiers to enter no-man's land and for taking over the MAC building. He then arranged to have the barrel checked. What happened to make him change his mind from having the barrel opened to dipping a rod into its unknown contents, it is not difficult to surmise. In the end he remarked: "There is extraneous matter in this barrel and I don't believe it contains the 50 gallons of fuel oil as required by the manifest. I am, therefore, returning the barrel to Israeli control." The Jordan representative immediately protested and demanded that the barrel be opened, but General Riley over-ruled and the matter of the barrel was considered closed much to the consternation of the Jordan government and the disappointment of the United Nations personnel who went to so much trouble to carry out their duties faithfully.

Commander Hutchison summed up the situation in those words: "Israel was guilty of falsifying records submitted to the United Nations; Israel was guilty of attempted smuggling and had revealed to the world it was contravening the Mount Scopus Agreement; Israel had ignored the inviolability of the United Nations Mixed Armistice Commission Headquarters and had taken it over by armed force; Israel had broken the General Armistice Agreement by ordering troops into no-man's land. All of this should have been flashed around the world—not only by Jordan but by the United Nations. Instead, the United Nations kept quiet . . ."[31]

The second incident occurred on December 13, 1952. A group of Israelis atempted to make an end run to the north of Jerusalem with a good-sized load of ammunition for Mount Scopus. Six U.S. Army manpacks were used for the haul. They included 1,000 rounds of rifle ammunition, 2,000 rounds of Sten-gun ammunition, six 81mm. mortar shells, six 2-inch mortar shells, three 90 volt dry batteries and 24 hand grenades with a tin of detonators. Commander Hutchison states, "The Israelis had almost reached their objective when they were surprised by Jordanian National Guardsmen. They fled, leaving the loaded manpacks on the ground. Three of the men lost their fatigue caps bearing names and numbers. One of the men must have been wounded, as bloodstains and a bandage were found near one of the packs. Twice during the night the Israelis tried to retrieve the equipment, but on both occasions they were driven back."

"The next day," Hutchison states, "the Israelis entered a counter-complaint, alleging that a group of Arabs had entered an ammunition supply camp in Jerusalem and stolen the manpacks. They also claimed that an Israeli guard had been wounded during the Arab raid."[32]

This Israeli attempt at distortion did not impress the Mixed Armistice Commission, which condemned Israel for trying to smuggle ammunition to Mount Scopus.

The Jordan government did not cease to express its deep concern to the successive Chiefs of Staff of the United Nations Truce Supervision Organization over what was happening on Mount Scopus. General Riley did little to assert United Nations authority over the demilitarized zone after the Military Agreement had been concluded on July 7, 1948; and when he made his belated and feeble effort in 1952 to inspect the area, "the Israelis could not furnish the keys to several rooms." In the fall of 1953, General Bennike, who replaced General Riley, and inherited an unsatisfactory situation on Mount Scopus, made a similar attempt, but the Jewish officer in charge informed him that he had no orders to allow the inspection. After contact with the Israeli authorities, the inspection was permitted, only to be disallowed to continue thirty minutes after it had started.[33]

General E.L.M. Burns, who replaced General Bennike in 1954, had no better luck. He said he considered it perfectly understandable that Jordan should be deeply concerned about Israeli encroachments on Mount Scopus. The zone, he explained, absolutely dominates the roads into Jerusalem, which is the nexus of all important roads connecting the larger towns of Arab-held Palestine. "If the Israelis," the General pointed out, "could connect up with the sort of fortess held by the detachment of Israeli police [who were probably regular soldiers] they would dominate and could eventually compel the surrender of Jerusalem and probably cause the collapse of Jordanian control of the area west of the Jordan River." He added, "the seizure or occupation of it by Israel would be a disaster for Jordan."[34]

Jabal el-Mukabbir

Besides, being a demilitarized zone, this area, comprising the old Government House, the Arab College, a Jewish Agricultural School and the lands around, has a special status.

The Government House building was being used as the headquarters of the United Nations Truce Supervision Organization for Palestine, the Arab College was empty and neglected after having been ransacked by the Israelis in an attempt to occupy it, while the Jewish Agricultural School was in operation.

The Israelis made several attempts to exert sovereignty over the area; and on January 22, 1958, the Security Council was obliged to draw their attention that "the status of the zone is affected by the provisions of the Israel-Jordan General Armistice Agreement and that neither Israel nor Jordan enjoys sovereignty over any part of the zone (the zone being beyond the respective demarcation lines.)"[35]

No-Man's Land (Between the Arab and Israeli-held Sectors of Jerusalem)

This area consists of open fields and demolished or damaged buildings. When a building is only partly damaged and the entrance is on the Israeli side, the Israelis have occupied such buildings against the protests of the Jordan government and the directives of the United Nations Truce Supervision Organization. The Tannous building near the Jaffa Gate is a case in point. Every effort of the Mixed Armistice Commission to dislodge the Israelis has failed and the United Nations did nothing about it.

The Latrun Area (on the Jaffa-Jerusalem Road)

This No-Man's Land area consists of agricultural land comprising approximately 15,500 acres wholly owned by the Arab farmers of the surrounding villages.

The Israelis first attempted to eliminate its status by suggesting its division between Jordan and themselves or exchanging it for territory further north; and when both these proposals failed, the Israelis began to encroach on the land through cultivation of as many plots as they could in an effort to establish a precedent, as they did in the demilitarized zones. Clashes ensued that necessitated Security Council intervention.

The natural and obvious thing to do was to permit the Arab farmers to cultivate their lands under United Nations protection. To leave the land fallow was to invite trouble.

Arab Villages Severed by Armistice Demarcation Line

When hostilities between Jordan and the Israeli authorities ceased, there were certain Arab villeges within the Little Triangle in the central sector of Palestine where the inhabitants had successfully defended themselves, their homes and lands against Zionist attacks until the cease-fire order of the Security Council became effective. Some of these villages and localities were later ceded to the Israelis under certain specific conditions explicitly prescribed in the General Armistice Agreement.

Article VI, paragraph 6, stipulated, "Where villages may be affected by the establishement of the Armistice Demarcation Line provided for in paragraph 2 of this article, the inhabitants of such villages shall be entitled to maintain and shall be protected in, their full rights of residence, property and freedom."

In the case of Arab villages located on the Israeli side of the demarcation line, the Article prescribed, "It shall be prohibited for Israeli forces to enter or to be stationed in such villages, in which locally recruited Arab police shall be organized and stationed for internal security purposes."

There is no ambiguity in the intent and meaning of these two provisions. The first applies to Arab villages situated on both sides of the armistice demarcation line and whose lands are severed by the line. In this case, the farmers were guaranteed their full rights in homes and property. This also meant that the villagers were to be allowed to cross over the line, cultivate their lands, gather their crops and remove them to their villages as they had been doing since time immemorial.*

---

*This practice is not uncommon in the case of border villages. During the Mandate, Bon Voisinage agreements were concluded between the British and French Mandatory Governments whereby the villagers of border villages on the Lebanese and Syrian frontiers were allowed to cross over, cultivate their lands and gather their crops.

When in 1945, these countries achieved their independence, the author with a British Assistant District Commisssioner visited Beirut and Damascus and concluded new Bon Voisinage Agreements with their governments.

In the case of Arab villages falling on the Israeli side of the armistice line, the provision is clear that internal security was to be the responsibility of locally recruited Arab police, and that Israeli forces were to be "prohibited from entering or being stationed in these villages."

After signature of the Armistice Agreement, the farmers of Arab villages on the Jordan side were in fact permitted to cross over and to cultivate their lands. But when it came to harvesting their crops, the farmers were prevented from doing so under the threat of military force, which resulted in clashes and in some instances in the loss of life. The Arab crops that year were gathered by the Israelis; and soon after, also the lands were seized and distributed among existing Jewish settlements or used for the establishment of new fortified frontier settlements.

As regards the second provision, the Israelis failed to establish the locally recruited Arab police that they undertook under the agreement to do. Instead they stationed their own Jewish frontier force and applied the same discriminatory and emergency regulations in force in Arab villages in the Galilee area. Some of the Arab lands were confiscated and the villagers could not move about freely, along with other restrictions. On October 29, 1956—the day the Israelis invaded Egypt—a curfew was imposed on the village of Kafr Qasem, followed by the massacre of fifty-one persons, which is fully discussed in Chapter XI.

The Arab inhabitants believed that the arrangements affecting them in the Armistice Agreement were only temporary measures for the period of the armistice. Had it been suspected that the situation would develop into incorporating their villages and lands into Israeli territory, it is certain that the Jordan government would not have agreed to the arrangement and more than likely that the villages would have continued to fight.

Functions of Special Committee on Jerusalem

Article VIII of the Israeli-Jordan General Armistice Agreement provides for the establishment of a Special Committee to formulate "agreed plans and arrangements":

1. designed to enlarge the scope and improve the application of the armistice;

2. for such matters as either party may submit to it, "which, in any case, shall include the following:

(a) free movement of traffic on vital roads, including the Bethlehem and Latrun-Jerusalem roads;

(b) resumption of the normal functioning of the cultural and humanitarian institutions on Mount Scopus and free access thereto;

(c) free access to the Holy Places and cultural institutions and use of the cemetery on the Mount of Olives;

(d) resumption of operation of the Latrun pumping station;

(e) provision of electricity for the Old City; and

(f) resumption of operation of the railroad to Jerusalem."

The Special Committee had its first meetings in 1949* under the chairmanship of General William Riley, Chief of Staff of the United

Nations Truce Supervision Organization at the time.

The Israeli position throughout the 1949 meetings of the Special Committee was that Article VIII was, with two exceptions, entirely in their favor. They claimed it gave them the right of access to Mount Scopus, the Jewish cemetery on the Mount of Olives, the Wailing Wall in the Old City, free movement of traffic on the Latrun-Jerusalem road, resumption of operation of the Latrun water pumping station and resumption of the railroad to Jerusalem.

The Special Committee's functions under Article VIII, they maintained, were merely to decide on the procedure to be adopted for the implementation of the points cited above, with no right for the Arab side to raise new issues.

In return, the Israelis said, Jordan would have access to Bethlehem through the occupied part of Jerusalem; and the Old City would be supplied with electricity from the main plant in the Israeli-held sector.

The Jordan delegation pointed out that its own interpretation of the meaning of Article VIII was far wider in scope and spirit than the Israelis allege. It maintained that the intent and purpose of the said article were to provide for normal civilian life to return to the Holy City for *all* sections of the population without exception. It is inconceivable, the delegation explained, that the article could have been designed to serve the interests of the Israelis in full and utterly disregard the interests of the Arab inhabitants of Jerusalem.

The Jordan-delegation then proceeded to present its point of view, as follows:

(1) The first paragraph of Article VIII stipulates that a Special Committee shall be established "for the purpose of formulating agreed plans and arrangements designed to enlarge the scope of this agreement." The words "to enlarge the scope" can only mean that the door is left open for both parties to proffer claims and counter-claims before the Special Committee, which they had no time to formulate during the hurried interval the Armistice Agreement was prepared.

(2) The first sentence of paragraph 2 of the said article lays down that the Special Committee "shall direct its attention to the formulation of agreed plans and arrangements *for such matters as either Party may submit to it.*" This provision reinforces the first argument that the parties are not restricted to the six specific items enumerated in the article, but are at liberty to enlarge on them, particularly since the words which follow make it clear that such matters, *in any case, shall include* the items specified, "on which agreement in principle already exists." The words "in any case" are very significant because they indicate that whatever is decided upon by the Special Committee, the enlarged program *must* include the items enumerated in the article.

(3) The meaning of the item on "free movement of traffic on vital roads, including the Bethlehem and Latrun-Jerusalem roads," is quite

---

*The Jordan Delegation was composed of Hamad el-Farhan and Abdullah el-Tal, with Capt. (later General) Ali Abu Nuwar acting as military adviser and Sami Hadawi acting as civilian adviser.

The Israeli Delegation was composed of Moshe Dayan and Avraham Biran.

obvious that the Special Committee is empowered to establish what in
its judgment are roads *vital to both parties*, but that such vital roads *must*
include the Bethlehem and Latrun-Jerusalem roads. If only the two
roads were intended, the article would have stated so without needing
to prefix the words "vital roads."

(4) The article also provided for "free access to the Holy places."
Here again it did not limit this free access to *Jewish* Holy places, nor did it
specify that Holy places means the Wailing Wall, as the Israeli claim
alluded. If it had meant either or both these cases, it would have said so
explicitly.

The Jordan delegation maintained that free access to the Holy places
meant for Moslems, Christians and Jews over the whole territory of
Palestine; not made available to Jews in both Arab and Israeli-held
territories and out-of-bounds to Moslems and Christians in the Israeli-
held area. If Jews are to be accorded rights and privileges in the Arab
area, then it is only reasonable to demand that Moslems and Christians
should be accorded the same treatment in a land that is theirs by right of
birth and occupation until expelled.

The Jordan delegation then presented the following plans and arrangements to the Israeli side and suggested that they form a package
deal and the basis for the discussion:

(1) *The Jordan government* agrees to permit access to the Jewish buildings on Mount Scopus, the Jewish cemetery on the Mount of Olives, the
Wailing Wall in the Old City, free movement of traffic on the Latrun-
Jerusalem road, resumption of operation of the Latrun water pumping
station and resumption of operation of the railroad to Jerusalem.

(2) *The Israeli government*, on its part, agrees to permit the return of
the Moslem and Christian inhabitants of Jerusalem to their homes; to
grant free access to the Holy places in Israeli-held territory, such as,
Nazareth and Nabi Rubin in Jaffa; free movement of traffic on vital
roads, such as, to Nazareth and Jaffa on festival occasions; to Gaza to
provide a link between Arab families living in Jordan and the Gaza Strip;
and free movement of traffic to Bethlehem. The question of providing
the Old City with electricity from the Israeli sector was dropped as it was
neither practical nor necessary any more.

(3) *Jerusalem* will continue to be administered as a divided city, the
Israelis having jurisdiction over the Jewish populated areas and Jordan
over the Arab quarters.

The Israeli delegation ridiculed the proposals and described them as
fantastic. The Israeli representatives were reminded that if they demanded for their citizens the right to lead a normal civilian life, they
must not deny the same right to the Moslem and Christian inhabitants.
With Israeli refusal to discuss Arab claims, the meetings came to an end.
Further meetings were held in 1950 and again they bogged down in
barren wrangling over the agenda, as a result of the extremely restricted
scope of action that the Israeli delegation sought to impose on it.

The Armistice Demarcation Line

The four General Armistice Agreements prescribe in identical terms that "No element of the land, sea or air military or para-military forces of either party, including non-regular forces, shall commit any warlike or hostile act against the military or para-military forces of the other Party, or against civilians in territory under the control of that Party; or shall advance beyond or pass over for any purposes whatsoever the Armistice Demarcation Lines . . . or enter into or pass the air space of that other Party." Further on, the agreements provide that "The basic purpose of the Armistice Demarcation Lines is to delineate the lines beyond which the armed forces of the respective Parties shall not move."[36]

Right from the start this invisible armistice demarcation line invited trouble. While the General Armistice Agreements prescribe that their provisions were "dictated exclusively by military and not by political considerations," anyone familiar with the land topography of Palestine, can easily see that the reverse was the result. The line appears to have been drawn to meet political pressures and considerations rather than military necessities. It coincided almost to the minutest detail with what the Zionists demanded from the British Mandatory Government in 1946 as the minimum boundaries of the Jewish state that they were willing to accept. The armistice demarcation line separated Arab villages from their fertile lands in the coastal and other plains and included in the Israeli-held territory lands through which the railway line and principal highways ran whether or not this damaged Arab interests. One sad example has been the fate of the Arab town of Qalqilya in the central sector. This town was one of the most prosperous in Palestine, owning extensive orange groves and serving as one of the main vegetable markets of the country. The demarcation line severed all its orange groves in favor of Israel, leaving it a bulging peninsula, landless except for its rocky areas towards the east and its inhabitants helpless as they watched the Israelis gather the fruits of the trees they and their fore-fathers had planted and tended for generations for export to world markets while they languished in distress and poverty.

With conditions being what they are along the entire length of the demarcation line it is no wonder that the Arab villagers attempt, from time to time, to cross over to "steal" what legitimately belongs to them and in the process lose their lives. It is only natural for such conditions to create a situation of revenge by those who lose their dear ones after having lost their lands and means of livelihood.

Commenting on such a unique situation, a former resident of Israel now in the United States cited the "acts of cruelty and manifestations of demoralization which are now occurring in Israel, particularly in the army, in its treatment of Arab refugees and infiltrees," said, "an average from five to seven such infiltrees are being shot by Israeli soldiers every week as a matter of military routine."[37] This atrocity was confirmed by *The New York Times*, which reported, "a total of 394 Arab infiltrees killed, 227 wounded and 2,595 captured in 1952."[38]

The only protest against such treatment came from Israeli poet Nathan Alterman. Writing in *Davar*, official organ of the Israeli Labor Party, the poet pointed out, "Jews have always been notoriously lax in their attitude towards illegal crossing of frontiers, false passports and other small formal offenses against the state and never looked upon

them as moral issues, certainly not as crimes punishable by death."
Alterman then exclaims with indignation: "Oh you Knesset members;
you former passport forgers; you infiltrees, grand-children of infiltrees,
how quickly you have learned the new morality of militarism!"[39]

The Israeli plea is that their military raids across the armistice demarcation line constitute retaliation. If the actual facts of the Palestine
problem were considered, it would become evident that the term is
wrongly applied. According to the dictionary, retaliation means "return
like for like, evil for evil"; and the word reprisal—often used as describing Israeli actions—means "to procure redress of grievances." Since it
was the Arabs, not the Jews, who were the first sufferers through
expulsion and dispossession by force of arms and are being prevented
from returning, it follows with reason that their efforts to retrieve their
rights and possessions, by whatever means, should more accurately be
classified as retaliation and reprisal against Israeli provocation.

Whatever the merits or demerits of the Israeli argument, the fact
remains that by taking the law into their own hands and crossing over
the armistice demarcation line by military force, the Israelis have violated their obligations under the United Nations Charter, the truce order
of the Security Council of July 15, 1948,[40] and the provisions of the
General Armistice Agreements.

The philosophy of so-called Israeli retaliation has been examined by
the Security Council each time an attack by the Israelis had taken place
and has been condemned in the statements made by the majority of the
council members, as well as in Security Council and Mixed Armistice
Commission resolutions. For example, in its resolution of January 19,
1956, the Security Council proclaimed that the alleged provocation that
Israel claimed had prompted its attack on Syrian territory "in no way
justifies the Israeli action." The resolution proceeded to "remind" Israel
that the Council had "already condemned military action in breach of
the General Armistice Agreements, whether or not taken by way of
retaliation."[41]

During the discussion in the Security Council of a second attack by
Israeli military forces on Syrian territory on March 16, 1962, the British
representative strongly condemned the Israeli "deliberate attack" and
demanded that their leaders drop their "policy of violence" in favor of
cooperation with the United Nations;[42] The late U.S. Ambassador Adlai
Stevenson also rapped the Israelis for reverting to military actions which
flagrantly violated United Nations resolutions. "This policy," he said
"contributed to the rapid rise of tensions in the Middle East during 1955
and 1956 and it can no more be countenanced today than it was then."[43]
It is worthy to note that the report of the Chief of Staff on the incident
was that there was no evidence to support the Israeli charge that the
attack on Syria was necessary to destroy a fortified post in self-defense.
He said his observers found no evidence of any such post "either
existing or destroyed" when they inspected the area.[44]

If the members of the Security Council had hoped that by their
statements and resolutions the Israelis would cease their aggression
across the armistice demarcation line, they were very much mistaken.
The council was once again seized with the problem of Israeli aggression

against the village of Sammu' on November 13, 1966. Condemnation of the Israeli action was in this case universal. The representative of the United Kingdom said it "constituted a flagrant violation of our Charter and of the Israel-Jordan Armistice Agreement; it has done nothing to enhance the security of Israeli citizens or the reputation of Israel."[45]

The representative of the United States was more vocal. He said his government condemns the raid "deeming it in clear violation of the solemn obligations undertaken by Israel in the General Armistice Agreements. And what makes it of course most deplorable," he added, "is the tragic toll in human lives of this inexcusable action." He went on to say, "The Government of Israel carried out (with the support of tanks, armored vehicles, heavy weapons and aircraft) a raid into Jordan the nature of which and whose consequences in human lives and in destruction far surpass the cumulative total of the various acts of terrorism conducted against the frontiers of Israel." He compared this latest Israeli aggression with "the retaliatory action at Qibya taken by the armed forces of Israel on October 14–15, 1953," the brutality of which also received world condemnation.

The fact that the Israeli action was naked aggression devoid of any justification, is borne out by the testimony of the United States representative in his statement that followed. He said: "My government is confident that the government of the Kingdom of Jordan in good faith fully adheres to and respects its obligations under the General Armistice. Its record of cooperation with the United Nations peace-keeping machinery in the Middle East speaks for itself," he concluded.[46]

The representative of France intervened also "to condemn unequivocally the military action planned and carried out by the Israeli authorities." He remarked, "What is difficult to understand is that an attack which has proved to be so deadly was launched against a country which is respectful of its international obligations."[47]

The U.S.S.R. representative told the council that by its "direct military attack on a densely populated part of Jordan, Israel had flagrantly and brutally violated the most important provision of the United Nations and this alone deserves our condemnation." He described the attack as "lawlessness and brigandage" and "an open and arrogant challenge to the Security Council."[48]

Following these and other condemnations, the Security Council adopted a resolution on November 25 censuring "Israel for this large-scale military action in violation of the United Nations Charter and of the General Armistice Agreement between Israel and Jordan;" and emphasizing "to Israel that actions of military reprisal cannot be tolerated and that if they are repeated, the Security Council will have to consider further and more effective steps as envisaged in the charter to ensure against the repetition of such acts."[49]

By this time, the Israelis had gotten used to Security Council condemnations and censures, which meant very little to them. For on April 7, 1967, Israeli jet planes attacked Syrian positions and flew as far as Damascus bombing villages and causing loss of life and much damage. One would have expected the Security Council would immediately invoke its warning of "further and more effective steps" against Israel.

Instead complete silence prevailed in the chambers of the United Nations.

Classification of Violations

Violations of the General Armistice Agreements may be classified under two main categories:

(1) Individual crossings of the armistice demarcation line; and

(2) Crossings by the regular armed forces—planned and organized under government supervision and control.

The majority of the violations under category (1) have been committed by the Palestine Arabs, particularly by the inhabitants of the villages falling along the armistice demarcation line who could see—as they still do—their homes, orchards, groves and fields, but are prevented from entering them. It was only natural for some of them to sneak back to their homes and fields in order to retrieve some of their belongings or to "steal" their own crops and fruits for their starving families. Others were child shepherds who wandered innocently across the line unaware that they were committing a violation.

Had the armistice demarcation line been drawn to follow village boundaries rather than made to sever all fertile Arab lands in favor of Israel, the problems which have since arisen and which continue to plague conditions on the armistice demarcation line might well have been minimized. Reporting to the Security Council on the situation, the Chief of Staff said: "The problem is particularly difficult because the demarcation line is long—about 620 kilometres—and because it divides the former mandated territory of Palestine haphazardly, separating, for instance, many Arab villages from their lands."[50]

Despite these difficulties, the Arab states made every effort within their power to curb crossings in order to reduce the unnecessary loss of human life. This is attested to by Commander E.H. Hutchison, who said: "During my three years on the Jordan-Israel Mixed Armistice Commission, I watched Jordan's attitude towards border control change from one of mild interest to a keen determination to put a stop to infiltration."[51] This was further affirmed in 1966 by the representatives of the United States and France both of whom paid tribute to Jordan's respect for her international obligations.[52]

As regards violations under category (2), it is a matter of United Nations record that all such attacks have been by the Israel regular armed forces. No Arab state has ever been brought before either the Mixed Armistice Commission or the Security Council accused of an attack by its regular armed forces on Israeli-held territory. This is confirmed by the testimony of the Chief of Staff before the Security Council on November 9, 1953. Asked "how many Israeli attacks were carried out by Israeli military forces in retaliation to the total violations by Israelis," General Bennike replied: "Of the 21 resolutions condemning Israel, adopted by the Israeli-Jordan Mixed Armistice Commission, four refer to action by Israeli armed groups, one to armed Israelis, four to Israeli forces, one to Israeli regular forces, one to Israeli troops, one to Israeli soldiers, one to an officer and Israeli security forces, one to Israeli armored cars, and one to Israeli regular army. The answer to your question is sixteen."[53]

The General was then asked to indicate whether there were "any organized attacks by the Arab Legion against Israeli settlements or villages;" and "Did the Arab Legion engage during the truce in any mass murders or mass destructions." To this he replied: "Jordan regular forces were condemned by the Mixed Armistice Commission for three violations of the General Armistice Agreement none of which was an organized attack by the Arab Legion against an Israeli settlement or village."[54]

Israeli Aggressions

The acts of aggression committed by the Israelis after the signing of the Armistice in 1949 are too numerous to enumerate. They range from army patrol and aircraft crossings of the lines for reconnaissance purposes to murder and destruction of villages. What is significant about these aggressions is that the attacks are carefully planned and meticulously carried out by the *regular forces* of the Israeli army under Government instructions.

The United Nations has not published at any time statistics on the violations committed and casualties suffered by the parties to the General Armistice Agreements. Such official statistics are not doubt vital to determine the relative responsibility of the parties for the unrest and tension prevailing in the area and in order to dispel the distortions created by the one-sided propaganda alleging that Arab infiltration—the so-called root of the problem—has, over the years, inflicted heavy losses on the Israelis that they could neither tolerate nor allow to pass unpunished.

However, a fairly accurate appraisal of responsibility may be gathered from the individual independent tabulations published by Commander E.H. Hutchison for the period June 1949 to October 15, 1954, when he served on the Israeli-Jordan Mixed Armistice Commission and by General E.L.M. Burns for the period January 1, 1955 to September 1956 when he was Chief of Staff. It is unfortunate that figures for all fronts since 1949 and for the period beyond September 1956 have not been made public by other members of the United Nations Truce Supervision Organization who came before or followed Commander Hutchison and General Burns in their cycles of duty.

Commander Hutchison stated that during the period under his review,[55] the Israelis were condemned for 95 violations and the Jordanians for 60 violations—a ratio of two to one. In regard to those killed and wounded, the verified figures were:

	Killed	Wounded
Israelis	34	57
Jordanians [Palestinians]	127	118

Here the ratio was for every one Israeli killed there were four killed on the Jordan side.

General Burns' comparative figures for the four sectors along the armistice demarcation line in respect of the period under his review,[56] were:

	Killed	Wounded
Israelis	121	332
Arabs	496	419

Here also the ratio for the twenty-one-month period works out at four Arabs killed for every one Israeli. This does not, however, include the 18 Israelis and 48 Jordanians reported killed as a result of the Israeli attack on the town of Qalqilya on October 10/11, 1956; nor the casualties suffered following the Israeli invasion of Egypt on October 29, 1956. Civilian losses within the Gaza Strip during the Israel occupation were estimated by neutral sources to have run into the thousands.

If the above figures of condemnation and casualties are any criteria for the purpose of fixing responsibility, then one is led to the obvious conclusion that it is the Israelis—not the Arabs—who are the principal violators of the General Armistice Agreements and the aggressors responsible for the tension along the armistice demarcation line. This conclusion is also arrived at by General Carl Von Horn who replaced General Burns as Chief of Staff. He said: ". . . it was Israeli policy to maintain a situation pregnant with threats of Arab attacks. It seemed to all of us in UNTSO that there were two reasons why this suited them. First, it ensured a high state of readiness and efficiency within their own army, which showed a marked tendency toward internal disputes immediately tension relaxed. Second, it enabled them to make sure that their plight received the maximum amount of attention in foreign and particularly American newspapers, with the natural corollary that sympathy, aid and money continued to flow into Israel in substantial quantities."[57]

According to the records of the United Nations, the Israeli armed forces launched over forty military attacks in one form or another on Arab territory between the date of the signing of the General Armistice Agreements and April 1967. The following is a list of the principal attacks as a result of which there has been loss of life and damage to property. These have been either condemned by the Mixed Armistice Commission or censured by the Security Council;

1. Aerial bombardment of El-Himmeh (Syria) on April 5, 1951.[58]

2. The villages of Falame and Rantis (West Bank) attacked on January 28/29, 1953.[59]

3. The villages of Idna, Surif and Wadi Fukin (West Bank) attacked on August 11, 1953.[60]

4. An Arab Bedouin encampment south of the Gaza Strip attacked by air and ground forces in the summer of 1953.[61]

5. The villages of Qibya, Shuqba and Budrus (West Bank) attacked on October 14/15, 1953.[62] Seventy-five people were killed; the villages were completely demolished.

6. The village of Nahhalin (West Bank) attacked on March 28/29, 1954.[63] Fourteen people were killed; the village was demolished.

7. The Arab Legion camp in 'Azzun (West Bank) attacked on June 27/28, 1954.[64]

8. The village of Beit Liqya (West Bank) attacked on September 1/2, 1954.[65]

9. Syrian territory attacked on December 8/9, 1954.[66]

10. The Gaza Strip attacked on February 8, 1955.[67] Thirty eight people were killed and 31 others wounded.

11. The Gaza Strip was attacked and the Egyptian post on Hill 79 was occupied on August 22, 1955.[68]

12. Khan Yunis and Bani Suheila (Gaza Strip) were attacked on August 31/September 1, 1955.[69] Forty-six people were killed and 50 others wounded.

13. Syrian territory was attacked on October 22/23, 1955.[70]

14. Kuntilla post (Sinai Peninsula) was attacked on October 28, 1955.[71]

15. Sabha post (Sinai Peninsula) was attacked on November 2/3, 1955.[72] Fifty people were killed and 40 men taken prisoners.

16. El-Buteiha and El-Koursi area (Syria) attacked on December 11/12, 1955.[73] Fifty people were killed and 28 taken prisoners.

17. Egyptian patrols in the Gaza Strip attacked on August 16/17, 1956.[74]

18. Umm el-Rihan (West Bank) attacked on August 28, 1956.[75]

19. The village of Rahwa (West Bank) attacked on September 11, 1956.[76]

20. The village of Gharandal (West Bank) attacked on September 13, 1956.[77]

21. The villages of Sharafa and Wadi Fukin (West Bank) attacked on September 25/26, 1956.[78]

22. The villages of Qalqilya, 'Azzum, Nabi Elias and Khan Sufin (West Bank) attacked on October 10/11, 1956.[79] Forty eight people were killed and 31 others wounded.

23. The invasion of Egypt began on October 29, 1956.[80]

24. The village of El-Tawafiq (Syria) was attacked on February 1, 1962.[81] The village was razed to the ground.

25. Syrian territory along the shores of Lake Tiberias was attacked on March 16, 1962.[82]

26. The villages of Nukheila, Abbasieh and Tell el-Aziziyat (Syria) were attacked from the air and ground artillery on November 13, 1964.[83]

27. The towns of Jenin and Qalqilya and the village of Manshiyat near Jisr el-Majami (West Bank) were attacked on May 27, 1965.[84] Four people killed and seven others wounded. A number of houses demolished.

28. The villages of Houla and Meis el-Jabal (Lebanon) were attacked on October 28/29, 1965.[85] One woman killed and two houses and three village cisterns demolished.

29. Syrian territory was bombed from the air by jet planes on July 14, 1966.[86] Jet fighters shelled Syrian positions, killing one woman and wounding nine civilians.

30. The village of Sammu' (West Bank) was attacked on November 13, 1966.[87] Eighteen killed, 130 wounded and 125 houses, including the school, clinic and mosque demolished.

31. On April 7, 1967, Israeli planes penetrated deep into Syrian territory and attacked Syrian targets.[88]

The Qibya Attack

Commenting on the Qibya attack of 1953, Father Ralph Gorman, an American Roman Catholic Priest who spent many years in Jerusalem, said: "Terror was a political weapon of the Nazis and is still used by the communists. But neither Nazis nor communists ever used terror in a more cold-blooded and wanton manner than the Israelis in the massacre of Qibya."

"The official report of the Palestine Truce Supervision," he pointed out, "removed any possible doubt that the Israelis, themselves in large part refugees from Hitler's terror, were perpetrators of this horrible slaughter of innocent men, women and children. It also reveals that it was an official act of the state, carried out by an official organ, the army," he added.

The Reverend Gorman then went on to describe the attack. He said: "The evening of October 14 was like any other for the 1,500 inhabitants of the peaceful village until 9:30 all hell let loose. Mortar shells began exploding from artillery that had been carefully aimed from Israel before dark. After the town had been partly demolished and many of its inhabitants buried in the rubble of falling homes or blown to bits by exploding shells, half a battalion of the regular Israeli army moved in and surrounded the village to cut off escape." Then followed, he said, "an orgy of murder that would be incredible if it had not been verified by reliable neutral testimony. Women and children as well as men were murdered deliberately, systematically and in cold-blood."

Rev. Gorman then stated, "The only response the Israelis have made to outraged protests of the civilized world has been one of defiance and self-justification. The Prime Minister excused the murderers. Israeli newspapers openly gloated over the deed and even American Zionists showed little concern other than a fear that American dollars might not continue to flow as freely as before into the coffers of the new state."[89]

The diary of Moshe Sharett, acting Prime Minister at the time of the Qibya massacre, published in October 1965 by his son in rebuttal of certain statements made by Ben Gurion against his father, are most revealing of the manner in which the attack was planned. The excerpts from the diary begin with October 14, 1953, the day the raid took place. Sharett writes in regard to the incident that precipitated the massacre: ". . . Today the Mixed Armistice Commission roundly condemned the killing (of a woman and two children at Yahud). *Even the Jordanian delegates voted in favor of the resolution. They took upon themselves to prevent such atrocities in the future. Under such circumstances, is it wise to retaliate?"* Sharett enquires.

Sharett then comments: "I came to the conclusion that we are again confronted with a situation like that other time when I had a raid called off and in so doing broke off the vicious circle of bloody revenge for a fortnight and more. If we retaliate, we only make the marauder bands' job easier and give the authorities an excuse to do something. I called

Lavon (Defence Minister) and told him what I thought. He said he would consult B.G." (Ben Gurion).

The diary continues: "In the afternoon, during a meeting with Lavon and others in connection with developments in the north, an Army representative brought Lavon a note from the UNTSO Chief of Staff Gen. Vagn Bennike, saying that *the Commander of the Jordan Legion, Glubb Pasha, had asked for police blood-hounds to cross over from Israel to track down the Yahud murderers.* Sharett then states that after Lavon read the note, the Army man asked: "Any change in plans?" Lavon answered: "No change."[90]

From this diary, it will be seen that the Jordan government after being satisfied that the killings were the work of its citizens, went so far as to ask for Israeli blood-hounds to follow the murderers inside Jordan-controlled territory. Notwithstanding the sincerity of the Jordan government, the Israelis made no change in their plans for the massacre of the innocent inhabitants of Qibya.

Summation

To sum up: A study of the texts of the General Armistice Agreements, the reports of the Secretary-General and those of the various Chiefs of Staff of the United Nations Truce Supervision Organization, as well as the resolutions of the Security Council on incidents occuring along the armistice demarcation line between 1949 and 1967 lead to the following conclusions:

(1) The General Armistice Agreements signed between the Arab states and the Israeli authorities are not peace treaties but only agreements intended to stop the fighting.

(2) The agreements were designed as a temporary measure to deal with the situation which had arisen in Palestine as a result of the establishment of the state of Israel.

(3) Both parties to the agreements, having voluntarily undertaken to do certain things, they are obligated to abide unreservedly by their undertakings.

(4) The armistice demarcation line is not an international boundary, a frontier or border limit; its objective is merely to separate the military forces of the disputing parties.

(5) The Security Council has accepted the interpretation of the UN Acting Mediator and the Chairmen of the Mixed Armistice Commissions that the provisions of the General Armistice Agreements preclude the parties from claiming sovereignty over the demilitarized zones and no-man's land. This interpretation was made clear in one instance and acquiesced to by the Syrian government and the Israeli authorities at the Armistice Conference held on July 3, 1949, prior to the signing of the Armistice Agreement on July 20, 1949, and on the strength of which the Syrian troops pulled out of the areas they then occupied.

(6) While sovereignty over the defensive areas by the parties concerned is not questioned, certain limitations have been placed on military personnel and equipment within the areas. These are restricted to defensive forces only.

(7) Military and para-military forces were to be totally excluded from the demilitarized zones; while normal civilian life for *both Arabs and Jews* was to be permitted under local administrations under the supervision of the Mixed Armistice Commissions.

(8) The Mixed Armistice Commissions were empowered to arrange for "the return of civilians to villages and settlements in the demilitarized zone, and for the employment of limited numbers of locally recruited civilian police in the zone for internal security purposes."

(9) The inhabitants of villages affected by the armistice demarcation line are entitled "to maintain, and shall be protected in, their full rights of residence, property and freedom." Israeli forces are "prohibited" from entering or being stationed in such villages in which "locally recruited Arab police shall be organized and stationed for internal security purposes."

(10) The Military Agreement on the Mount Scopus demilitarized zone in Jerusalem places the zone under "United Nations protection;" while the General Armistice Agreement with Jordan places the zone east of the armistice demarcation line in Jordan territory. Jurisdiction over the zone is the responsibility of the "UN Commander."

(11) The Mixed Armistice Commissions were entrusted with the task of ensuring the observance and implementation of certain provisions of the General Armistice Agreements; and in regard to the meaning of certain clauses, the interpretation of the Mixed Armistice Commissions shall prevail.

(12) The Armistice Agreements provide authority for the free movement of the United Nations Truce Observers within the demilitarized zones and along the armistice demarcation line in order to carry out their duties.

(13) Israeli presence on the Gulf of Aqaba is illegal and in violation of the Security Council directives of July 15, 1948, of November 4, 1948 and the provisions of the General Armistice Agreement with Egypt.

(14) Neither party has the right to repudiate the Armistice Agreements or any of their provisions.

An objective comparison between these basic provisions and the actions of the Arab states, on the one hand, and the Israelis, on the other, since 1949 will reveal that the Arab states have faithfully carried out their obligations whereas the Israelis have violated every provision cited and that the United Nations failed to assert its presence in the area by enforcing compliance.

Israeli attitude in Palestine can best be illustrated by drawing upon the experiences of General Carl Von Horn during the period he was Chief of Staff of the United Nations Truce Supervision Organization. Von Horn stated, "time and time again in the course of frank discussions with Israeli officers and officials, I had heard them openly repudiate the idea of objectivity. Their flat statement," he said "was 'you are either for or against us'. Even nastier," he added, "was an Israeli tendency to immediately brand objectivity as anti-Semitic; a convenient label which could be smeared on to any UN soldier whose impartial report did not weigh down in favor of the Israelis."

In reviewing his relations with Arabs and Israelis, General Von Horn remarked that UNTSO personnel had "from time to time incurred a certain degree of animosity" in their dealings with the Arabs, but never, he said, "in the same implacable and frenetic way." He went on to testify that "the Arabs could be difficult, intolerant, and indeed often impossible, but their code of behavior was on an infinitely higher and more civilized level." He then pointed out that "all came to this conclusion in UNTSO," which he described as "strange, because there was hardly a man among us who had not originally arrived in the Holy Land with the most positive and sympathetic attitude towards the Israelis and their ambitions for their country."

General Von Horn went on to explain, "after two or three years in daily contact with officials, soldiers and private individuals on *both* sides, there had been a remarkable change in their attitude." He found it, he said, "sad but very significant" that when he asked what their most negative experiences had been during their service with UNTSO, the reply was almost invariably: "The consistent cheating and deception of the Israelis."[91]

PALESTINE AS RESULT OF ARMISTICE AGREEMENTS 1949

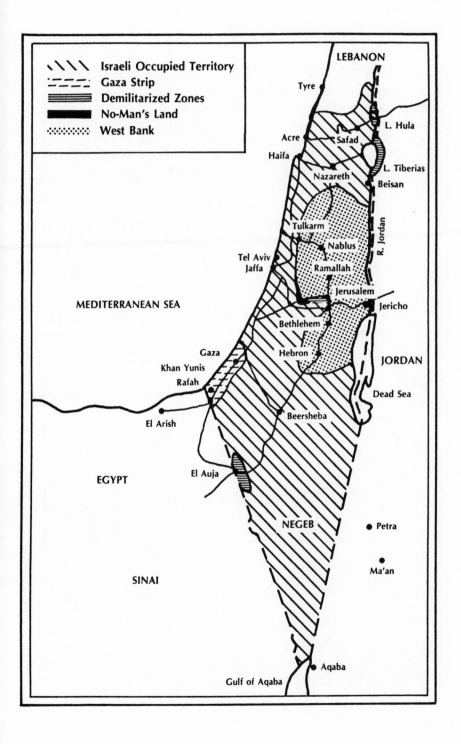

JERUSALEM ACCORDING TO THE GENERAL ARMISTICE AGREEMENT
1949

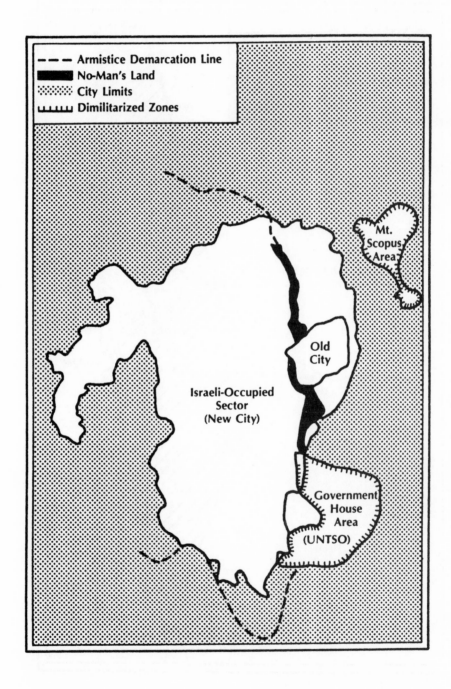

IX   United Nations Efforts for Settlement

Appointment of Mediator

With the abolition of the Palestine Commission, which was supposed to take over the administration of the country progressively from the departing Mandatory Power, Count Folke Bernadotte was appointed UN mediator and entrusted with the task of bringing about a settlement.

After surveying the situation and arranging for a truce, the UN mediator presented the parties on June 28, 1948, with a tentative plan, the salient points of which were:

(a) The Arab areas of Palestine be united to Jordan and that Jordan, so constituted, should form a union with Israel.

(b) The union should handle economic affairs, foreign policy and defense for both Israel and Jordan.

(c) Subject to the instrument of union, Jordan and Israel would each control its own internal affairs.

Attached to the proposals was an annex dealing with territorial matters. In it, Bernadotte suggested that all or part of the Negev be included in Jordan, in return for which all or part of Western Galilee would go to Israel. He further proposed that Jerusalem should be Arab, that Haifa be a free port and Lydda a free airport.[1]

Bernadotte's proposals were rejected by both parties; and on September 17, 1948, together with his French aid Colonel Serot, Bernadotte was assassinated in the Israeli-occupied sector of Jerusalem by men wearing the uniform of the Israeli army. "No action was taken by the Israeli authorities for twenty-four hours to apprehend the murderers. Then Ben Gurion roused himself and took action. Most of the members of the Stern Group were rounded up and many were arrested, but the assassins were never caught."[*]

Moshe Menuhin, commenting on the assassination, said: "And thus Israel got away with murder. The United Nations demanded that Israel bring the assassins to justice; the answer was that she could not find the murderers." Menuhin then points out, "Count Bernadotte was the first martyr in the service of United Nations reconciliation efforts in Palestine—a saint to the Arabs and, perhaps as is usually the case, an anti-Semite in the eyes of the fanatical Jewish political nationalists." He adds, "The saddest part is that Count Bernadotte's plan was the only answer to the Arab-Israeli war. And another thought: To this day it is almost a crime to recall the murder of Count Bernadotte because 'it may be a disservice to the best interests of poor little Israel'. Forgotten is the name of the noble man who was a victim of ungrateful, land-hungry jingoists."[2]

On September 16, 1948—one day before his assassination—Count Bernadotte presented to the General Assembly his final recommendations for a solution of the Palestine problem. He drew the attention of the General Assembly that "The Jewish state was not born in peace as was hoped for in the Resolution of November 29, but rather . . . in violence and bloodshed."

The main point in his report was his insistence on the necessity for prompt and firm action by the United Nations. He then advised the General Assembly that the refugees' "unconditional right to make a free choice (between return and compensation) should be fully respected." He added: "It is, however, undeniable that no settlement can be just and complete if recognition is not accorded to the right of the Arab refugee to return to the home from which he has been dislodged. It will be an offense," he continued, "against the principles of elemental justice if these innocent victims of the conflict were denied the right of return to their homes while Jewish immigrants flow into Palestine, and indeed, at least offer the threat of permanent replacement of the Arab refugees who have been rooted in the land for centuries."

On the question of property, Bernadotte remarked that "there have been numerous reports from reliable sources of large scale looting, pillaging and plundering, and of instances of destruction of villages without apparent military necessity. The liability of the Provisional Government of Israel to restore private property to its Arab owners and to indemnify those owners for property wantonly destroyed, is clear," he said.

The mediator's report also recommended the modification of the Partition Plan in such a way as to include the Negev in the Arab state area and in return, Galilee and the enclave of Jaffa in the Jewish state.[3] His intention was apparently to give each side a solid and homogeneous block of territory, instead of the crossovers, pockets and corridors in the United Nations plan. The towns of Lydda and Ramle were to return to the Arabs, and Jerusalem was to be placed under United Nations jurisdiction.

---

*Bernadotte's assassination is reminiscent of the murder of Lord Moyne by the Stern Gang in Cairo in 1944, because the British policy in Palestine he had suggested was contrary to Zionist aspirations.

The report caused much consternation among the Israelis. By this time they had experienced the taste of victory and were not going to allow it to slip through their fingers. Bernadotte was highly respected in United Nations and international circles, and the Israelis feared that his recommendations would receive universal support. His murder removed any chance of approval of his recommendations.

Resolution on Return and Compensation

On December 11, 1948, the General Assembly met and, among other things, resolved "that refugees wishing to return to their homes and live at peace with their neighbors should be permitted to do so at the earliest practicable date, and that compensation should be paid for the property of those choosing not to return and for loss of or damage to property which under principles of international law or in equity, should be made good by the governments or authorities responsible."

At the same time General Assembly Resolution 194 went on to establish a Conciliation Commission and instructed it "to facilitate the repatriation, re-settlement and economic and social rehabilitation of the refugees and the payment of compensation . . ."

It also instructed the commission "to take steps to assist the governments and authorities concerned to achieve a final settlement of all questions outstanding between them."[4]

The tragedy of this resolution was threefold: its lateness; the absence of effective machinery for execution; and the absence of any admission of United Nations responsibility, thus leaving compliance to the pleasure of the parties concerned. The intervening period of seven months between the date the state of Israel was proclaimed and the adoption of the resolution, saw nearly one million homeless and destitute Palestine Arabs still searching for safety, shelter and food, while many died from starvation or exposure. On the other hand, the Israelis were given ample opportunity to consolidate and strengthen their hold over Palestine. Once confident that the United Nations did not possess the power or willingness to assert its authority and enforce compliance, the Israelis simply ignored it—and continue to do so—claiming in 1965 that Resolution 194 was "obsolete by the course of events."[5]

On December 14, 1950, the General Assembly met once again, and this time, "*noting with concern* that agreement has not been reached . . . repatriation, resettlement, economic and social rehabilitation of the refugees and the payment of compensation have not been effected, *recognizing* that . . . the refugee question should be dealt with as a matter of urgency . . . *directs* the United Nations Conciliation Commission for Palestine to . . . continue consultations with the parties concerned regarding measures for the protection of the rights, property and interests of the refugees."[6]

The vagueness and mildness of this belated resolution, though it recognized the urgency of the refugee problem, did nothing to bring it to an end. This was added encouragement to the Israelis in their intransigence. They were now certain—if they doubted it before—that the United Nations was incapable of doing anything not acceptable to them.

From this date on, no further action was taken except to affirm and reaffirm annually the right of the refugees to repatriation or compensation under the resolution of December 11, 1948, leaving the Palestine Arabs in the squalor of refugee camps and the Israelis in occupation of Arab homes and property.

Palestine Conciliation Commission

The Commission began its functions soon after its appointment by first meeting in Beirut, Lebanon and later in Lausanne, Switzerland. It then reported to the General Assembly that "the exchange of views . . . must be considered not only as bearing upon one of the specific tasks entrusted to the Commission by the General Assembly resolution of December 11, 1948, such as the refugee question or the status of Jerusalem, but also as bearing upon its general task of conciliation of the points of view of the parties with a view to achieving a final settlement of all questions outstanding between them."[7]

The Commission also reported that it had presented the parties with a *Protocol* "which would constitute the basis of work" and asked them to sign it. The Protocol, signed on May 12, 1949, provided that the Commission, "anxious to achieve as quickly as possible the objectives of General Assembly Resolution 194 of December 11, 1948, regarding refugees, the respect for their rights and the preservation of their property, as well as territorial and other questions, has proposed to the delegations of the Arab states and to the delegation of Israel that the working document attached hereto (map of partition) be taken as a basis for discussions with the Commission."

The Commission added that "the interested delegations have accepted this proposal with the understanding that the exchange of views which will be carried on by the Commission with the two parties will bear upon the territorial adjustments to the above indicated objectives."[8]

At this stage, things looked as if one possible solution of the Palestine problem might be in sight. But the Commission went on to report that when it then asked the two parties to make known their views on outstanding questions, the delegation of Israel submitted proposals regarding the territorial questions, according to which it demanded that *the international frontiers of Mandatory Palestine be considered the frontiers of Israel*, with one provisional and temporary exception, namely, the central area of Palestine then under Jordanian military authority, in which the Israelis consented to "recognize the Hashemite Kingdom of Jordan as the *de facto* military occupying Power," without entering into "the future status of the area" for the time being.[9]

When the Arab delegations protested that these unique proposals constituted a repudiation by the Israelis of the terms of the Protocol signed on May 12, 1949, the Israel delegation retorted, *"it could not accept a certain proportionate distribution of territory agreed upon in 1947 as a criterion for a territorial settlement in present circumstances."*[10]

It is worth recording in this respect that during the debate on the report of the UN mediator in November 1948, in which he suggested certain territorial changes, it was the Israeli representative who strongly objected to any alteration in the boundaries as resolved in the Partition Resolution of 1947 and argued that "It was logical that any conciliation effort should make the November 29th resolution its basis." At a subsequent meeting, the Israeli representative said, "in the view of his delegation, the Assembly's resolution of November 29, 1947, is a valid international instrument of international law, while the conclusions in the mediator's report were merely the views of a distinguished individual which were not embodied in any decision of a United Nations organ."[11]

Is it not ironic that the UN Partition Resolution should be regarded as a "logical" basis for "any conciliation effort" and "a valid international instrument of international law" in November 1948 and no longer so hardly a year later because the Israelis had achieved their objectives?

Concerning the refugee and Jerusalem issues, the delegation of Israel adopted similar inflexible attitudes incompatible with the provisions of the General Assembly resolution of November 29, 1947 (on partition) and December 11, 1948 (on repatriation and compensation), the acceptance of which the Israelis had indicated—by signing the Lausanne Protocol of May 12, 1949.

When its initial efforts for a political settlement failed, the Commission retired to United Nations headquarters in New York and concerned itself with the less important duties of preparing lists of individual Arab property in Israeli hands and valuing it; arranging for the release of blocked Arab bank accounts in Israel; and reiterating from time to time that its services were available to the parties if called upon.

Lacking power and not possessing the machinery to enforce its wishes, the Commission was unable to carry out its task of protecting "the rights, property and interests of the refugees" pending a final settlement.

This callous attitude of the United Nations has one and only one explanation, that the Palestine problem was by now regarded as one of those chronic problems to be shelved for time—not justice and equity—to solve.

Between 1953 and 1961, the Commission took no direct action but waited for the parties to make contact with it for a solution. But, on May 9, 1961—fourteen years after the Commission was established and entrusted with the task of finding a solution to the Palestine problem—the Commission made one final effort to explore, by means of a special representative, the precise views of the parties as to what action might usefully be taken for the implementation of paragraph 11 of Resolution 194(III).[12]

Dr. Joseph E. Johnson, President of the Carnegie Endowment for International Peace since 1950, was selected; and he left for the Middle East on August 31, returning to New York on September 20, 1961. During this period, he visited Beirut, Amman, Cairo, Gaza, Jerusalem and Tel Aviv, and had conversations with high Government officials, the Secretary-General of the League of Arab States, the Director of United Nations Relief and Works Agency for the Arab Refugees (UNRWA). He also visited refugee camps and vocational training centres and talked with area officers and local officials.

On his return, Dr. Johnson informed the Commission that high officials of the host countries and of Israel had expressed the view that it might be possible to take practical steps with regard to the refugee problem without prejudice to the positions of the governments on other aspects of the Palestine problem. In the light of this preliminary statement, Dr. Johnson was asked to make a second trip to the Middle East and to submit a report in time for consideration by the Seventeenth Session (1962) of the General Assembly.

Dr. Johnson submitted his proposals to the Palestine Conciliation Commission in time for the next session of the United Nations, but for some unexplained reason, the report was not circulated to the members of the United Nations, and was not dealt with by the General Assembly.*

Israeli Membership in United Nations

The Israelis had no intention from the start of giving up one inch of territory or allowing the return of a single refugee to his home. They signed the Lausanne Protocol for the purpose of gaining admission to membership of the United Nations. Without that, the new state's sovereignty and acceptance into the community of nations would have remained shaky.

It should be noted that Israel's first application for membership was rejected in December 1948 because it was then felt that the Jewish state did not fulfill the requirements of the United Nations Charter. At that time, the Israelis had encroached upon and were still in occupation of, territory assigned to the proposed Arab state and the international zone of Jerusalem; while scores of thousands of Palestinian Arabs swarmed the surrounding Arab countries as refugees.

In 1949, the Israelis once again sought admission. Concurrently, the Conciliation Commision was conducting negotiations in Lausanne, Switzerland. Anxious to gain admission, the Israelis could not again afford to display patent disregard for the will of the United Nations. The signing of the Lausanne Protocol on May 12, 1949 coincided almost to the hour with the approval of Israel's admission into membership of the United Nations on May 11, if the time difference between Lausanne and New York is taken into account. The signature, of which member-states have been informed, gave the impression to the opposing members that the Israelis were now ready to surrender the extra territory occupied beyond that assigned to the Jewish state under the Partition Plan, and to allow the Palestine Arabs to return to their homes.

This deception was later officially admitted with impunity by the Israelis in these words: "Some members of the United Nations wished at this opportunity to test Israel's intentions with regard to the refugees, boundaries and Jerusalem issues, before approving its application for admission. In a way, Israel's attitude at the Lausanne talks aided its

---

*On the suggestion of a friendly member of the Commission, the author was able to see Dr. Johnson and to read his report. The reason why circulation to member-states was withheld was—as the author understood it—because it was not favorable to Israel.

Delegation at Lake Success in its endeavour to obtain the majority required for admission."[13]

Once admission was secured by such a ruse, Israel had no further need to honor her pledges to the United Nations.

It is significant to note that, in approving Israel's second application for membership, the General Assembly did not overlook the special relationship between Israel's existence and previous resolutions of the Assembly. Nor was Israel's special obligations to implement these resolutions ignored.

Of some ninety states admitted into membership since 1949, Israel was the only state that was accepted on the condition that specific resolutions of the General Assembly would be implemented.

Despite the verbal assurances of the Israeli representative before the Assembly, the *Preamble* of the resolution of admission included a safe-guarding clause as follows: "Recalling its resolution of November 29, 1947 (on partition) and December 11, 1948 (on repatriation and compensation), and taking note of the declarations and explanations made by the representative of the government of Israel before the *ad hoc* Political Committee *in respect of the implementation of the said resolutions*, the General Assembly . . . decides to admit Israel into membership in the United Nations."[14]

Here, it must be observed, is a condition and an undertaking *to implement* the resolutions mentioned. There was no question of such implementation being conditional on the conclusion of peace on Israeli terms as the Israelis later claimed to justify their non-compliance.

It should further be noted that, in the Israeli Proclamation of Independence dated May 14, 1948, the Israeli leaders promised that they would be "ready to cooperate with the organs and representatives of the United Nations in the implementation of the Resolution of the Assembly of November 29, 1947."[15]

Israel today claims sovereignty by reason of the Partition Resolution; it also claims that its sovereignty cannot now be touched even by the United Nations. The fact that Israel has not fulfilled the stipulations in the resolution that gave it birth and has failed to live up to the promises and obligations it undertook when admitted into membership of the United Nations, makes that sovereignty—legally and morally—null and void and leaves Israel's presence in Palestine limited to brute force which, in other cases, has been condemned by Western democracy.

Internationalization of Jerusalem

Efforts were also made by the Conciliation Commission to obtain agreement of the parties on the internationalization of Jerusalem.

Israel has from the beginning resisted to the utmost the internationalization of the city. When the Trusteeship Council called upon Israel in 1949 to submit to United Nations authority "in the light of her obligations as member of the United Nations," the Israeli answer was to transfer their parliament and government from Tel Aviv to Jerusalem and to declare Jerusalem their capital. In response to the request of the Trusteeship Council "to revoke these measures and to abstain from any action liable to hinder the implementation of the General Assembly resolution of December 9, 1949,"[16] the then Prime Minister, David Ben Gurion, countered with a declaration, "the United Nations . . . saw fit . . . this year to decide that our eternal city should become a *corpus separatum* under international control. Our rebuttal of this wicked counsel," he said, "was unequivocal and resolute: The government and Knesset at once moved their seat to Jerusalem and made Israel's crown and capital irrevocably and for all men to see."[17]

This challenge to world authority and to all Moslems and Christians throughout the world who look toward the Holy City for inspiration, was allowed to stand. It might be regarded today as contributing to the tension and instability in the area. So instead of peace, brotherhood and love coming out of Jerusalem the Holy City has been turned into a hot-bed of hatred and strife between the three communities.

Violation and Defiance of UN Authority

The state of Israel came into being as a result of an act of the United Nations and, as such, the Israelis are obligated to the World Organization to respect and comply, *unreservely*, with all its principles and stipulations. But no sooner was the Jewish state established, when the Israelis began to violate the provisions of the very resolution that brought their state into existence and all subsequent resolutions calling upon the Israelis to do certain things.

The principal resolutions that stand unimplemented against the Israeli record in respect to the 1948 War, are:

(1) *No. 181 (II) of November 29, 1947* (on partition)—defining the boundaries of the Jewish state and providing guarantees for the rights of the Arab inhabitants.

(2) *No. 194 (III) of December 11, 1948* (on refugees)—providing for the exercise of the right of the refugees to make a free choice between return to their homes and compensation.

(3) *No. 303 (IV) of December 9, 1949* (on Jerusalem)—declaring the Holy City a *corpus separatum* under United Nations jurisdiction.

(4) *No. 273 (III) of May 11, 1949* (on admission of Israel to membership of UN)—The United Nations "*decided* to admit Israel into membership of the United Nations" after it had taken "*note* of the declarations and explanations made by the representative of the Government of Israel before the *Ad Hoc* Political Committee in respect of the implementation of its Resolutions of November 29, 1947 (on territory) and December 11, 1948 (on refugees)."

(5) *No. 394 (V) of December 14, 1950* (on rights, property and interests of the refugees)—directing the Conciliation Commission on measures for "the protection of the rights, property and interests of the refugees" pending final settlement.

Israeli arguments for non-compliance with their obligations under the charter and non-implementation of the provisions of the resolutions cited, are: The Arab states having attacked the state of Israel, the Israelis are no longer bound by the Partition Resolution; territory won in battle beyond that assigned to the Jewish state under the Partition Plan is not returnable. On the internationalization of Jerusalem, the Israelis reacted by declaring the Holy City the capital of Israel with retroactive effect to May 15, 1948.

As regards the refugees, the Israelis claim that having abandoned their homes and lands of their own free will, the refugees have thereby forfeited their rights of return and to reclaim their property.

As for "the protection of the rights, property and interests of the refugees," the Israelis regard any United Nations control over property situated in Israel as derogatory to the sovereignty of the Jewish state and interference in the internal affairs of a member-state.

In the light of the chronological order of events of the period, the Israeli arguments are neither logical nor reasonable. It will be recalled that Arab rejection of the partition plan was in 1947 for obviously legitimate reasons; the entry of the Arab armies into Palestine was in May 1948; hostilities ceased in July 1948; the United Nations' call to Israel to permit the refugees to return to their homes was in December 1948; the Lausanne Protocol by which both parties agreed to settle their dispute on the basis of the resolution of November 29, 1947, (on territory) and resolution of December 11, 1948 (on refugees) was signed on May 12, 1949; and last but not least, Israeli implementation of these two resolutions was made a condition for Israel's admission into membership of the United Nations.

The fact that agreement was reached after the cessation of hostilities rendered immaterial the positions and actions of either party during the period which preceded the date of the signing of the Lausanne Protocol and Israel's declaration of readiness to implement the said resolutions. In effect, the agreement meant that whatever the causes or the responsibilities, these were to be ignored as both parties lent their attention to a settlement based on the Protocol signed at Lausanne, Switzerland. But the Israelis, after achieving their objective, decided to repudiate their obligations.

Israel policy has since been:

"Force of arms, not formal resolutions will decide the issue."[18]
"These resolutions no longer live, nor will they rise again."[19]
"All that we have taken we shall hold."[20]

X The Arab Refugee Problem

The Palestine Tragedy

When the Palestine tragedy occurred in 1948, the conscience of the world was moved and prompt action was taken to bring relief to the victims. But through political obstruction inside and outside the United Nations, the injustice has been allowed to linger and the distress has been prolonged until now it may be included in the category of problems that the world tends to accept as chronic and something it must learn to live with. Thus, the initial impulse of conscience became blunted and the calamity was allowed to continue indefinitely. Instead of a just solution being imposed by the United Nations on the defaulting party under at least the threat of sanctions if compliance could not be effected by other means, meager relief is doled out to the victims in the hope that time will solve the problem.

Statements have been heard from time to time that, after all, the Palestine Arabs are not the only refugees in the world; that there is no reason for granting them preferential treatment.

There is one basic difference, however, which few recognize, between the refugees from European countries, China, Cuba and those who migrated when India and Pakistan became independent, on one side and the Palestine Arabs, on the other. The former were *not* ousted by their governments but left of their own free will because they either disagreed with, or did not wish to live under the changed political conditions. There is no law or policy in all these countries to prevent their returning if they wished to do so. The Palestine Arabs, on the other hand, were *forcibly expelled and dispossessed* by an alien people who established themselves as a government; they are still eager to return to their homeland and are only prevented from doing so by those who now occupy their homes and lands.

United Nations failure to protect the Arab inhabitants and to fulfill the guarantees it voluntarily undertook to uphold Arab rights, property and interests in the territory set aside for the Jewish state, has, by its inaction, encouraged the aggressor and removed all chances of a peaceful settlement.

Solutions have been offered from time to time, but all invariably ignored the Palestine Arabs' natural rights to their country. One of the proposals made was resettlement of the refugees in Arab countries. The obvious answer to this suggestion was given by the late UN Secretary-General in his report for 1959. Dag Hammorskjold warned: "No reintegration would be satisfactory, or even possible, were it to be brought about by forcing people into their new positions against their will. It must be freely accepted, if it is to yield lasting results in the form of economic and political stability."[1]

Attitude of the Refugees

There is a myth current outside the Arab world that the refugees would accept to be resettled where they are, outside Palestine, and that it is the Arab governments that block resettlement for political reasons. This is the reverse of the truth. The Arab governments refuse resettlement because the refugees themselves refuse it, not the other way round.

The attitude of the refugees has been made clear since 1948. They are unwilling to accept anything short of their full rights to their homes and country. This expression of desire has not altered during the years and has been conveyed annually to the General Assembly by the agency responsible for their relief (UNRWA). Here are some examples:

In one instance, the UNRWA director reported, "the great mass of the refugees continues to believe that a grave injustice has been done to them and to express a desire to return to their homeland." On the question of the Israeli stand, he said: "The government of Israel has taken no affirmative action in the matter of repatriation and compensation . . ."[2]

In another instance, the director told the General Assembly, "the past and present drove home to each of us, even more forcibly, the truly tragic plight of the Palestine refugees . . . They have existed," he said, "by virtue of charity meted out on a meager scale." He then drew attention that "for the most part they have lived without opportunity for self-advancement and—worst of all—their hopes for the future have tended to grow dimmer than brighter." He ended by pointing out that, "viewed by any standard, the plight of these people stands out as a dark stain on human history."[3]

One would imagine that such reports would spur the General Assembly to action in order to alleviate the sufferings of these unfortunate victims of political events. But four years later, the new Commissioner-General of UNRWA had occasion to report, "All that he has so far seen and heard since assuming his present responsibilities confirms the view recorded in previous reports that the refugees in general strongly maintain their insistence on the idea and aspiration of returning to their homes . . . The refugees" he added, "have also expressed the wish that they should be enabled to receive redress for the loss they have suffered without prejudicing their claims to repatriation or any other political rights mentioned in resolution 194 (III). The modalities of implementing that paragraph of the General Assembly resolution may be differently conceived by the refugees," he said, "but what is not in doubt is that their longing to return home is intense and wide-spread." The Commissioner-General went on to say, the refugees "express their feeling of embitterment at their long exile and at the failure of the international community, year after year, to implement the resolution so often reaffirmed. They feel that they have been betrayed and their resentment is directed not only against those whom they regard as the chief authors of their exile, but also against the international community at large whom they hold responsible for the partition and loss of their homeland, which they regard as an offence against natural justice."

"One further point," the Commissioner-General said, "should be made regarding the general attitude of the refugees. In their own eyes they are not refugees at all in the sense in which that term is used to describe persons who have uprooted themselves and broken with their past in order to seek a new life in new surroundings and in a new country. The Palestine refugees regard themselves rather as temporary wards of the international community whom they hold responsible for the upheaval which resulted in their having to leave their homes. As they see it, the international community has a duty to enable them to return to their homes and meanwhile, to provide for their maintenance and welfare."[4]

In 1965, the Commissioner-General once again drew attention to the attitudes and feelings of the refugees which, he said, continue unchanged. "From their standpoint, a nation has been obliterated and a population arbitrarily deprived of its birthright. This injustice," he pointed out, "still festers in their minds and they hold the United Nations responsible for their lot and for extending assistance to them until a solution can be found to their problems. Their longing to return to their homes, encouraged by the General Assembly's declaration on repatriation and compensation in paragraph 11 of resolution 194 (III) and referred to in many subsequent resolutions, remains unabated. During the past year," the Commissioner-General added, "their emotions have, if anything, increased with the additional focus for their feelings provided by the Palestine Liberation Organization, which came into being in June 1964. According to a declaration of September 1964 by the Council of Kings and Heads of State of the League of Arab States, the Organization was established 'to consolidate the Palestine entity and as a vanguard for the collective Arab struggle for the liberation of Palestine'." The Commissioner-General pointed out that "apart from the view expressed by that organization and by the Arab governments, the refugees themselves use every opportunity to stress the intensity of their aspirations, and hopes to return to their former homeland and to urge the Commissioner-General to convey their views to the General Assembly. From this stand point and from such information as has come to his attention, the Commissioner-General believes that the refugee problem has not grown any less complex or less dangerous to the peace and stability of the region."[5]

In his report for 1965–1966, the Commissioner-General emphasized, "as year succeeds year, there is no sign that the refugees are becoming any less embittered by their conviction that a grave injustice has been done to them through the loss of their homes and country and the continued deprivation of any benefit from the property they left behind. The implications for peace and stability in the Middle East of the continued existence of the Palestine refugee problem thus remain as grave as ever."[6]

It is neither suprising nor the work of politicians, as the Israelis claim, that the Palestine Arabs—old and young—should, after this lapse of time, still insist upon their right of return to their homes and country. The demand is genuine. Apart from the need to redress the injustice inflicted upon them, it should be noted that it is part of the Arab character to be attached to the soil where their ancestors had lived and are buried. Their removal has created in them a spiritual emptiness which no amount of material compensation can satisfy.

With new generations of Palestinians growing up imbued with such ardent love for their usurped homeland that transends the amenities and opportunities foreign lands may have to offer, it is easy to discern why the chances are remote for the Palestine problem to be solved on the basis of the *status quo*.

With their patience exhausted, is it any surprise that Palestinians formed the resistance movement in 1964?[7]

Refugee Living Conditions

The deplorable conditions under which the refugees had been living were further aggravated by the situations which arose as a result of the June 1967 War; the Israeli attack on the refugee camp of El-Karameh; the troubles of Jordan in 1970–1971; and those of Lebanon.

A Commissioner-General of UNRWA described the life the refugees live as one of "bitterness, frustration and disappointed hopes. During the long period of their dependence on international charity," he said, "theif life has been one of hardship and privation. The relief accorded by UNRWA, though indispensable," he pointed out, "has been no more than a bare minimum . . . The rations are meager and unvarying and would hardly sustain a person who depended solely on them for any long period . . ." the Commissioner-General added.

He then stressed, "whatever differences of opinion there may be about certain aspects of the problem, it is clear that a large part of the refugee community is still living today in dire poverty, often under pathetic and in some cases appalling conditions. Despite the sustained efforts of UNRWA and of the host governments and other collaborating agencies, there are families," he pointed out, "who still live in dwellings which are unfit for human habitation: some in dark cellars, others in crumbling tenements, others in grossly over-crowded barracks and shacks . . . Nearly all the UNRWA camps are extremely over-crowded with five or more persons living in one small room. They lack adequate roads and pathways and many camps are deep in mud in winter and in dust in summer. There are rarely any sewers or stormwater drainage. The water supplies are communal and often inadequate, particularly during the hot summer months. Yet the refugees living in the camps (who constitute about two-fifths of the total number of refugees receiving relief) are, on the whole, probably better housed and better cared for than many of the remaining three-fifths living outside the camps in such dwellings as they have been able to provide for themselves. Understandably, UNRWA is under constant pressure from these less fortunate refugees to expand its camps and build more shelters."

"I am in no doubt," continued the Commissioner-General, "that a large category of refugees is genuinely in need of the relief dispensed by the agency and that these refugees would face starvation or at least extreme privation if this relief ceased. Their dependence on help from others is not due to unwillingness to work, but to the simple lack of jobs which they can do. As to the attitude of the Arab governments towards the employment of the refugees, the Commissioner-General has seen much to show that the authorities in the host countries are adopting a helpful and humane attitude to the question of enabling the refugees to find work and support themselves, even though this reduces the opportunities open to the local population."

It seemed to the Commissioner-General that it would be useful to consider what future awaited the Palestine refugees if the deadlock over repatriation continued. Without attempting a detailed forecast, he offered three general observations:

(1) A large hard core of refugees will continue to live in poverty and dependence on the charity of their fellow men for the indefinite future. How large this hard core may be is conjectural but even years hence (assuming that no solution of the refugee problem is found) it would seem that it must still include most of the refugees now living in the Gaza Strip, a substantial part of those living in Jordan and a significant number of those in the other host countries. If it seems intolerable that so large a number of human beings should spend their lives in perpetual dependence and that their fellow men should be asked to shoulder indefinitely the burden of supporting them, then it should be remembered that this would appear to be part of the price that has to be paid for the continuing lack of a solution to this problem. It should be remembered also that, however heavy the load imposed on others may be, the cruelest burden is that borne by the refugees themselves;

(2) The remaining refugees, not included in this hard core, will probably continue to improve their ability to support themselves at a rate depending on (a) the general economic development of the region and the creation of new opportunities of employment and (b) the employability of individual refugees (the latter depending in large measure on the education and training that they received); until their self-support is securely established, they (as well as the hard core) will continue to need assistance of the kind provided by the agency;

(3) There is a danger that bitterness and resentment may continue among the refugees against those whom they hold responsible for the tragedy that befell them and against the international community in general for its failure to provide a remedy; that this bitterness and

resentment may be diffused more widely and rooted more deeply throughout the Arab world as the *diaspora* of the Palestine refugees continues; and that, as a result, hope of a solution of the refugee and other related problems may diminish rather than increase as time goes on.

The Commissioner-General concluded by pointing out that the refugees regard the UNRWA rations not merely as a form of assistance from the international community, which they are entitled to receive so long as their problem remains unsolved, but also as a recognition of their status and position while they await repatriation or compensation.[8]

Refugees of 1948 War

According to United Nations records, the number of persons who left their homes in 1948, was in the neighborhood of 900,000. The years that followed saw more and more Arabs expelled.

Of the persons who fall under the established definition of "Palestine refugees," 1,757,269 are registered with the agency as of June 30, 1978. The registrations are distributed in the agency's area of operation as follows:

Lebanon	–	211,902
Syria	–	198,435
East Jordan	–	682,561
West Bank	–	310,268
Gaza Strip	–	354,103
		1,757,259[9]

These figures do not include, however, Palestinians who have lost their means of livelihood but not their homes, and as such, do not qualify for relief under the United Nations definition of refugee. They also do not include persons who have been able to re-establish themselves in the host countries and are therefore not in need of relief; or Palestinians who are now scattered throughout the world.

Basis of Relief Rations

The refugees are presently maintained by the United Nations on a diet made up of the following basic rations and other supplies:

1. *Basic dry rations*
   A monthly ration for one person consists of:
      10,000 grams of flour
       600 grams of dried beans
       600 grams of sugar
       500 grams of rice
       375 grams of oils and fats.
   This ration provides about 1,500 calories per day per person. In winter, the monthly ration is increased by

300 grams of dried beans
400 grams of flours
It then provides about 1,600 calories per day per person.
2. *Other supplies*
One piece of soap (150 grams) per month to each ration benefi-
ciary. One and one-half liters of kerosene have hitherto been
allocated to ration beneficiaries and to babies and children registered for services, in camps in Jordan, Lebanon and Syria during
five winter months. In Gaza, one liter has been allocated to these
beneficiaries, whether or not they live in camps, during five winter
months. For the future, it is planned to issue kerosene only on a
hardship basis in all host countries.[10]

The 1,500 calories provided the refugees per day in summer and the
1,600 calories in winter are below the minimum required for an individual. These do not include meat, vegetables or fruits, which the refugee
must either find elsewhere or learn to do without.

Problem Before the United Nations

The Palestine Arabs have repeatedly expressed their resentment at
having to receive charity. They have considerable property in the
Israeli-occupied part of Palestine, the income from which would be
sufficient to maintain them on a more decent standard of living than the
meager seven cents per person per day level doled out to them by the
United Nations. The income from this property—the patrimony of an
entire nation—runs into the hundreds of millions of dollars. The capital
value of the agricultural lands, farmsteads, cattle, machinery, city properties, contents of private homes and businesses, motor vehicles, etc.,
which the Israelis seized, adds up to billions of dollars. Some of these
properties have been sold, others are leased; and the proceeds from the
transactions are being used for the settlement of new Jewish immigrants, of whom few were ever refugees.

The annual debates of the Palestine question in the Special Political
Committee are generally intense, but the ultimate result is the adoption
of a resolution of extended help, leaving the cause of the problem to
fester and grow. A spokesman of the Palestine Arabs told the Committee, in unequivocal terms, "The establishment of the Palestine Liberation Organization was an expression of the Palestinian Arabs' determination to continue the struggle for those rights, which had been taken
away from them by invading British colonialists and Zionists and by the
United Nations, and given to total strangers from all parts of the world.
Although the Organization had the support of the Arab Governments, it
had not been established by them but was a manifestation of the vitality,
initiative and spirit of sacrifice of the people of Palestine themselves in
dealing with their problem. Its formation had been proclaimed by the
First Palestine Arab National Congress held at Jerusalem on May 28,
1964 and attended by 424 Palestinian representatives. The Congress had
declared the unequivocal determination of the people of Palestine to
liberate their homeland from foreign occupation and domination. The
establishment of the Organization had constituted the turning-point in

the history of the Palestinian Arabs and a repudiation of the claims of those who would have the United Nations believe that the question of Palestine no longer existed and that it was only the refugee problem which was on the agenda.

"After seventeen years of patient waiting," the spokesman went on to say, "they had lost all faith in the United Nations, but the establishment of the Organization had re-awakened their hopes and afforded them an opportunity to renew the struggle for their homeland, their strong and genuine attachment to which could not be shaken by the lapse of time. Wherever they were now residing," he said, "the more than two million Arabs of Palestine formed a single national entity which had its home in Palestine from time immemorial."[11]

Another spokesman was no less emphatic on the subject of the rights of the Palestine Arabs. He warned that "The Palestine Arabs, the lawful owners of the country, continued to exist and they had one goal: to repossess their homeland and exercise their right to self-determination. Whether the refugees became self-supporting or not, whether UNRWA continued to function or not, nothing would deflect them from their determination to achieve that objective. Their rights and their national identity would not be weakened by the passage of time and their just cause was supported by all the Moslem and Arab peoples and by freedom-loving nations throughout the world. The Palestine problem," he pointed out, "was an example of colonialism in its ugliest form and a case of genocide in the era of the United Nations. It constituted a violation of human rights and a denial of the right of self-determination."[12]

During the debates of 1964, the representatives of Afghanistan and Malaysia introduced a draft resolution calling for the appointment of a custodian to administer Arab property in Israeli-occupied territory.*[13] The sponsors explained that the provisions of the draft were humanitarian and not political. It was designed solely to enable the Arab refugees from Palestine to receive the income from the property that they owned in their ancestral land. "That was simply a matter of common sense and justice," they said. The representative of Afghanistan pointed out, "he could not see any reason why Moslem or Christian Arabs should not continue their ownership of property which belonged to them in a town or village in Palestine, even if the town or village had been occupied by the Israeli authorities since 1948. To refuse them that right," he added, "would be an act of racial and religious discrimination condemned by the whole world."[14]

The Israeli representative opposed the draft resolution on the grounds that the Arabs had rejected the Partition Plan and they could not now claim its implementation; that the proposed measure would constitute a limitation upon Israel's sovereignty; that the United Nations could not intervene in the internal affairs of any state; and that the Arabs have been unwilling to conclude a peace treaty with Israel.

---

*A similar proposal to appoint a custodian of Arab property in Israeli occupied territory, sponsored by Afghanistan, Malaysia, Pakistan and Somalia, was again made in 1966. It was defeated by 38 votes to 36, with 36 abstentions (Draft Resolution No. A/SPC/L.128 of November 9, 1966—UN Document A/6506 of November 15, 1966).

The representative of Malaysia replied that, in the first place, he wished to explain, "It was essential to bear in mind that the proposed text did not call upon the committee or the General Assembly to come to a decision on the substance of the matter, or to pass any kind of judgment, but merely requested, in accordance with international practice and custom, the appointment of a custodian to administer the disputed property in the best interests of its owners."

Commenting on the four objections raised by the Israeli representative, the representative of Malaysia replied as follows:

First, "Whether they [the Arabs] accepted partition or not, the situation was a *fait accompli* and the new state occupied land which had not previously belonged to it, so that the question whether the property now belonged to its own nationals, to aliens or to enemies was still in debate."

Secondly, "The question of Israel's sovereignty had to be viewed in the context of international principles and the obligations placed on that state, when it was created by a United Nations resolution."

Thirdly, "If a state had certain obligations that it refused to fulfill, it was the duty of the General Assembly to ask it to do so."

Fourthly, "In fact, the property in question should be treated as enemy property which was subject to duly established *International Law,* which drew a distinction between what was called the acquired rights of a new state, rights that were already in existence before the new state came into existence and rights of enemy property. The question whether a belligerent might confiscate the private property of enemy nationals on its own soil was controversial. The state of Israel," he added, "claimed precisely to have a right, under its domestic laws, to expropriate and confiscate all property within its territory. However," he pointed out, "since the end of the eighteenth century and after the Second World War, the outright confiscation of enemy property had been eschewed, and the principle of indemnification had been affirmed by treaty.[15] The purpose of the immunity of private property from confiscation was to avoid throwing the burdens of war upon private individuals. Furthermore," he went on, "there was some doubt as to whether the confiscations that might have been made would be recognized by other states or by international tribunals."[16]

It is obvious from the annual debates in the Special Political Committee that the majority of the members of the United Nations have the desire to do in Palestine what they know is right and what is just; but the world organization, when acting as a body, is generally influenced to remain equivocal in pressing for Israeli compliance. Instead of facing the facts squarely and placing responsibility for the deadlock where it belongs, the United Nations contends itself each year with applying palliatives in the form of charity to the victims of its ill-conceived decision of partition of 1947 and a superficial call to both parties "to settle their differences either by direct negotiation or through the Conciliation Commission"—as if the Arabs are equally to blame for the tragedy.

According to the Israelis, they claim there is nothing to settle: the Palestine Arabs are out and must remain out; their properties have been confiscated for the use of new Jewish immigrants and cannot be returned; and all that remains to be done is for the Arab states to settle for peace with Israel on the basis of the *fait accompli*.

Misconceptions About the Problem

The Arab states are accused of keeping the dispute alive because of their refusal to resettle the refugees in their own territories. But there is *no* resolution of the United Nations calling on the Arab states to do so; there *are*, however, resolutions calling on the Israelis to permit the refugees to return to their homes and compensate those who do not wish to return. Nevertheless, the Arab states have shown every willingness to open their borders to those refugees who wish to settle in Arab lands after they have been allowed to exercise their right of free choice between repatriation and compensation, as laid down in paragraph 11 of resolution 194 (III). This willingness was clearly expressed by Ambassador Kamil Abdel Rahim on behalf of the other Arab states. He told the General Assembly: "The Arab countries would be quite prepared to welcome all those who preferred to stay out of Israel, but they had no power over the overwhelming majority of refugees who want to go back."[17]

There prevails in certain circles an assumption that the Arab states are using the refugees as pawns in the game of power politics with Israel. The additional charge is that the Arab states have both mistreated and neglected the refugees and have made no effort to alleviate their sufferings.

The real facts have long been obscured by Israeli disinformation. But Dr. John H. Davis, former Commissioner-General of the United Nations Relief and Works Agency (UNRWA), who could speak with authority on the subject, has exploded the misconceptions about the situation.

In a speech delivered before the Conference of Voluntary Agencies in Geneva, Switzerland, on January 18, 1961, Dr. Davis declared that "the Palestine refugee problem has defied political solution, not because of alleged 'whims' of Arab politicians or the reputed 'shiftless" nature of the refugees, but because of the 'depth and universality' of the conflict of basic feeling between Arabs and Israelis."

"The reason," he pointed out, "is a 'widespread lack of understanding' of the problem." He listed what he termed as five major 'misconceptions' about the situation:

1. *That the Palestine Arab people are shiftless and prefer international charity to working for a living.*
Dr. Davis countered that this is not true—The Palestinians are "generally industrially inclined and have a strong desire to be self-supporting. As of 1948, the Palestine economy and culture were about the most advanced of any in the Middle East."

2. *That the Arab host governments have mistreated the refugees by neglecting them and even holding them as hostages in their struggele with Israel.*
Dr. Davis replied that "the truth is that in general the host governments have been sympathetic and generous within their means."

3. *That the conniving of unprincipled Arab politicians had held the refugees idle.*

Dr. Davis declared that Arab politicians "quite accurately voice the deep feelings and aspirations" of their peoples, refugees and non-refugees alike, when they refuse to "accept Israel as a permanent component of the Middle East. It is the basic feelings of the peoples on both sides of the Palestine issue rather than politicians' whims, that have prevented and still prevent a political solution to the Palestine problem."

4. *That a political solution would mean an end to the refugee problem.*
Dr. Davis pointed out that, politics aside, there is the human aspect of the problem—namely, that a large portion of the adult male refugee population is unemployable. The older generations were farmers or unskilled laborers and the younger are untrained and all of them are now living in countries where the demand for such workers is already fully met.

5. *That internal pressure should now be applied to host governments to force them to solve the refugee problem more quickly.*
Dr. Davis said, "in view of the human aspect of the problem alone and without regard to political factors (important as they are), the host governments cannot themselves solve the Palestine refugee problem. To pressure them to do so would tend to increase economic and political instability in these countries, which in turn, would tend to delay rather than facilitate a permanent solution."[18]

Right of Refugees to Homes and Property

The Partition Resolution provides that the Arab inhabitants of the Jewish state shall be protected in their rights and property. In addition, the *Israeli Proclamation of Independence* of May 14, 1948, while guaranteeing political equality and other freedoms for all its citizens, provided, "The state of Israel will be ready to cooperate with the organs and representatives of the United Nations in the implementation of the resolution of the Assembly of November 29, 1947, and will take steps to bring about the economic union over the whole of Palestine."[19] This Proclamation was made *after* the Zionists had already expelled and dispossessed at least 300,000 Arabs, but still needed world opinion on their side.

Now, Israel disclaims any responsibility for the Palestine tragedy and has consistently refused to comply with United Nations resolutions. The former director of UNRWA reported to the General Assembly in 1958, the "reintegration of the refugees into the economic life of the Near East either by repatriation or by resettlement" will continue to be hampered so long as the government of Israel will take no "affirmative action to facilitate the implementation of General Assembly resolution 194 (III) of December 11, 1948 concerning repatriation and compensation."[20]

Israel's refusal to allow the refugees a choice between return to their homes and compensation is part and parcel of the political policy that motivated the decision of expulsion and dispossession in 1948.

Zionist treatment of the Palestine Arabs has been amply recorded for all time by British historian Arnold Toynbee in his *A Study of History*. He wrote:

"If the heinousness of sin is to be measured by the degree to which the sinner is sinning against the light that God has vouchsafed to him, the Jews had even less excuse in A.D. 1948 for evicting Palestinian Arabs from their homes than Nebuchadnezzar and Titus and Hadrian and the Spanish and Portuguese Inquisition had had for uprooting persecuting and exterminating Jews in Palestine and elsewhere at diverse times in the past. In A.D. 1948 the Jews knew, from personal experience, what they were doing; and it was their supreme tragedy that the lesson learned by them from their encounter with the Nazi Gentiles should have been not to eschew but to imitate some of the evil deeds that the Nazis had committed against the Jews."[21]

In a lecture at McGill University in Montreal, Canada, Professor Toynbee told his Jewish audience "The Jewish treatment of the Arabs in 1947 was as morally indefensible as the slaughter by the Nazis of 6,000,000 Jews." He also pointed out, "The most tragic thing in human life is when people who have suffered impose suffering in their turn." When told during a subsequent debate with the Israeli ambassador that the Nazi action was planned and carried out in cold blood, Toynbee retorted: "I still feel that the massacres of Arab civilians by the Israeli armed forces were carried out cold-bloodedly and with a purpose. It is impossible," he said, "to be more than 100% wicked. A murder is a murder. If I murder one man," he pointed out, "that makes me a murderer. I don't have to reach 6,000,000 or even 1,000," he added.

On the question of the return of the refugees, Toynbee drew attention to the fact that the Jews had acquired most of the land in Israel by dispossessing the Arabs. "To put it bluntly," he said, "that is robbery and I am sure it is on the Jewish conscience. What I have said has given the Jews a bit of a shock treatment. I have said aloud a bit of what is being said inside your conscience. I say listen to your own inner voices," Toynbee advised his Jewish audience.[22]

The attitude of the Israelis towards their Arab victims has been condemned repeatedly by people of conscience inside and outside Israel. In one instance, Rabbi R. Benjamin, writing from Israel, said: "In the end we must come out publicly with the truth: That we have no moral right whatever to oppose the return of the Arab refugees to their land . . . that until we have begun to redeem our sin against the Arab refugees, we have no right to continue the Ingathering of Exiles. We have no right to demand that American Jews leave their country to which they have become attached and settle in a land that has been stolen from others, while the owners of it are homeless and miserable."

Benjamin went on to say, "We had no right to occupy the house of an Arab if we had not paid for it at its value. The same goes for fields, gardens, stores, workshops. We had no right to build settlement and to realize the ideal of Zionism with other people's property. To do this is robbery. I am surprised that Rabbi Herzog and all those who speak in the name of Jewish ethics and who always quote the Ten Commandments should consent to such a state of affairs."[23]

Another case of condemnation comes from the late William Zukerman, Editor of the *Jewish Newsletter* (New York). He declared: "The fact that they [the Arab refugees] fled in panic because of a real, or imaginary, danger is no excuse for depriving them of their homes, fields and livelihoods." He pointed out, "No people is exempt from panic in war time; least of all the Jews . . . To deprive them [the Arabs] of their homes and property because they, like most humans, sought safety for themselves and their children, is a grave act of injustice . . . It is a reversal," he said, "of all the moral principles upon which the Jews have based their civilization and their way of life from the days of the Prophets to the present." Zukerman then enquires: "How can a people which has for centuries led a life as refugees and experienced all the bitter pain of exile, begin its political renaissance with an act of injustice against other refugees? The most tragic aspect of this entire affair," he added, "is not only that a grave collective injustice has been committed, but that the majority of Israelis and *Diaspora* Jews justify and glorify it as an act of patriotic pride, historic justice and heroism. Not until this appalling spiritual confusion is cleared up, can any practical measures be undertaken,"[24] he concluded.

Refugees of June 1967 War

The tragedy of the Palestinian people did not stop at their expulsion in 1948. It was re-enacted with greater ferocity in 1967. During the Six-Day War, the impetus of the Israeli attack took them right through the West Bank.

Surprised by the suddenness of the attack, and terrified by modern war weapons, such as napalm with which they had had no previous experience, the Arab villagers fled in panic, along with some refugees from the 1948 War who had been settled in camps in the West Bank.

Altogether, about 200,000 people fled during the brief war. Another 210,000—mostly from the Gaza Strip—impelled by fear, the dynamiting of their homes, or loss of their menfolk, joined them.[25] These were followed in subsequent years by individual expulsions. The total number of persons who fled their homes or were expelled in this second exodus, was about 416,000 persons. This does not include Syrians expelled from the Golan Heights and Egyptians from the Sinai Peninsula.

Initially, the Security Council adopted a resolution calling on Israel "to ensure the safety, welfare and security of the inhabitants of the areas where military operations had taken place, and to facilitate the return of those inhabitants who had fled the area since the outbreak of hostilities."[26]

Another action taken by the United Nations after the cease-fire was to squeeze out of the Israelis a reluctant promise to re-admit the refugees, who were mostly assembled in makeshift camps along the east bank of the Jordan River.[27] Out of the original 200,000, over 176,000 filled in the appropriate return forms under the supervision of the International Red Cross. The return of the refugees was set for July 1967, but only 14,027 were allowed back, plus another 1,847 were admitted under a family reunion plan.*

---

*A great deal of propaganda accompanied the return of the 14,027 refugees—the Israelis

In addition to actual expulsions, whether or not accompanied by large-scale destruction of dwellings, there is another form of pressure used by the Israelis in order to empty the occupied territories of their inhabitants. This is economic pressure. It takes many forms—hidden and overt, coarse and subtle. It is only the high morale of the Arabs living under occupation, plus the financial aid they receive from the Jordan government that enables the West Bankers to hold on.

The General Assembly did not cease at every annual session of the United Nations to call upon Israel to allow the repatriation of those refugees who wish to return to their homes and to compensate those who do not wish to return and for losses sustained, in accordance with Resolution 194 (III) of December 11, 1948.

In 1974, the General Assembly went a step further by considering the Palestine question from all its aspects and adopting the following resolution by a vote of 89 in favor, 8 against (the U.S.A., Israel, Bolivia, Chile, Costa Rica, Iceland, Nicaragua and Norway), and 37 abstentions:

The General Assembly:

Deeply concerned that no just solution to the problem of Palestine has yet been achieved, and recognizing that the problem of Palestine continues to endanger international peace and security,

Recognizing that the Palestinian people is entitled to self-determination in accordance with the Charter of the United Nations,

Expressing its grave concern that the Palestinian people had been prevented from enjoying its inalienable rights, in particular its rights to self-determination,

Guided by the purposes and principles of the charter,

Recalling its relevant resolutions which affirm the right of the Palestinian people to self-determination,

1. *Reaffirms* the inalienable rights of the Palestinian people, including:
   (a) The right to self-determination without external interference;
   (b) The right to national independece and sovereignty;

2. *Reaffirms* also the inalienable right of the Palestinians to return to their homes and property from which they have been displaced and uprooted, and calls for their return;

3. *Emphasizes* that full respect for and the realization of these inalienable rights of the Palestinian people are indispensable for the solution of the question of Palestine;

---

providing photographers and journalists to cover the event. Commenting on this propaganda, Ian Gilmour and Dennis Walters, British Members of Parliament, in a joint statement said:

"The Israeli attitude to the refugees becomes clearer when their return rather than their expulsion is considered. Most people in Britain probably believe that Israel has agreed to their return and that repatriation is now satisfactorily proceeding.

"Nothing could be farther from the truth. Certainly, on one day, in front of television cameras, 144 were allowed to return over the Allenby Bridge. Unfortunately, there was no television to record that over the other bridges on that same day, more than three times that figure were still going in the other direction. And since July 10, so far as we could establish, not one single refugee has been allowed to return and the sad traffic of exodus has continued at a rate of about 1,000 a day."[28]

4. *Recognizes* that the Palestinian people is a principal party in the establishment of a just and durable peace in the Middle East;

5. *Further recognizes* the right of the Palestinian people to regain its rights by all means in accordance with the purposes and principles of the Charter of the United Nations;

6. *Appeals* to all States and international organizations to extend their support to the Palestinian people in its struggle to restore its rights in accordance with the Charter;

7. *Requests* the Secretary-General to establish contacts with the Palestine Liberation Organization on all matters concerning the question of Palestine;

8. *Requests* the Secretary-General to report to the General Assembly at its thirtieth session on the implementation of the present resolution;

9. *Decides* to include the item entitled 'Question of Palestine' in the provisional agenda of its thirtieth session."[29]

As in the case of the other resolutions of the United Nations on Palestine, the response of the Israeli authorities assisted by the U.S. government was negative as they continued in their defiance of the authority of the World Organization.

Total Palestinian Population

The estimated number of Palestinians subjected to expulsion and dispossession as a result of the creation of the state of Israel in 1948 and dispersed to various parts of the Middle East soon after the tragedy, was as follows:

Jordan (East Bank)	1,150,000
West Bank (controlled by Jordan)	700,000
Gaza Strip (controlled by Egypt)	450,000
Lebanon	400,000
Syria	250,000
Kuwait	250,000
Saudi Arabia	50,000
Other Arab States	250,000
Israel	500,000
Scattered in other countries	200,000
	3,200,000

These Figures have been altered since that time, taking into account transfers, births and deaths. As of 1988, it is estimated that the total number of Palestinians affected by the creation of the state of Israel in 1948 exceeds five million.

XI   The Arab Minority in Israel

Israeli Promises and Responsibilities

Israel claims it is the only democratic nation in the Middle East where all citizens enjoy full and equal rights without distinction as to race, color, or religion. Accordingly, Israel poses as a freedom-loving nation, fulfilling all the requirements of the United Nations Charter, the Universal Declaration of Human Rights and the United Nations Partition Resolution that gave birth to the Jewish state.

That this claim has gone unchallenged does not substantiate it. While the Jewish majority in the country may enjoy full rights and liberties, it is certainly not true of the Arab minority—Moslem and Christian. A nation's democracy is judged not by the form of government it has or by the method of its voting or the number of its political parties, but the manner and extent of the equalities and freedoms enjoyed by all of its citizens without discrimination.

The creation of Israel was made possible as a result of the United Nations Partition Resolution of November 29, 1947, which explicitly laid down the conditions under which the Jewish state and Arab state were to come into existence. The resolution stipulates in Section B (10) (d) and Section C (1) and (2) that the constitution of the proposed state shall, *inter alia*, embody provisions which shall guarantee "to all persons equal and non-discriminatory rights in civil, political, economic and religious matters and the enjoyment of human rights and fundamental freedoms;" and shall make "no discrimination of any kind between the inhabitants on the ground of race, religion, language, or sex."

The use of the imperative word "shall" in the resolution was not accidental but deliberate, in order to ensure full freedom and equality for Moslem, Christian and Jew.

In addition, complete equality was guaranteed to the Arab inhabitants in the countless statements of Zionist leaders in their demand for a Jewish state. David Ben-Gurion, arguing the Zionist case for a Jewish state before the Anglo-American Committee of Enquiry on Palestine in 1946, made the following statement: "We will have to treat our Arab and other non-Jewish neighbors . . . as if they were Jews but make every effort that they should preserve their Arab characteristics, their language, their Arab culture, their Arab religion, their Arab way of life, while making every effort to . . . gradually raise their standard of life."[1]

The zeal and ethusiasm which Ben-Gurion—who was later to become the first Prime Minister of Israel—displayed as Chairman of the Zionist Organization in Palestine, may have persuaded the Committee that the Arabs had nothing to fear from a Jewish state whose leaders promised not only that "nothing shall be done which may prejudice the civil and religious rights of the non-Jewish communities in Palestine" as the Balfour Declaration states, but also that every phase of Arab life and culture will be preserved and improved.

In 1948, the Jewish state still needed international support. To assure the United Nations and world opinion that the attitude of Zionist leaders towards the Arab minority had not altered, Israel's Proclamation of Independence *guaranteed* that the state "will be based on principles of liberty, justice and peace as conceived by the Prophets of Israel; will uphold the full social and political equality of all its citizens, without distinction of religion, race, or sex."[2]

These laudable principles proved to be mere lip-service after the state was established. The Arabs living in the Israeli-occupied territory of Palestine have been condemned to a life of deprivation, restriction, confiscation of property, degradation and second-class citizenship within their ancestral homeland since 1948.

Population and Land

The number of Arabs who remained in occupied Palestine after the establishment of the state of Israel on May 14, 1948, was estimated to be about 170,000 persons. Of these, 119,000 were Moslems, 35,000 were Christians, and 15,000 were Druze. About 32,000 were city dwellers, 120,000 were villagers, and 18,000 were Bedouins (nomads).

By the end of 1966, the Arab minority stood at 233,000 Moslems, 58,500 Christians, and 31,000 Druze, making a total of 312,500.[3] By the end of 1977, the figure is estimated to have reached 500,000 souls.

The Arab inhabitants are concentrated mostly in that part of the Galilee region which was originally assigned to the Arab state under the Partition Plan; the second largest concentration is in the "Little Triangle" in the center of the country bordering the West Bank; and the third largest is in the south (the Negev).

Economically, the Arabs of Israel have been hard pressed as a result of discriminatory and restrictive laws. About 70% of their land has been either expropriated or confiscated as a result of these laws; they are discriminated against in education, jobs, and the availability of water for irrigation; and their movements remained restricted from 1948 to December 1966 by the need for a permit for each trip, which was not easy to obtain.*

Soon after the establishment of the Jewish state, the Israelis confiscated large tracts of land belonging to the Arabs who did not leave the country. 438,000 acres (exceeding total Jewish land holdings in Palestine in 1948) was at first confiscated; and the Israeli government announced its intention of confiscating a further 400,000 acres. This land grab policy has had disastrous effects on the Arab inhabitants of Israel.

According to an article by Tawfiq Zayyad, the mayor of Nazareth, the average area belonging to an Arab village was, in 1948, 16,500 dunums (4.05 dunums to the acre). In 1974, this area was down to 5,000 dunums. The average area per head in an Arab village went down from 16 dunums in 1948 to less than one dunum in 1974. For example: Nazareth was deprived of most of its agricultural land, while its population tripled from 15,000 in 1948 to 45,000 persons. The village of Umm El-Fahm, with a population of 4,000 in 1948, owned 140,000 dunums. Today, this same village is left with only 12,000 dunums while its population has increased to 17,000 persons. The villages of Et-Taybeh and Et-Tira have each lost 23,000 dunums. The same is true of other Arab villages in Israel.

The average area of arable land in an Arab village was, in 1974, 2,000 dunums as against 9,136 dunums in 1948. Since the population of the average Arab village in Israel had increased by three or four times, there is naturally a sharp decrease in the extent of dunums held per person.[4]

Restrictive and Discriminatory Measures

While it is true, as Israelis so often point out, that members of the Arab minority are enfranchised and can stand for election to the Israeli Parliament (Knesset), this is small recompense for the hardships and discriminations that they have to put up with in everyday life. Unfortunately, their sense of insecurity and lack of contact with the outside world makes protest difficult. Furthermore, there is no reason to assume that, had the Palestine Arabs remained in their country and obtained political independence, they would not have progressed politically, socially and economically, as their Arab brothers have progressed in the neighboring countries. Indeed, it is legitimate to argue that the Palestine Arabs would have developed faster than their neighbors because they started from a higher socio-economic base. The spotty and limited progress achieved by the Arab minority is too high a price for the insecurity of this minority and its severance from the rest of the community that fled the country.

---

*The hardships imposed by the laws and regulations in operation, and the arbitrariness with which they are implemented, can be verified by an examination of the laws and by reference to:
(a) Don Peretz, *Israel and the Palestine Arabs* (Middle East Institute, Washington D.C., 1958);
(b) Walter Schwarz, *The Arabs in Israel*, (Farber, London, 1959);
(c) *New Outlook* (an Israeli periodical), March/April 1962 issue;
(d) Sabri Jiryis, *The Arabs in Israel*, (Haifa 1965), published originally in Hebrew, later confiscated. Translated into Arabic in 1967 (Beirut: Palestine Research Center) 2 Vols.
   Regarding area of land expropriated (estimated at 1.2 million dunums, or 300,000 acres) see *Jerusalem Post*, June 29, 1954.

Restrictive and discriminatory measures are justified by the Israeli authorities on the grounds of security, although the Arab minority has at no time threatened the security of the state. Samuel Divon, David Ben Gurion's Advisor on Arab Affairs, summed up official opinion when he said to Walter Schwarz in an interview in 1958:

"Ben Gurion always reminds us that we cannot be guided by subversion which the Arab minority has *not* engaged in. We must be guided by what they *might* have done if they had been given the chance."[5]

Such a position represents Israeli attitude more honestly than the assurances given by the Jewish Agency for Palestine to the Anglo-American Committee of Enquiry in 1946 pledging equal treatment for Arabs in a Jewish State,[6] or stated in Israel's Proclamation of Independence.[7]

Legislation Governing Arab Minority

Legislation applicable to the Arab inhabitants in Israel since 1948 includes:

1. *The Military Emergency Regulations 1948*[8]—Don Peretz sums up the effect of these regulations on the Arab inhabitants as follows: "Arabs in these areas lived under a complex of legal restrictions. Their movement into, out of, and within security zones was regulated by the military. Legal residents could be banished and their properties confiscated. Whole villages could be removed from one area to another. The final authority regarding violations of emergency regulations was a military court, whose decisions were not subject to the jurisdiction of the Civil Courts of Appeal."[*9]

2. *Civil Emergency Laws and Regulations***—Explaining these laws, Don Peretz said: "Every Arab in Palestine who had left his town or village after November 29, 1947, was liable to be classified as an absentee under the regulations. All Arabs who held property in the New City of Acre, regardless of the fact that they may never have travelled farther than the few meters to the Old City, were classified as absentees. The 30,000 Arabs who fled from one place to another within Israel, but who never left the country, were also liable to have their property declared absentee."[10]

3. *The Land Acquisition Law (Confirmation of Past Actions and Compensation)*[11]—The purpose behind this law was to legalize 1948–1949 seizures of Arab lands and to ensure future acquisitions. Arab citizens of Israel protested this new act of injustice to the Israeli Parliament, to the United Nations, and to western powers; but without result. They were joined in

---

*The past tense used by Peretz does not mean that the regulations had stopped being in force at the time of writing. As indicated earlier, they were abolished only at the end of 1966. The other discriminatory regulations discussed further on are still in force.

**The Abandoned Areas Ordinance 1949, *State of Israel Laws*, Vol. I, pp. 25–26; The Absentee Property Regulations 1948, *Jerusalem Post*, December 19, 1948; The Emergency Regulations (Cultivation of Waste Lands) 1948–1949, *State of Israel Law*, Vol. II, pp. 70–77.

their protest by a very few enlightened Jewish Israelis who condemned the law as "oppressive, prejudicial and discriminatory."

Another Jewish writer, Derek Tozer, following a visit to the Middle East, described these laws as "extraordinary, even in modern times. The military governor," he said, "will declare an Arab area a prohibited zone, thus debarring entry to any Arab wishing to tend his land. The 1953 law is then invoked and agricultural lands become liable to confiscation, since the owners have failed to tend the till their lands themselves. This means that the property of the Arabs automatically becomes the property of the State."[12]

David K. Elston, columnist of the *Jerusalem Post*, attacked the Land Acquisition Law as "perhaps the most serious factor creating embitterment among all Arabs." He pointed out that in Galilee, twenty villages had been deprived of their property by the Jewish collectives, which "arrogated to themselves, through long-term leases granted by the Minister of Agriculture, lands of Arabs who were free from guilt or wrong-doing."[13]

Dr. Shereshevsky of the *Ihud* Party, described the Land Acquisition Law as "robbery of land from people, inhabitants of the state." He pointed out: "They are agricultural people, like you, citizens like you. There exists only one difference between them and you: they are Arabs and you are a Jew. This difference seemed to you so great and decisive that you were ready to trespass on all that is required by the Law of Israel and its traditions."[14]

Moshe Keren, another Jewish writer, described the law as "wholesale robbery with a legal coating," and added: "The future student of ethnology will wonder how it came to pass that it was the Jewish people, striving to build their state on the foundations of justice and righteousness and having themselves been the victims of unparalleled acts of robbery and expropriation, that should have been capable of doing this to a helpless minority."[15]

4. *Law of Limitation, March 1958*—This law requires Arab landowners without a registered title to produce evidence that they have been in continuous undisputed possession of their lands for fifteen years,* or forfeit them to the Israeli government.

Under the Ottoman Empire and British Mandate laws, landowners had to prove possession and cultivation for ten consecutive years to obtain title deeds. This meant that with the new law a significant number of Arab landowners now had to produce fresh evidence of possession, which was difficult and often impossible for them to obtain.

As indicated earlier, the cumulative effect of laws and regulations so far referred to has been to expropriate about 70% of the land belonging to the Arab minority. It is obvious that this process has nothing to do with security and everything to do with the Israeli hunger for land.

5. *The Law of Return and the Nationality Law*[16]—Under these two laws the right of Israeli residence and nationality is automatically and uncon-

---

*The original period in the bill was fifty years, but owing to many protests, including one from the author published in *The New York Times*, the period was reduced to fifteen.

ditionally conferred upon a Jew, of whatever nationality, the moment he steps on Israeli soil. Palestinian Arabs, on the other hand, are not so privileged, even within their own country. The fact that Palestine Arabs were born in the territory occupied by the Israelis is insufficient to confer upon them automatic citizenship, notwithstanding the specific stipulation in the United Nations Resolution on Partition.[17]

To become an Israeli citizen, an Arab must be naturalized under the provisions of the Nationality Law. This is only possible by proving:

(a) that he was born in the country;

(b) that he lived in Israeli-occupied territory three out of the five years preceding the date of his application for citizenship;

(c) that he is qualified for permanent residence;

(d) that he is settled or intends to settle permanently in the country; and

(e) that he has a sufficient knowledge of the Hebrew language (though Arabic is regarded as an official language);

and because all this is at the discretion of the Minister of the Interior, many Arabs are still denied citizenship.

After this law was passed, the Minister of the Interior admitted in Parliament that racial discrimination existed in Israel. But he pointed out that this stemmed not from the Nationality Law, but from the Law of Return by which only Jews are given the right of return. The former law, he argued, intended to distinguish between those whose loyalty to Israel was sure and those who had to prove it.[18]

Commenting on this law, the Hebrew newspaper *Haaretz* reminded Israelis of the Jewish struggle for minority rights in other countries and of Israeli neglect of Arab rights.[19]

Derek Tozer, previously quoted said: "The official policy of the government [of Israel] is unequivocal. Arabs, like Jews in Nazi Germany, are officially Class B citizens—a fact which is recorded on their identity cards."[20]

Israelis as Rulers

While posing to credulous foreigners as enlightened protectors of their Arab minority, the Israelis have discreetly kept them submissive by methods which, if they had been carried out against Jews elsewhere, would have had the world press in an uproar. Here are some illustrations:

1. In October 1948, the Christian villagers of Ikret in western Galilee were removed from their village and told that their removal was necessary for security reasons; that they would be allowed to return to their homes within fifteen days. For this reason, the villagers took only the clothing required for their temporary absence. But the fifteen days period dragged on, first, into months and then into years. Tired of broken promises, the villagers petitioned the courts of justice; and the verdict ordered the Israeli army to permit the return of the villagers. The army responded by destroying every house in the village, choosing Christmas Day 1951 for their action. Not even the church was spared: and, to add insult to injury, the church bell was removed to a nearby

Jewish settlement and used, not to call people to prayer, but to announce the time for meals.

Archbishop George Hakim, head of the Greek Catholic community, cabled a strong protest to the Israeli authorities against this unwarranted wholesale destruction of a Catholic village and the desecration of its church. Following a visit to the ruined village, the archbishop wrote to Rabbi Hertzog, Minister of Religious Affairs, and said: "From above the churchyard, overlooking the village, I could not but ponder over these atrocities, and ask what would the Righteous God—in Whom we both believe—keep in store for these crimes that are being committed by a people or a state and what would be the verdict of the international conscience?"

2. On September 16, 1953, the Christian inhabitants of Kafr Bir'im were expelled from their village, subsequently destroyed. The Israeli magazine *Ner* described the incident as follows: "Further proof of the intensification of the measures against the Arabs of Israel lies in the complete demolition of the village of Kafr Bir'im, the Maronite inhabitants of which were expelled by the military authorities in 1948 and are at present dispersed in adjacent Arab villages. The Maronite Patriarch and Bishop Mubarak had interceded on behalf of these villagers. Promises were lavishly made that they would be permitted to return to their homes and lands. In fulfillment of these promises, the village has been razed to the ground."[21]

3. On Good Friday 1954, the Christian cemetery in Haifa was desecrated, 73 crosses were smashed and trampled underfoot. The Christian communities demonstrated in protest and expressed their condemnation. Since 1948, over 350 Christian churches and Moslem mosques have been destroyed.

Replying to Israeli press charges alleging that he was conducting a campaign of defamation against Israel, the late Monseigneur MacMahon, Head of the Pontifical Mission in the Arab countries, said: "It is neither a campaign nor defamation when the Catholic press throughout the world expresses indignation over the destruction of villages and churches in Israel."

The Kafr Qasem Massacre*

On the eve of the 1956 attack on the Suez Canal on October 29, 1956, the Israeli Frontier Force entered the village of Kafr Qasem, a border village in the "Little Triangle," imposed a curfew while the villagers were still in their fields. As they returned unsuspecting from their fields, 51 of them were murdered and 13 others were wounded. Among the dead were 12 women and girls, 10 boys between the ages of 14 and 17 years, and 7 children between the ages of 8 and 13 years.[22]

---

*Kafr Qasem is a border village. Under the terms of the Armistice Agreement with Jordan, Israeli forces are *prohibited* "to enter or to be stationed in such villages, in which locally recruited Arab police shall be organized and stationed for internal security purposes" (UN Document S/1302/Rev. 1 of June 20, 1949, Article VI, para. 6). The Israeli police or army had no legal right to enter the village; their entry and the massacre that followed could not have occurred without the full knowledge and acquiescence of the government, as the investigation later proved.

At first, efforts were made to hush up the matter, but when news of the massacre leaked out, and it transpired that the soldiers' orders had been shoot to kill, the Israeli government had no alternative but to hold a trial. The cruelty of the massacre became all the more evident when it was realized that only thirty minutes separated the announcement of the curfew from its application, and that the villagers had given no cause whatsoever for the treatment they received.

The revelations made during the trial are shocking, even in a world used to cruelty. But the sentences and later treatment received by the accused are even more shocking. According to the Hebrew daily *Haaretz*, "the eleven officers and soldiers who are on trial for the massacre of Kafr Qasem have all received a 50% increase in their salaries. A special messenger was sent to Jerusalem to bring the checks to the accused in time for Passover. A number of the accused had been given a vacation for the holiday." The paper added: in court, "the accused mingle freely with the spectators; the officers smile at them and pat them on the back; some of them shake hands with them. It is obvious that these people, whether they will be found innocent or guilty, are not treated as criminals, but as heroes."[23]

The *Jewish Newsletter* carried an item on the attitude of hatred on the part of Israeli security forces toward the Arab citizens of Israel. Private David Goldfield is reported to have resigned from the Security Police in protest against the holding of the trial. When he appeared as a witness, he testified: "I feel that the Arabs are the enemies of our state . . . When I went to Kafr Qasem, I felt that I went against the enemy and I made no distinction between the Arabs in Israel and those outside its frontiers." When asked by the judge what he would do if he met an Arab woman who wanted to get into her home and was not in any way a threat to security, the witness replied: "I would harbor no sentiments, because I received an order and I had to carry it out."[*24]

---

*This feeling of hatred for the Arab is not engendered in one lone individual, but is apparently part of the Israeli policy of indoctrination of the youth of Israel.

According to an item of news which appeared in the Hebrew weekly, *Haolem Hazeh* of Tel Aviv, the editors are reported to have "talked to hundreds of Jewish children, boys and girls, of different social classes and of ages varying from 6–13 years, about the Arabs of Israel and what they thought should be done with them. Of these children 95% said that they should be murdered. A small percentage were a little compassionate and human. They opined that the Arabs should be detained in concentration camps or else deported to the Negev." The editors, it was stated, "attributed this wicked propensity to the children's family life, to their social environment and to the education they receive in schools."

But "a mother wrote to the editors saying that her son's reply was due solely to the education he was receiving in school and not to his home life or to his private associations."

"However, this malicious tendancy," the weekly pointed out, "is not uncommon among Jewish rank and file. The wholesale massacre on the eve of the Sinai campaign of 49 innocent Arab farmers in Kafr Qasem village—boys and girls, men and women some of whom were visibly pregnant—was the outcome of scholastic education, all of which infuse xenophobic feelings against the Arabs."

Another expression of violent hatred for the Arab came from an Israeli Jew studying in the United States. In a letter to an Arab lawyer, the late Elias Koussa who lived in Haifa, dated November 4, 1956, Bertram H. Appleby wrote: "As soon as my medical course ends, I shall return to Israel to devote my life to fighting her enemies, especially the enemy within, a people without conscience, morality, humanity, or simple intelligence. We Zionists can easily read your mind, your intentions—to make Israel accept a huge percentage of Arab refugees, to

On February 26, 1959—two years and four months after the massacre—the commander of the Border Police who gave the order, was sentenced to "a token fine of *two cents* for exceeding his authority by imposing an absolute curfew on an Arab village in Israel in 1956."[25] It would be difficult to find an example of greater cynicism in the history of mankind!

The Koenig Memorandum

A secret document, referred to as the Koenig Memorandum, which sets out to analyze the situation of the Arab minority in Israel and to suggest ways to handle them, was written by Israel Koenig, the northern district commissioner of the Ministry of Interior, and was submitted in April 1976 as a memorandum to the Prime Minister of Israel and other authorities on the subject of how to handle the Palestinian Arabs of the Galilee District.

The Israeli newspaper *Al-Hamishmar*, which published the full text of the memorandum on September 7, 1976, commented: ". . . [the memo] includes dangerous evaluations and statements that, if accepted as authorized positions, would cause conflict between the Jewish majority and the Arab minority." *The Jerusalem Post*, in its editorial of September 9, 1976, admitted that the Koenig memo . . . "is a system of wholesale discrimination against the Arabs which he hopes will cause their ranks to be depleted."

Listed below are a number of the major ideas from this racist document. The memorandum describes the Arab mentality as oriental, Levantine, superficial and backward, and suggests:

1. Forbidding any leniency in the treatment of the Arab, and advocates stringent control by the police, the army, and prison authorities;
2. Imposing upon the Arabs a dishonest leadership in the form of a national Arab party administered secretly by the Israeli Intelligence Agency;
3. Establishing a special intelligence system to spy on the leaders of the [largely Arab] Communist Party and others in order to destroy their credibility;
4. Imposing the most severe measures against Arab student leaders, closing the door to universities in the face of Arab students, putting obstacles in the way of their education, and at the same time facilitating the emigration of Arab youth and forbidding their return;
5. Keeping the Arabs busy 24 hours a day searching for a livelihood, so that they would not have time to think about their general welfare or national educational needs;

---

renounce pieces of territory, the larger the better, to give up special privileges, special schools, special everything. But your evil plans (or should I say plots?) will not succeed, now as in the past. Believe me, everything you do, everything you speak, is being noted and when the day of reckoning comes, all these will be atoned for."

6. Adopting a strong policy against the Arabs by imposing stiff taxes and fines that would deprive them of the financial and economic means to improve their standard of living or social status;

7. Cancelling their social security benefits and confining such benefits for Jews only;

8. Confiscating Arab lands for the establishment of new Jewish settlements thereon;

9. Obstructing any natural increase in the Arab population, and to take such action as would reduce their number.*

The Israeli Prime Minister of the time, when approached to deny that this was Israeli policy and to denounce the memorandum, refused to do so. In 1976, the Israeli Parliament approved a plan for the Judaization of the Galilee area. This plan has two objectives: (1) to deprive the Arab inhabitants of their remaining lands by further confiscations; and (2) to change the demographic structure of Galilee, which is presently populated by an Arab majority.[26]

Denial of Equal Political Rights to Arab Citizens

According to recognized principles of democratic government and practices, minorities are free to establish their own political parties and to adopt the platform they desire. In parliament and the cabinet they are usually represented in proportion to their voting strength.

In the Israeli-occupied territory of Palestine, however, the Arab minority is not permitted to exercise its political rights and prerogatives in the same manner and to the same extent as is the Jewish majority. Although the United Nations Partition Resolution of 1947 makes it an imperative condition that the Jewish state shall constitutionally *guarantee* "to all persons equal and non-discriminatory rights in political matters," the Israeli authorities have denied these rights to their Arab minority.

According to Israeli sources the Moslem and Christian Arab citizens comprise 11% of the total population of the country. As such, they have an undisputed right to representation in all branches of the Israeli government. Nevertheless, for many years they were prevented from forming their own political parties. For election to parliament, an Arab candidate had to run on the ticket of one of the existing Jewish parties and abide by its platform whether he agreed with its principles or not. Attempts were made by some of the Arab leaders to organize an Arab front that would be entrusted with safeguarding the rights and interests of the Moslem and Christian Arab communities. The Israeli authorities took steps to thwart the efforts of the sponsors, by withholding travel permits to the meeting place. In addition, the sponsors were required to report to the police stations at certain inconvenient hours of the day to ensure their non-attendance. Such action was unjustified and humiliating, particularly when it is usually taken against criminals whose surveillance becomes necessary "in the interests of public security."

---

*According to Israeli newspaper *Yediot Aharanot*, of August 5, 1975, the 18th Congress of Talmudic Studies in Jerusalem—presided over by then Israeli Prime Minister Yitzhaq Rabin—recommended that "a Jewish doctor should not help a non-Jewish woman to conceive."

Even after the official ban on Arab parties was lifted, however, true representation in Israel's parliament continues to be denied to Palestinians. The discrimination institutionalized in the Zionist state cannot be successfully challenged in Knesset debate alone, and thus renders the formal right to build Arab-led parties a hollow victory.

Dr. Harold E. Fey, former senior editor of the *Christian Century*, wrote: "The Arabs have no alternative but to elect those who are nominated for them. They do not have an independent party and are prevented from forming one." Dr. Fey went on to say that the Arabs "do not deny that Israel may be a democracy for the majority, but they know it is something less than that for the minority, the Class B citizens."[27]

The Arabs are not only prevented from forming their own political parties; they are also deprived of their full share of political representation. The Israeli parliament has 120 seats of which few are occupied by Arabs sitting as members of Jewish parties. As such, they are not in a position to protect Arab rights and interests, especially when these clash with the policy of the Jewish majority. When an Arab member of parliament is courageous enough to table an objection in the interests of the Arab minority, his voice is the only one heard in favor, even within his own party.

The presence of these Arab members of parliament enables Zionist propaganda to tell the world that the Arabs of Israel enjoy full political freedom. This creates the false impression that Israel fulfills all of the requirements of a democratic state.

A comparison with the situation in nearby Jordan—which, incidentally, is described by Israel as far from being a democratic country—will reveal a totally different picture. In Jordan, the Christian inhabitants comprise less than 10% of a total population of 2,100,000 persons. According to their numerical strength, Christians were entitled to three out of the forty seats in both Houses of Parliament. Instead, they occupied six seats.

Another analogy may be drawn from the executive and administrative branches of government. In Israel, the cabinet does not include a single Arab minister. There are no Arabs holding the post of undersecretary or director of a department. Their number in the general government services is insignificant. In contrast, Jordan had two cabinet posts occupied by Christians—one representing the East Bank and the other the West Bank. In addition, there are many Christians who hold the office of undersecretary, director of a department and other senior positions. Christian representation in the general services far exceeds the ratio based on population.

Summation of Israeli Violations

The Israelis are guilty of violating the basic principles regarding minority rights, as laid down in the UN Charter, the Universal Declaration of Human Rights, and the Partition Resolution. The following summary pinpoints the abuse of these international obligations:

1. *"No person shall be subjected to arbitrary exile."*—
Israel has expelled about 35,000 of the Arab inhabitants from their

homes and villages to other parts of the country and refuses to allow them to return.

2. Guarantees *"to all persons equal and non-discriminatory rights"*—

Israel has placed the Arab minority in a class B category; restricted their movement; discriminated against them in employment, in political representations, in government service, in education, in health facilities, etc.

3. *"Everyone has the right to freedom of movement and residence within the borders of the state"*—

Israel has prohibited the free movement of the Arab minority and imposes forced residence on some for little or no cause.

4. *"Everyone has the right to leave any country, including his own, and to return to his country"*—

Israel prevents the travel of Arabs outside the country unless they undertake to sign away their right of return.

5. *"No expropriation of land owned by an Arab in the Jewish state shall be allowed except for public purpose"*—

Israel has so far expropriated 1,250,000 dunums of fertile Arab land and is in the process of confiscating more, using the claim of "public purpose;"

6. *"Palestine citizens residing in Palestine . . . shall, upon recognition of independence, become citizens of the state"*—

Israel, while granting immediate citizenship rights to a Jew the moment he steps on Palestine soil, withholds such rights from the Arab inhabitants who have been born and live there;

7. *The control and administration of Waqf (pious foundation property)* "shall be exercised in accordance with religious law and the dispositions of the founders"—

Israel has taken over such properties and is utilizing the proceeds from the sale or lease thereof for the settelement of new Jewish immigrants, contrary to the "dispositions of the founders."

Commenting on Israel's treatment of non-Jews, James Warburg, former banker and writer on international affairs, said: "Nothing could be more tragic than to witness the creation of a Jewish state in which the non-Jewish minorities are treated as second-class citizens—in which neither a Jew's Christian wife nor their children can be buried in the same cemetery as their father." Warburg then remarked: "It is one thing to create a much-needed refuge for the persecuted and oppressed. It is quite another thing to create a new chauvinistic nationalism and a state based in part upon medieval theocratic bigotry and in part upon the Nazi-exploited myth of the existence of a Jewish race."[28]

With this record, Israel's claim to be a democratic state in which all citizens enjoy equal rights and freedoms, is without foundation. What is written into a constitution or law is meaningless unless the implementation is consistent with the spirit. At any rate, Israel has no constitution, and with regard to its laws it has already been established that they violate minority rights.

XII Repatriation and Compensation

Task of Palestine Conciliation Commission

The Palestine Conciliation Commission, having failed in the task entrusted to it by the UN General Assembly in Resolution 194 (III) of December 11, 1948, to bring about a peaceful settlement between the parties (see Chapter IX), turned its attention to the second task entrusted to it under Resolution 394 (V) of December 14, 1950, namely:

"To establish an office which, under the direction of the commission shall:

(a) make such arrangements as it may consider necessary for the assessment and payment of compensation in pursuance of paragraph 11 of General Assembly Resolution 194(III);

(b) work out such arrangements as may be practicable for the implementation of the other objectives of paragraph 11 of the said resolution;

(c) continue consultation with the parties concerned regarding measures for the protection of the rights, property and interests of the refugees."[1]

Legal Interpretations and Historical Precedents

At the same time, the Secretariat of the United Nations sent, for the guidance of the Commission, two working papers:

One, dealing with the "legal interpretation of paragraph 11, subparagraph 1 of General Assembly Resolution 194 (III) of December 11, 1948, on:

1. The right of refugees to return to their homes;
2. Payment of compensation."[2]

The second, on "The Historical Precedents for Restitution of Property and Payment of Compensation to Refugees".[3]

Under the first paper, the matter was said to present itself under two different aspects, namely:

(a) Payment of compensation to refugees not choosing to return to their homes;

(b) Payment of compensation to refugees for loss of or damage to property.

As regards (a), the compensation claims for property of refugees not choosing to return to their homes was recognized to rest on general legal principles and must be considered in the light of the Assembly's decision that refugees should be given the choice either to return to their homes and live at peace with their neighbors, or to receive compensation for their property if they choose not to return.

As regards (b), the compensation claims for "loss of or damage to property which, under principles of international law or in equity, should be made good by the governments or authorities responsible," it was opined that from the legislative history of paragraph 11 of the Resolution of the General Assembly, the cases which the assembly particularly had in mind were those of looting, pillaging and plundering of private property and destruction of property and villages without military necessity.

All such acts, the working paper stated, are violations of the laws and customs of war on land laid down in the Hague Convention of October 18, 1907, the rules of which, as stated in the Nuremberg Judgment in 1939, "were recognized by all civilized nations and were regarded as being declaratory of the law and customs of war." Articles 28 and 47 of the Hague Regulation, annexed to the Convention, provide *explicitly* that pillage is prohibited. Article 23(g) prohibits destruction or seizure of the enemy's property unless such destruction or seizure be imperatively demanded by the necessities of war. Article 46 protects private property, and Article 56, paragraph 1, provides that the property of municipalities, that of institutions dedicated to religion, charity and education, the arts and sciences, even when state property, shall be treated as private property. In addition to these rules, Article 3 of the Convention makes the explicit provision—particularly important in this connection—that a belligerent party which violates the provisions of the regulations shall, if the case demands, be liable to pay compensation.

The opinion was also expressed that from the expression, "loss of or damage to property which under principles of international law or in equity shall be made good," whereby the wording became similar to that generally used in mixed claim conventions, it may be assumed that the General Assembly, on the other hand, did not wish to limit the claims to cases as just mentioned. It would, therefore, seem necessary to give the provision in question a somewhat wider application and to consider each on its merits.

Under the second paper—'Historical Precedents for Restitution of Property and Payment of Compensation to Refugees'—the purpose, it was stated, was "to furnish some background for this principle and to recall similar historical situations where claims of restitution of property

or payment of compensation were put forward. Such historical background became important during World War II when the question arose
whether, according to international law, the Allied Nations at the end of
the War could protect the property interests of the Axis refugees."

The matter was considered at an International Law Conference held
in London in 1943 under the auspices of the Institut de Droit International, the International Law Association, the Grotius Society, and the
Allied University Professors' Association.

A collection of historical precedents where states were known to have
safeguarded the property, rights and interests of refugees, was compiled and presented to the conference for consideration. The following
three precedents are worth mentioning because they bear similiarity to
the positions of both Jewish victims of Nazi Germany and Palestine Arab
victims of the State of Israel:

1. *Treaty of Nijmegen of September 17, 1678 (Between Spain and France)*—
"*Article XXI*—All the subjects of the one part as well as the other, both
ecclesiastic and secular, shall be re-established in the enjoyment of their
honor, dignities and benefices of which they were possessed of before
the war as well as in all their effects, movables and immovables and
rents upon lands seized and occupied from the said time as well as on
the occasion of the war as for having followed the contrary party.
Likewise in their rights, actions, and successions fallen to them, though
since the war commenced without nevertheless, demanding or pre-
tending anything of the fruits and revenues coming from the seizing of
the said effects, immovables, rents and benefices till the publication of
this present treaty." (This treaty followed the war of 1675–1678 between
France and Holland. The war had spread into the Spanish Netherlands,
and although it was the Dutch who fought, it was Spain which lost to
the French).

2. *Treaty of London of April 19, 1839 (On independence and neutrality)
Belgium—Article XVI*—"The sequestrations which have been imposed in
Belgium during the troubles, for political causes, on any property or
hereditary estates whatsoever shall be taken off without delay, and the
enjoyment of the property and estates above mentioned shall be immediately restored to the lawful owners thereof."

3. *Peace Treaty with Turkey of August 10, 1920* (signed but not ratified.
This treaty provided for the compensation of Armenian refugees who
had fled from Turkey)—
Article 144—(1) The Turkish government recognizes the injustice of the
Law of 1915 relating to Abandoned Properties (Emwal-il-Matroukeh),
and of the supplementary provisions thereof, and declares them to be
null and void, in the past as in the future.

(2) The Turkish government solemnly undertakes to facilitate to the greatest possible extent the return to their homes and
re-establishment in their businesses of the Turkish subjects of non-
Turkish race who have been forcibly driven from their homes by fear of
massacre or any other form of pressure since January 1st, 1914. It
recognizes that any immovable or movable property of the said Turkish
subjects or of the communities to which they belong, which can be
recovered, must be restored to them as soon as possible, in whatever

hands it may be found. Such property shall be restored and without compensation of any kind to the present owners or occupiers, subject to any action which they may be able to bring against the persons from whom they derived title."

Global Assessment of Refugee Property

Reinforced by the new directions granted to it in Resolution 394(V) of December 14, 1950, and guided by the interpretations in the two working papers in their possession, the Palestine Conciliation Commission should have approached their task differently. The office the Commission was authorized to establish should have commenced its operations by visiting the refugee camps and finding out from them who wished to return to their homes; obtain particulars of their immovable properties; and gather information relating to the extent and estimated value of their losses in movable property, etc.

Once this information was available, the Commission's next move should have been to consider ways and means to protect "the rights, property and interests of the refugees" as instructed, which were then being violated by the Israeli authorities on a large scale, and then embark on the other issues involved.

Instead, the Commission proceeded by a route which was detrimental to "the rights, property and interests of the refugees." In a matter of months, the commission estimated that the extent of the land abandoned by the Arab refugees was 16,324,000 dunums, of which 4,574,000 dunums were cultivable. The demilitarized zones and the No-Man's land area were not included in the estimate. The term "land," the commission stated, denoted immovable property; buildings and trees were regarded as an integral part of the soil on which they stood and valued with it. The total value of the property of the Arab refugees was estimated at one-hundred million Palestine pounds ($280,000,000 at the then rate of exchange), made up as follows:

Palestine Pounds

Rural land	69,500,000	
Urban land, excluding Jerusalem	21,500,000	
Jerusalem lands	9,000,000	PP. 100,000,000.-

This estimate, the commission stated, was based on the value of the land for its existing use, as measured by the revenue that it would produce. In estimating the revenue, due regard was paid to urban and rural property tax assessments, which were suitably adjusted to allow for the increase in value between the date of assessment and November 29, 1947, which was adopted as the date of valuation. The commission admitted that no account was taken of potential development value, except in the case of development value which can be ascribed to the normal growth of towns. No value was placed on uncultivable land outside urban areas even though such land had high value as potential building sites.

With regard to movable property, the commission stated that it was unable to make a valuation of all such property, since some categories do not lend themselves to a global evaluation, and since there were no means of knowing what property the refugees took with them and what they left behind. It, therefore, confined itself to an attempt to estimate the approximate value of the movable property that belonged to the refugees before their exodus. Account was taken of the following items of property: Industrial equipment, commercial stocks, motor vehicles, agricultural equipment and livestock, and household effects.[4]

The Commission used a book method which may be applicable in western countries, but certainly not acceptable in the Middle East. However, the Arab states and the Palestinian Arabs naturally rejected the Commission's conclusions outright because it was not compensation that the Palestinian Arabs demanded but return to their homes and property.

For the sake of argument, to prove the absurdity of the figures arrived at by the Commission, two comments are made:

1. The Commission estimated the value of Arab property in Jerusalem to be PP.9-million. In 1946, the Palestine government appointed the Fitzgerald Committee to make recommendations for the division of the Holy City into Arab and Jewish municipal areas. The committee assessed Arab property within the suggested Arab zone (excluding Arab property in the Jewish zone and the Old City regarded as an historical site and therefore not taxable since Turkish times), to be exactly double the figure of the Commission, namely, P.18,000,000.*

If this great difference could occur in a small section of Jerusalem, one can readily understand the gross error that exists in the valuation of the rest of the country!

2. The Commission stated that "no value was placed on uncultivable land outside urban areas."[5] Land in the vicinity of towns has always had greater value than agricultural land whether it was capable of cultivation or not; and where the land was non-taxable under the Rural Property Tax Ordinance, the owner could afford to wait for better prices. In many cases, Palestinian owners constructed buildings on such lands outside urban areas and enjoyed exemption from both forms of taxation.

Israeli Legislation for Confiscation of Refugee Property

While the Palestine Conciliation Commission was engaged with paper work, the Israelis were busy enacting legislation for the liquidation of the identity of Arab lands and the confiscation of their ownership.

The legislation enacted during the first two years of Israel's existence to deal with the confiscation and disposal of Arab lands in Palestine, was:

The Abandoned Areas Ordinance 1948;
The Absentee Property Regulations 1948;

---

*Palestine Government: *The Fitzgerald Report*, The Palestine Gazette Extraordinary No. 1541 of December 18, 1946. (When the author pointed out this discrepancy to the commission, he was informed that the commission was unaware of the report).

The Emergency (Cultivation of Waste Lands) Regulations
1948–1949.

According to these laws, the Israeli government empowered itself to declare a conquered, surrendered, or deserted area to be an abandoned area; and conferred emergency powers on the Minister of Agriculture and the newly created post of Custodian of Absentee Property.

The crucial provision in these three regulations was the definition of an absentee. Any person was declared to be an absentee who was, on or after November 29, 1947 (the date of the Partition Resolution):

(a) a citizen or subject of any of the Arab states;
(b) in any of these states for any length of time;
(c) in any part of Palestine outside of the Israeli-occupied areas; or
(d) in any place other than his habitual residence, even if such place as well as his habitual abode were within Israeli-occupied territory.

According to Jewish author Don Peretz: "Every Arab in Palestine who had left his town or village after November 29, 1947 was liable to be classified as an absentee under the regulations. All Arabs who held property in the New City of Acre, regardless of the fact that they may never have travelled farther than a few meters to the Old City, were classified as absentees. The 30,000 Arabs who fled from one place to another within Israel, but who never left the country, were also liable to have their property declared absentee. Any individual who may have gone to Beirut or Bethlehem for a one-day visit during the latter days of the Mandate, was automatically an absentee."[6]

Having empowered the Custodian and the Minister of Agriculture to assume control of absentee property and waste lands respectively, the Israeli government moved a step further in 1950 in the direction of legalizing the occupation of Arab refugee property and establishing a firmer constitutional basis. It did so by passing a law through the Israeli parliament to replace the various emergency regulations.

Thus, the Absentee Property Law 1950, besides confirming most of the privileges bestowed on the Custodian by virtue of earlier regulations, empowered him to sell absentee property. The Law also gave legal recognition to the *de facto* distribution of all Arab lands, which had already taken place.

The Absentee Property Law further empowered, in Section 19 (a)(1), the Custodian to sell Arab property to the Development Authority at a price not less than its official value. This so-called official value was fixed in the law to be as follows:

1. In the case of property within the limits of towns, and industrial buildings in rural areas in which mechanically driven machinery is used: 16:⅔rd times the net annual value of the property as assessed for taxation purposes for the year 1947–1948.

2. In the case of rural lands, including the buildings thereon and fruit plantations: If the land belongs to the categories of citrus, bananas, or village built-on areas: 300 times the amount of tax charged on citrus for 1947–1948. All other taxable land: 75 times the amount of tax charged on it for the year 1947–1948; non-taxable land: no value!

The said Law also provided Section 32 for the following deductions to be made from the official value where the property is sold or where it was released and returned to its Arab owner. The latter incidence never occurred:

(a) A remuneration of 4%—as the share of the state;
(b) Any expenses (including travelling expenses, costs of legal proceedings, the remuneration of advocates, agents, or other persons employed by the Custodian in connection with the property) incurred for the purpose of safeguarding, maintaining, repairing or developing any property of an absentee, plus interest at the rate of 6% per annum from the day on which the expenses were incurred.

On paper, the basis of assessment of property in urban areas follows the recognized principles of valuation in Western countries and tends to give the impression that the Israelis were being just. There is, however, one important difference: Whereas this principle is applied to the actual income obtainable from the property in the open market under normal circumstances, the Israeli formula of the official value is being applied to an "assessment made purely for taxation purposes" and had no relation whatsoever with the true capital value of the property. Besides, rents were controlled during the years of the war and those that followed until the termination of the Mandate in 1948, while prices of buildings soared to great heights.

As regards land in rural areas, it is not clear on what basis, if any, the so-called official value was calculated. It certainly was not the market value, because the rural property tax was based on 10% of the average of a low annual yield after deducting two-thirds of the assessed yield to cover costs of production. Land included fixtures, such as buildings, which were ignored in the fixing of the tax; while land of low productivity value and land classified as non-cultivable were not taxed. Although such undeveloped land may not have had any agricultural value, it had great potential value in cases where it was located close to urban areas.

Although the Absentee Property Law empowered the Custodian to sell absentee property to a Development Authority', this authority was only created several months after the law was promulgated.

The Development Authority (Transfer of Property) Law 1950, empowered the Development Authority, *inter alia*, "to buy, rent, take on lease, take in exchange or otherwise acquire property." It was also empowered "to sell or otherwise dispose of" property. But its power to sell or otherwise transfer the right of ownership of property was limited to the following conditions:

1. Such transfer of ownership can be made only to the state, the Jewish National Fund, certain government-approved institutions, or local authorities.

2. "The right of ownership of land so acquired may not be retransferred except with the consent of the Development Authority to one of the bodies" in the aforementioned categories; and

3. Transactions of this nature, involving the transfer or retransfer of ownership must be "effected by decision of the government in each individual case."

Commenting on this law, Don Peretz said:

"The Development Authority Law was based upon a sort of legal fiction. It was not desired to transfer abandoned land to government ownership, as this would be interpreted as confiscation of the abandoned property. The government was disinclined to take such a step, which would have been unfavorably regarded abroad, and no doubt, opposed. The substitution by the government of ownership in place of possession of the abandoned property would have exacerbated the relations between Israel and the Arab people. However, it was not practical to dispose of the absentees' property without some legal status unless administratively, and this, too, was quite undesirable. It was necessary to find a means of disposing of the property legally. The Development Authority Law passed by the legislature of the state was based upon a principle which Israel had always approved, namely, the obligation of payment for land transferred to Jews."[7]

According to the Director of the Development Authority, "the first million dunums of absentee property which he purchased from the custodian were resold to the Jewish National Fund for about 12-million Israeli pounds, a greater sum than he had paid for it."[8]

The question arises: Was this seizure of Arab property legal? And did the laws and regulations enacted by the Israeli authorities conform with the spirit and purposes of the 1947 Partition Resolution that created the state of Israel?

It will be recalled that the UN General Assembly in recommending the creation of the Jewish State in 1947, resolved that the rights of Arabs—including property rights—shall be protected; and that "no expropriation of land owned by an Arab in the Jewish State shall be allowed except for public purposes." The resolution also stipulated that "in all cases of expropriation, full compensation as fixed by the Supreme Court shall be paid previous to dispossession."

The resolution went on to prescribe that the provisions just quoted shall, among others, be embodied in the fundamental laws of the state (of Israel), and no law, regulation, or official action shall conflict or interfere with these stipulations, nor shall any law, regulation or official action prevail over them."

The resolution also resolved that the aforementioned provision, with others, "shall be under the guarantee of the United Nations, and no modifications shall be made in them without the assent of the General Assembly of the United Nations."[9]

Despite these United Nations stipulations and guarantees, the Israeli authorities enacted the 'laws and regulations' cited earlier and took 'official actions' against the Palestinian Arabs which deviated basically from the terms of the Partition Resolution, the provisions of the UN Charter and the Universal Declaration of Human Rights that explicitly decrees that "no one shall be arbitrarily deprived of his property."[10]

Identification and Valuation of Refugee Property

With nothing further to be done in the Middle East, the commission retired to United Nations Headquarters in New York, and established the Identification and Valuation Office.*

From the start, it was realized that the work was not going to be conclusive if it is confined mainly to documents without personal contact with the refugees themselves and possible visits to the ground.

The only sources of information available to the Land Specialist were the micro-films prepared by the Palestine government before the date of the termination of the Mandate and the Urban and Rural Property Tax records. The micro-films covered only the lands the titles to which had been settled by 1948 under the provisions of the Land (Settlement of Title) Ordinance and had already been entered in the Land Registers. The total area of such land did not exceed one-fifth of the total land area of Palestine. The remaining four-fifths consisted of unregistered land held under possessory titles, that is, right of ownership was not absolute but claimed by possession which, in some cases, was disputed while areas were approximate and locations not properly definable.

The tax records for the settled lands were compiled by the Official Land Valuer and showed accurate names of owners and areas but no other description, while those with respect to non-settled land were compiled by specially appointed Village Tax Distribution Committees. The Committee merely entered the names of the individuals who were liable for the payment of the tax without regard of whether they were the actual owners or not: areas were shown approximate and fluctuating in extent depending on the standing of the individual with the Committee; and the amount of tax following suit. Cases were known where some tax-payers paid more tax than was due on the land in their possession, while others were favored with less.

In the case of non-cultivable land, and land of low productivity value, these were non-taxable, and the Committee saw no reason to include them in the Tax Distribution Lists since the lists were for taxation purposes and not ownership.

Another omission from the tax lists was that of fixtures on the land such as buildings. Neither the Land Law nor the rural tax law required registration of such fixtures. So, in effect, the records of identification compiled by the United Nations are inconclusive because they do not represent a true picture of the situation on the ground.

The Commission was informed of these anomalies, and it was suggested that once the Identification Schedules have been compiled in New York, that they should be posted in areas where refugees are known to exist, and they should be asked to inspect them and submit their objections on a prescribed form. In this way, it was thought possible to obtain information about buildings which exist on the land, and at the same time make other alterations which may be deemed necessary.

It was also suggested to the Commission that the refugees should be asked to submit, on another prescribed form, information relating to

---

*The author was engaged in December 1952 as Land Specialist to take charge of the work because of his position in the Palestine government as Official Land Valuer and Inspector of Urban Assessments and being the officer in charge of maintaining an up-to-date record of land area ownership between Arabs and Jews.

their losses in movable property, such as the contents of homes, business premises, motor vehicles, agricultural implements, etc.

The Commission rejected both suggestions and gave instructions that the work of identification should proceed on the basis of the documents available. With regard to movable property, the Commission remained silent on the subject.

On the question of valuation, it was suggested that, in order to relieve the Land Specialist of criticism, he should be assisted by qualified local people acting as committees to lay down the basis for the valuation of individual property in the various parts of the country. This suggestion was also rejected.

The work of identification and valuation of property continued to be carried out on the basis of the micro-films and other documents made available to the Commission in New York under the supervision of the new land expert and was completed in 1964. He presented the Commission with a working paper on the Methods and Techniques of Identification and Valuation of Arab Refugee Immovable Property Holdings in Israel;[11] and with this his responsibilities came to an end. Copies of the results of the work of the Land Expert were made available to the League of Arab States and to the Jordan. A 1983 study by the author estimates the value of those property losses to be $169 billion at 1988 prices.

Arab States Protest Israeli Confiscations

On March 23, 1953, representatives of the Arab states to the United Nations submitted to the Commission a joint memorandum concerning Israel's wrongful disposal of Arab property in the territory under its control. The Arab representatives called on the commission to take expeditious and effective measures to safeguard the property of the refugees.

On July 1, 1953, the Arab representatives sent a follow-up letter to the Commission in which they reaffirmed that the contents of their memorandum of March 23 were viewed by their respective governments as extremely important, a concern with a situation that might be seriously detrimental to the interests of the Arab refugees.

The action taken in pursuance of those two communications was related by the Commission in its Thirteenth Progress Report of 1953.[12] It stated that the chairman of the Commission had been told by the Israeli representative to the United Nations that any action taken would not impair any legal claims of the Arab refugees, and that his government would provide the Commission with further information.

On the face of it, such a statement appeared satisfactory; but, on July 7, 1953, the Israeli representative informed the Commission in writing that the government of Israel was prepared to discuss the payment of compensation in practical terms.

On July 29, 1953, the Commission rightly replied that "It was on the question of the manner in which Arab property was being dealt with and not on the question of compensation that the Commission sought information." The letter went on "to recall that in its Resolutions of

December 11, 1948 and December 14, 1950, the General Assembly had given the Commission a responsibility in connection with the property rights of the refugees."

This latter remark is significant because it clearly indicated that the Commission fully recognized the nature of the task entrusted to it by the General Assembly, namely, to take "measures for the protection of the rights, property and interests of the refugees." The Commission's letter to the Israeli representative also included the following specific questions:

1. Has the disposal of property belonging to Arab refugees now residing outside the borders of Israel been authorized by the government of Israel?

2. If so, under what conditions is this disposal to be carried out and to what extent, if any, has it already been put into effect?

3. If such property has been disposed of, is the money realized being held in the name of the original owner to be paid to him at some future date as compensation for the loss of his property, if he chooses not to return?

4. Have the necessary measures been taken to ensure the restitution of their property to such refugees as might be repatriated?

The Israeli representative replied on August 23, 1953, to the effect that:

1. The disposal of property has been authorized by the government of Israel and effected in accordance with the provisions of the Absentee Property Law of 1950;

2. Under the above Law, this property became vested in the Custodian of Absentee Property and had been transferred to the Development Authority under the Development Authority Law;

3. Funds realized in consideration for the property were treated in accordance with the provisions of the Absentee Property Law and the counter-value was credited to the property for which it had been received; and

4. The policy of the government of Israel was to ensure integration of those refugees who were legally authorized to enter Israel.*

The ambiguity and evasiveness of the Israeli replies to the clear questions of the Commission are apparent. It was specifically the Absentee Property Law, on which the Israelis relied, that the Arab states had protested as illegal and in violation of the provisions of the Partition Resolution. The Israeli attitude should have prompted the Commission to investigate whether the laws and regulations enacted and the official actions taken were in conformity with, or in violation of, the stipulations and guarantees in the Partition Resolution. Unfortunately, the matter was not pursued further by the Commission, and the Israelis were

---

*The term refugee here gives the impression that Palestinian Arabs are intended. This is not so, because any returning Arab would obviously go back to his home and property. At any rate, no such Arabs have been allowed to return. Since the Israelis have been referring to Jews who emigrate to Israel from Arab countries as refugees, it is safe to say that the term applies to the integration of Jewish immigrants, not Arab returnees.

permitted to proceed unhindered in their policy of confiscation and liquidation of Arab land, rights and interests in their homeland.

On March 1, 1956, representatives of the Arab states to the United Nations once again submitted a joint communication to the Commission requesting it to assume its full responsibility and to adopt a policy of vigorous and effective action "for the protection of the rights, property and interests of the refugees." The delegations pointed out that the Commission in discharging this task should take into consideration the points raised by the Arab Delegations in the debates at the previous sessions. The Commission was also requested to report to the General Assembly "on the causes and various forms of Israeli infringements and actions which affect the legitimate and inherent rights, property and interests of the refugees, and are in any way prejudicial to them."

In addition, the Commission was asked to prepare and submit to the General Assembly a complete report on the Arab property in the territory occupied by Israel. This report should include, among other things, how the property is controlled and managed and what measures are being taken to preserve it; a complete statement of account, showing the income and rentals derived from the different types of properties; and an appraisal of the manner followed by the Israeli authorities for fixing the rent, as well as the basis upon which the rent is calculated. These should then be compared, wherever possible, with cases involving freely held Jewish property of similar characteristics and location.

The joint communication concluded with the statement that the Commission was duty-bound, more than ever before, to take vigorous and effective action with the view of protecting the rights, property and interests of the refugees without any further delay.

What action the Commission took on this letter besides acknowledging it was never known. No annual reports were presented by the Commission to the General Assembly in 1956 and 1957; and the report for 1958, made no mention of the points raised by the Arab governments.

The matter continued to be raised by the Arab representatives to the United Nations at each session of the General Assembly, but all that happened was that a record was made of what was said. It soon became clear that the United Nations had no intention of doing anything as the situation in the Middle East continued to deteriorate.

German Reparations Versus Israeli Confiscations

Palestinian Arab losses as a result of the creation of the state of Israel in 1948 run into the billions of dollars. The type of losses sustained by the Palestinian Arabs can be compared in a great measure with the losses suffered by the Jews at the hands of the Nazis.

In the latter case, the government of the Federal Republic of Germany made amends to the victims of Nazi persecution in the amount of 85.3 billion German marks by January 1978, of which the state of Israel became the recipient of 3,450 million marks even though the Jewish state was not in existence when the Nazi crimes were committed, and the Jewish victims never had any connection with Palestine.* (For full details, see Appendix)

The Palestinians do not begrudge the Jewish victims of Nazi persecution receiving reparations for losses sustained and restitution of property where this was possible; but they expect that justice should be equally applied to others in similar circumstances without discrimination. If Jews could claim compensation for "personal injuries, for time spent in concentration camps, or for loss of professional careers resulting from Nazi actions," and are able to regain possession of property which it was alleged they were "forced to sell because of racial discrimination"** then by the same token the Palestinian Arabs are entitled to receive compensation for similar losses sustained and to regain possession of their homes and lands in the same manner. However, unlike many Jews in Nazi Germany, the Arabs of Palestine did not sell their property, and they refuse to do so to this day. It was seized and later confiscated by the Israeli authorities without the consent and against the wishes of the rightful owners. If, therefore, justice ordains that forced sales for fear of racial persecution can be annulled even though the Jewish owners had received the value of their property at the time of the sale, it follows with stronger reason and in equity that property confiscated by Israel against the expressed decisions of the United Nations, must also be returned to its lawful owners.

The Israelis refuse to this day to restore property to its legitimate owners, to pay rent for property being used, or to compensate their Arab victims for losses sustained.

---

*According to the *Toronto Star* of June 9, 1978, "Bonn plans fund to compensate Jews" in an additional amount of some $288 million. The money is "to be distributed among Nazi victims who are not eligible under the existing compensation programs."

**According to *The New York Times* of August 14, 1959, "The Supreme International Restitution Court in Berlin has recognized the claims of four Jewish families for the return of valuable estates and houses sold to foreign diplomatic agencies during the Nazi era." The Tribunal, the highest restitution court for West Berlin and West Germany," ruled that the property was to be returned to the former owners because they had been forced to sell for fear of racial persecution under the Hitler regime."

XIII   Violation of Human Rights

Zionist-Israeli Goals

Israeli violation of the human rights of the Palestinian people was not spontaneous or unplanned; it was inherent from the start in the goals and aspirations of the Zionist movement which called for the establishment of a Jewish state on Arab lands, but somehow free of its Moslem and Christian inhabitants.

When the Jewish state was created in 1948, the Israelis proceeded to rid themselves of the indigenous Arab population by the most brutal and inhuman methods, using murders and massacres to hasten the Arab exodus. In the process, the pattern of destruction of Arab villages and homes, to prevent the inhabitants from returning, was described by Dr. Shahak as "chillingly radical." He said: "An Arab village would be invaded; then every house, every garden wall, every cemetery and its tombstones would be razed, literally to the ground. The purpose was to make the Arab presence disappear."[1]

But Israeli violations did not stop at that; they were intensified and reached their climax following the June 1967 War when some Israelis began to believe that, with the occupation of the Sinai Peninsula, the Gaza Strip, the Golan Heights and the West Bank, they were well on the way toward the objective of the dreamed-of empire of David and Solomon.

Conventions and Laws Governing Human Rights

The international conventions and agreements governing the status of subject populations that are applicable to the Israeli occupation of Arab territories, are:

The Hague Convention of 1907
The United Nations Charter of 1945
The Universal Declaration of Human Rights of 1948
The Fourth Geneva Convention Relative to the Protection of Civilian
    Persons in Times of War of August 1949

The Israeli authorities accepted their obligations under these international instruments; signed the Universal Declaration of Human Rights soon after Israel was admitted into the membership of the United Nations in 1949; and ratified the Fourth Geneva Convention on July 6, 1961.

The Fourth Geneva Convention is intended to cover the conduct of foreign military occupation. The conditions by which the Convention becomes relevant and must be observed, are defined in Article 2, which reads as follows:

"The Convention shall also apply to all cases of partial or total occupation of the territory of a High Contracting Party even if the said occupation meets with no resistance. Although one of the Powers in conflict may not be a party to the present Convention, the Powers who are parties thereto shall remain bound by it in their mutual relations. They shall, furthermore, be bound by the Convention in relation to the said Power, if the latter accepts and applies the provisions thereof."

Article 4 of the said Fourth Convention, adds:

"Persons protected by the Conventions are those who, at a given moment and in any manner whatsoever, find themselves, in a case of conflict or occupation, in the hands of a Party to the conflict or Occupying Power of which they are not nationals."

The civilian persons in the occupied territories are similarly considered protected persons according to the provisions of Article 42 of the Hague Convention of 1907. They also enjoy the rights provided for in the Charter of the United Nations and in the Universal Declaration of Human Rights.

The applicability of the Fourth Geneva Convention to the occupied Arab territories has been explicitly recognized both by the International Conference of the Red Cross[2] and by the General Assembly of the United Nations, which, in the operative paragraphs of its resolution,

"1. *Affirms* that the Geneva Convention Relative to the Protection of Civilian Persons in Time of War of August 1949, applies to the Arab territories occupied by Israel since 1967;

"2. *Calls upon* the Israeli occupation authorities to respect and comply with the provisions of that Convention in the occupied Arab territories."[3]

U.N. General Assembly concern for the human rights of the population of the occupied territories began as early as July 4, 1967—less than a month after the end of the June 1967 War and after it became known that the Israelis were violating their obligations under the provisions of the Fourth Geneva Convention in relation to the Arab civilian population.

On that date, the General Assembly adopted a resolution that affirmed that human rights should be respected in the areas occupied by Israel, and recommended that all governments, including Israel, respect and uphold the principles of the Fourth Geneva Convention Relative to the Protection of Civilian Persons in Times of War.[4] This resolution was reaffirmed on December 19, 1967.[5]

UN Investigates and Condemns*

In view of persistent reports of repressive practices by the Israeli occupation authorities, the General Assembly took measures to investigate the situation in the occupied territories. On December 19, 1968, it established a Special Committee to Investigate Israeli Practices Affecting Human Rights in the Occupied Territories.[6] Since that date, the Israelis have consistently refused to allow the Special Committee to enter the occupied territories to carry out its investigations.

Israel's primary argument against allowing the Special Committee access was that it should not be obliged to do so unless similar investigations were undertaken on the condition of Jewish citizens of Arab countries. This was regarded as constituting a clear evasion, as such an investigation—and the overall question of the status of Jewish-Arab minorities—does not fall within the provisions of the Fourth Geneva Convention. The Israelis further stated that they would not be bound by any provisions of the Geneva Conventions in the conduct of their occupation.[7]

Despite the obstacles raised by the Israelis to conceal the true nature of the occupation, the Special Committee did gather valuable evidence of Israeli violations of human rights. The two reports[8] submitted by the Committee to the General Assembly, formed the factual basis for many of the later General Assembly condemnations of Israel.

The first General Assembly resolution condemning Israeli violations of human rights in the occupied territories, was adopted on December 11, 1969. In the preambular paragraph to this resolution, the Assembly noted that it was "gravely alarmed by fresh reports of collective punishments, mass imprisonments, indiscriminate destruction of homes, and other acts of oppression against the civilian population in the Arab territories occupied by Israel."

In its operative paragraphs, the resolution expressed grave concern at the continuing reports of violations of human rights in the occupied territories and "condemns such policies and practices as collective area punishment, destruction of homes, and the deportation of the inhabitants of the territories occupied by Israel." The resolution further called upon Israel to desist from such practices and to comply with the Fourth Geneva Convention and the Universal Declaration of Human Rights," and other relevant resolutions adopted by the various international organizations."[9]

---

*For Israeli violations of human rights committed against the Palestinian Arabs who were expelled in 1948, see Chapter X; and for those against the Arabs who remained behind under Israeli rule, see Chapter XI.

After 1969, Israel was repeatedly censured or condemned by the United Nations for its violation of the human rights of the Arab civilian populations in the occupied territories. In essence, the numerous resolutions adopted called upon the Israelis, among other things, to rescind forthwith all repressive measures and to desist from all policies, such as:

(a) The annexation of any part of the occupied Arab territories;

(b) The establishment of Israeli settlements in those territories and the transfer of parts of Israel's civilian population into the occupied territories;

(c) The destruction and demolition of villages, quarters and houses, and the confiscation and expropriation of property;

(d) The evacuation, transfer, deportation and expulsion of the inhabitants of the occupied Arab territories;

(e) The denial of the right of the refugees and displaced persons to return to their homes;

(f) The ill-treatment and torture of prisoners and detainees;

(g) Collective punishment.[10]

However, the most severe critic of Israeli violations of human rights in the occupied territories came from the UN Commission of Human Rights. On March 8, 1968, the Commission dispatched a telegram to the Israeli government calling upon it to desist from destroying the homes of the civilian populations of the occupied territories; and on May 7, the UN sponsored International Conference on Human Rights adopted Resolution No. 1 which "*expresses* its grave concern for the violation of human rights in the Arab territories occupied as a result of the June 1967 hostilities."

Thereafter, the Commission on Human Rights adopted annual resolutions concerning the violation of the human rights of the Arab civilian populations. In summary, these deplored "Israel's continued violations of human rights in the occupied territories, particularly the acts of destroying homes of the Arab civilian population, deportation of inhabitants and resorting to violence against inhabitants expressing their resentment to occupation," and called upon Israel "to put an immediate end to such acts."[11]

But the most significant of them all, was the Resolution adopted on March 23, 1972 which, in a way, placed Nazi and Israeli actions on the same level. After "noting that the Charter of the International Military Tribunal of Nuremberg, as confirmed by General Assembly Resolution 3(1) of February 13, 1946, and Resolution 95(1) of December 11, 1946, has considered as war crimes the grave breaches later enumerated in the Geneva Conventions of August 12, 1949", the commission decided that it "*Considers* that grave breaches of the Fourth Geneva Convention committed by Israel in the occupied Arab territories constitute war crimes and an affront to humanity."[12]

Other UN bodies also censured Israel. The General Conference of UNESCO adopted a resolution that "noted with anxiety" that it was "apparent from the Director-General's report that the populations of occupied territories were not enjoying their inalienable and inviolable rights to national education and cultural life." It invited the Director-General to "exercise full supervision of the operations of cultural and educational institutions" in the occupied territories. It urgently appealed to Israel to refrain from any act that has the effect of hindering the exercise of rights to national education and cultural life.[13]

The World Health Assembly of the World Health Organization (WHO) took similar action. It adopted a resolution which, after noting that Israel was bound to observe the relevant provisions of the Fourth Geneva Convention, *"draws attention* that Israel's violations of the basic human rights of the refugees, displaced persons and the inhabitants of the occupied territories, constitute a serious impediment to the health of the population of the occupied territories" and *"calls upon* Israel to refrain from any interference with the activities of the International Committee of the Red Cross in the occupied territories."[14]

Israeli Defiance

Israel's response to its obligations under the UN Charter, the Universal Declaration of Human Rights, and the Fourth Geneva Convention, was one of impudent defiance. Summarized, these violations are:

1. The annexation of any part of the occupied territories, such as, the eastern part of Jerusalem under a so-called unification scheme. This has been strongly opposed and condemned by the United Nations on more than one occasion. Even the US government looked with disfavor on the Israeli action.

2. The establishment of Israeli settlements on Arab lands in occupied territories and the transfer of parts of the Jewish population into the occupied territories. By the end of 1977, seventy-seven settlements had been established—31 in the West Bank area (21 in the Jordan Valley, 7 in the Hebron area, and 3 on the hill-tops. Others are in course of construction); 17 in the Rafah area of the Gaza Strip; 26 in the Golan Heights; and 3 in the Sinai Peninsula, south of the port of Eilat.[15]

3. The destruction and demolition of villages, quarters and houses, and the confiscation and expropriation of Arab property, such as the total destruction of the villages of Yalu, Emwas and Beit Nuba in the Latrun area, and the Arab quarter around the Wailing Wall in the Old City of Jerusalem.

The number of Arab buildings destroyed during the seven-year period commencing 1967, was 19,152 (10,897 in the Gaza Strip, 6,255 in the West Bank, and 2,000 in the Goland Heights).[16] No figures are available for the Sinai Peninsula.

4. The extent of land expropriated or confiscated during the same period, exceeded a million and a half dunums (4.05 dunums to an acre), or one-sixth of the total area of the West Bank and one-third of the Gaza Strip. Thousands of Bedouins were forcibly evicted from their lands, and about 100,000 dunums were confiscated.

The same activity took place in East Jerusalem where 22,000 dunums of Arab land in the Old City and its suburbs were confiscated with the eviction of tens of thousands of Arabs who used to live and work there.

After the demolition of about 800 Arab buildings, 13 new Jewish settlements were constructed to form "a ring around Jerusalem" as the authorities described it. As a result, a serious demographic change occurred causing a forcible decrease in the number of the Arab inhabitants from 140,000 in 1967 to 70,000 in 1974.

"The demolition of houses," said Israeli lawyer Felicia Langer, "is one of the most cruel punishments imposed administratively by the military governor without any decision of any court of law. The victims are always the innocent families of the detained, knowing nothing of what sort of crime their son or brother is suspected."[17]

5. The deportation and expulsion of inhabitants from the occupied territories runs into the thousands of Palestinian activists and political leaders. The purpose behind these is to deprive the Palestinian inhabitants of their leadership and moral supporters, remarked Felicia Langer.[18]

6. Denial of the right of displaced persons to return to their homes. The United Nations has annually called upon the Israelis to allow the displaced persons to return to their homes, but without success.

Israeli Imprisonments and Detentions

Israeli Lawyer Felicia Langer—a longstanding defender of Palestinian prisoners—stated:

"In addition to confiscation of land, expulsions, and demolition of houses, there is another means of intimidation: The military trials. The military courts have imposed many thousands of years of imprisonment on Palestinians without any possibility of appeal against the judgments in the West Bank, Gaza, and Golan. Not only those who hold arms and fight—to which they have a right as a sacred privilege to fight against foreign occupation—are sentenced in these courts. There is nothing lawful in the eyes of the authorities—a peaceful demonstration, spreading a leaflet, giving a glass of water to a son or husband or daughter or father suspected of subversive activity. The fathers and mothers, the wives and the sisters are obliged by the law to announce to the authorities if they suspect that their loved ones are acting against the Israeli authorities.

"Now, in accordance with a law enacted in 1973, the Israeli government is kidnapping Palestinians from neighboring countries and bringing them for trial before military courts in Israel. The offence can be merely membership in any Palestinian or other organization which is considered by the Israeli authorities to be dangerous to the security of Israel. Ten Lebanese, Syrians and Iraqis were kidnapped four years ago and sentenced to six years each according to that law, contrary to all sacred maxims of the law of nations.

"Now we have new kidnappings. In a piratic action in July against the Palestinians in Lebanon, a Greek ship, which was on its way to Lebanon, was stopped by the I.D.F. 160 miles away from Israeli territory. Three of the passengers are still in an Israeli prison, their crime being their intention to help their brothers in Lebanon who are attacked with Israeli weapons and her instigation, as part of an imperialist conspiracy against the Palestinian people and progressive forces in Lebanon . . .

"The use of torture during the investigations is a method, and I declare it as a lawyer who has dealt with thousands of cases. I have seen marks of torture on the bodies of hundreds of my clients. I knew prisoners who grew mad as a result of torture [or who were] half paralyzed after a treatment by electric shocks . . . Many people have died in prisons as a result of torture, or are condemned to a slow death because of lack of medical treatment . . .*[19]

Israeli Acts of Torture

The accusation of torture of detainees and prisoners by the Israeli authorities is confirmed from many unimpeachable sources, some of which are:

1. Langer's testimony in the last paragraph of the previous section is that of an eye-witness who cannot be repudiated. Her exposure of Israeli torture tactics has brought her into conflict with the Israeli authorities.

2. On February 26, 1968, the International Committee of the Red Cross, in a report on conditions in the Tulkarm Prison, stated: "A number of detainees have undergone torture during the interrogation by the military police. According to the evidence, the torture took the following forms:

(a) Suspension of the detainee by the hands and the simultaneous traction of his other members for hours at a time until he loses consciousness.

(b) Burns with cigarette stubs.

(c) Blows by rods on the genitals.

(d) Tying up and blind-folding for days.

(e) Bites by dogs.

(f) Electric shocks at the temples, the mouth, the chest and testicles."

3. In a letter dated October 1976 from Amnesty International to the Israeli Prime Minister Yitzhaq Rabin, Amnesty stated:

"The conclusion seems unavoidable that abuses in the past, directed against Arab detainees, have had a brutalizing effect on the conduct of the law enforcement agencies, and strong counter measures by your government are clearly a matter of great urgency, especially now that relevant authorities, including the Minister of Police and the courts, have admitted that unnecessary force had in at least some cases been used during interrogation. Amnesty International therefore respectfully repeats its request for an independent inquiry into all aspects of this problem."

4. On June 19, 1977, *the London Sunday Times* published the result of a five-month independent on-the-spot inquiry by an Insight Team into Israel's use of torture against Palestinian detainees and prisoners. Its findings were, in part, that "torture of Arab prisoners is so widespread

---

*For a fuller record of Israeli violations of the human rights of the Arab population, see *With My Own Eyes: Israel and the Occupied Territories 1967–1973*, by Felicia Langer (London: Ithaca Press, 1975).

and systematic that it cannot be dismissed as rogue cops exceeding orders. It appears to be sanctioned as deliberate policy."

The "Insight Team's" report on the torture of Palestinian detainees and prisoners went unnoticed by the western media.

XIV Racism and Racial Discrimination

Elimination of Racial Discrimination

In 1945, the major powers, with representatives of the smaller nations, gathered in San Francisco and drafted the Charter for the proposed United Nations Organization which was to replace the defunct League of Nations; in 1948, the United Nations adopted the Universal Declaration of Human Rights; and in 1949, the Fourth Geneva Convention Relative to the Protection of Civilian Persons in Times of War, came into effect. But notwithstanding these international agreements, the scourge of racism and racial discrimination continued to be practised in certain countries.

On November 20, 1963, the UN General Assembly proclaimed the Declaration on the Elimination of All Forms of Racial Discrimination, which provides in Article 1: "Discrimination between human beings on the ground of race, color, or ethnic origin is an offence to human dignity and shall be condemned." The resolution went on to affirm that "any doctrine of racial discrimination or superiority is scientifically false, morally condemnable, socially unjust and dangerous." It expressed its alarm at the manifestations of racial discrimination still in evidence in some areas of the world, some of which are imposed by certain governments by means of legislative, administrative or other measures."[1]

In 1965, the International Convention on the Elimination of All Forms of Racial Discrimination went a step further by proclaiming in Article 1: "In this convention, the term racial discrimination shall mean any distinction, exclusion, restriction or preference based on race, color, descent, or national or ethnic origin."[2]

If these principles were compared with conditions in the world today, it will become clear that two countries qualify as nations practicing racism and racial discrimination as a policy on a governmental basis. These are: The Union of South Africa for apartheid policies, and the state of Israel for its discriminatory treatment of the Palestinians both within and outside Israel.

South Africa was condemned by the United Nations on more than one occasion, and certain sanctions have been imposed upon it; but in the case of Israel, the Jewish state managed during many years— through the power and influence of Zionism in the capitals of the western world—to remain clear of the arm of the United Nations. However, this could not go on for ever as more and more injustices of a racist character were being inflicted with impunity against the Palestinian people and could no longer be ignored.

United Nations Equates Zionism with Racism

In 1975, the case against Israel was brought before the UN General Assembly. Dr. Fayez Sayegh, delegate of Kuwait, arguing in favor of the draft resolution, said: "The Zionism of which the draft resolution speaks, is a concrete political ideology, articulated by a concrete political organization which launched a concrete political movement at a precise moment in time, which created political institutions, and which manifested itself in concrete practices which had the effect of excluding some people on the basis of their being non-Jews and including others on the basis of their being Jews—Jewishness being defined officially by Zionism as an ethnic and not strictly a religious definition."[3]

The Israeli representative, in an attempt to confuse the issue and to inject an accusation of anti-Semitism, equated the attack on Zionism as an attack on Judaism, and alleged that it was "born of a deep, pervading feeling of anti-Semitism."[4]

On November 10, 1975, the General Assembly, by a vote of 72 in favor, 35 against, and 27 abstentions, adopted a resolution which "determines that Zionism is a form of racism and racial discrimination."[5]

After the passage of the resolution, attacks appeared in the press of the United States and Canada against the United Nations describing it as an impotent organization, and against the nations which voted in favor of the Resolution accusing them of being stooges of the oil-rich Arab States.

To understand the resolution, a student of Middle East affairs put it this way:

The resolution is not:
    an attack against world Jewry by a mass of anti-Semitic people or
        governments;
    an attempt by communist and Third World nations to take over or
        wreck the United Nations;
    the result of a vast purchase of votes by oil-rich Arab states.
The resolution is:
    an expression of resistance to Israeli intransigence in their refusal
        to deal with the Palestinian people;
    an attempt to isolate Israel in the United Nations for her disregard

of numerous UN resolutions and appeals to respect the human rights of Palestinians in the territories occupied in 1967;

an attempt to isolate Israel for her refusal to withdraw from those territories;

a criticism of Israel as a Jewish state, i.e., a state founded on principles according to which Jews enjoy privileges not shared by non-Jewish citizens;

a reaction against policies pursued by western nations—especially the United States—which ignore the plight of the Palestinian people and attempt to reach a solution to the Middle East problem through exclusion of the Palestine Liberation Organization from negotiations;

an attempt to show solidarity with the Palestine struggle subsequent to the Sinai Agreement in regard to which Egypt pursued national, as opposed to regional interests.[6]

The nations which supported the resolution actually did so as a matter of principle and on the basis of the evidence presented. They categorically oppose the apartheid policies and practices of South Africa and as such, they could not very well remain indifferent to the racist policies and practices of Zionism and its off-spring Israel.

Speaking in the General Assembly after the vote, the Israeli representative said: "For us, the Jewish people, this is no more than a piece of paper, and we shall treat it as such."[7] He was later reported to have angrily torn up a copy of the resolution in the presence of the UN membership.[8] He made no effort, however, to defend the principles of Zionism by rebutting the evidence presented.

The U.S. representative, on the other hand, joined the Israeli bandwagon. Ambassador Daniel Moynihan vehemently attacked the resolution and told the General Assembly: "There appears to have developed in the United Nations the practice for a number of countries to combine for the purpose of doing something outrageous." He added: "The United States rises to declare before the General Assembly, and before the world, that it does not acknowledge, it will not abide by, and will never acquiesce in the infamous act." Moynihan then referred to the description made by the U.S. representative on the Social, Humanitarian and Cultural Committee to the effect that "it was obscene," and he continued to declare that "the abomination of anti-Semitism . . . has been given the appearance of international sanction," alleging that "the General Assembly today grants sympathetic amnesty—and more—to the murderers of the six million Jews." He went on to describe the findings of the General Assembly as "a lie which the United Nations has now declared to be a truth."*[9]

Two pertinent points arise out of this erratic outburst by Ambassador Moynihan: The first, he proved it to be a lie that the United States is the champion of the United Nations. It appears that the U.S. government

---

*Ambassador Daniel Moynihan was about to run for a seat in the U.S. Senate, which he later won, in traditionally pro-Israel New York.

will support the world organization only if it follows United States policy. The second, the representative of the United States has given the Israelis support for their disrespect and non-compliance with resolutions of the United Nations.

Had United States opposition to the resolution been based on arguments capable of refuting the substance of the evidence which brought about its passage, one would perhaps feel sympathy for the logic of the United States position; but for the representative of a great power to make attacks of a general character and fail to prove that the majority of nations was wrong, indicates bias, and reflects adversely on the government of the United States.

Apart from the denunciations of the equation between Zionism and racism in general terms, the only argument that appeared in print was the usual claim that Zionism is synonymous with Judaism. The Canadian Zionist Federation, for example, argued that "the separation of Zionism from Judaism is like separating Muhammad from Islam and Christ from Christianity."[10]

The analogy is as preposterous as it is absurd. Judaism is based on the Five Books of Moses; Christianity on the Teachings of Christ; and Islam on the Revelations made to the Prophet Muhammad. In essence, the three faiths are identical in their religious and human values of love, humanity, humility, tolerance and equality, and none justify a political movement based on occupation and oppression.

Grounds Supporting the UN Resolution

Zionism—unlike Judaism—lacks any religious significance, and uses Judaism as a means to further its political objectives. Furthermore, it has capitalized on the persecution and oppression of Jews in Christian Europe down through the ages, and on what the Nazis did to the Jews during World War II—neither of which calamities exists anywhere in the world today.

It would be too lengthy a process to enumerate all the evidence and arguments to prove the racist and racial discriminatory policies, laws, and practices of the Zionist-Israeli hierarchy. Suffice it to repeat here one example that has already been dealt with at some length in an earlier chapter. The Israeli Law of Return confers the rights of entry automatically and unconditionally upon any Jew, of whatever nationality, the moment he steps on Israeli soil, even though he may never before had set foot in Palestine. This same right is denied to a Palestinian Arab who was born, raised, owns property in Palestine, and lived there all his life, as well as his ancestors before him. How can a country that enacts such a law be described as a democracy? And how can the label of racism and racial discrimination against such a country be questioned or defended? This law is unique in its principles, and does not exist even in South Africa's apartheid.

Article 13(2) of the Universal Declaration of Human Rights gives "everyone the right to leave any country, including his own, and to return to his country;" and while the Israeli government is a signatory to this universal declaration and insists that its provisions should be applied to Soviet Jews, it has flouted its provisions with impunity where the Palestinian Moslems and Christians are concerned.

Even Arabs who have at no time left the territory that came under Israeli jurisdiction, were denied the same rights as alien Jews. To become an Israeli citizen, an Arab must be naturalized under the provisions of the Nationality Law. This is only possible by proving that he was born in the country; that he lived in Israeli-occupied territory three out of five years preceding the date of his application for citizenship; that he is entitled to permanent residence; and that he has a sufficient knowledge of the Hebrew language. Even if the Arab met all these requirements, it was still up to the discretion of the Minister of the Interior to grant or refuse the application.

The Israeli Minister of the Interior admitted in parliament that racial discrimination did exist in Israel. But he pointed out that this stemmed, not from the Nationality Law but from the Law of Return, which endowed only Jews with the right of return.[11]

Also during the debate in the Israeli Parliament, Israeli Professor M.R. Konvitz expressed fears that such a law might be unfavorably compared with Nazi legislation, since it embodied "a principle of exclusion which constitutes religious discrimination." He argued that though the law might offer temporary advantages at a time when large numbers of displaced persons have to be settled, thereafter it would undoubtedly be considered discriminatory.[12]

After the Bill became law, the *Jewish Newsletter* warned that the Law of Return revives a dangerous racist theory that smacks of the slogan of a previous generation. "A German is a German wherever he is;"[13] while Rueven Grass, a religious immigrant from the United States, compared the law to the Nazi laws because "it gives immigration privileges to anyone who is Jewish under the Nuremberg Laws' definition, i.e., having a Jewish grandparent."[14]

XV Terrorism

Terrorism Classified

The objective of terrorism is the same in all cases, namely, to harass, obstruct, kill and destroy an institution or structure that the so-called terrorist perceives as the enemy. But the underlying causes leading up to such acts, differ and can be variously classified. Setting aside those acts of purely personal vengeance, two basic categories of terrorism can be defined:

1. There is the violent act by the indigenous population to destroy or disrupt a foreign oppressive or tyrannical institution that by its forceful occupation of the land has violated the legitimate rights and offended the fundamental values of the inhabitants;

2. There is the act of a minority group that intends to force or enforce its will upon the majority and thereby achieve the surrender of principles and rights maintained by the people being acted against.

These two types of acts are premeditated political terror, which are calculated to effect a change in the political process; they are fundamentally antithetical.

Under the first category, fall such cases as the operations of the resistance movements of Europe during World War II, which were launched by the local inhabitants against the invading Nazi and Fascist armies of occupation, and even within the Nazi and Fascist states themselves by dissident citizens.

The Allied powers described their members as freedom fighters and supported them morally, militarily and financially. The Nazis and the Fascists, on the other hand, called them terrorists, saboteurs, murderers, and the like, and tried to exterminate them by all means at their disposal, because their activities were intended to destroy the political and military strength of the enemy and to re-establish freedom and liberty. Although this type of action might terrorize the ruling or military institution, it cannot be conceived as a depraved terrorism in the true sense of the word. For all its negative attributes, the world has seen fit to exonerate this type of so-called terrorism as a struggle for human freedom, liberty, and dignity, and to endow it with almost religious sanction.

The second category comprises the unique case of Palestine where an alien element was brought into the country against the wishes of the indigenous inhabitants and who, once they became a sizable minority and militarily strong, were engaged in wresting the country from its original inhabitants. There, the Zionist movement, after enjoying British patronage and protection for its program to achieve political hegemony over the land, turned against its erstwhile patron when the latter began to show signs of vacillation. It should be noted that the British Mandatory authorities were in the country against the wishes of the Arab inhabitants, and therefore were regarded, for all intents and purposes, as themselves intruders.

One must therefore be careful not to confuse the image of the French underground movement during World War II with the Zionist underground subversive organizations (the Hagana, the Irgun Zvei Leumi, and the Stern Gang), which were attempting to remove, first the British Mandatory government, and then the Arab inhabitants, both of which stood in the way of their achieving their goal in Palestine.

Zionist Terrorism

When the time was right and the demoralized British were committed to abandon their mandate over Palestine, as well as their self-imposed responsibilities to safeguard and protect the rights of the non-Jewish communities of the country, the Zionist momentum was smoothly channelled into achieving, through terror, what they had at first expected the British to achieve for them, namely, the seizure of Palestine, the demographic purgation of Palestine's native majority (the Moslem and Christian Arabs), and the proclamation of the pure Jewish nation state. The Zionist action against the British Mandatory was more in the nature of a palace coup carried out by a colonialist alien group against a foreign colonial power, with the indigenous Arab inhabitants of the country serving as the victims.

The Zionists' subsequent campaign of terror against the Arab majority was designed to reach the ultimate goal of the movement in a land free of its Moslem and Christian inhabitants; and this was partly accomplished in 1948 with the help of Britain and the United States in the lead.

The Character of Zionism

When the Israeli leaders of today use international platforms to indignantly protest the Palestine Arabs' justification to fight for their rights in their homeland, they should be reminded of their own Zionist record, of how they acquired the homes, lands, property and country of those whom they now call terrorists.

The Israelis are the last entitled to condemn acts of terrorism and violence, kidnapping, holding of hostages, and even murder, because they were the first to indulge in such evil practices against innocent people in Palestine. As an established state recognized by the United Nations, they have, since 1967, added such refinements as torture of prisoners and detainees, collective punishment, expulsion and deportation, destruction of property and confiscation of Arab lands.

Terrorism and violence was a trade-mark of Zionist history. The late David Ben Gurion and Golda Meir, Menachem Begin, Moshe Dayan, and the rest of the Israeli higher echelon, who were mostly born outside Palestine and therefore alien to it, happen all to have been either members of the Jewish Agency for Palestine during the period of the mandate, which planned and coordinated Zionist underground terrorist activities,[1] or were active members of the illegal underground terrorist organizations whose members were being sought by the Palestine government for trial before the courts of justice for their criminal offences.*

The Zionists believed that the shortest route to ousting the British from Palestine, and later expelling and dispossessing the Palestinian Arab inhabitants and establishing a Jewish state would be through the process of terrorism and violence. They planned their strategy accordingly, which they began to implement at the start of World War II while Britain was engaged in a deadly struggle with Nazi Germany.

It would fill whole volumes to document the actions committed by the Zionists in Palestine during the period 1939 to 1948. Suffice it to draw attention to some of the more outstanding incidents taken from the record published by the Palestine government in 1946.[2]

Israel Honors its Terrorists

"After the creation of the state of Israel, classified terrorism gave way to the outwardly more respectable terrorism, designed to cow and subjugate the Palestinians and their Arab sympathizers, which the state with all its resources can mount," wrote correspondent David Hirst. Describing "Palestinian violence by contrast [as] reactive, small-scale, but easily branded as barbaric," Hirst "condemns that of an Israel which was built on terrorism and continues to glorify its terrorists to this day."

Hirst then cites the case of Marcelle Ninio, an Egyptian Jewess, who, in 1954, was one of the Israeli agents who planted bombs in United States institutions in Cairo and Alexandria in order to disrupt the then improving Arab-American relations. The criminals were caught red-

---

*There was a ransom for the capture of Menachem Begin—the planner, among other atrocities, of the blowing up of the King David Hotel in July 1946, and architect of the Deir Yasin massacre in April 1948. As Prime Minister of Israel from 1977–1983, he received the red carpet treatment on visits to the capitals of the western world; and in October 1978 was awarded the Nobel Prize, and a prize and citation by the National Council of Churches in the U.S.A. for his part in the Camp-David peace negotiations.

handed, the leader committed suicide in prison, two were executed by
hanging, and the rest, including Marcelle Ninio, were sentenced to
terms of imprisonment.[3]

David Hirst then notes that Marcelle Ninio "was repatriated after the
June 1967 war" to Israel and that she had recently married. He added:
Golda Meir (then Prime Minister), who attended the wedding, called
her a heroine. Dayan, who was there too, told her that the "war was
success enough that it led to your freedom."[4]

This glorification of Zionist terrorism is no surprise. Here is another
example: The bodies of the two Stern gangsters who assassinated Lord
Moyne in Cairo in 1944, were given heroes, military burials on Mt. Herzl
after lying in state in the Jerusalem Hall of Heroism. In this case, the
bodies of the two murderers who were hanged in Cairo for their crime,
were exchanged in 1975 for twenty Egyptian prisoners-of-war.[5]

Author Arthur Koestler aptly comments on the Dr. Jekyll and Mr.
Hyde character of the present-day Israeli leadership who, as Zionist
leaders, "preached resistance but denied indignantly acting against the
law. They alternately tolerated, fought against or engaged in terrorism,
according to the opportunity of the moment, but all the time carefully
maintained the fiction of being guardians of civic virtues; and the habits
of hypocrisy which they learned from the Mandatory Administration,
they partly carried over into the new born state."[6]

Terrorism and the United Nations

Following the Munich incident of September 5, 1972, in which eleven
Israeli and four Palestinian commandoes lost their lives, the United
Nations Secretary General Kurt Waldheim arranged to inscribe on the
agenda of the XXVIIth (1972) session of the General Assembly an item
entitled International Terrorism.

Western nations unreservedly supported the move of the Secretary-
General to examine terrorism in abstract terms. But Israel continued to
whip up emotion throughout the capitals of Europe and the Americas,
urging their governments to take unilateral measures within their own
countries to deal specifically with Arab terrorism and acts of violence
against Israeli interests and personnel, and offered its help to this end.

Asian and African states, however, whose memories of the sufferings
they had endured at the hands of the colonial powers were still fresh in
their minds, and who had to fight for their own freedoms, were unwilling to go along with the item as worded. They pointed out that, while
they condemn isolated and individual acts of violence and terrorism,
they would continue to rule out actions by liberation movements from
being classified as terrorism.

Many of those who objected to the item of the agenda as proposed
came from countries that until recent years, had to fight for their
liberties. Before independence, they were described by their overlords
as terrorists, but after independence they became recognized as the
founding fathers of the state and their so-called terrorism was transformed overnight into legitimate means of achieving desired and noble
ends. The French and American revolutions are clear examples; while

the Israelis claim similar recognition. The turn to terrorism by the Palestinians is simply another example of resort to all means to achieve what are regarded as legitimate political ends, not only by the Palestinians themselves, but by the majority of the world community.

In order to meet the objectives of the Afro-Asian group, the representative of Saudi Arabia proposed an amendment to include a study of the underlying causes of terrorism. The proposed final text of the item was then made to read:

"Measures to prevent international terrorism which endangers or takes innocent human lives or jeopardizes fundamental freedoms, and studying causes of those forms of terrorism and acts of violence which lie in misery, frustration, grievance and despair, and which cause some to sacrifice human lives, including their own, in an attempt to effect radical changes."

The proposed amendment separates between acts of violence to regain a lost right—as in the case of a liberation movement—and acts of violence against individuals or groups, to perpetuate an injustice.

During the height of the anti-Arab abuse and consideration of the item by the General Assembly, the Lebanese president addressed an appeal to the world and the United Nations in which he said:

"Before considering a curb on violence undertaken by a group of people in a continuous state of despair and provocation, we should tackle the causes of this despair and put an end to provocation."[7]

Such an approach was a sensible one, but who was there to listen? Israeli Foreign Minister, Abba Eban, explained the position of his government differently. He declared:

"The immediate problem in the Middle East is not the quest for a peace settlement, but control of the commandos. Israel is prepared to strike against commandos operating from neighboring countries if their governments are unable or unwilling to eliminate them."[8]

Since the difference between the two points of view was great, nothing came out of the discussion at the United Nations. Meanwhile, on October 15, 1972, Israeli jet planes struck deep inside Lebanese and Syrian territories—this time without previous provocation that the Israelis could claim as an excuse. On October 16, 1972, Golda Meir confirmed to the Israeli Parliament that Israel's new policy was to attack the Palestinian commandos wherever they are without having to wait for them to strike first.

XVI The Palestine Resistance Movement

Palestine Resistance to Balfour Declaration and Mandate*

Until 1939, the Palestinians, in their own limited and perhaps unsophisticated way, made every effort to defend themselves against the Zionist invasion of their homeland with the help of British military might. In the years 1920, 1921, 1923, 1929 and 1933, they rioted and many innocent lives on both sides were lost needlessly. In every case, the riots benefitted the Zionists by arousing sympathy for their cause abroad, increasing Jewish immigration and raising the much needed funds for their projects and maintenance.**

In the period 1935 to 1938, with Jewish immigration becoming a flood, the Palestinians became alarmed and rose in open rebellion against the mandate which necessitated the bringing into the country of additional military reinforcements.

---

*Palestine Arab resistance to Zionism goes back many decades. For a study of the development of Palestinian resistance to Zionism since 1882, see *Information Paper No. 14*, June 1974, by Dr. Walter Lehn, University of Minnesota, published by the Association of Arab-American University Graduates (AAUG), North Dartmouth, Mass.

**The 1929 riots—the worst till then—were claimed to have been inspired by the Zionist Organization because of its financial difficulties due to the depression in the United States. Jewish immigrants in Palestine began to demonstrate against the Jewish Agency and to demand "either give us bread or return us from whence you brought us,"

The Palestine government was obliged to open relief works for the Jewish unemployed, but this was not enough.

To get out of its difficulties, the Zionist Organization sent secretly, agents into the Arab villages to distribute postcards (which the author saw at the time) showing the Haram Esh Shareef (the third holiest shrine in Islam) with the sign of the Star of David on top and the picture of Theodor Herzl at the bottom.

The Arab villagers believing that the Jews were about to occupy their holy place, rose up in arms. The result: Money and Jewish youth flowed into the country.

When the rebellion lasted longer than the British expected, and with all signs in 1939 indicating that war with Nazi Germany was immiment, the British government decided it could not afford to deal with the situation in Palestine and at the same time prepare to meet the Nazi danger. It thereupon solicited the help of the neighboring Arab states— the Emir of Trans-Jordan in particular—to intervene to put a stop to the bloodshed, promising it would deal justly with Palestinian grievances after the War.

The Palestinian Arabs acquiesced in the mediation of their fellow-Arabs at the time and laid down their arms, little realizing that it was the beginning of their forfeiting initiative and control over their own destiny, which was to cost them the loss of their country.

After the establishment of the state of Israel in 1948, the Palestine problem—which until then was a dispute between the Palestinian Arabs on the one hand, and the British Mandatory and the Zionist Organization on the other—was overnight transformed into an Arab states-Israeli conflict in which the Palestinians no longer figured as a party and were from then on referred to, and dealt with, as mere refugees in need of shelter and maintenance.

During the period of 1948–1964 the Palestinians' political activity was minimal and any resistance was unorganized because of their dispersion; while the Arab states—until then still uninvolved and unaffected directly by the creation of the state of Israel—paid lip-service to the Palestinian cause, and their representatives at the United Nations merely delivered speeches at the annual sessions and returned to their countries to lead their normal lives.

Thus, the Palestine question, as a political issue, was shelved and less and less was said about it, while the Israelis attempted to suppress the Palestinian national identity and hurried to consolidate their hold over Arab homes and lands in order to face the world with an accomplished fact, and to build up their military strength to forestall any attempt by the Arabs to dislodge them at any future date. The only action the United Nations took was to raise funds to help feed the destitute Palestinian refugees who were languishing in refugee camps in neighboring Arab countries.

To the Israeli leadership, the Palestinians had become, after the first initial period, a people who were now extinct. This belief made the late Golda Meir declare in 1969: "It was not as though there was a Palestinian people and in Palestine considering itself as a Palestinian people and we came and threw them out and took their country away from them. They did not exist."[1] But the years that followed proved otherwise.

Emergence of El-Fateh and El-'Asifa

During this period, a new generation of Palestinians was born—most of them in refugee camps. They realized the blunders their elders had committed by relying on the Arab states to do for them what they ought to have done for themselves. Contrary to Israeli belief, these young men and women did not forget Palestine even where they were born in exile; they grew up incensed by the injustice that was inflicted upon them and resentful at having to subsist on international charity. They therefore decided to do something about it, and El-Fateh and El-'Asifa were formed.

Little is even now known outside the Arab world about El-Fateh and El-'Asifa except what the Zionist and Israeli press claim them to be—a group of terrorists, marauders, saboteurs, cut-throats bent on creating trouble and hurting little Israel. But if one were to investigate the causes that led up to their creation and studied the objectives of the organization in relation to similar movements that spring up in times of stress, a logical explanation for their deeds may be reached.

The letters of the word Fateh are made up of the Arabic initials of the term Palestine Liberation Movement if read backwards while El-'Asifa—the military branch of Fateh—means storm. Their early members were a group of dedicated young Palestinian men and women who had experienced the Palestine tragedy as children but were not responsible for it.

On New Year's Day 1965, El-Fateh issued its first communique, which in part read as follows:

> "Sixteen years have elapsed while our people live detached from their cause which has been shelved at the United Nations as a problem of displaced refugees, whereas the enemy plans, with all his means, on the local and international levels, for an extended stay in our homeland . . . In the light of this distressing fact, and because of the adverse effect of the lapse of time, the 'Asifa forces have been launched forth to reiterate to the enemy and the world at large that this people did not die and that armed revolution is the road to return and to victory."[2]

The principles of El-Fateh organization were no different from those of liberation movements established in any other country, namely, to remove the evils and injustices imposed upon the Palestinians and to regain their right of freedom and security.

In a way, one can easily compare the set-up of this Arab organization with that of the American Revolution. In the Declaration of the Causes and Necessity of Taking Up Arms adopted in 1775 by the Second Continental Congress at Philadephia, the freedom-fighters declared:

> "In our native land, in defence of the freedom which is our birthright, and which we enjoyed till the late violation of it—for the protection of our property, acquired solely by the honest industry of our forefathers and ourselves, against violence actually offered, we have taken up arms. We shall lay them down when hostilities shall cease on the part of the aggressors, and all danger of their being renewed shall be removed, and not before."

If the American people—whose homes and country were not taken away from them by the British government, and whose very existence was not threatened with extinction—were within their human and legal rights to adopt the stand they did, surely the Palestinian Arabs, after thirty years of pleading, solicitation, argument, appeal and protest at the doors of the United Nations and the great powers, have a stronger right to adhere to the principles of the American Declaration and to take up arms in defence of their property and homeland.

With such a principle in mind, and guided by the fact that every liberation movement in Asia and Africa had to fight and make great sacrifice for its freedom, the Palestinian resistance movement had no alternative but to take up arms.

It should be noted that the loss of contact with homeland and property since 1948 through terror and armed force does not in any way derogate the right of an individual or change the character of the guilty and aggrieved parties. Having been denied a peaceful return to their homes and property for three decades, the Palestinian Arabs believe the only way left open to them is to take measures against those who expelled and dispossessed them. To describe the Palestinians as the aggressors and the Israelis as the victims, is a misstatement of history.

Admittedly, no peace-loving person can honestly endorse aggression for whatever reason and from whatever source; but human patience is not inexhaustable in the face of a stubborn adversary. The Palestinian Arabs used every peaceful approach for thirty years. They appealed to the United Nations, to the western powers, and to world opinion, with no avail. Under such circumstances, they have no alternative but to turn toward armed resistance.

Birth of the Palestine Liberation Organization

In 1964, the Palestine Liberation Organization came into existence; was recognized by the Arab states as the representative and spokesman of the Palestinian people; and accepted as a member of the League of Arab States.

The aim of the organization is the liberation of Palestine, a task which is deemed to be a defensive measure, necessitated by the needs of self-defence—a right provided for and upheld in the Charter of the United Nations. The organization declared its readiness from the start to befriend all nations that love freedom, justice and peace; and urged all such nations to support and assist the people of Palestine in their struggle to restore what legitimately belongs to them in their own country, and to enable them to exercise their national sovereignty and freedom.*

The Israelis became alarmed and charged that these objectives were aggressive, aimed at the sovereignty of the state of Israel; they protested to the United Nations, describing them as a source of danger to Israeli security.

---

*On December 6, 1971, UN Resolution 2787 (XXVI) confirmed in Article 1: "The legality of the peoples' struggle for self-determination and liberation from colonial and foreign domination and alien subjugation . . . as well as the Palestinian people, by all available means consistent with the Charter of the United Nations." Article 3 called upon all states "dedicated to the ideals of freedom and peace to give all their political, moral and material assistance to peoples struggling for liberation, self-determination and independence against colonial and alien domination."

The Palestine National Charter

In June 1968, a National Covenant, consisting of 33 articles, was adopted by the Palestine National Council (See Appendix C). The following are some of its principal provisions:

Article 1—Palestine, the homeland of the Palestinian Arab people, is an inseparable part of the greater Arab homeland, and the Palestinian people are a part of the Arab Nation.

Article 2—Palestine, within the frontiers that existed under the British Mandate, is an indivisible territorial unit.

Article 3—The Palestinian Arab people alone have legitimate rights to their homeland, and shall exercise the right of self-determination after the liberation of their homeland, in keeping with their wishes and entirely at their own accord.

Article 4—The Palestinian identity is an authentic, intrinsic and indissoluble quality that is transmitted from father to son. Neither the Zionist occupation nor the dispersal of the Palestinian Arab people as a result of the afflictions they have suffered can efface the Palestinian identity.

Article 5—Palestinians are Arab citizens who were normally resident in Palestine until 1947. This includes both those who were forced to leave or who stayed in Palestine. Anyone born to a Palestinian father after that date, whether inside or outside Palestine, is a Palestinian.

Article 6—Jews who were normally resident in Palestine up to the beginning of the Zionist invasion are Palestinians.*

Affiliated Resistance Organizations

The Palestine Liberation Organization serves as umbrella organization for eight guerrilla groups.**

(continued from page 195)

On November 30, 1973, the General Assembly, in Resolution 3070 (XXVIII), reaffirmed the right of a "people's struggle for liberation . . . including armed struggle," and condemned "all governments which do not recognize the right to self-determination and independence of peoples . . . including the Palestinian people."

*The contents of this article were interpreted by the Zionist-Israeli propaganda machine—and constantly quoted to confuse its true meaning—to mean that all Jews who entered Palestine after 1917 must leave the country including their off-spring. This is not so.

What the Article actually means is that Jews who were in Palestine prior to 1917 are regarded as Palestinian citizens, and the status of those who entered the country after the issue of the Balfour Declaration to date, is covered by the statement made by Yasir Arafat, chairman of the Palestine Liberation Organization, before the UN General Assembly on November 13, 1974, namely, that the Palestine of tomorrow includes "all Jews now living in Palestine who choose to live with us in peace and without discrimination," provided that they "turn away from the illusory promises made to them by Zionist ideology and Israeli leadership."

**The eight guerrilla groups which make up the membership of the Palestine Liberation Organization, are:
El-Fateh—Represented by Yasir Arafat.
The Democratic Front for the Liberation of Palestine—Represented by Nayef Hawatmeh.
The Popular Front for the Liberation of Palestine—Led by Dr. George Habash.
The Popular Front for the Liberation of Palestine, General Command—Represented by

Control over the policy, strategy and administration of the Palestine Liberation Organization is guided by four branches, namely:

1. *Palestine National Council*—Consisting of more than 500 members representing every walk of Palestinian life in areas where Palestinians are known to exist.

2. *Palestine Central Council*—Consisting of a 55-member policy-making body selected by the National Council from among its members to function while it is in recess.

3. *Executive Committee*—Consisting of 15 members representing *El-Fateh* and the various other guerrilla groups which adhere to the laid down policies. Membership is elected by the legislative arm of the Palestine Liberation Organization.

4. *Palestine Liberation Army*—This serves as the regular army of the Palestine Liberation Organization. The Army is headed by the Chairman of the Executive Committee as commander-in-chief.

P.L.O. Joins United Nations

On October 14, 1974, the UN General Assembly, by an overwhelming majority vote of 105 in favor, with four against (United States, Israel, Bolivia, and the Dominican Republic), and 20 abstentions, adopted the following 71-nation co-sponsored resolution:

"*Considering* that the Palestinian people is the principal party to the question of Palestine,

Invites the Palestine Liberation Organization, the representative of the Palestinian People, to participate in the deliberations of the General Assembly on the question of Palestine in plenary meetings."[4]

On November 13, 1974, Yasir Arafat, Chairman of the Palestine Liberation Organization, and representative of the Palestinian people, appeared before the General Assembly, was accorded the respect due to a head of state, and made a statement on behalf of the Palestinian people. The full text of his speech is found in the records of the General Assembly for 1974.

Mr. Arafat concluded his speech with an offer to the Jews of co-existence, couched in the following words:

"In my formal capacity as chairman of the Palestine Liberation Organization, and as leader of the Palestinian revolution, I proclaim before you that when we speak of our common hopes for the Palestine of tomorrow, we include in our perspective *all* Jews now living in Palestine who choose to live with us in peace and without discrimination.

In my formal capacity as chairman of the Palestine Liberation Organization, and leader of the Palestinian revolution, I call upon

---

Ahmad Jabreel.
The Arab Liberation Front—Led by Abdul Rahim Ahmad
The Palestine Liberation Front—Led by Abul 'Abbas.
The Palestinian Popular Front—Led by Dr. Samir Ghosheh.
As-Saiqa—Represented by Zuheir Mohseh.

Jews, one by one, to turn away from the illusory promises made to them by Zionist ideology and Israeli leadership. Those offer the Jews perpetual bloodshed, endless war and continuous thralldom.

We invite them to emerge from their moral isolation into a more open realm of free choice, far from their present leadership's efforts to implant in them a Massada complex.

We offer them the most generous solution that we might live together in a framework of just peace in our democratic Palestine.

In my formal capacity as chairman of the Palestine Liberation Organization, I announce here that we do not wish the shedding of one drop of either Arab or Jewish blood; neither do we delight in the continuation of killing, which would end once a just peace, based on our people's rights, hopes and aspirations is finally established."

To the membership of the General Assembly, he said: "Today, I have come bearing an olive branch and a freedom-fighter's gun. Do not let the olive branch fall from my hand. I repeat: Do not let the olive branch fall from my hand."[5]

On November 25, 1974, the General Assembly adopted a resolution by a vote of 95 in favor, 17 against (which included the United States and Israel), and 19 abstentions, granting the Palestine Liberation Organization observer status with the right "to participate in the sessions and the work of the General Assembly; in the sessions and the work of all international conferences convened under the auspices of the General Assembly; and in the sessions and the work of all international conferences convened under the auspices of other organs of the United Nations."[6]

Resolutions of the Palestine National Council (1979)

The fourteenth session of the National Council that was held in Damascus, Syria, between January 15 and 22, 1979, reaffirmed "the resolutions of the political declaration stressing the necessity of representing all the Palestinian resistance organizations and all national Palestinian forces in the P.L.O. institutions, including the Central Council and the Executive Committee. In addition:

"It condemned internal fighting and divisions within the Palestinian revolution and condemned any faction that resorts to violence to settle differences and calls for punishment of those responsible;

The Palestine National Council calls upon all Palestinian resistance organizations to adopt a political and educational program that would strengthen national unity among the masses on the basis of the political program, and on the basis of democratic dialogue without any accusations or condemnations: In accordance with the principles of the political program concerning a democratic front, all P.L.O. institutions, offices and popular organizations must be based on this principle and open to proportional representation."

The National Unity Program, presented to the council by P.L.O. Chairman of the Executive Committee, Yasir Arafat, was unanimously approved as follows:

On the Palestinian Level

1. To hold fast to the inalienable national rights of our people in their homeland, Palestine, including their right to return, their right to self-determination without any external intereference, and their unconditional right to establish an independent state on their national soil.

2. To defend the P.L.O. and to confirm it as the sole legitimate representative of our people, the leader of their national struggle, and their spokesman in all Arab and international forums.

3. To affirm our firm determination to pursue and escalate armed struggle and all forms of political and popular struggle, particularly inside the occupied territories.

4. To stress that the Palestine cause is at the core and essence of the Arab-Israeli conflict, and to reject all resolutions, agreements, and settlements which do not recognize, or which undermine, our people's rights in their homeland, including their right of return, to self-determination and to establish their independent national state. We declare our absolute rejection of UN Security Council resolution 242.

5. To reject and confront the self-rule plan in the occupied homeland, which consolidates Zionist settler colonialism in our land, denies the rights of our people, and denies our people's goal of national independence.

6. To reaffirm the unity of the Palestinian Arab people inside and outside the occupied homeland, and their unified representation within the P.L.O.; to confront all plans and attempts to partition our people and to by-pass the P.L.O. and to strive to support the struggle of our people under occupation and to consolidate their unity and steadfastness.

7. To support the Palestinian National Front in the occupied territories as an inseparable part of the P.L.O., and to provide it with all means of political and financial support that would enable it to mobilize the masses to confront the Zionist occupation and its plans.

8. To affirm the attachment to Palestine as the historic homeland of the Palestinian people for which there is no alternative; to fight all plans for resettlement or for the creation of an alternative homeland put forward by the Zionist-imperialist enemy.

On the Arab Level

1. To confirm that the confrontation and resistance to the Camp David Accords is the responsibility of the Arab masses and their national and progressive forces.

2. To support and consolidate the Confrontation and Steadfastness Front and to expand it on the basis of resistance to the imperialist Zionist conspiracy; to affirm our objective of liberating all Arab and Palestinian occupied land and of fulfilling the inalienable national rights of the Palestinian people; to provide all possible popular and material support to the Steadfastness and Confrontation Front.

3. The P.L.O. calls upon all national and progressive parties, movements and forces in the Arab world to back and to offer all forms of popular and material support to the Steadfastness and Confrontation Front.

4. (a) The P.L.O. stresses that it firmly abides by the unity, Arabism and independence of Lebanon, and reasserts its respect for Lebanese sovereignty and its commitment to the Cairo Agreement;

(b) The P.L.O. highly values the role which the Lebanese people and their national and progressive forces have played, and continue to play, in support and in defence of the struggle of the Palestinian people.

5. (a) The P.L.O. reaffirms the special nature of the relations which bind the Palestinian and Jordanian peoples, and expresses its concern for maintaining this cohesion between the two fraternal peoples.

(b) The P.L.O. declares its attachment to the Rabat and Algiers Arab Summit resolution which confirms that the P.L.O. is the sole legitimate representative of the Palestinian people, and confirms our people's right to establish an independent national state.

6. The P.L.O. stresses its right to struggle on the Arab and international level via any Arab territory for the liberation of Palestine.

7. The P.L.O. declares that its relations with any Arab regime, are defined by these regimes' commitment to the Algiers and Rabat resolutions and by their rejection of the Camp David Accords.

8. The P.L.O. calls upon all the Arab nationalist forces and on all nationalist and friendly regimes to support the Egyptian people and their national movement to enable them to confront Sadat's conspiracy.

On the International Level

1. The role which the United States is playing against our Palestinian people and their national struggle, and against the Arab national liberation movements and their goals, represents a blatant aggression against our people and their national cause. The P.L.O., together with all the factions of the Arab liberation movement and forces, and with the nationalist and progressive regimes, declares its determination to resist U.S. policy, objectives and practices in the area.

2. The P.L.O. confirms the importance of its alliances with the socialist states led by the U.S.S.R., as a national necessity in confronting U.S.—Israeli conspiracies against the Palestine cause and the Arab liberation movement and its achievements.

3. The P.L.O. stresses the importance of consolidating its ties and co-operation with the friendly non-aligned Islamic and African states, which support the P.L.O. and its struggle for the realization of Palestinian national rights of return, self-determination, and establishing an independent national state.

4. The P.L.O., as a national liberation movement, declares its support for all national liberation movements in the world, particularly in Namibia and South Africa, and expresses its intentions of developing its relations with these movements, affirming that the struggle against imperialism, Zionism and racism is a common cause.

5. The P.L.O. declares its adherence to the achievements of Palestinian struggle on the international level, including the international recognition of the P.L.O. and the national rights of the Palestinian people in their homeland, Palestine. These achievements have materialized in UN resolutions since 1974, especially resolutions 3236 and 3237 that confirm

the right of the P.L.O. to participate in all meetings and conferences on the Palestine issue, and consider such agreements or discussions null and void in the absence of the P.L.O.

On the Organizational Level

1. All the Palestinian revolution's factions and the Palestinian forces participate in the P.L.O.'s institutions, primarily the National Council, the Central Council, and the Executive Committee, in accordance with the principles of democracy and fraternal relations.
2. The Palestinian leadership is a collective one. Decision-making is the responsibility of all, in its adoption and implementation, on the basis of democracy and the commitment of the minority to the majority's decision, according to the political and organizational program and to the resolutions of the National Council.
3. Full guarantee of the exercise by the P.L.O.'s departments, institutions and apparatuses of their prerogatives, according to their functions, as stipulated by the P.L.O.'s internal code. The Executive Committee forms specialized councils on a *frontal* basis, to put forth plans and supervises their execution by the P.L.O.'s institutions, especially in the military, informational, and finance fields.
4. The Executive Committee and the Central Council are to be formed according to what is agreed and as stipulated by the internal code and the National Council resolutions.[7]

Functions of the Palestine Liberation Organization

It is generally—but erroneously—assumed that the functions of the Palestine Liberation Organization are confined to political and military matters. The Palestine Liberation Organization is as well organized as is humanly possible under the conditions in which the Palestinians live, scattered as they are throughout the Arab world and abroad. Today, the diaspora Palestinians have a complex of institutions in the political, social, cultural, economic, medical and trade union realms about which little is known. There has been a parallel effort, intensified after 1982, to develop these national institutions inside occupied Palestine, in the West Bank and Gaza. Briefly, there are:[8]

1. *Trade Unions*—Palestinian trade unions are democratic organizations, in which officials are elected by the membership. All Palestinian trade unions are linked to the Palestine Liberation Organization in various ways. The unions are represented by delegates in the Palestine National Council, and are also engaged in day-to-day cooperation with the Palestine Liberation Organization. The P.L.O.'s department for popular organizations, whose staff includes representatives of the unions, deals with the regular problems encountered by Palestinian workers and professionals. The P.L.O. offers help to these unions in fields ranging from finance to intercession with Arab governments on behalf of the right of the Palestinian workers to work in Arab countries where they are refugees without work permits. In the West Bank and Gaza, as well as inside Israel, the Palestinian unions provide the only

protection for Palestinian workers against the harsh and discriminatory military laws governing labor relations between Palestinian workers and Israeli Jewish owners.

2. *Medical Services*—The major institution affiliated with the P.L.O. is the Palestine Red Crescent Society (PRCS)—which is equivalent to the Red Cross Societies in western countries—established in 1969. Its president was the delegate who signed the Agreements of the International Red Cross and the Geneva Conventions on behalf of the Palestine Liberation Organization.

The P.R.C.S. has participated in several international conferences and has branches in the occupied territories, almost all Arab countries, and supporting societies in Sweden, France, Switzerland, Britain and the United States.

The P.R.C.S. renders medical service to the Palestinian community —civilian and commando alike. Along with its extensive work in the West Bank and Gaza, it operates at present seven hospitals in Syria, Lebanon and Egypt, and several clinics in the border villages of South Lebanon. Each hospital has an operating room, X-ray section, laboratory, out-patient clinic and an emergency room. The society also has four medical complexes in Syria and Lebanon, each with an out-patient clinic, dental clinic, laboratory, pharmacy and dressing room. It has organized over 25 popular clinics in Syria, Lebanon, Egypt, and the Sudan. Each refugee camp in Syria and Lebanon has at least one of these. In the villages, camps, and towns of the West Bank and Gaza, the P.R.C.S., along with several other P.L.O.-related medical committees, provides general as well as emergency care for Palestinians living under occupation. Their work includes sending mobile clinics to isolated villages that have no other access to medical or public health services.

3. *Education*—The Palestine Liberation Organization has organized an educational program for Palestinian students in Kuwait. This program was necessitated by the exceptionally large number of Palestinians of school age who are resident there as a result of the large influx of Palestinians into Kuwait that followed the 1967 war.

The program provides educational facilities for 38% of school-age Palestinian children in Kuwait. The P.L.O. Planning Center has also an educational section that has evolved a philosophy of Palestinian education and designed educational material for Palestinian children. It organizes summer programs and courses for Palestinian teachers, and has been building model kindergartens.

4. *Welfare Services*—The P.L.O. assumes responsibility for the welfare of the children of commandos killed in action. The first of the organizations dedicated to this end, the Association of Workshops for the Children of Palestinian Martyrs, was established by *El-Fateh* in January 1970. It offers vocational training for orphans or children from fatherless families, but has the additional economic purpose of producing readymade clothes, furniture and embroidery for the purpose of refugee camps at prices consistent with the very low income of these camps.

5. *Industrial Training*—Under the banner of Samed (meaning resolute, steadfast),—the P.L.O. has established institutions for textiles, carpentry, embroidery, and other arts and crafts, in which Arab youth of

both genders but mostly Palestinians are trained. The produce is sold in the Arab markets and abroad with a marginal profit to cover expenses.

6. *Research Center*—The Palestinian Research Center, established in 1964, had an extensive library on the Palestine problem, and has published over 300 studies by prominent writers. Its publications are distributed throughout the Arab world, and are available for distribution in almost all other countries.

It published an Arabic intellectual monthly Journal, known as '*Shu-oon Filastiniya*' (Palestinian Affairs). The center's contribution to a better understanding of the Palestine problem has been considerable. The Center's library came under heavy assault during Israel's siege of Beirut in 1982. While some of the collection was moved out in time to be saved, large parts of the archives were destroyed. Publication of the Journal has not yet resumed.

7. *Information Offices*—The Palestine Liberation Organization has its own information offices or members attached to the information services of the League of Arab States, throughout the world. They supply the public with information on the Palestine problem, attend conferences which affect the Palestine issue, give speeches and appear on television and radio, and write letters to the press from time to time. Since the Palestinian diplomatic initiative of 1988 began, and especially since the Declaration of an independent State of Palestine, many of these offices have been accorded various levels of diplomatic status. In countries around the world where this is the case, P.L.O. representatives carry out traditional diplomatic tasks as well as their continuing educational work.

8. *The National Fund*—The funds necessary for the running of the operations of the Palestine Liberation Organization and its branches, are derived mostly from some of the Arab governments. Further funds come from: (1) a fixed tax levied by certain Arab governments on Palestinians who live and work in their countries: (2) loans and contributions from friendly nations and Arab peoples; (3) any additional source approved by the National Council.

The Palestine National Fund is in charge of all monies received, and finances the Palestine Liberation Organization and its branches according to an annual budget, prepared by the Executive Committee and approved by the National Council. It develops the fund's revenues, and supervises the expenditures of the Palestine Liberation Organization and its organs.

Perhaps the most striking feature of the Palestine Liberation Organization since its creation in 1964, has been its ability to survive and develop in the face of extreme obstacles, trials and tribulations, both in the Middle East and abroad. It is of particular significance that the PLO retains its ability not only to organize the national life of diaspora Palestinians throughout the world, but as well to take responsibility for reflecting, in the international arena, the political gains of those Palestinians resisting Israel's continued occupation. The conviction of the Palestinian people in the justice of its cause and the readiness of its youth to make the supreme sacrifice, has strengthened the determination of the organization to hold up the banner of freedom and to fight the sacred battle until victory is achieved.

This belief and determination is being implanted in the generations of the future, and will be found in the oath with which the refugees' school-day begins as the children stand to attention and recite:

Palestine is our country,
Our aim is to return.
Death does not frighten us.
Palestine is ours,
We shall never forget her.
Another homeland we shall never accept!
Our Palestine, witness O God and History,
We promise to shed our blood for you![9]

XVII   The Arab Boycott of Israel

Zionist Pressures

The only action the Arab States were capable of taking against the Israelis in the first instance for their expulsion and dispossession of the Palestinian people and the occupation of territory beyond that allotted to the Jewish state under the Partition Resolution of 1947, was to impose an economic boycott against the state of Israel and such foreign companies and firms that support the Jewish state, until such time as the Israelis redress the wrong they have committed against the Palestinian people and come to terms with their Arab neighbors. The boycott has been in place since 1948.

Every effort is being made by Israel and its Zionist supporters to discredit the boycott as being discriminatory on religious grounds. Accusations of a religious or racial nature are frowned upon in western countries, and the Israeli propaganda machine hopes that through its supporters in the west, the Zionists will be able to force the Arab states to lift the boycott against Israel.

Consequently, from time to time, campaigns are launched in the capitals of the western world that distort the issue and mislead the public in order to undermine the economic relations between foreign companies and the Arab markets, and to disrupt friendly relations between the Arab states and other countries.

These campaigns have spread the myth that the Arab boycott is directed against Jewish companies and companies that have Jews on their boards of directors or a substantial number of Jews in their employ; and that the boycott was anti-Semitic in character, applied purely on emotional and prejudicial grounds.

The Arabs have remained determined to proceed undeterred in their application of the rules governing the boycott of Israel as one of the means to protect their interests and security.

The Arabs realize that, for their boycott against Israel to succeed, they must include world Zionism which provides the state of Israel with the moral, political and financial support it needs to wage war against the Arabs; to consolidate its occupation of Arab homes, lands and territories; and encourages it in its expansionist-racist policies. The Zionists also back Israeli intransigence and defiance of the provisions of the UN Charter, the Universal Declaration of Human Rights, and the numerous resolutions of the United Nations that deal with withdrawal from occupied Arab territories, and the restoration of the political and human rights of the Palestinian people. So, the Arabs regard the international Zionist movement, for all intents and purposes, as an enemy that must be boycotted on all levels if the economc isolation of the State of Israel is to succeed.

However, the Arab states do not wish their own relations with foreign governments and companies to be impaired, and therefore, they have officially and repeatedly affirmed that they will not discriminate against Jewish individuals or firms which respect the Arab boycott of Israel. A statement issued by the General Union of the Arab Chambers of Commerce, Industry, and Agriculture, reaffirms this position in the following words:

> "The Arab boycott is directed against Israel, but not against the Jewish people. Jewish firms outside Israel receive from the Arabs the same treatment as non-Jewish firms. There is no discrimination. Any firm, irrespective of the creed or race of its owners, share-holders, or managers, will be able to deal with the Arab countries so long as it does not breach the regulations of the Arab boycott of Israel."

In an article under the title of "Boycott—A Two-Edged, Flexible and Powerful Weapon," the *Middle East Economic Digest* stated:

> "Israel's most persistent claim is that the boycott is anti-Jewish, and not just anti-Zionist. This particular point has been strongly and justifiably denied by the Boycott Office. Its Commissioner-General Mohammad Mahgoub, said last February: 'We don't differentiate between one race or nationality and the other. A company is black-listed because it plays a role in helping Israel's economic, industrial or military efforts . . .
>
> To prove my point, there are many firms owned by Jews that operate freely in the Arab world, while there are others owned by Moslems and Christians that are black-listed because they deal with Israel'."[1]

In confirmation of the accuracy of the above two statements, it should be noted that the non-Jewish Ford Motor Company is on the Arab boycott list because it has an assembly plant in Israel; while the Jewish firm that manufactures Levi's jeans sells its products freely throughout the Arab world.

Principles of the Arab Boycott Regulations.[2]

The Arab boycott operates on two levels, namely:

1. Direct Arab-Israeli contact is absolutely forbidden. The boycott can be described as a political-economic-social blockade of the Jewish state and will be lifted only if and when peace is restored in the area;

2. The second form of the boycott is of an international character and applies to the following categories:
   — Firms that have branches in Israel.
   — Firms that have assembly plants in Israel.
   — Firms that have agencies or main offices in Israel for their Middle East operations.
   — Firms that give patents, trade marks, copyrights, etc. to Israeli companies.
   — Firms (and private or public organizations) that purchase shares in Israeli companies or factories.
   — Firms that purchase parts made in branches located in Israel.
   — Technical or consultant firms that offer their services to Israel.
   — Airplanes that fly to Israel may not continue into Arab airspace.
   — Foreign companies that are owned by known active Zionists.
   — Foreign companies that are wholly or partially owned by Israeli nationals.
   — Foreign firms that act as agents for Israeli companies or products.
   — Foreign firms that own part of an Israeli company.
   — Foreign companies whose officers or directors are Israeli nationals, or whose managers are members of a joint foreign-Israeli chamber of commerce.
   — Subsidiaries or branches of boycotted firms.

It will be noted from the above that at no time does the word Jew appear in the Arab Boycott of Israel Rules; and where reference is made to officers, directors, or managers, it means Israeli nationals or active Zionists, not Jews.

Furthermore, the Rules are not directed against legitimate foreign investors who wish to trade with the Arab markets, be they Jews or gentiles. This was made clear in a statement published by the League of Arab States in January 1976 at the height of Zionist pressure upon the U.S. government to legislate against the Arab boycott. The statement read:

"All the Arabs are saying is that it is not in their national interest to trade—directly or indirectly—with the state of Israel that has waged war against them; and that Arab organizations and companies should not buy, sell to, or otherwise deal with any companies that are involved in the Israeli economy through investment or other tangible support. Hence, any company has the option of choosing, on the basis of its own interest, between doing business in the Arab markets, or establishing an Israeli connection."[3]

The criticism raised against the involvement of third-country organizations and individuals in the Arab boycott, ignores present-day economic realities and the close link between economic, technological and military capabilities. We live in an increasingly inter-dependent world in which multi-national firms conduct business across many national boundaries, producing component parts in subsidiaries located in different parts of the world, and then putting them together in a final product. The origin of the components of any product is not usually put on the label, but such flow of component parts and semi-finished products is a common occurrence in international trade relations and production policies. Hence, a primary boycott has to be supplemented by a secondary one if it is to achieve the objective it was started to achieve; and here is where the subsidiary company comes in.

Furthermore, a company that invests in the Israeli economy, provides Israel with technical assistance, or buys Israeli-made products for its own use or distribution in other markets, is indirectly contributing to Israel's war-making capacity. Such a company is relieving the Israeli govenment of the responsibility of solving its people's economic problems; thus allowing it to concentrate its efforts and resources on strengthening its armed forces, to hold on to occupied Arab lands, and to resist international pressures for a just and equitable solution to the Palestine problem.

Thus, it should be borne in mind that, even though companies in third countries have to be aware of—and abide by—the requirements of the Arab boycott if they are interested in doing business in the Arab world, the boycott itself is not aimed at third-countries or third-country companies.

Boycott Precedents

Economic weapons, such as blockades, embargoes, and boycotts have been used by many nations in the past and are still being used by a number of nations at the present time. Sovereign nations have always felt that they have the right to use their economic resources and capabilities in defence of their vital interests.

The Arab boycott of Israel is not novel; and its principles are no more severe than those imposed by the Zionists themselves against the people of Palestine between 1920 and 1948; by the Allied blockade and embargo against Germany in two world wars; by American and world Jewry against Nazi Germany in 1933; by the trade restrictions established by the United Nations against South Africa's apartheid policies; and there has recently been talk of imposing boycotts and sanctions against governments that violate the human rights of their citizens.

The *first* Jewish boycott imposed against the Palestinian Arabs as found in the Constitution of the Jewish Agency for Palestine was during the period of the Mandate. The constitution provided: "Land is to be acquired as Jewish property, the title to the lands acquired is to be taken in the name of the Jewish National Fund to the end of that the same shall be held as the inalienable property of the Jewish people."

On the question of labor, the constitution provided: "In all works or undertakings carried out or furthered by the agency, it shall be deemed to be, as a matter of principle, that Jewish labor shall be employed."

Both these provisions were described by Sir John Hope-Simpson, who was invited to Palestine by the British Mandatory in 1930 to look into the Arab grievances, as resulting "in land purchased from Arabs becoming extraterritorialized and ceases to be land from which the Arab can gain any advantage now or in the future." In regard to labor, Sir John commented: "The principle of the persistent and deliberate boycott of Arab labor in the Zionist colonies is not only contrary to Article 6 of the Mandate, but it is, in addition, a constant and increasing source of danger to the country."[4]

The *second* boycott was the global boycott launched by American and world Jewry against Germany hardly six months after the Nazi Party had come into power on January 30, 1933. Samuel Untermeyer, a Zionist with extensive Wall Street backing in New York financial interests, went on the air on WABC Radio on August 6, 1933, and made a plea for the boycott of German goods and services. Excerpts from his statement follow:

"Our campaign is twofold—defensive and constructive.

On the defensive side will be the economic boycott against all German goods, shipping and service.

On the constructive side will be an appeal to the League of Nations to construe and enforce the labor union provision of the Versailles Treaty and the written promise made by Germany, while the Treaty was under negotiation, to protect its minorities, which have been flagrantly violated by its defranchisement and persecution of the German Jews.

"What we are proposing and have already gone far towards doing, is to prosecute a purely defensive economic boycott that will undermine the Hitler regime and bring the German people to their senses, by destroying their export trade on which their very existence depends.

"They have flaunted and persisted in flaunting and defying world opinion. We propose to, and are organizing world opinion to express itself in the only way Germany can be made to understand. Hitler and his mob will not permit their people to know how they are regarded by the outside world. We shall force them to learn in the only way open to us . . . The object-lesson we are determined to teach them is so priceless to all humanity, that we dare not fail.

"Each of you, Jew and gentile alike, who has not already enlisted in this sacred war, should do so now and here. It is not sufficient that you buy no goods made in Germany, you must refuse to deal with any merchant or shop-keeper who sells any German-made goods or who patronizes German ships or shipping . . .

"In conclusion, permit me again to thank you for this heartening reception, and to assure you that, with your support and that of our millions of non-Jewish friends, we will drive the last nail in the coffin of bigotry and fanaticism that has dared raise its ugly head to slander, belie and disgrace twentieth century civilizations."[5]

The *third* boycott was that launched by American and Canadian Jews in 1975–1976 against Mexican tourist resorts because the Mexican representative to the United Nations voted in favor of the General Assembly Resolution which "determines that Zionism is a form of racism and racial discrimination." The boycott was so effective, costing Mexico the loss of millions of dollars, that the Mexican Government was compelled to capitulate and to make amends said to be to the satisfaction of the Israeli government before the boycott was lifted.

Anti-Boycott Legislation

Zionist pressure in the United States was such that the government was obliged to enact certain anti-boycott legislation to appease the Zionist lobby, but when the unique law came into operation, it was described as having little, if any, effect on the boycott situation.

Similar pressure was being brought on the Canadian government, but Prime Minister Pierre Trudeau retorted:

> "The government must not be hypocritical because Canada has its own boycotts. Trade with Rhodesia is [sic] forbidden, as is trade in strategic goods with communist countries. The Arab boycott is similar to United States boycotts of Cuba and China. The United States orders its Canadian subsidiaries not to trade with Cuba."[6]

Having failed to get its federal government to follow the example of the U.S. government, the Canadian Zionist lobby turned its attention to the Province of Ontario. Premier William Davis, returning from a trip to Israel where he was lavishly entertained, was prepared to champion the Israeli cause in the Ontario Parliament. A bill was introduced, passed two readings, but was then referred to the Justice Committee for further consideration. The author was among those who appeared before the committee to point out the deficiencies of such an enactment, which could only hurt Canada whose trade deficit with the Arab world in 1977 was close to $1-billion. The bill was described as being like one who cuts off his nose to spite his face. Canada, it was pointed out by more than one speaker, needs the Arab world much more than the Arab world needs Canada, for there is nothing the Arab world needs that cannot be obtained from another country. Notwithstanding, the bill was enacted into law in October 1978.

XVIII Israeli Policy of Expansion

Zionist Goals in Palestine

On the face of it, Zionism began with the seemingly innocuous objective of securing a refuge for the persecuted Jews of Europe. But when it obtained a foothold in Palestine through the Balfour Declaration of 1917, it began to clamor for statehood, and when it achieved this statehood, it began to plan for expansion.

The limits of so-called *Eretz Israel*, as loosely defined by the Zionist movement, coincide with the ancient biblical and historical boundaries of the so-called Promised Land, namely from the Nile to the Euphrates—to include the whole of Palestine, Jordan, southern Lebanon, and parts of Syria and Iraq as well as a part of Saudi Arabia.

Each time the Arabs draw attention to the dangers to Arab territories of Israeli policies of expansion, they are met with an emphatic denial of any such intention. Israel belittles the Arab accusation as a mere illusion and claims that all the Israelis now wish, is to live in peace in their own homes and on their own lands. Even when attention is drawn to the Israeli occupations that occurred between 1948 and 1967, they argue that these took place as a result of the Arab attacks on the Jewish state.

The Palestinian Arabs never had any doubts about Zionist intentions. They were always aware that these included—as a first step—the establishment of a Jewish state to be followed by territorial expansions at times of their own choosing. British officials in Palestine during the period of the Mandate also saw this very clearly and warned the Arab inhabitants and their own government. Even before the Mandate over Palestine was announced, the British Chief Military Administrator in Palestine saw fit to report to his goverment that the Zionists "appear bent on committing the temporary Military Administration to a partialist policy before the issue of the Mandate. It is manifestly impossible," the report said, "to please partisans who officially claim nothing more than a national home but in reality will be satisfied with nothing less than a Jewish state."[1]

Commenting on this report Michel Ionides, who spent many years in the Middle East in the services of the Trans-Jordan and Iraqi governments, said: "The Arabs were up against stiff odds. Officially, a Jewish state was not intended. The British government had said so and the Zionists did nothing to remove that belief. The Arabs saw the tongue in the Zionist cheek, the British did not."[2]

While the Zionist movement set its eye steadily on Palestine as the State of the Jews (*Der Judenstaat*, as Theodor Herzl, the father of Zionism, called it in his booklet by the same title published in 1896), it allowed flexibility in the drawing up of the frontiers of the proposed state. Thus, according to Herzl, "the northern frontier is to be the mountains facing Cappodocia [in Turkey]; the southern, the Suez Canal. Our slogan shall be—The Palestine of David and Solomon."[3]

On another occasion, the area was described as from the Brook (presumably meaning the Nile), to the Euphrates.[4] On October 29, 1899, Davis Triestsch wrote to Theodor Herzl: "I would suggest to you to come round in time to the greater Palestine program before it is too late . . . The Basel Program must contain the words 'great Palestine' or 'Palestine and its neighboring lands' otherwise it's nonsense. You do not get the ten million Jews into a land of 25,000 kilometres."[5]

In 1919, the Zionist Delegation to the Paris Peace Conference circulated a plan of a Zionist state, the boundaries of which appear to have been narrowed down, as follows:

"The boundaries of Palestine shall follow the general lines set out below:

Starting on the north at a point on the Mediterranean Sea in the vicinity of Sidon and following the watersheds of the foothills of the Lebanon as far as Jisr El-Kara'on, thence to El-Bire, following the dividing line between the two basins of the Wadi El-Korn and the Wadi Et-Teim, thence in a southerly direction following the dividing line between the eastern and western slopes of the Hermon, to the vicinity west of Beit Jenn, thence eastward following the northern watersheds of the Nahr Muganiye, close to and west of the Hejaz railway.

In the east, a line close to and east of the Hejaz railway terminating in the Gulf of Aqaba.

In the south, a frontier to be agreed upon with the Egyptian government. (*Note*: It has been indicated that the southern border would extend from El-Arish in northern Sinai to Aqaba in the south).

In the west, the Mediterranean Sea."*[6]

---

*The Zionist demands comprise, in current terms:
  (a) The whole of Mandated Palestine;
  (b) Southern Lebanon, including the towns of Tyre and Sidon, the headwaters of the River Jordan on Mount Hermon, and the southern portion of the Litani River;

An explanatory note then followed, stating: "The boundaries above outlined are what we consider essential for the necessary economic foundation of the country. Palestine must have its natural outlets to the sea and the control of its rivers and their headwaters. The boundaries are sketched with the general economic needs and historic traditions of the country in mind, factors that necessarily must also be considered by the Special Commission in fixing the definite boundary lines. This commission will bear in mind that it is highly desirable, in the interests of economical administration, that the geographical area of Palestine should be as large as possible so that it may eventually contain a large and thriving population which could more easily bear the burdens of modern civilized government than a small country with a necessary limitation of inhabitants."

The explanatory note went on to say: "The economic life of Palestine, like that of every other semi-arid country, depends on the available water supply. It is, therefore, of vital importance, not only to secure all water resources already feeding the country, but also to be able to conserve and control them at their sources. The Hermon is Palestine's real 'Father of Waters,' and cannot be severed from it without striking at the very root of its economic life . . . The fertile plains east of the Jordan, since the earliest biblical times, have been linked economically and politically with the land west of the Jordan . . . It could now serve admirably for colonization on a large scale."[7]

In May 1942, a conference of American European and Palestinian Zionists was held at the Biltmore Hotel, New York, under the sponsorship of an Emergency Committee for Zionist Affairs. The participants expressed their desire to insist on a full implementation of the Basel Program.[8] On May 11, 1942, the conference adopted a set of resolutions known collectively as the Biltmore Program. In particular, they called for:

"The immediate establishment in Palestine of a Jewish Commonwealth as an integral part of the new democratic world;
The rejection of the White Paper of 1939;[9]
Unrestricted Jewish immigration and settlement in Palestine;
The formation and recognition of a Jewish military force under its own flag."[10]

In October 1942, the Zionist Organization of America and Hadassah adopted the Biltmore Program, as did subsequently the Mizrahi and Labor groups in Palestine, though the Labor Organization did not rule out the possibility of bi-nationalism.[11] Then on November 6, 1942, the General Council of the World Zionist Organization endorsed the program, stamping it as the official policy of Zionism at large, so helping to

---

(c) Syria—The Golan Heights, including the town of Kuneitra, the River Yarmuk, and El-Himmeh Hot Springs;
(d) Jordan—The whole of the Jordan Valley, the Dead Sea, and the eastern highlands up to the outskirts of Amman, thence running southwards along the Hejaz railway to the Gulf of Aqaba—Leaving Jordan with no access to the sea;
(e) Egypt—From El-Arish on the Mediterranean Sea, in a straight southerly direction to the Gulf of Aqaba.

ZIONIST PROPOSALS FOR A "JEWISH STATE"
As submitted to the Paris Peace Conference 1919

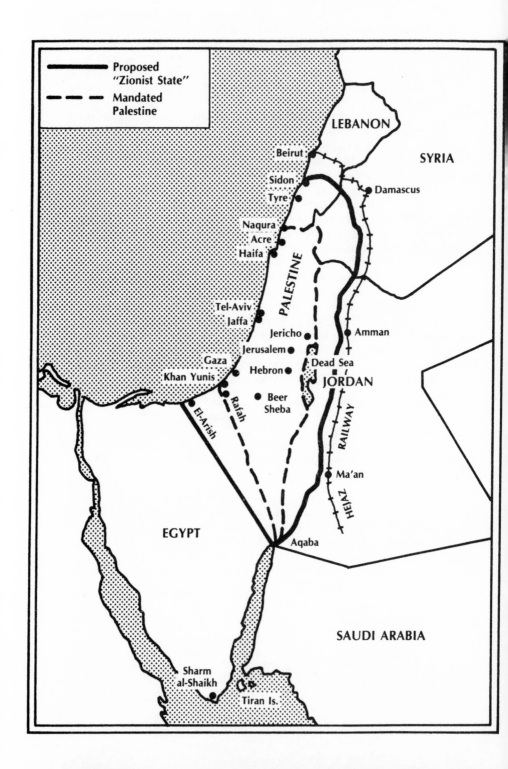

build up a climate in which Zionist statehood would be acceptable to the world.[12]

On May 3, 1943, General Patrick J. Hurley, personal representative of President Roosevelt in the Middle East, reported to the President that "The Zionist organization in Palestine has indicated its commitment to an enlarged program for:

1. a sovereign Jewish state that would embrace Palestine and probably eventually Transjordan;

2. an eventual transfer of the Arab population from Palestine to Iraq; and

3. Jewish leadership for the whole Middle East in the fields of economic development and control."[13]

Testimony of Zionist intentions of seizure of Palestine and beyond is contained in an account given by Geoffrey J. Morton, who spent many years in Palestine as Assistant Superintendent of Police and was credited with ending the activities of Zionist terrorist leader Stern. Morton had this to say:

> "I knew one missionary . . who in 1942 accepted an invitation to lecture on her experiences (with mass evacuations) to a *soi-disant* cultural organization in Jerusalem.
>
> It was arranged that she should be conveyed by car to the scene of the meeting. To her surprise, she was blindfolded for the journey and never knew where she was taken.
>
> Her audience turned out to be a gathering of obviously important people in the Jewish world who questioned her in detail about the problems involved in mass evacuation of the population. They made no bones about wanting to evict the Arab population when the British withdrew . . .
>
> At this meeting, she was shown a map of the future Jewish empire. It did not include Egypt, but it did include the whole of Palestine, Jordan, Syria, the Lebanon, and strangely enough, Cyprus."[14]

The 1967 occupation of the Sinai Peninsula and the Gaza Strip, the Golan Heights, the West Bank of the Jordan, can be better understood with these Zionist territorial aims in the background. These occupations in 1967 are in complete harmony with Zionist territorial aims of 1897, as later narrowed by the proposals submitted to the Paris Peace Conference of 1919, but they do not derogate from the ultimate aims of Zionism.

Zionist Declarations of Expansion

Declarations of an aggressive and expansionist character have been made from time to time by the Zionist and Israeli leaders without regard to what effect they may have on the Arabs whose territories the Zionists seek. A sample of these, which appeared before the June 1967 War, give an indication of Israeli strategy:

1. *David Ben Gurion*—In 1937, when the Zionist Congress was debating the partition plan proposed by the Palestine Royal (Peel) Commission, Ben Gurion, then Chairman of the Jewish Agency for Palestine, is reported to have explained to the press: "The debate has not been for or

against the indivisibility of *Eretz Israel*. No Zionist can forego the smallest portion of *Eretz Israel*. The debate was over which of two routes would lead quicker to the common goal."[15]

2. *Chaim Weizmann*, then president of the World Zionist Organization, defending the non-inclusion by the Peel Commission of southern Palestine within the proposed Jewish frontiers, remarked: "It will not run away."[16]

3. *David Ben Gurion*—The state "has been resurrected in the western *part* of the *land*" of Israel and that independence has been reached "in a *part* of our small country. Every state consists of a land and a people. Israel is no exception, but it is a state identical neither with its land nor with its people. It has already been said that when the state was established, it held only 6% of the Jewish people remaining alive after the Nazi cataclysm. It must now be said that it has been established in only *a portion of the land of Israel*. Even those who are dubious as to the restoration of the historical frontiers, as fixed and crystallized from the beginning of time, will hardly deny the anomaly of the boundaries of the new state."[17]

4. *David Ben Gurion*—On another occasion, he stated: "I accept to form the Cabinet on one condition, and that is, to utilize all possible means to expand toward the south."[18]

5. *Moshe Dayan*—As chief of the Israeli Army, he declared: "It lies upon the people's shoulder to prepare for the war, but it lies upon the Israeli army to carry out the fight with the ultimate object of erecting the Israeli Empire."[19]

6. *Menachem Begin*—Then leader of the *Herut* (later *Likud*) Party and later Prime Minister: "I deeply believe in launching preventive war against the Arab states without further hesitation. By doing so, we will achieve two targets: Firstly, the annihilation of Arab power; and secondly, *the expansion of our* territory."[20]

7. *Spokesman of the Herut Party declared in New York in 1956*—"Peace with the Arab countries is *impossible* with the present boundaries of Israel, which leave Israel open to attack. Israel should take the offensive immediately and capture strategic points along its border, including the Gaza Strip and then should take over the British-backed Kingdom of Jordan."[21]

8. *Chaim Weizmann*—During a visit to Jerusalem on December 1, 1948, he told his audience: "Do not worry because part of Jerusalem is not now within the state. All will come to pass in peace. Again I counsel patience. Fear not, my friends, the old synagogues will be rebuilt anew and the way to the Wailing Wall will be opened again. With your blood and sacrifices you have renewed the covenant of old. Jerusalem is ours by virtue of blood that your sons shed defending it."[22]

Such statements, coming as they did from the Israeli leaders, can mean one thing, and only one thing—expansion. Ben Gurion referred to the state of Israel as established in a portion of the land of Israel; the Israeli Chief of Staff called for a fight to establish the Israeli empire; and the Herut Party called for the occupation of the Gaza Strip and the Kingdom of Jordan. Is this all irresponsible talk? Or does it mean something?

If the western world is willing to trust in the peaceful declarations of the Israeli leaders, the Arabs, out of bitter experience, can no longer be fooled. The Zionists have always claimed that they wished to live in peace with the Arabs in Palestine where, they said, there was enough room for both peoples to live side by side; but events have shown that such peace was dependent upon not only the establishment of a Jewish state in Palestine, but that the Palestine Arabs shall not be there to enjoy the promised peace within their homeland but watch it from neighboring Arab territories as refugees.

Israeli Invasion of Egypt in 1956

The reasons the Israelis gave for their action varied. In a communique issued on the eve of the invasion, the Israeli Ministry of Foreign Affairs described the campaign in terms of both a preventive war and a retaliatory raid.[23] General Moshe Dayan's order to his troops read: "Today the Southern Forces will fight across the border and will enclose the Nile Army in its own country."[24] When asked to explain the Israeli action, the liaison officer for Armistice Affairs at the Ministry of Foreign Affairs qualified the terms of the official communique and confirmed that "this was not just a retaliatory raid, but that the Israeli forces were going to stay in Sinai."[25]

In announcing the invasion of Egypt to the Knesset, David Ben Gurion was even more explicit. He said: "The army did not make an effort to occupy enemy territory in Egypt proper and limited its operations *to free the area from northern Sinai to the tip of the Red Sea.*" Referring to the occupation of the Island of Tiran, south of the Gulf of Aqaba, he described it as "the Island of Yotvat, south of the Gulf of Eilat, which was liberated by the Israeli army."[26] (It should be noted that Eilat itself, constructed on the site of the Arab village of Umm Rashrash, had been occupied merely half a month after Israel had signed the Armistice Agreement with Egypt in which the Israelis undertook to respect the demarcation line defined in the agreement; this line excluded Eilat).

On the question of the Armistice Agreement with Egypt, Ben Gurion stated: "The armistice with Egypt is dead, as are the armistice lines, and no wizard or magician can resurrect these lines."[27]

Ben Gurion's statement that his troops did not occupy territory in Egypt proper; the selection of the words free and liberated, and the use of Hebrew terminology for centuries-old Arabic names in Arab territory, leave no doubt that the purpose of the Israeli attack was in fact neither a preventive war nor a retaliatory raid, as was at first claimed, but a well planned campaign to occupy the whole of the Sinai Peninsula and the Gaza Strip under the Israeli program of expansion.

On November 2, 1956, the UN General Assembly, meeting in special emergency session to consider the British-French-Israeli aggression against Egypt, adopted a resolution urging "as a matter of priority that all parties now involved in hostilities in the area agree to an immediate cease-fire and, as part thereof, halt the movement of military forces and arms into the area." The resolution further urged the parties to the Armistice Agreement "promptly to withdraw all forces behind the

Armistice Lines, to desist from raids across the armistice lines into neighboring territory, and to observe scrupulously the provisions of the Armistice Agreement."[28]

The Israelis resisted the General Assembly order to withdraw, every inch of the way, even though five subsequent resolutions had been adopted calling for Israeli withdrawal. It was not until President Eisenhower threatened the Israelis with sanctions and made the following declaration that the Israelis complied:

"Should a nation which attacks and occupies foreign territory in the face of United Nations disapproval be allowed to impose conditions on its withdrawal? . . .

If we agree that armed attack can properly achieve the purpose of the assailant, then I fear we will have turned back the clock of international order. We will have countenanced the use of force as a means of settling international differences and gaining national advantage.

If the United Nations once admits that international disputes can be settled by using force, then we will have destroyed the very foundation of the oganization, and our best hope for establishing a real (new) world order."[29]

The threat of economic sanctions and President Eisenhower's statement had immediate effect on the Israelis who began their withdrawal four days later. But their withdrawal was not a peaceful one. General Burns, Chief of the Truce Supervision Organization, reported: "As the Israelis withdrew across the Sinai, they began a systematic destruction of the surfaced roads, the railway, the telephone-lines, and what few buildings there were along the railway and at one or two road-junction points." The General's reaction was: "God had scorched the Sinai earth, and His Chosen People removed whatever stood above it." He then added: "When the United Nations Emergency Force found out what was going on, Mr. Hammarskjold protested vigorously to the Israeli government, that this destruction was a breach of the undertaking they had given to facilitate the efforts of U.N.E.F. directed toward maintaining peaceful conditions, and it certainly was not cooperation to destroy the roads by which we had to advance. By the time the destruction had ceased, the Israelis had already thoroughly demolished about 70 kilometres of roads."[30]

The Gulf of Aqaba

One outcome of Israeli withdrawals was that Israeli shipping was allowed to pass through the Gulf of Aqaba. To lend legality and provide a precedent for this change, an amendment to the Maritime Law was adopted in 1958 by a vote of 62 to 1 with the Arab states abstaining. Article 16, as amended, reads:

"There shall be no suspension of the innocent passage of foreign ships through straits that are used for international navigation between one part of the high sea and another part of the high seas or the territorial sea of a foreign state."*

The Israeli delegate described the Article at the time as a "clear-cut decision preventing suspension on any legal ground of the free passage of ships of all nationalities through the Strait of Tiran to and from the Gulf of Aqaba." The Saudi Arabian representative, on the other hand, declared that his government would not recognize the article, which he described as specially tailored to fit a special case.

It should be noted that the decision was merely a *recommendation* and is binding only on those nations that ratify it. Refusal by any nation to recognize the provisions of the article can in no way be construed to be a violation of the UN Charter. Egypt made it clear at the time that so long as the UN Emergency Force remained at Sharm Esh-Sheikh, Israeli shipping will be able to pass through the Strait of Tiran. This did not mean that Egypt had accepted the changed situation or that a precedent had been established that would alter the *status quo* existing up to 1956.

The Arab stand continues to be that the Strait of Tiran has been Arab territorial waters from time immemorial; that there is no international ageement to which Egypt is a party declaring it otherwise; that Egypt was still technically at war with the Israelis; that Egypt was obligated to take all measures to defend its security; and that Egypt cannot permit the approach of its enemy to within 500 yards of its shore.**

On October 14, 1948, the Israelis attacked and occupied the town of Beersheba and the El-Auja area—both of which were assigned to the Arab state under the Partition Resolution of 1947. On October 19, 1948, the Security Council took a decision ordering "the withdrawal of both parties from any positions not occupied at the time of the outbreak;"[31] and on November 4, 1948, the council once again called upon the parties "to withdraw those of their forces which have advanced beyond the positions held on October 14."[32]

On February 24, 1949, an armistice was concluded between Egypt and the Israeli authorities, whereby the Israelis were permitted to hold what they had acquired in violation of the truce orders. But in the direction of the Gulf of Aqaba, the Israelis were limited to within half the distance between the Gulf shoreline and the area they then actually held. This is quite explicit from the provisions of Annex II (b) to the General Armistice Agreement, which prescribed that the armistice demarcation line in the south shall run "from point 402 down to the southernmost tip of Palestine, by straight line marking half the distance between Egypt-Palestine and Transjordan-Palestine frontiers."[33] The

---

*The International Law Commission in 1956 found no grounds for considering the Strait of Tiran an international waterway subject to the rules appropriate to such waterways. See letter by Harvard Professor Roger Fisher in *The New York Times*, June 10, 1967.

**The mouth of the Gulf of Aqaba is bordered by Egypt on the west and by Saudi Arabia on the east. The passageway into the Gulf is interrupted in the center by the Islands of Tiran and Sanafir. The passageway between the islands and the Saudi Arabian coast is not navigable; that between the islands and the Egyptian coast is three miles in width, but only 500 yards are navigable, and these closer to the Egyptian coast.

Israelis were thereby excluded from access to the Gulf of Aqaba. But, on March 10, 1949—only thirteen days after they had signed the Armistice Agreement with Egypt—the Israelis launched an attack on the southern Negev which brought their forces up to the Gulf of Aqaba coastline. Therefore the Israelis were in the Gulf of Aqaba region solely as a result of brute force in violation of the Armistice Agreement they willingly signed.

The June 1967 War

Because it is more sensitive to threats to Israel than threats to the Arabs, public opinion in the West at first believed that the June 1967 War began with Egypt's closing of the Strait of Tiran to Israeli shipping in May and with the entry of Egyptian troops into the Sinai Peninsula; and that the Israelis were compelled to attack to prevent the destruction of their state. Because of this propaganda, the Israelis were able to get moral, political and financial support from many western nations that at the same time branded the Arab states as the aggressors. Actually, President Nasser's actions were merely precautionary in answer to Israeli threats against Syria in April of that year. Because these Israeli activities went almost unnoticed in the western press, very few people realized their occurrence at the time.[34]

In 1966, all signs indicated that the Israelis were intent on war and another bid for expansion; and the year 1967 appeared best suited for that. Israel's internal problems had become precarious; there was much dissatisfaction; differences increased between the Oriental and western Jews; the economy of the country was unstable; the number of unemployed had reached the figure of about 100,000 (about 10% of its labor force) and was on the rise; and emigration had exceeded immigration for the first time since the 1920s. Something had to be done to draw attention of world Jewry to Israel's plight.

Two conferences of world Zionist leaders were held in West Jerusalem to deal with the situation, but apparently their help was not as quickly forthcoming as the situation demanded. Hence the Israelis had to decide on more drastic measures. Funds and immigration were urgently needed, and both these could best be obtained through war with the Arabs.

There were other reasons why the Israelis selected the year 1967 for their attack. First, inter-Arab differences were at their highest, and therefore the Arabs were least able, militarily, to resist any thrust that the Israelis might make. There were signs that fences were being mended, and the Israelis could not afford to wait and see Arab unity and preparedness frustrate their plans. Second, the 1968 U.S. presidential elections were approaching, and the Israelis felt confident that their influence in the United States was sufficiently strong to make the Jewish vote a factor to be reckoned with in preventing a repetition of U.S. interference to dislodge them, as President Eisenhower did in 1957. The fact that certain presidential aspirants visited Israel before announcing their candidacy, strengthened the Arab belief that Israel played a big role in the election of a U.S. president. Furthermore, six senators up for

re-election, also visited Israel and returned to applaud its accomplishments.

To escape world condemnation and win public support, the Israelis
used the closure of the Strait of Tiran to Israeli shipping and the entry of
Egyptian troops into the Sinai Peninsula as a pretext to launch their June
1967 attack and the occupation of the Sinai Peninsula, the Gaza Strip,
the Golan Heights and the West Bank, including Jerusalem.

While the Israelis were preparing for war, President Lyndon Johnson
issued a warning thirteen days before the Israeli strike against Egypt.
The warning was addressed to all nations of the Near East to the effect
that "the United States is firmly committed to the support of the political
independence and territorial integrity of all nations of that area;" that
the United States strongly opposes aggression by anyone in the area, in
any form, overt or clandestine;" and that the United States has "always
opposed the efforts of other nations to resolve their problems with their
neighbors by the aggression route."[35]

In substance, the declaration of President Johnson was identical with
that made by President Eisenhower in 1957. But a world of difference
separated them when it came to honoring their contents. President
Eisenhower firmly ordered the immediate withdrawal of the Israeli
forces to their original positions; but President Johnson's attitude after
the Israeli attack had succeeded, changed to one of support of the Israeli
position both inside and outside the United Nations, despite the clarity
of the U.S. commitment.

Statements have since appeared indicating that President Johnson
had in fact been informed—and approved—of the Israeli plans by Prime
Minister Levi Eshkol during the latter's visit to the White House shortly
before the attack of June 5, 1967 began. In his memoirs, which were
published after he had vacated the presidency, President Johnson made
the startling charge that Israel had double-crossed him in May-June
1967. Prime Minister Levi Eshkol, he stated, had promised that Israel
would delay military action to keep the Tiran Strait open while he
attempted to negotiate with Egypt's Nasser. Johnson believed that he
had a couple of weeks in which to solve the problem and conveyed this
information to Egypt's president. This story is strongly supported by the
fact that Nasser kept the Egyptian air force on the ground to avoid
giving the Israelis any cause to fear an Egyptian attack.

United States military, intelligence, and diplomatic officials unanimously insisted that Egypt planned no immediate hostile action, and
this fact was communicated to Israel. Vice-President Zakaria Mohieddin
agreed to confer with President Johnson in Washington on June 7, 1967.
But on June 5, Israel struck first at Egypt, then at Jordan and Syria.

In the light of these circumstances, Israel could be accused of double-
crossing President Johnson in order to gain advantage of a military
surprise at a moment when Nasser believed that no hostilities were
likely. However, Johnson concealed the facts of this double-crossing not
only from the American Congress and people, but also from his European allies.

In Arab eyes, President Johnson became an accomplice after the fact,
as many regarded the U.S. government as an accomplice before the fact.

Johnson's announced the policy—previously quoted—of preserving the political and territorial integrity of every state in the area had after all meant only for Israel.*[36]

U.S. policy in subsequent years, confirms the obvious, that the government was now committed to permitting the Israelis to remain in occupation, if not of all the territories occupied, in at least those parts which it considers necessary for its security. The Arabs became more convinced of this after the U.S. representative at the United Nations used the veto in the Security Council to block the passage of a draft resolution calling for Israeli withdrawal.

When President Richard Nixon took over the White House, the Arabs believed that he would follow the wisdom and courage of President Eisenhower to whom he was in 1957 Vice-President. Instead, he exceeded the Johnson Administration's support for Israel, so much so as to earn the reputation of being the President who had done more for Israel than all the Presidents who came before him.

To suggest that Egypt was, in 1967, planning to attack Israel denies history. The evidence is all here that it was the Israelis who were preparing for an attack on Syria long before President Nasser asked the U.N. Emergency Force to leave the Gaza Strip and Sharm Esh-Sheikh. For Nasser, the movement of Egyptian troops into the Sinai Peninsula was merely a defensive measure to counter-balance the Israeli build-up on the Syria borders and in order to deter aggression. He made that clear not only in his official pronouncements, but also in answer to messages he received from President Johnson.

A sampling of Israeli statements made before the June 1967 War and after it, shows a wide gap: The statements preceding the war, invariably contained assurances and pledges regarding Israel's innocence of expansionist designs. The statements made after hostilities had ceased, explicitly disclosed Israel's intention to hold on to certain occupied Arab territories.

Statements Made by Israeli Leaders Before the War

1. *Michael Comay*—Then Israeli representative at the United Nations, told the Special Political Committee on November 8, 1966, in rebuttal of Arab accusations of Israeli expansionist designs on Arab territories: "I would like to inform the committee quite categorically that the government of Israel covets no territory of any of its neighbors, nor does it feel obliged to hand over its territory to any of its neighbors. We are all members of the United Nations. We have signed the Charter obliging us to respect each other's political independence and territorial integrity.

---

*Correspondent Anthony Pearson disclosed in two articles published in *Penthouse* magazine (May–June 1976) which were later incorporated in his book *Conspiracy of Silence: Attack on the USS Liberty* (London: Quartet Books, 1978) that "at a series of secret meetings in Tel Aviv and Washington between CIA officers, the Israeli General Staff, selected politicians, and inner members of the Johnson Administration, it was decided to promote a contained war between Israel and Egypt." The war, when it started, went beyond the contained war to which President Johnson had agreed—hence the double-crossing.

My government fully and unreservedly accepts this obligation towards the other 120 Member States of the United Nations."[37]

2. *Levi Eshkol*—Then Prime Minister, in an address in the Israeli Parliament: "told Arab countries that Israel has no aggressive designs."[38]

3. *Moshe Dayan*—Then Minister of Defence, said: "We have no invasion aims. Our only target is to foil the Arab armies' aim of invading our country.*[39] On another occasion, he was quoted as saying: 'Soldiers of Israel, we have no aims of territorial conquest."[40]

4. *Gideon Rafael*—Then Israeli delegate to the United Nations, read the following statement by the Israeli Defence Minister to the Security Council on June 5, 1967—the day of the Israeli attack: "We have no aims of conquest. Our sole objectives are to put an end to the Arab attempt to plunder our land, and to suppress the blockade."[41]

5. *Levi Eshkol*—Declared on the day of the attack: "We do not demand anything except to live in tranquility in our present territory."[42]

Statements Made by Israeli Leaders After the War

1. *Levi Eshkol*—"A new political reality in the Mideast" has been created;[43] "Israel intends to keep the former part of Jerusalem and the Gaza Strip. Israel without Jerusalem is Israel without a head."[44]

2. *Abba Eban*—As Foreign Minister, said: "Israel will, under no circumstances, return to the 1949 Armistice Agreements."[45] "Sometimes you cannot gain peace and security without territorial gains."[46] "If the General Assembly were to vote by 121 votes to 1 in favor of Israel returning to the Armistice lines . . . Israel would refuse to comply with that decision."[47] "Israel has no intention of squandering the position won by its Middle East war victory and will hold lands captured from the Arabs until a satisfactory peace settlement is reached."[48] "The military victory is neither stable nor successful unless it is ratified by peace. What happened in 1967 happened because in 1957 Israel had been persuaded to give up the fruits of victory. This time there will be a different map of Israel . . . Israel does not have to be recognized. Israel exists."[49]

3. *Yisrael Galilee*—As Minister of Information, said: "Israel cannot agree to return to the status quo before this [conflict] happened."[50]

4. *Yigal Allon*—As Minister of Labor, said: "We must have depth, especially in the central part of the country and the vicinity of Galilee and Jerusalem."[51]

5. *David Ben Gurion*—There are "no grounds for Israeli negotiations on Old Jerusalem."[52]

6. *Moshe Dayan*—As Minister of Defence, said: "The Gaza Strip is Israel's, and steps will be taken to make it part of this country."[53] "Israel

---

*Compare this statement with that made by General Mordechai Hod, Commander of the Israeli Air Force, who indicated that the plan of attack had been in preparation for sixteen years. He said: "Sixteen years' planning had gone into those initial 80 minutes" (The air strike against Egypt on June 5, 1967). "We lived with the plan, we slept on the plan, we ate the plan. Constantly we perfected it." (From an article by Randolph and Winston Churchill, published in *The Times* (London), July 16, 1967, p. 7).

ISRAELI-OCCUPIED TERRITORIES (1967)

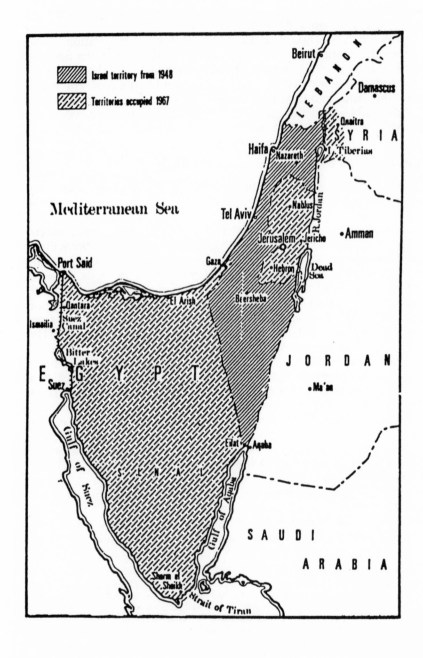

must not return to its 1948 borders. We need to consider the reality of 1967 and the map of 1967. We need, not only permanent borders, but borders that will ensure peace."[54] "There are about a million Arabs whom we don't want, I should say as citizens of Israel, in the Jordanian part. We certainly don't want Egypt to go back to the Gaza Strip. This is the same story like Sinai . . . I don't think that we should in any way give back the Gaza Strip to Egypt or the western part of Jordan to King Hussein." Asked whether there was any way whereby Israel could absorb the huge number of Arabs whose territory Israel now occupies, he said: "Economically, we can; but I think that it is not in accord with our aims in the future. It would turn Israel into either a binational or poly-Arab-Jewish state instead of the Jewish state, and we want a Jewish state . . . We want a Jewish State like the French want a French state."[55] "On no account will we force ourselves to leave, for example, Hebron. This is a political program, but more important, it is a fulfillment of a people's ancestral dream."[56]

7. It was reported from Jerusalem that all maps issued by the Israeli Department of Surveys with markings of the 1949 armistice lines have now been classified as antiquated and historical.[57]

8. The Israeli government declared that the areas occupied as a result of the June 1967 War, are no longer recognized as enemy territory. This action has the double purpose, on the one hand, of overcoming criticism that the Israelis, in their treatment of the civilian Arab inhabitants, are contravening the 1949 Geneva Conventions; and, on the other hand, of acquiring freedom of action to expropriate their property.[58]

Israeli Expansionist Policy Confirmed

Merely for the sake of argument, one could say that the foregoing quotations only suggest a growing appetite for territory on the part of the Israelis, not premeditated expansionism. This might be so. However, the record of events indicates that, given the slightest chance, Israel has not taken long before actually expanding. It ought to be remembered that the circumstantial evidence of expansionist intensions is *not* limited to the immediate past of a year ago; nor are the expansionist acts limited to the aftermath of the June 1967 War*.

Israel's expansionism can be said to be based on her occupation of Egyptian, Jordanian and Syrian territories, and her refusal to withdraw in spite of the Security Council Resolution to this effect No. 242 of November 22, 1967, and in spite of blanket condemnation in the UN Charter of occupation of the territories of other states by member states.

But it is not intended to use the evidence of occupation in broad

---

*Addressing a youth group in the Golan Heights in July 1968, Moshe Dayan is reported to have told his audience:

"Our fathers had reached the frontiers which were recognized in the Partition Plan; our generation reached the frontiers of 1949; now the Six-Day War generation has managed to reach Suez, Jordan and the Golan Heights. This is not the end. After the present ceasefire lines, there will be new ones. They will extend beyond Jordan—perhaps to Lebanon, and perhaps to central Syria as well." (Quoted from *The Times* London, June 25, 1969).

terms. It will be assumed, for the sake of argument, that Israel is willing to negotiate partial withdrawal, against certain Arab concessions. Therefore, the expansionist acts will, by elimination, involve those areas occupied by Israel and declared non-negotiable by Israeli leaders, that is, areas that Israel states it will unequivocally refuse to include in any negotiations agenda. The non-negotiable areas are those occupied in excess of the territory set aside for the Jewish state in the Partition Plan of 1947 as later extended under the provisions of the General Armistice Agreements and held until June 5, 1967, plus parts of the territories occupied in the June 1967 War. These last, include East Jerusalem, Gaza, the Golan Heights and certain parts of the West Bank needed to provide Israel with "secure borders", according to the Israelis.

As regards the City of Jerusalem, its occupation is irrevocable, according to Israeli official sources at all levels. In fact, Abba Eban, as Israeli Foreign Minister, declared at the United Nations on June 16, 1967 that even if the whole membership voted against the annexation measures taken by Israel (regarding the Arab parts of the City and a few villages surrounding it), Israel would still not budge or remove these measures.

There is hardly any more need to establish the case that Israel, like Zionism, the ideology underlying it, is expansionist. The establishment of the state in 1948 against the will of the Arab majority and on its land, was an act of aggression, colonialism in the classical sense. To have further occupied more than the Partition Plan allowed it, made of Israel an expansionist state. To have occupied yet more territory in June 1967, and to announce blatantly the determination not to give up several parts of this territory, confirms the expansionist label, if confirmation is still needed. To accept such a situation is not only a travesty of justice, but also poses grave dangers to the safety and security of the region and world peace.

Attack on U.S. Ship Liberty

The story of the June 1967 War would be incomplete if reference is not made to the Israeli attack on the U.S. ship *Liberty* on June 8, 1967 in which 34 American seamen were killed and 164 were wounded. The Israelis claimed at the time that the attack was a mistake and the U.S. government publicly accepted this explanation, although both knew it was a lie. The facts—revealed nine years later—prove that the attack was deliberate; that there was connivance between Israelis and the U.S. government to launch what has been described as a contained war against Egypt to cut President Nasser to size; and reduce Soviet influence in the region. The Israelis took advantage of the opportunity and, contrary to agreement with the United States, decided to extend the war into one of expansion. The *Liberty* was about to inform Washington of Israeli plans, and an attempt was made to sink the ship with all hands and to blame the Egyptians.

Reporter Anthony Pearson, who was in the Middle East at the time covering the war, stated that two questions puzzled him: Why did the Arabs continue to fight after all seemed lost? And why did the Israelis viciously attack an unarmed American communications vessel? He decided to investigate; and after failing to find a publisher for his book, published his findings in *Penthouse* magazine in two installments.

In the first article, Pearson stated his conclusion that the fateful attack was "not an accident but a deliberate, ruthless, well-planned attempt to sink a U.S. spy ship that had uncovered the secret machinations by which Israel helped to prolong the Six-Day War." He gave a minute-by-minute account of the attack and went on to say:

"For two years, the CIA had been deeply committed to reshaping events in the Mideast to suit a whole new State Department policy calling for a reduction of Soviet influence in the area, the discouragement of leftist nationalism, and the re-instatement of American influence.

"Richard Helms, the CIA chief, was still pursuing a policy of over ten years' standing that allowed for all intelligence operations inside Israel to be conducted through Mossad (the Israeli intelligence agency). There was no CIA station chief in Tel Aviv, and officers working under cover in the American Embassy there acted in full consort with officers of Israeli intelligence—each side supposedly having total access to the information of the other.

"In 1965, after President Nasser had exposed an illegal American arms deal to Israel, James Angleton (head of CIA counter-intelligence), conducted a number of meetings with Mossad officers to decide how and when to get rid of Nasser. It was impossible to overthrow the president within Egypt by any sort of coup. First, his charisma had to be undermined and his popular support destroyed. Nasser's constant and increasing threats against Israel, and his assurances to his people that the Israeli menace would be defeated, suggested to the CIA that an Egyptian loss of face could be achieved by calling Nasser's bluff—by actually making him confront Israel.

"At a series of secret meetings in Tel Aviv and Washington between CIA officers, the Israeli General Staff, selected Israeli politicians, and inner members of the Johnson Administration, it was decided to promote a contained war between Israel and Egypt—a war that would not affect the territorial lines between Israel and Syria and Jordan.

"The plan was organized in Israel by a group that included Yigal Allon, Intelligence Chief Meir Amit, Aharon Yariv, head of Army Intelligence, Shimon Peres, Ezer Weizmann, Air Force Chief Mordechai Hod, David Hacohen and Moshe Dayan. Their liaison officer in Washington was Eppy Evron, who dealt directly with Angleton at the CIA and Eugene Rostow at the State Department.

"In principle, they agreed that the situation of an increasing hardline by Nasser combined with the Soviet build-up in Egypt and Syria, should be exploited to rouse maximum public opinion for war, and that the Israeli army should be placed on full alert to induce action by either Damascus or Cairo. In these circumstances, the Kenesset would have to give its approval for war. And when this war was launched—the Israelis assured the Americans—it would be fought to a pre-designed American plan for containment."

The conspiracy began to unfold on May 30, 1967: "Robert Anderson, an American special envoy, was sent to Cairo to talk to Nasser. He met the Egyptian President on June 1 and succeeded in persuading him to consider an option of detente with the United States. As a gesture of goodwill, Nasser said he would send his Deputy, Zacharia Mohieddin, to Washington on June 5. This message was transmitted to Washington, and within two hours of its receipt by the State Department, the Israeli secret service knew every detail of it. That same day—June 1—the Israeli Knesset gave a majority vote for war, and Moshe Dayan was appointed Minister of Defence.

"The joint Israeli-CIA plan for war had aimed for an initial strike date in the second week in June. And the USS *Liberty* had been dispatched by the CIA to arrive off Sinai before the planned hostilities began—in order to make certain that the Israelis didn't overstep the objectives of the containment plan.

"Right up to the moment of attack, Eppy Evron was assuring his Washington contacts that Israeli troop movements were simply a precautionary measure against the build-up of Arab troops. Evron believed he could tell the American government anything he liked. He didn't know about the *Liberty* and her mission.

"Thus, as war began, the listening devices on the *Liberty* were tuned to transmissions from both the Arabs and Israelis. With radar monitoring, it was possible to carefully map the movements and positions of troops, armor, and aircraft, showing the true progress of battle. All this information was being transmitted in full to the National Security Agency in Washington. Selected parts were also passed on to the United Nations in New York.

"It was clear to the observers on the *Liberty* that the decoding capabilities of the Arabs had failed to crack Israeli codes. But the Israelis had penetrated Egyptian and Jordanian codes from the moment the war began . . . Somewhere between Amman and Cairo, in a relay station in Sinai, the messages were being blocked by the Israelis, then reconstructed and passed on so swiftly and effectively that there was no apparent break. In the language of intelligance, this type of interference is called 'cooking'.

"The first batch of these messages transmitted from Cairo advised Hussein of a bad military situation on the Egyptian front. The Israelis blocked these and recorded them by misinforming the King that three-quarters of the Israeli Air Force had been destroyed over Cairo and that the 300-plus aircraft was now picking up on radar approaching Jordan were Egyptian jets raiding targets in Israel . . .

"Throughout the first day of fighting, the Israelis continued to cook messages in order to give both sides the impression that the war was going favorably for the Arabs. There was no chance of the plan going wrong, because Hussein had broken off diplomatic relations with Syria (over an allegation of sabotage by the Syrian Secret Service) a week before the Israelis attacked, and he was not in communication with Damascus. No Israeli interference with messages between Cairo and Damascus was necessary because the Syrians, although told of the bad situation in Sinai, were also being told their flank was still covered by the Jordanians. This encouraged them to withdraw troops from the

Golan towards Damascus, in order to cover the road from Amman as a second line to the Jordanian Army.

"Another group of cooked transmissions on June 6 and 7 falsely informed Hussein that the Egyptians were counter-attacking in Sinai and needed support from Jordan in the form of an attack against the Israeli positions in the Hebron area. To make this attack, Hussein had to withdraw his forces from a planned offensive that had been designed to cut Israel into two [in the Tulkarm-Natanya area]. The Egyptians were also misled into believing the Jordanians were making a successful attack in Hebron, and they in turn counter-attacked during the early hours of June 8 and ignored a United Nations call for a cease-fire.* The Israelis gained enough time from this to enable them to capture all the Jordanian territory they needed to finish off the Egyptians in Sinai, and to move their troops right up to the east bank of Suez immobilizing the Canal.

"In Washington, on the evening of June 7, Avraham Harman, the Israeli Ambassador, had been called to the State Department and told by Eugene Rostow that the Israeli attack on Jordan and Egypt had to stop immediately and that no move was to be made against the Syrians on the Golan. A cease-fire was being implemented at the request of the Arabs by the United Nations.

"Harman argued his country was acting against Arab aggression . . . No mention was made by Rostow of the *Liberty*, but four hours later, in Tel Aviv, orders were passed from the offices of the Minister of Defence and the Commander of the Air Force to undertake a surveillance of an American communications ship operating off the Sinai coast. Then, four hours after the surveillance orders, at 1:30 p.m. Tel Aviv time, further orders were issued from the same sources to attack and sink the ship (Israeli officials, however, say that no written orders were ever issued). Aircraft were called upon to knock out all communications antennae in the first strike. Subsequent strikes would completely immobilize the ship, preparatory to final torpedo hits from MTB's. It was imperative that the ship should be destroyed.

"For the Israelis, *Liberty* was an unknown factor. On June 8, Israel was still three days away from her final objectives. It was possible that drastic measures might have to be taken at any time. The Israeli leaders were afraid that the continued presence of the *Liberty* off Sinai, monitoring their activities for both the U.S. government and the United Nations, might wreck their plans. If the ship was sunk with all hands, the attack would be blamed on the Egyptians, or perhaps on Russian fighters from a Soviet fleet carrier. It would also serve the purpose of involving the Americans directly and committing them totally to Israel's side. It was a daring plan—a vicious plan—but certainly well-coordinated and well-executed. It seems surprising that it failed. Everything seemed stacked against the *Liberty*.

---

*Soon after the cease-fire, the author visited Amman; and while waiting for an audience with King Hussein, he was informed by a high-ranking official of the palace whom he knew before, that the loss of the West Bank was due to false information supplied by Nasser that the Israeli Air Force had been destroyed and that the Egyptian Army was advancing in Sinai. Not until his research in 1978 did the author learn the truth.

"An hour before the first Israeli air surveillance, U.S. intelligence reported to the Joint Chiefs of Staff that Israeli monitors had broken into the *Liberty's* coding banks, deciphered her codes, and had transmitted a warning to Israel's military-intelligence headquarters. The Americans were informed that the Israelis were reacting badly and might possibly take some sort of action against the ship.

"The Joint Chiefs of Staff immediately ordered a message transmitted to the *Liberty* warning her to withdraw to the Sixth Fleet at once. This message was rated by navy intelligence as pinnacle, which meant that it had the highest priority . . . As the pinnacle message left Washington, it became the first of three remarkable communication errors—if indeed they were errors. The *Liberty* should have received the message by 9 a.m. ship's time. She never did . . .

"Within two hours, a second message to the *Liberty* was misrouted . . . This one was dispatched from the Sixth Fleet Commander . . . advising McGonagle (the Commander) of his dangerous position and ordering him to withdraw. It was a back-up message to the pinnacle . . . This message was misrouted . . .

"The third and final message lost in this strange tangle of confused misroutings, left the *Liberty* for the *Little Rock* via Naples, advising the Sixth Fleet Commander of the extent of the attack then taking place . . . In fact, the *only* message received that day was the open-channel Mayday sent immediately after the coded pinnacle to the *Little Rock*.

"The Navy has never satisfactorily explained how three messages of such vital importance, rated red-urgent and sent via the pinnacle code route could all have been misrouted. The vague explanation was bad management. Soon after the attack on the *Liberty*, one naval statement announced that it had taken place because of misplaced communications. No known official naval enquiry into the communications incident ever took place. In fact, the strangest part of the whole *Liberty* affair has increasingly seemed the U.S. government's anxiety to excuse and cover up an attack on one of its own ships."[59]

In his second article, Anthony Pearson reveals how the U.S. "government aided and abetted Israel in sweepig the real facts about the *Liberty* under the carpet;" how "The *Liberty*, which was furnished with extremely sophisticated intelligence equipment, had been monitoring Arab and Israeli transmissions from her post off Gaza;" and how "the communications experts on board had discovered that the Israelis were intercepting messages between the Arab leaders and then changing them and retransmitting them—a procedure known as cooking. These cooked messages," Pearson stated, "led King Hussein of Jordan and president Nasser of Egypt to believe that the war was actually going well for the Arabs and encouraged them to continue fighting. This ploy gave Israel the time it needed to consolidate its growing victory. It allowed the Israelis to destroy the confused Arab armies and seize Arab territory.

"What no one knew—except those at the highest levels of the Israeli and American governments—was that Israel was violating a predetermined plan formulated by the CIA top officials of the Johnson Administration, the Israeli General Staff, and leading Israeli politicians.

According to this plan, Israel should have fought a contained war with the Arabs—which would not have affected the territorial lines between Israel and Syria and Jordan. But the *Liberty* had discovered Israel's violation of this scheme, and on the evening of June 7, the Israeli Ambassador in Washington was told that the attacks had to stop. Eight hours later, orders were given in Tel Aviv to destroy the ship.

"The attack would have been totally successful. It failed only because a Mayday distress call from the *Liberty* had reached the Sixth Fleet, six-hundred miles to the northwest. Two flights of four jet fighters were immediately launched to save the ship. The Israelis intercepted the call and pulled back while there was still time to make the only possible excuse-error and mistaken identity."

". . . On June 10, 1967, they [the Israelis] were masters of Sinai as far as the very eastern banks of the Suez Canal, of the Jordan West Bank, of Jerusalem, and a big chunk of the Syrian Golan Heights. The attack on Syria had been almost as big a shock to the world as was the whole sudden war. It was significant that *Liberty* was the only neutral voice able to tell the United Nations in New York and the Defence and State Departments in Washington that the Israelis were making moves to conquer the Golan Heights. The transmissions from *Liberty* exposing the Israeli Golan attack plans could have saved Syria if they had gone through. The Israelis were in violation of a United Nations negotiated cease-fire. The attack on the ship, however, stopped communication, and the Israelis had their way.

"The *Liberty* had been only a small obstacle against a determined Israeli plan for reshaping the Mideast in Israel's own interests, and the attack on the ship was an indication of that country's determination to expand. To achieve their aim, the Israelis were prepared to push aside the restraining hand of their American ally with the same contempt that they felt for the threatening arm of their enemies. America had forbidden the conquest of Jordan. The *Liberty* attack was the Israeli reply. Old-timers in the State Department could well say: 'We told you so:' But the cost of thirty-four lives and so much pain and injury left a burning anger in many places. According to former CIA Patrick McGarvey, who was coordinating intelligence reports from the Joint Chiefs of Staff when the *Liberty* attack became evident, an order was immediately issued for an air strike against the Israeli torpedo base at Haifa which had launched the torpedo boats. That order was quickly counter-manded by the White House."

In the United States, "the story had received some publicity immediately after the attack, but there was a strange lack of interest shown in any follow-ups. Jack Anderson, the Washington columnist, raised questions about the *Liberty's* role as a spy ship, expressed the opinion that the attack was no accident, and exposed the facts that initial congressional hearings on the matter were totally secret and apparently leak-proof, and that there was a good deal of friction among the representatives concerning the issue. On the Hill, and in the White House, the State Department, the Pentagon, and the intelligence community, the *Liberty* affair was suddenly shrouded in secrecy. A presidential citation was issued for the ship, and Commander McGonagle was cited for the Medal of Honor. Beyond that necessary routine, there was silence."*

Pearson commented: "One of the most outrageous aspects of this cover-up was the manner in which the American commendations for the ship and McGonagle's Medal of Honor were submitted to the Israelis. According to a member of the Senate Foreign Relations Committee's staff at the time, the citations were censored by Israel before they were awarded. All reference to the nationality of the attackers was deleted, and McGonagle's citation read simply jet aircraft and motor torpedo boats. The citation awarded to the ship referred only to foreign jet fighter aircraft and motor torpedo boats."**

Pearson ended his article with this statement: "But what is most significant is that the United States was unable to expose Israel's connivances without exposing its own. And the Israelis, constantly fighting for the survival and dignity of their country, could only regard the destruction of the *Liberty* and the following cover-up as vital to the destiny of a whole people and of a country that is as much a holy vision as a home. Perhaps that is how those who were responsible for the attack can sleep and dream—but never remember."[60]

Following the publication of the *Penthouse* articles, Anthony Pearson published a book on the incident and added some interesting details.[61]

Pearson discloses in his book something *Penthouse* did not include, and that was that the *Liberty* was closely accompanied by a U.S. nuclear-powered submarine, the *Andrew Jackson*, which was forbidden and therefore unable to come to the *Liberty's* aid, although its crew could photograph the attack through its periscope.

A Pentagon general is reported to have told Pearson that the *Andrew Jackson* was sent to accompany the *Liberty* because, in the event of the small chance of Israel being defeated, the Israelis planned a Doomsday missile attack on Cairo, Baghdad and Damascus that would have brought in the Soviet Union. (The general and Pearson take it for granted that Israel had a nuclear capability in 1967 which it had attained partly with the help of the CIA). It was stated that the U.S. submarine was capable of knocking out all the Israeli missile sites in the Negev. The general is said to have been uncertain whether the Israelis knew of this—in which case they would have had an additional reason for attacking the *Liberty*—but he believes they did not.

Finally, in the more speculative area, the General suggests that the reasons why the NSA messages never reached the *Liberty* was that "the close cooperation of the CIA with Israeli intelligence had reached such a peak in 1967 that our whole intelligence network was thick with people

---

*Compare this United States position of secrecy and silence even when American lives were lost with that of the *Pueblo*, captured by the North Koreans in January 1968 without the loss of any lives, and the publicity the incident received which eventually ended up in being produced as a film.

**Those who have had an opportunity to see the plaque placed in the United Nations building in New York in honor of the memory of UN Mediator Count Folke Bernadotte who was assassinated in Jerusalem in September 1948, will have observed that the Israeli nationality of the assassins in that case was also omitted.

involved in that cooperation—not necessarily agents—just guys who were helping along the close cooperation of the Agency and Mossad." Pearson speculates that the affair has been hushed up by the United States because Israel threatened to retaliate by exposing the CIA's destabilization policies against the radical Arab states in the 1960's.

Peter Mansfield, who reviewed the book, concluded by stating: "Of course we cannot be certain about this, but there is enough fact and convincing circumstancial evidence in this book to cause the deepest alarm, not only to Americans but to any citizens of the world, about the consequences of the U.S.-Israeli alliance. There is one slightly encouraging possibility suggested by this book. Could it be that Israel's relative intelligence failure in 1973 was due to the double-cross of 1967 and a consequently greater reluctance on the part of the Americans to cooperate with Mossad?[62]

XIX   Israel and the United States

Israel's Favored Position

The state of Israel is often referred to as the favored child or the creation of the United States, and as such, its continued existence and well-being are regarded as the responsibility of that country. In fact, the United States is committed to the survival and security of Israel.

There is all the truth in this statement. Had it not been for the active part played by the White House in 1947 and 1948, the Jewish state would never have come into existence; the Palestine tragedy, with all its human sufferings, would not have occurred; the tension and instability which plagued the region since 1948, would not have arisen; and the United States position in the Arab world would not have been damaged to the extent it has.

The Senate Committee on Foreign Affairs, after hearing the views on American foreign policy of retired Foreign Service officers, who had done service in the Middle East, declared: "It was unanimously agreed that the manner in which Israel was created had an unfortunate effect on our relationship with the Arab nations."[1]

There are many who recognize the error of early American judgement and consider the creation of the Jewish state a mistake. But instead of attempting to redress the wrong committed, they lulled themselves all these years into a sweep-it-under-the-rug attitude and relied on time to heal Arab wounds and bring the two peoples together, forgetting that at no time has it been possible to fraternize between right and wrong. This short-sighted policy has not only proved dangerous; it has encouraged the Israelis into believing that whatever they do, and no matter how far they go in their intransigence and defiance of their international obligations and human decency, the United States—government and people—would always be there to lend them the support they need.

United States "special relationship" with Israel was openly disclosed in a statement made by a Deputy Secretary of State before the Mid-American Conference at Stillwater, Oklahoma, on May 8, 1964, which was attended by the author. John D. Jernagen, defending the Israeli position on the Arab refugee question, stated:

"Against great odds, Israel has built a thriving economy, a sound social structure and a stable, domestic government. Does it not deserve our admiration and friendship?

At the least, should we not refrain from trying to force that country to make concessions that it believes would weaken its economy and social structure and endanger its security?

We certainly have to think twice or thrice about these questions and to weigh carefully whether what we urge Israel to do would in fact injure it. Israel is a friend of the United States and of the west. It has a western outlook, uninfluenced by the communists. One of our major policy objectives is to persuade more countries to adopt this attitude."

He went on to say:

"Israel is a refuge for Jews from countries where they have been endangered, oppressed, suffered discrimination. United States public opinion, influenced by our strong Biblical tradition, has considered it our duty to support the establishment and maintenance of this refuge."

Ironically, while the United States has been unwilling to give displaced Jews special immigration privileges in the U.S., it was willing to do so in Palestine at Arab expense.

Commenting on the publicity given to Israel's achievements, Richard J. Marquardt, in a letter to the press, enquires with wonder: "How much longer will the American public be exposed to this kind of sentimental mythology? I recognize that many persons of the Jewish faith need to have repeated to them the stories of Israel's miracles and of that country's legendary figures. They apparently have a deep need for heroic symbols with which to identify. This is quite understandable. But what of the remaining 97% of the American population?"

Marquardt then comments: "Our appetite for these highly biased tales is not an insatiable one, and I, for one, am bored to distraction with Israel, its spectacular accomplishments, propaganda, a blatant mixture of pathos and boasting . . . With some three-and-a-half billion dollars available to it from various foreign sources since its creation, why shouldn't Israel have accomplished something?"[2]

A noted professor from Canada aptly remarked:

"The material achievements of Zionism have tended to blind the eyes of many in the west to its real character, just as the material achievements of Nazism and Fascism blinded many to the evil inherent in those two creeds.

The destructive character of Zionism, arises from the fact that, like the rabid nationalisms already mentioned, it is determined to do something for its adherents, no matter what the cost to other people.

For countries of the western world to link their Middle East policies in any way with support of such an 'ism' is to court disaster."[3]

The Zionist Lobby

In concert with the geo-political strategic advantages the U.S. gains from its "special relationship" with Tel Aviv, Israel's strength in the United States, stems from two sources: the *first*, is derived from the complex of American Zionist organizations. Even though card-carrying Zionists represent—by Zionism's own figures—less than 10% of American Jews, the movement is highly organized, munificently financed and closely disciplined. The economic pressures, social ostracism and excommunication the Zionists are able to exercise over American Jews who may fall out of line with their policies, has had the effect of cowing American Jewry—with few exceptions—into submission. Many American Jews—wittingly or unwittingly—while striking an I-am-not-a-Zionist-but attitude, utilize their wealth, influence and economic standing in the country to advance Israeli objectives, placing them above United States interests and security.

The *second* source of Israel's strength in the United States is derived from the influence and pressure that the Zionist lobby is able to exert on American policy-makers, the U.S. government, religious institutions and the information media.*

Those who have kept pace with the gradual deterioration of the situation in the Middle East since 1948, will readily admit that the blame, in a large measure, rests with:

1. American news media for distorting the facts, witholding the truth, or misleading the American people;

2. The U.S. politician who allows himself to be influenced or pres-

---

*In 1963, the U.S. Foreign Relations Committee conducted an investigation into the foreign agent aspect of American Zionist groups in the United States for the purpose of checking abuse. The report of the committee disclosed, according to sworn testimony, the firm control maintained by the Jewish Agency for Israel in Jerusalem over Zionist and some non-Zionist activities in the United States. Large sums, obtained from the United Jewish Appeal, were funnelled back to the United States from Israel. The money was used to support the indoctrination of U.S. Jews themselves in Zionist politics and culture.

Senator William F. Fulbright, chairman of the committee, referred to the Zionist operation as a conduit through which more than $1,000,000 a year passed for political lobbying and propaganda in the United States—all from tax-free funds raised ostensibly for humanitarian purposes. The Senate-record—which runs into some 220 pages—disclosed that:

1. More than $5,000,000 of mainly United Jewish Appeal Funds were returned to the United States from Israel in five-and-a-half years for political lobbying and propaganda purposes.
2. Some $300,000 of United Jewish Appeal funds were used to gain control of the Jewish Telegraphic Agency (news and propaganda distributor to the Jewish press).
3. United Jewish Appeal funds, returned through foreign agent channels, were used to create and maintain the Presidents Conference of Major Jewish Organizations (Union of American Hebrew Congregations, B'nai B'rith, etc.).
4. The Synagogue Council of America received funds as did the Zionist lobbyist I.L. Kenen (to the latter alone, $38,000 in one year).
5. Christian supporters of Zionism were given tours of Israel and were paid to run the American Christian Palestine Committee (succeeded by the American Christian Association for Israel). (See Records of Hearings of Meetings of Committee on Foreign Relations, U.S. Senate, 88th Congress, 1st Session, Part 9, May 23, 1963, pp. 1211–1424 & 1695–1782).

sured into supporting a one-sided policy inconsistent with the professed principles of the United States of what is right and just;

3. The U.S. Government for its unqualified moral, political, military, and economic support of the Israeli aggressive and espansionist policies.

Judging from the events which followed the June 1967 War, many U.S. politicians are no more than puppets on a string manipulated by the Zionist/Israeli lobby when it comes to matters concerning the Middle East.

Former Senator William Fulbright, in an interview on Face the Nation on October 7, 1973, declared: "The Israelis control the policy in the Congress and the Senate;" and that, "On every test on anything the Israelis are interested in, in the Senate, the Israelis have 75 to 80 votes" (out of 100 votes). He then cited two illustrations to prove his point: The bill which granted Israel $500-million in military and economic aid that year; and the Jackson Amendment banning trade with the Soviet Union until that country liberalized the emigration of Soviet Jews to Israel. (In contrast, no similar bill was ever introduced in the Senate banning aid to Israel until the latter allowed the Palestinian refugees to return to their homes under the principles of the Universal Declaration of Human Rights, and in accordance with the provisions of the numerous Resolutions of the United Nations.

On the first point, Senator Fulbright said: "I wish to do nothing to injure them" (the Israelis), but "I do not approve of their expansionism. I wish to do everything reasonable for their security and to guarantee that they will not be driven into the sea, as they say; that they will have as much security within their legitimate borders as we can give them. On the other hand, I do not approve of this unlimited expansion. I think other people have rights too in this area. That's the policy I've tried to follow; that is what I thought was this administration's policy; and when you see what's going on in Congress with the Jackson Amendment in the Senate and the House already voted on, and the co-sponsors in the Senate, how can you say the supporters of Israel in the United States don't control the Congress?"

When told this was a fairly serious charge, the Senator replied: "The charge is a fact of life. It is a fairly serious charge to say that your colleagues in the Senate—some 70 of them—are controlled by a power group rather than by their own vision of what they think are proper principles of freedom and right."

With regard to the trade bill with the Soviet Union, Senator Fulbright said: "I have no objection—in fact I approve of all private people complaining and criticizing the Russians. I am perfectly willing, and have done it myself. I do not think that's a part of the trade bill. I think that's a distortion of the trade bill and it's against the interests of the United States to mix those two up together. The trade bill stands on its own basis; its either good or bad from that point of view, and not trying to reform the internal government of Russia."

In the following elections, Senator William Fulbright lost his seat.

United States Double-Standard Policy

The Arabs accuse the U.S. government of following a double standard policy in matters relating to the Middle East, but the U.S. government denies that, claiming that its policy in the Arab-Israeli conflict is one of impartiality, objectivity, and fairness.

Referring to the series of tragedies in the troubled Middle East, Robert Pierpont, White House correspondent for CBS News, stated March 7, 1973, that "the United States appears to have lost its sense of fair play and justice, and seems to be operating on a double standard." This double standard, Pierpont pointed out, is present even when it comes to terror and murder. "For so long", he said "Americans have become used to thinking of the Israelis as the good guys and the Arabs as the bad guys, that many react emotionally along the lines of previous prejudices." Pierpont went on to say that "both sides have killed innocents, both sides have legitimate grievances and illegitimate methods of expressing them. Perhaps the Arabs' action was more irrational—sheer terror. At least it was not backed by a relatively rational government which justifies its actions as necessary."

Pierpont contrasted the recent Israeli air attack on "Palestinian refugee camps some 130 miles from their own territory and snuffing out 30 or 40 lives in the process [where] there was no outcry in this country" (the United States) with the Munich incident where "the United States, from President Nixon on down, expressed outrage;" and when the two Americans and one Belgian were killed in Khartoum, the President expressed shock and a deep sense of grief; Secretary of State William Rogers suggested the death penalty for the criminals; while Senator Hugh Scott said: "I hope they shoot them all, and the sooner the better."

Pierpont concluded by advising the application of a "more studied balance and fair play to the difficult problems of the Middle East."[4]

Arab reaction to the partial attitude of the U.S. government—particularly after the October 1973 War and the imposition of the oil embargo—was best illustrated in a letter published in *The New York Times*. The writer began by stating: "Defamation of the Arab character seems to be the accepted style nowadays in United States communication media. Arabs are characterized as cheaters, blackmailers, stabbers-in-the-back and warmongers."

The writer then made the following comparisons:

When the Arabs use their oil as a weapon to persuade the United States that supplying weapons to Israel helps perpetuate her conquest of Arab land—that is blackmail;

When the United States uses wheat as a weapon to force Russia to release Soviet Jews to go to Israel to occupy more Arab homes—that is humanitarianism;

When Israel wages a pre-emptive attack and occupies Arab territories—that is self-defence;

When the Arabs wage an offensive to liberate those same territories—that is invasion;

When Israel sneak-attacked the Arabs on June 6, 1967—that was heroic;

When the Arabs struck back on October 6, 1973—that was barbaric, even though the first attacked Arab armies on Arab land, and the latter attacked Israeli armies in the Sinai and the Golan Heights and not in Israel.

The writer went on to say: "The absence of the traditional American sense of justice and fair play is nowhere more emphasized than in the case of the Palestinians versus Israel. It is the result of the constant appeasement of Israel by the Fourth Estate. There is no sacred institution left in American which is not the subject of the media's scrutiny. Israel, it seems to me, is beyond such scrutiny for fear of anti-Semitic accusations, and because of the crisis of conscience hanging over the Western mind, among other things."

"Because of such reasons," he said, "Israel became the spoilt child of the United States. A spoilt child can kick others and take away their toys. When, in turn, they try to take their toys back, she runs crying to her mother, who protects her and encourages her to be more aggressive. The Palestinians, on the other hand, are the neglected children, and their relatives, the Arabs are the bad guys. Consequently, any action initiated by the Palestinians and the Arabs in their just struggle to regain their rights, is characterized as destructive and aggressive."

"This kind of myth-information," the writer concluded, "does not tend to serve the very best interests of the American people. It is not fair to the Arabs, and, in the long run, it won't help the Israelis."[5]

On paper, the U.S. representative to the United Nations will vote annually in favor of a resolution calling upon the Israelis to allow the repatriation of those refugees who wish to return to their homes and to compensate those who do not wish to return and for losses sustained, in accordance with Resolution 194(III) of December 11, 1948. In practice, the U.S government will resist any United Nations pressure on Israel to implement. (In contrast, the U.S. government will use every opportunity to support and encourage Zionist and Israeli demands for the liberalization of the emigration of Soviet Jews to Israel.)

The U.S. government consistently states that its policy is to support people in their bid for self-determination, sovereignty and independence; yet, in November 1974, it voted against such a right being granted by the General Assembly to the Palestinian people; and when the matter came before the Security Council in 1976, the U.S representative vetoed the draft resolution.

The U.S. government repeatedly declared that it does not approve of Israeli occupation of Arab territories, the annexation of East Jerusalem, the displacement of the Arab inhabitants, the destruction of buildings and the confiscation of land, the establishment of Jewish settlements in occupied areas, and the torture of detainees and prisoners; yet it will do nothing about it, and continues to support the Israelis to the maximum militarily and economically, thereby encouraging them to maintain their position of intransigence and defiance. (In contrast, the United States will withhold military and economic aid from any country that has attacked another. Somalia is a typical example: During its war with Ethiopia, President Jimmy Carter made it clear that Somalia would receive no aid from the United States so long as it had troops on Ethiopian territory.)

Furthermore, everytime a draft resolution was placed before the Security Council condemning Israel for its so-called retaliatory attacks on refugee camps in which hundreds of innocent men, women and children are killed, the U.S. representative used the veto; and in cases where the matter was debated before the General Assembly, the United States voted against any resolution of condemnation of Israel.

And when the General Assembly adopted a resolution that determine that Zionism was a form of racism and racial discrimination, the U.S. representative vehemently attacked the resolution describing it as "infamous, obscene, and uncivilized."

On May 23, 1967—thirteen days before the Israeli military forces crossed the armistice demarcation lines into Arab territories—President Johnson, who became aware of the clouds of war which were gathering over the Middle East, reiterated U.S. commitments toward the area in clear terms. He issued the following warning:

"To the leaders of all the nations of the Near East, I wish to say what three American Presidents have said before me—that the United States is firmly committed to the support of the political independence and territorial integrity of all the nations of that area.

The United States strongly opposes aggression by anyone in the area, in any form, overt or clandestine. This has been the policy of the United States led by four Presidents—Truman, Eisenhower, Kennedy, and myself—as well as the policy of both of our political parties.

The record of the actions of the United States over the past twenty years, within and outside the United Nations, is abundantly clear on this point.

We have always opposed—and we oppose in other parts of the world at this very moment—the efforts of other nations to resolve their problems with their neighbors by the aggression route. We shall continue to do so. And tonight we appeal to all other peace-loving nations to do likewise. I call upon all concerned to observe in a spirit of restraint their solemn responsibilities under the Charter of the United Nations and the General Armistice Agreements. These provide an honorable means of preventing hostilities until, through the efforts of the international community, a peace with justice and honor can be achieved."[6]

The following day, Arthur Goldberg, the United States Chief Delegate at the United Nations, made the following statement before the Security Council:

"We are fully aware, as are all the members of the Council, of the long-standing underlying problems of the area. But no problem of this character can be settled by warlike acts. The United States' opposition to the use of aggression and violence of any kind, on any side of this situation, over the years, is a matter of record. As our actions over many years have demonstrated, and as President Johnson reaffirmed in his statement yesterday, 'the United States is firmly committed to the support of the political independence and territorial integrity of all the nations of that area. The United States strongly opposes aggression by anyone in the area, in any form, overt or clandestine.'

My country's devotion to this principle has been demonstrated concretely—not only in the Suez crisis, where we stood against old allies, but consistently through the years. In fact, in the most recent debate in this council involving this area (For background, see Department of State Bulletin of December 26, 1966, p. 974). We made very clear the United States commitment to the solution of all problems of the area by exclusively peaceful means and by recourse to the armistice machinery.

In this spirit, I am authorized to announce that the United States, both within and outside the United Nations, is prepared to join with other Great Powers—the Soviet Union, the United Kingdom and France—in a common effort to restore and maintain peace in the Near East."[7]

In the face of such determined warning and undertaking by the United States, if for no other reason, the Arabs felt secure and were not themselves going to start a war with Israel and get involved with the U.S. government.

When the territorial integrity of Egypt, Jordan and Syria was violated, the Arabs truly believed that President Johnson would honor the United States' firm commitment of stopping the aggression and demanding immediate and unconditional withdrawal of the Israeli forces, as President Eisenhower—one of the three Presidents mentioned by President Johnson—had done in 1957 when the Israelis invaded the Sinai Peninsula. Instead, President Johnson reversed himself and demanded of the Arabs to bow to Israeli demands for a peace treaty with Israel for secure and recognized boundaries before withdrawal.*

A feeling of utter despair and disbelief pervaded the Arab world, especially when the Arabs observed United States opposition to the condemnation of aggression as a matter of principle; the withholding of support of a resolution for Israeli withdrawal from territories occupied; and abstention twice in the General Assembly and once in the Security Council when resolutions on Jerusalem were adopted calling upon Israel "to rescind all measures already taken and to desist forthwith from taking any action that would alter the status of Jerusalem."[8] It was only then that the Arabs realized that the warnings of the U.S. president were solely for the protection of Israel and not against anything that the Israelis might do.

Aid to Israel from American Sources

United States aid to Israel falls into three categories, namely:

---

*Compare this attitude by President Johnson with his prompt action following the Soviet invasion of Czechoslovakia in 1968.

The U.S. government then demanded the immediate convening of the Security Council and presented the council with a draft resolution condemning the invasion as a violation of the territorial integrity of a member state and demanded immediate withdrawal. The resolution failed because it was vetoed by the Soviet Union.

Direct governmental assistance;
Tax-free donations and contributions;
The sale of Israeli Bonds.

It is not the business of the Arabs what funds the Israelis receive from American Jews so long as this aid does not affect them adversely. But they are certainly very much concerned over the aid the Israelis receive in the nature of direct governmental assistance and from the tax-free status of contributions going to Israel from the United Jewish Appeal. These monies are being used mainly to perpetuate an injustice against the Palestinian people and to continue the occupation of Arab territories. Such aid further encourages the Israelis in their arrogant, intransigent and defiant attitudes towards the United Nations and its resolutions on the Palestine question.

The U.S. government admits that its aid to Israel is to serve two purposes:

(a) To assist Jewish immigrants to settle in Israel;
(b) To maintain a balance of military power between Israel and the Arab States.

If the Israelis were to be within the provisions of International Law, the Charter of the United Nations, the Universal Declaration of Human Rights, and were to comply with the directions in the numerous resolutions adopted by the General Assembly and the Security Council, there would be no need to maintain a so-called balance of military power between them and the Arab states, because there would be no conflict of interests between them, and therefore no need for military precautions.

The extent of the financial aid that the state of Israel has received from the United States during the fiscal years 1948 to 1977, amounted to a total of $25,600.3 million, broken up as follows:

1. *From the U.S. Government (Military and Economic)*

	(In millions of dollars)	
1948–1975	6,562.3	
1976	2,425.0	
1977	2,100.0	11,087.3

Calculated on the basis of an estimated American population of 220 million persons, and on the average of the two years 1976 and 1977 of say 2.3 billion per annum, this financial assistance to Israel costs the United States about $6-million a day, or over $10 per year for every man, woman and child living in the country—much more than any assistance granted by the federal government to any state in the Union!

2. *From Other United States Sources (In millions of dollars)*

Source	1948–1975	1976	1977	1948–1977
Private Institutions	3,363.0	470.0	465.0	4,298.0
Private Individuals	2,301.0	538.0	460.0	3,299.0
Israeli Bonds	2,611.0	264.0	282.0	3,157.0
Loans (Commercial)	2,060.0	120.0	120.0	2,300.0
Investments	1,410.0	52.0	87.0	1,549.0
Totals	11,745.0	1,444.0	1,414.0	14,603.0

Note: The monies received by Israel from the United States under (1) and (2) above, namely, $25,690.3 million, works out at $7,300 per Israeli.

The funds donated or contributed to the United Jewish Appeal (U.J.A.) and sent to Israel are tax-free because they are supposed to be used for humanitarian purposes. But this is not altogether true. It has already been pointed out that part of the tax-free dollars finds its way back to the United States to be used for "the indoctrination of United States Jews themselves in Zionist politics and culture," as well as for "lobbying and propaganda purposes."

Disclosures of other abuses in the use of these tax-free funds comes to light from time to time. Some of these are:

1. The American Council for Judaism pointed out that, "few contributors to the United Jewish Appeal know that the Jewish Agency for Israel —recipient of 80% of U.J.A. dollars going abroad—has IL. 150,763,332 invested (in 1965) in profit-making corporations. These 'relief' dollars go into El Al Airlines, Zim-Israel Navigation Co. and construction, agricultural and other firms operating on a profit basis. Last month" (September 1965), "S.Z. Shragai, head of the Jewish Agency's immigration department, offered British Zionists new apartments in Israel for $100 to $333 down, paying off the rest with a loan from the Jewish Agency for 30 years at 6% . . ."[9]

2. The Jewish National Fund was accused of diverting relief funds for other profit-making ventures. This accusation was made by the *Jerusalem Post* (Israel) newspaper. It wrote: "The Jewish National Fund is diverting funds contributed by world Jewry for reclamation work into setting up joint contracting companies with private firms." The paper complained that "these companies receive the bulk of J.N.F. work—although their work is more expensive according to the managers of a large contracting firm." The *Post* then comments that it was not known "if the J.N.F. was legally entitled to engage in private contracting," but pointed out that, even if so, "it was unethical to take donations from abroad and use them to set up such companies."[10]

3. Tax-free dollars, intended for humanitarian purposes, find their way also as contributions to election funds of certain friendly Senators and Congressmen; to pay honoraria to selected speakers at fund-raising or other functions; to meet the expenses of free trips to Israel of politicians, churchmen, and members of the media; and to meet entertainment expenses of such persons who might be of service to Israel.

Commenting on these tax-free donations, James Warburg, a prominent financier of the United States Jewish community, enquired: "Why should all contributions to the United Jewish Appeal be tax-deductible when so large a proportion of them flow directly or indirectly into the hands of a foreign government that openly engages in propaganda attempting to influence the policy of the government of the United States?"[11]

Another comment on the methods used to obtain these tax-free donations comes from the late Henry Hurwitz, a prominent Jewish writer. Hurwitz said: "as is well known, a very large proportion of the supposedly *voluntary* philanthropic donations are extracted from business and professional men on threats of punitive economic and social sanctions. This must be described as what it is—a species of terrorism. Such terrorism has become a most effective technique in large Jewish fund-raising."[12]

In 1958, Senator E. Flanders of Vermont saw the dangers to United States interests in Israeli policies in the Middle East and recognized that the funds which go to Israel from the United States in the form of charity, were being utilized for other than charitable purposes. He therefore presented the Senate with a draft resolution in the following terms:

"Whereas the unrest in the Arab world is caused primarily by the forcible occupation of Arab land by the government of Israel, and Whereas the expansion of the population of Israel threatens an added seizure of Arab territory, and

Whereas the over-population of Israel is largely financed by tax-free contributions from American citizens,

Therefore, be it

Resolved that the Treasury investigate the uses to which tax-free contributions of American citizens are put when sent to Israel, to see whether they tend to exacerbate Middle East turmoil rather than relieve unavoidable distress to the end that the tax-free status may be justified or withdrawn."[13]

It was no surprise to see the failure of the draft resolution.

XX United Nations Peace Efforts and Failures

Failures of UN Peace Efforts (1948–1967)

Soon after the Palestine tragedy occurred in 1948, the UN General Assembly appointed Count Folke Bernadotte, of Sweden, as Mediator to "promote a peaceful adjustment of the future situation in Palestine." He was assassinated by the Israelis on September 17, 1948 because his proposals conflicted with Israeli goals.

The second effort for a settlement was made by the Palestine Conciliation Commission, and this also failed, with the result that the matter was shelved and the Palestinians were left to languish in refugee camps while the Israelis were busy consolidating their position in Arab homes and Arab lands until the June 1967 War broke out with more territories occupied and more people fleeing or expelled from their homes.

The Jarring Mission (1967–1973)

Since the June 1967 War, peace in the Middle East centered around Security Council Resolution No. 242 of November 22, 1967, which provides, among other things, for "Israeli withdrawal from territories occupied, the termination of all claims or states of belligerency, freedom of navigation, the achievement of a just settlement of the refugee problem, and guarantee of the territorial inviolability and political independence of all states in the area." Ambassador Gunnar Jarring, of Sweden, was appointed special representative and entrusted with the task of implementing the provisions of the said Resolution in a third attempt to conclude a peace agreement between the parties.

From the beginning, the governments of Egypt and Jordan signified their willingness to comply with the provisions of the Security Council Resolution and notified the special representative accordingly. But the

Israeli authorities dilly-dallied to gain time and in order to confront the world with an accomplished fact. The lack of progress toward peace prompted the General Assembly to adopt a resolution in which it "noted with appreciation the positive reply given by Egypt to the special representative's initiative for establishing a just and lasting peace in the Middle East," and called "upon Israel to respond favorably to the special representative's peace initiative."[1]

Ambassador Jarring spent much time in the Middle East shuttling between the various capitals in the area. In the end, he made one final attempt to break the deadlock. On February 8, 1971, he presented the governments of Egypt and Israel with an aide-memoire in which he stated:

"I wish to request the governments of Israel and the United Arab Republic to make to me at this stage the following prior commitments simultaneously and on condition that the other party makes its commitment and subject to the eventual satisfactory determination of all other aspects of a peace settlement, including in particular a just settlement of the refugee problem:

Israel would give a commitment to withdraw its forces from oc-cupied United Arab Republic territory to the former international boundary between Egypt and the British Mandate of Palestine on the understanding that satisfactory arrangements are made for:

(a) Establishing demilitarized zones;

(b) Practical security arrangements in the Sharm Esh-Sheikh area for guaranteeing freedom of navigation through the Strait of Tiran;

(c) Freedom of navigation through the Suez Canal.

The United Arab Republic would give a commitment to enter into a peace agreement with Israel and to make explicitly therein to Israel, on a reciprocal basis, undertakings and acknowledgements covering the following subjects:

(a) Termination of all claims or states of belligerency;

(b) Respect for and acknowledgement of each other's sovereignty, territorial integrity and political independence;

(c) Respect for and acknowledgement of each other's right to live in peace within secure and recognized boundaries;

(d) Responsibility to do all in their power to ensure that acts of belligerency or hostility do not originate from or are not committed from within their respective territories against the population, citizens or property of the other party; and

(e) Non-interference in each other's domestic affairs."

Ambassador Jarring added: "In making the above-mentioned sugges-tion, I am conscious that I am requesting both sides to make a serious commitment, but I am convinced that the present situation requires me to take this step."

Egypt's answer was a definite yes; but Israel's reply was a categorical no. It accused Ambassador Jarring of exceeding his functions and refused to cooperate with him unless he altered his position.

Much surprise was expressed over Israel's negative attitude because many then believed that the Israelis were truly and sincerely anxious for a just and lasting peace, and here was their opportunity. No was Israel's answer to the efforts of the four permanent members of the Security Council who tried to intervene; and no was the Israeli reply to even the continuation of Ambassador Jarring's mission of mediation. No was also the answer to the attempts of the ten distinguished leaders of Africa who tried to intervene in 1971; and another no was the Israeli response to the considered views of the Non-Aligned Nations. This brought to an end the mission of Ambassador Jarring.

UN Recognition of Palestinian National Identity

Between 1948 and 1969, the United Nations dealt with the Palestinians merely as refugees in need of shelter and maintenance. But, in 1969, the General Assembly specifically and formally recognized, for the first time, the inalienable rights of the Palestinian people, declaring that the Assembly:

"*Recognizing* that the problem of the Palestine Arab refugees has arisen from the denial of their inalienable rights under the Charter of the United Nations and the Universal Declaration of Human Rights, *Gravely* concerned that the denial of their rights has been aggravated by the reported acts of collective punishment, arbitrary detention, curfews, destruction of homes and property, deportation and other repressive acts against the refugees and other inhabitants of the occupied territories, . . .

"*Reaffirms* the inalienable rights of the people of Palestine;

"*Draws the attention* of the Security Council to the grave situation resulting from Israeli policies and practices in the occupied territories and Israel's refusal to implement [United Nations] resolutions;

"*Requests* the Security Council to take effective measures in accordance with the relevant provisions of the Charter of the United Nations to ensure the implementation of these resolutions."[2]

In 1970, the General Assembly, reasserting its previous demands for Israel withdrawal from territories occupied in 1967, for the observance of the right of return of the refugees, and for the cessation of violations of human rights, advanced to acknowledge the central position of the Palestine issue in the Middle East situation, in the following words:

"*Recognizes* that the people of Palestine are entitled to equal rights and self-determination, in accordance with the Charter of the United Nations.

Declares that full respect for the inalienable rights of the people of Palestine is an indispensable element in the establishment of a just and lasting peace in the Middle East."[3]

In 1973, the General Assembly adopted a resolution that dealt with the situation in Africa as well as in the Middle East. The assembly recognized in this resolution that armed struggle was a legitimate part of a liberation movement, declaring that the assembly:

"*Reaffirms* the inalienable right of all people under colonial and foreign domination and alien subjugation to self-determination, freedom and independence . . .

"*Also reaffirms* the legitimacy of the people's struggle for liberation from colonial and foreign domination and alien subjugation by all available means, including armed struggle;

"*Condemns* all governments that do not recognize the right to self-determination and independence of peoples, notably the people of Africa still under colonial domination and the Palestinian people.[4]

Middle East Conflict Before the General Assembly

In 1972, the Palestine problem and the situation in the Middle East came before the XXVIIth session of the United Nations. The debate concluded with the toughest resolution so far adopted against the Israeli authorities. It once again deplored the non-compliance by Israel "to respond favorably to the special representative's peace initiative;" it declared once more that "the acquisition of territories by force is inadmissible and that consequently territories thus occupied must be restored;" and it reaffirmed that "the establishment of a just and lasting peace in the Middle East should include the application of both of the following principles:

(a) withdrawal of Israeli armed forces from territories occupied in the recent conflict;

(b) termination of all claims or states of belligerency and respect for and acknowledgement of the sovereignty, territorial integrity and political independence of every state in the area and its right to live in peace within secure and recognized boundaries free from threats or acts of force."

The resolution then invited Israel "to publicly declare its adherence to the principle of non-annexation of territories through the use of force:" and reaffirmed once more that "any changes carried out by Israel in the occupied Arab territories in contravention of the Geneva Conventions are null and void and consequently calls upon Israel to rescind forthwith all measures and to desist from all policies and practices affecting the demographic structure or physical character of the occupied Arab territories."

The resolution also called upon "all states not to recognize any such changes and measures carried out by Israel in the occupied Arab territories and invites all states to avoid actions, including actions in the field of aid, that could constitute recognition of that occupation."

Furthermore, the resolution recognized that "the respect of the rights of the Palestinians is an indispensable element in the establishment of a just and lasting peace in the Middle East.[5]

The resolution was adopted by 86 votes to 7 with 31 abstentions. Six Latin American countries of the 134 United Nations members voted with Israel in opposition, while the United States abstained.

By its abstention, the U.S. government down-graded United Nations efforts to uphold the principles of its charter and other international instruments, such as the Universal Declaration of Human Rights and the Fourth Geneva Convention of 1949. It also encouraged the aggressor to continue to defy the community of nations and to keep the Middle East in a continued state of tension.

The deadlocked situation of no-war no-peace and Israeli construction activities in occupied territories had all the indications that the Israelis had no intention of relinquishing any parts of the occupied territories and were merely bidding for time to conclude their program of expansion by the pretext of wanting peace through direct negotiations.

Middle East Conflict Before Security Council

In June 1973, the government of Egypt made one final attempt at a peaceful settlement by coming, once again, to the Security Council in the hope that the Council would recognize the seriousness of the situation and act before it is too late.

On June 6, 1973, the Security Council met. Muhammad El-Zayyat, then Foreign Minister of Egypt, presented the case for his country. After reviewing the conditions under which the state of Israel came into being, he pointed out that the legal borders of the state of Israel were those defined in General Assembly Resolution No. 181(II) of November 29, 1947, which recommended the partition of Palestine into a Jewish state, an Arab state and an International Zone of Jerusalem and Environs under United Nations jurisdiction. In June 1967, El-Zayyat said, the Israelis violated the international boundaries between Palestine under the British Mandate and its neighbors.

El-Zayyat then referred to the numerous resolutions adopted by the General Assembly and the Security Council and declared: "Egypt accepted the principle of the appointment of a Special Representative of the Secretary General, who was to be Ambassador Gunnar Jarring; Egypt gave him its active support and sincere co-operation when, on February 8, 1971, after four long years of arduous work, he addressed to us, and to Israel, his two identical aide-memoirs. Seven days later, on February 15, Egypt gave him the serious commitments that he had asked for, including readiness to enter into a peace agreement with Israel if Israel also carried out all its obligations under the Charter and as requested by Ambassador Jarring's mandate and authority. After a year of challenge, frustration and immobility, he again tried to work. It was suggested in February 1972 that the parties should exchange, through Ambassador Jarring, clarifications of their positions on the various subjects dealt with in the Council resolution of November 1967 with a view to formulating provisions for inclusion in a peace treaty. Again, Egypt accepted in an effort to break the impasse. Again Israel scuttled this latest and last effort, insisting that the so-called Jarring initiative of February 8 was outside his terms of reference. In a word, Israel threw out the last long six years. It has aimed, and I am sure it is still aiming, at keeping the *status quo* in order to perpetuate its occupation and, again I repeat, to terrorize us into surrender."[6]

On the question of Israel's request for direct negotiations, El-Zayyat replied: "Israeli leaders keep insisting on direct negotiations with Arab States with no prior conditions. Egypt accepted to have any talks without prior conditions. But do not let us be fooled. Everything, they claim, would be negotiable. In the same breath, the Israeli government has declared and notified you, Mr. President, and this Council officially by notifying Ambassador Jarring, that it poses a very heavy pre-condition. In its communication to Ambassador Jarring dated February 26, 1971, Israel says it would not withdraw to the pre-June 5 boundaries: to wit, it will have to take a part of Egypt and part of Syria and part of Jordan. This is a pre-condition. Another pre-condition is the pre-condition of occupation. The peace diktat imposed by the victor upon the vanquished is a pre-Charter concept that the United Nations system has outlawed. Basic norms of contemporary international law contain a ruling on the non-validity of treaties imposed under occupation under the threat or use of force. Article 17 of the Organization of American States, signed at Bogota in 1948, states: 'No territorial acquisitions or special advantages obtained either by force or by other means of co-ercion shall be recognized.' But this is perhaps too old, it is 1948. Let us see whether there is some fresh affirmation. The principle has been clearly stated and solemnly codified in the United Nations Vienna Convention of the Law of Treaties concluded by the United Nations Conference on the Law of Treaties in Vienna on May 23, 1969. Article 52 of that Convention stated: 'A treaty is void if its conclusion has been procured by the threat or use of force in violation of the principles of international law embodied in the Charter of the United Nations'."[7]

El-Zayyat then referred to a symposium held by seven former Israeli chiefs of staff and stated that they were all in agreement on the following points: (1) They believed that the Arab leaders are now ready and willing to sign a peace agreement with Israel on the basis of Israeli withdrawal to the international borders before June 5, 1967; (2) They agree that it is preferable for Israel to disregard this Arab readiness for peace and to hold out in the hope of complete capitulation. That capitulation is to come within 30 years; (3) They feel there is now no military danger at all from the Arab countries. They believe the contrary to be true.[8]

In the light of this disclosure, El-Zayyat pointed out that "while the military occupation remains, Israel continues its active war. It continues to change the physical character and demographic composition of the occupied Arab territories in order to create what it has always called new facts and to confront the world with them. To that end, Israel resorts to lawless practices, such as the total destruction of towns and villages, mass deportation of inhabitants and, most important, establishment of Israeli military and para-military settlements in the Arab territories—concerning which these generals have said: 'What we build must stay; it is not prefabricated'."[9]

The Organization of African Unity Assembly of Heads of State and Government, representing 41 African States, delegated six of its foreign ministers to participate in the deliberations of the Security Council on the situation in the Middle East, and present the Council with the resolutions of the organization. Excerpts from the statements of two of the delegated foreign ministers are given here:

The Foreign Minister of Tanzania—"Since the Israel aggression of 1967, that country has continued to occupy several parts of territories belong-ing to independent Arab states . . . It has been rightly stated that this situation is a threat to international security and that, hence, this council must not only talk and express pious sentiments without taking firm and concrete action to dislodge the aggressor and to put right the situation brought about by that aggression. For us in Africa—the situation is not only a continuing menace to the territorial integrity of Egypt, but is also a situation that we view as a direct threat to our own security.

"Our concern with the situation in the Middle East does not spring only from the fact that an African state is a victim of aggression. It stems also from the fact that Israel has now developed an immunity to international public opinion comparable to that of the minority racist regimes in southern Africa . . . the Organization of African Unity, the Conference of the Non-Aligned States and Governments in Georgetown, Guyana, governments, institutions and individuals have called upon Israel to withdraw from Arab territories, with no favorable response from the government of Israel. It has continued to flout world public opinion and has completely continued to disregard it. Once it painted the picture of a small country threatened with extinction. In fact, when the representative of Israel spoke yesterday, the same picture again was painted in this council. Yet now it is proving itself not as a country that is threatened but as the country that is threatening others. Further, it has begun to propound and to practice aggression and expansionism, and its behavior has continued to be that of an aggressor. It has continuously committed acts of aggression against some of the Arab States and it has continued to practice its policy of expansionism by holding on to countries occupied as a result of aggression while arrogantly maintaining that it does not envisage withdrawing back to the borders existing before the war of aggression in 1967. Recently, it has embarked on acts of terrorism as a policy of state and these acts of terrorism have been endorsed by the highest levels of Israeli leadership.

"This organization cannot accept that position. It is a position which, if endorsed, will mean the endorsement of the acquisition of territories through the use of force. It is a position which, if accepted, will mean acceptance of aggression as a policy in international relations. It is a position which, if we endorse it, will really mean endorsing the rule of the jungle, that is, a world without law. Surely this is not what this organization was established to defend and perpetuate . . .

"Fulfilling the mandate entrusted by the Tenth Summit Conference of the Organization of African Unity, the Tanzanian delegation wishes to make an earnest appeal to the council to take decisive measures to arrest and to terminate the trend of lawlessness and injustice in the Middle East. We call upon the Security Council to decide, here and now, on effective measures calculated to eliminate the consequences of the 1967 war of aggression; to restore the legitimate rights of the Palestinians who are now compelled to live in exile in conditions of squalor and utter frustration; and to establish conditions where a just and lasting peace can prevail in that region."[10]

The Foreign Minister of Nigeria, as one of the six foreign ministers delegated to speak on behalf of the Organization of African Heads of State and Government, representative of all 41 independent African States, "unanimously adopted a resolution which noted with deep concern that, despite the numerous resolutions of the Organization of African Unity and the United Nations calling upon Israel to withdraw from all occupied African and Arab territories, Israel not only persisted in refusing to implement those resolutions but also continued to practice 'a policy of intimidation with a view to creating in the said territories a state of *fait accompli* aimed at serving its expansionist designs.' The resolution went on further to deplore the systematic obstruction by Israel of all the efforts exerted to reach a peaceful solution to the problem at both the international and the African levels and to recall in that respect the negative attitude of Israel toward the 1971 mission of the ten African heads of state mandated by the Organization of African Unity to work for the implementation of Security Council resolution 242 (1967) of November 22, 1967, which stipulated in particular the withdrawal of Israeli forces from the occupied territories in conformity with the principle of the inadmissibility of the acquisition of territories by force."

The Foreign Minister added that "the resolution, *inter alia:*

"2. *Strongly condemns* the negative attitude of Israel, its acts of intimidation and its obstruction of all efforts aimed at a just and equitable solution of the problem in accordance with the Security Council resolution 242 of November 22, 1967;

"3. *Calls once more* for the immediate and unconditional withdrawal of Israeli forces from all occupied African and Arab territories;

"4. *Declares* that all changes effected by Israel in the occupied territories are null and void, and pledges not to recognize any changes leading to a fait accompli or likely to jeopardize the territorial integrity of the countries that are victims of the Israeli aggression;

"5. *Recognizes* that the respect of the inalienable rights of the people of Palestine is an essential element in any just and equitable solution, besides being an indispensable factor for the establishment of permanent peace in the region;

"6. *Reaffirms* in the name of African solidarity and by virtue of Article 11, paragraph 1(c) of the OAU Charter its active and total support for the Arab Republic of Egypt in her legitimate struggle to recover entirely and by all means her territorial integrity;

"7. *Draws* the attention of Israel to the danger threatening the security and unity of the African continent as a result of its continued aggression and refusal to evacuate the territories of the states victims of that aggression and declares that the attitude of Israel might lead OAU member states to take, at the African level, individually or collectively, political and economic measures against it, in conformity with the principles contained in the OAU and UN charters;*

"8. *Earnestly calls* upon the Big Powers supplying Israel with arms and military equipment of all kinds and granting it moral and political support that enables it to strengthen its military potential, to refrain from doing so;

"9. *Strongly supports* the Egyptian initiative requesting the United Nations Secretary-General to report to the Security Council on the explosive situation prevailing in the Middle East, and expresses the

---

*Because of continued Israeli lack of response to the appeals of African states, by the end of 1973, 34 African states had cut off diplomatic relations with the state of Israel.

hope that the Security Council shall take every appropriate measure to implement immediately the relevant resolutions adopted by the United Nations, so that a just and durable peace may be established in the region."

The Foreign Minister of Nigeria ended by stating that "we have come to demonstrate our solidarity with the United Nations and our faith in its resolutions. We have come to plead humbly that every effort should be made to implement the resolutions which you adopt here in the Security Council and appeal through you, Mr. President, to the friendly state of Israel to pay more heed to the resolutions of the United Nations and to show some consideration for the legitimate concerns of Africa . . ."[11]

The Conference of Foreign Ministers of Non-Aligned Countries also sent a delegate to the Security Council in the person of the foreign minister of Guyana, to present to the Council the resolution adopted by the conference at its meeting held in Georgetown, Guyana, in August 1972. The resolution read by the foreign minister expressed, *inter alia*, "the solidarity of non-aligned countries with Egypt, Jordan and Syria in their legitimate struggle to recover by every means their territorial integrity; it called for the full restoration of the rights of the Arab people of Palestine; it acknowledged unequivocally that the acquisition of territory through force is wholly impermissible, and recorded the intention of non-aligned countries to follow closely the evolution of the situation in the Middle East."[12]

The Israeli response, in a nutshell, centered on the premise that "Israel will under no circumstances relinquish its right under international law to have the boundary of peace established for the first time in the Middle East through negotiation and agreement; nor will Israel acquiesce in any other change in the substance, balance or interpretation of resolution 242 (1967)." The Israeli representative, Yosef Tekoah, accused Egypt of attempting "to tamper with resolution 242 (1967), and especially to exclude determination of secure and recognized boundaries from the process of agreement between the parties," which he claimed "has been the main obstacle to progress in the search for peace." Tekoah then explained that "the purpose of resolution 242 (1967) is to establish a new situation and not to restore the one created by the provisional military armistice lines, a situation of vulnerability and peril that," he claimed, "resulted in the 1967 hostilities. It is clear," he admitted, "that the secure and recognized boundaries are not defined in the resolution, being dependent," he said, "on negotiation and agreement. There is no rule or principle in international law that prevents agreed border changes in peace treaties even when recognized boundaries already exist."[13]

On July 24, 1973, the Security Council voted on a draft resolution that in essence, merely reiterated previous resolutions. Its main provisions were:

"*Emphasizing* its primary responsibility for the maintenance of international peace and security,

"*Emphasizing further* that all members of the United Nations are committed to respect the resolutions of the Security Council in accordance with the provisions of the charter,

"Reaffirming resolution 242 (1967) of November 22, 1967,

"Conscious that the rights of the Palestinians have to be safeguarded,

"2. *Strongly deplores* Israel's continuing occupation of the territories occupied as a result of the 1967 conflict, contrary to the principles of the charter;

"3. *Expresses* serious concern at Israel's lack of co-operation with the Special Representative of the Secretary-General;

"4. *Supports* the initiatives of the Special Representative of the Secretary-General taken in conformity with his mandate and contained in his aide-memoire of February 8, 1971;

"5. *Expresses* its conviction that a just and peaceful solution of the problem of the Middle East can be achieved only on the basis of respect for national sovereignty, territorial integrity, the rights of all states in the area and for the rights and legitimate aspirations of the Palestinians;

"6. *Declares* that in the occupied territories no changes that may obstruct a peaceful and final settlement or may adversely affect the political and other fundamental rights of all the inhabitants in these territories should be introduced or recognized; . . ."[14]

Thirteen nations out of the fifteen, voted in support of the resolution; China abstained because it did not consider the resolution went far enough; but the United States representative vetoed its adoption.

The United States veto was regarded by the Arab states as a slap in the face and an affront to the majority of the United Nations membership, which supported the implementation of the provisions of Security Council resolution No. 242 of November 22, 1967, as the only hope for a peaceful settlement of the crisis in the Middle East. What the Arabs could not understand is how the U.S. government could sponsor a resolution in 1967 calling for Israeli withdrawal and then turn around in 1973 and veto the resolution of implementation. Arab disappointment in the United States position may have contributed to the October 1973 War that followed.

Appointment of Committee to Consider Palestinian Rights

The General Assembly, at its thirtieth session (1975), requested the Security Council to act to enable the Palestinian people to exercise their rights. The Assembly also called for the participation of the Palestine Liberation Organization, on an equal footing with other parties, in all negotiations on the Middle East held under United Nations auspices, requesting the Secretary-General to make efforts to secure the invitation of the PLO to the Peace Conference on the Middle East.[15]

In another resolution adopted on the same day, the General Assembly expressed its concern that no just solution to the problem of Palestine has yet been achieved; that the problem of Palestine continues to endanger international peace and security; and that no progress has been achieved toward:

(a) The exercise by the Palestinian people of its inalienable rights in Palestine, including the right of self-determination without external interference and the right to national independence and sovereignty;

(b) The exercise by Palestinians of their inalienable right to return to their homes and property from which they have been displaced and uprooted.

Under the same resolution, the General Assembly established the Committee on the Exercise of the Inalienable Rights of the Palestinian People. The mandate of the Committee was to formulate recommendations for a program of implementation designed to enable the Palestinian people to exercise their inalienable rights, including:

(a) The right to self-determination without external interference;

(b) The right to national independence and sovereignty;

(c) The inalienable right of the Palestinians to return to their homes and property from which they have been displaced and uprooted."[16] The committee, after holding several meetings, submitted its first report in May 1976.[17] Excerpts from its statements and recommendations on the right of return of the Palestinians, follow:

"It was emphasized that the inalienable rights of the Palestinian people to self-determination could be exercised only in Palestine. Consequently, the exercise of the individual right of the Palestinian to return to his homeland was a *conditio sine qua non* for the exercise by this people of its rights to self-determination, national independence and sovereignty.

"In this respect, it was pointed out that Israel was under binding obligation to permit the return of all the Palestinian refugees displaced as a result of the hostilities of 1948 and 1967. This obligation flowed from the unreserved agreement by Israel to honor its commitments under the Charter of the United Nations, and from its specific undertaking, when applying for membership of the United Nations, to implement General Assembly resolutions 181(II) of November 29, 1947, safeguarding the rights of the Palestinian Arabs inside Israel, and 194(III) of December 11, 1948, concerning the right of Palestinian refugees to return to their homes or to choose compensation for their property. This undertaking was also clearly reflected in General Assembly Resolution 273(III). The Universal Declaration of Human Rights, as well as the Fourth Geneva Convention Relative to the Protection of Civilian Persons in Time of War of August 12, 1949, also contained relevant provisions concerning these rights. The states directly involved were parties to this convention.

"The opinion was expressed that whatever modalities or procedures were envisaged for the implementation of the right of return of the Palestinians—whether such return would be carried out by phases or by quotas according to a definite timetable—that right should be absolute for every Palestinian and must have priority over any other form of substitute arrangements, such as compensation. The Palestinians should be afforded the widest practical opportunities to exercise their right of return, in regard both to the time element and to procedural conditions. Only those Palestinians who would choose not to avail themselves of those opportunities after a predetermined period of time should be considred as opting for compensation instead of actual repatriation . . .[18]

To implement the right of return, a two-phase program was proposed:

"Phase One

The first phase involves the return to their homes of the Palestinians displaced as a result of the war of June 1967. The committee recommends that:

(i) The Security Council should request the immediate implementation of its resolution 237 (1967) and that such implementation should not be related to any other condition;

"Phase two:

The second phase deals with the return to their homes of the Palestinians displaced between 1948 and 1967. The committee recommends that:

(i) While the first phase is being implemented, the United Nations in co-operation with the States directly involved, and the Palestine Liberation Organization as the interim representative of the Palestinian entity, should proceed to make the necessary arrangements to enable Palestinians displaced beteen 1948 and 1967 to exercise their right to return to their homes and property, in accordance with the relevant United Nations resolutions, particularly General Assembly Resolutions 194(III);

(ii) Palestinians not choosing to return to their homes should be paid just and equitable compensation as provided for in Resolution 194(III);

"The Right to Self-Determination, National Independence and Sovereignty

" . . . The evacuation of the territories occupied by force and in violation of the principles of the Charter and relevant resolutions of the United Nations is a *conditio sine qua non* for the exercise by the Palestinian people of its inalienable rights in Palestine . . .

"(a) A time-table should be established by the Security Council for the complete withdrawal by Israeli occupation forces from those areas occupied in 1967 . . .

"(b) The Security Council may need to provide temporary peace-keeping forces in order to facilitate the process of withdrawal;

"(c) Israel should be requested by the Security Council to desist from the establishment of new settlements and to withdraw during this period from settlements established since 1967 in the occupied territories . . .

"(d) Israel should also be requested to abide scrupulously by the provisions of the Geneva Convention . . .

"(e) The evacuated territories . . . should be taken over by the United Nations, which . . . will subsequently hand over these evacuated areas to the Palestine Liberation Organization as the representative of the Palestinian people: . . .

"(g) As soon as the independent Palestinian entity has been established, the United Nations, in co-operation with the states directly involved and the Palestinian entity, should . . . make further arrangements for the full implementation of the inalienable rights of the Palestinian people, the resolution of outstanding problems and the establishment of a just and lasting peace in the region, in accordance with all relevant United Nations resolutions . . ."

Presenting the recommendations to the General Assembly in 1976, the committee chairman said, *inter alia:*

"Never in the history of nations have the actions of an international organization had such a decisive effect on the destiny of a people than those of the United Nations on that of the Palestinian people . . .

"The question of Palestine, which was introduced on April 2, 1947, to the United Nations by the United Kingdom, has borne and still bears the character of a problem of self-determination, which the United Nations to date has not been able to resolve in a just and, therefore, durable manner.

"As a result, the question has remained before the United Nations in a state of uncertainty ever since the very first days of the Organization, which has devoted more time, discussion and effort to its solution to any other item without succeeding in bringing about a just and durable solution . . . This situation does not mean that the United Nations is incapable of promoting a peaceful solution of this question . . .

"This task must be recognized to be both important and difficult. Important because, for the first time, the United Nations is dealing in a specific manner with the question which lies at the heart of the Middle East conflict. Difficult, because the implementation of the rights of the Palestinian people is the subject of diverging, if not diametrically opposed, interpretation . . .

"Our Committee, as you will have noted, has based itself, in its work, solely on the relevant decisions and resolutions of the General Assembly and the Security Council, whether the matter concerned the refugees, the withdrawal from the occupied Arab territories, or the implementation of the right to self-determination of the Palestinian people . . .

" . . . the mandate of the committee, (is) neither to resolve the question of the Middle East nor to reaffirm the rights of Israel, but to define ways and means to ensure recognition of the inalienable rights of the Palestinian people . . ."[19]

In June 1976, the committee report came before the Security Council where the chairman made the following statement:

"The present world situation requires that the Security Council carefully study the recommendations submitted to it so that a settlement of the question may be found, since as everyone knows, such a settlement is essential for the establishment of peace in the Middle East. We believe that such action is all the more appropriate in that the United Nations must bear a great part of the responsibility for the tragedy which the Arab people of Palestine are now experiencing.

"It is in the interests of the state of Israel as well that a real and lasting peace be established in the Middle East.

"Ruthless, blind and unjust force can build nothing that cannot be destroyed by an even greater force based on justice and law.

"The Israeli leaders have too much imagination and too great a sense of political responsibility not to understand that time is working against them. Unfortunately, we must recognize the fact that they are now beginning to count far too many lost opportunities, (The chairman then quoted Mendes-France): 'When a people wishes to free itself of an occupier although the occupier may be militarily more powerful, it will always be successful. This was the case in Vietnam, in Algeria, in Madagascar, in Angola. The same will hold for Palestine'."[20]

The Security Council had debated the Palestine question in the context of the Committee's reports, and had considered a draft resolution declaring that the council:

"Affirms the inalienable rights of the Palestinian people to self-determination, including the right of return and the right to national independence and sovereignty in Palestine, in accordance with the Charter of the United Nations".[21]

The resolution had received ten votes in favor; one against (U.S.A.) and four abstentions. The resolution failed due to the U.S. veto.[22]

The Council again took up the Committee's report in October 1977. The committee chairman again emphasized that the committee's

"mandate was not to deal with the Middle East question in its entirety, but, rather, to seek ways and means of implementing the inalienable rights of the Palestinian people. In other words, the task of our committee consists, above all, in righting the basic imbalance that has always characterized the various United Nations approaches to the Palestine question. Far from being an advocate of partiality, the committee has tried to redress that regrettable imbalance and to give the Palestine question its rightful place and its true dimension . . ."[23]

The chairman stressed that the inalienable rights of the Palestinian people had been recognized by most countries, adding that:

"Israel's right to exist is no longer challenged by anyone. But Israel in turn must recognize the legitimate rights of its neighbors. The world is now thirsting for peace and security. Israel has no right to continue to pose constant threats to the very survival of our planet . . ."[24]

The Committee's report was endorsed by the General Assembly in November 1976[25] and again in December 1977;[26] the Assembly on both occasions re-endorsed the right of return of the Palestinian people.

Origins and Evolution of Palestine Problem (1917–1977)

Pursuant to a General Assembly Resolution dated December 2, 1977,[27] the Committee on the Exercise of the Inalienable Rights of the Palestinian People, appointed a special unit and requested it to prepare a study on the Origins and Evolution of the Palestine Problem, as follows:

"The study should place the problem in its historical perspective, emphasizing the national identity and rights of the Palestinian people. It should survey the course of the problem during the period of the League of Nations Mandate and show how it came before the United Nations. It should also cover the period of United Nations involvement in the problem."

The study was prepared in two parts:

Part I—Surveys the historical origins during the period 1917–1947, during most of which Palestine was governed under a mandate granted by the League of Nations.[28]

Part II—Covers the evolution of the Palestine Question from the time it was taken up in the United Nations to the end of the year 1977.[29]

A third study on the Right of Return of the Palestinian People was also prepared and submitted to the committee.[30] In its introduction, the unit stated:

"The right of a person to return to his home in his native country traditionally has been included among an individual's fundamental rights. Only in the case of criminals was its denial regarded as a justifiable punishment, exile or banishment being regarded as one of the more severe punishments. Jurists were more concerned with securing the right of a person to leave his country freely, without unjustified interference from his ruler or government. The right of the individual to return home was taken as a corollary to the basic right of freedom of movement once this was established.

"In cases where persons had been forced to leave their country because of *force majeure*, such as war, the right of return could not be questioned. So natural was this principle considered, so axiomatic a corollary to the fundamental right to life, that juridical works paid little attention to a principle considered self-evident.

"The right of return normally would be a personal, an individual right. Only when large groups have been displaced from their homes would it assume a collective dimension. But it is rare that the right of return should be invoked on a national scale, that there should be a situation where the greater part of an entire nation should be uprooted from its land, be exiled and then denied the right of return. In our times a notable case in this dimension is that of the Palestinian people, forced to flee their ancestral land by reason of military and political action and then to find the right of return denied them on political and legal grounds.

"In the case of the Palestinian people, the individual or personal right of return assumes a special significance for, without its restoration, the exercise of the collective or national right of self-determination, itself guaranteed by a variety of international instruments, becomes impossible. Unable to exercise the fundamental right of self-determination during the period of the Mandate, although recognized in the Covenant of the League of Nations as a provisionally independent nation, The Palestinian people have struggled to regain this right since 1947, when the United Nations became involved in the Palestine issue and recommended the partition of Palestine into two states—one Palestinian Arab and the other Jewish. While Israel declared independence on May 14, 1948, on the basis of the United Nations partition resolution, war and politics (both Israeli and Arab) prevented the Palestinian state envisaged in the resolution from coming into existence. Instead, the first great exodus of Pales-

Bitter Harvest   260

tinians fleeing from their homeland took place in 1948, and the second wave followed in the 1967 Middle East War. From then on, the majority of the Palestinian people have been in exile, unable to return to their country, despite the right of those wishing to return to their homes and live at peace with their neighbors in Palestine having been endorsed repeatedly by the General Assembly since 1948.

"For two decades, from 1953 to 1973, the Palestinian issue was treated essentially as a refugee problem. Eventually, in 1974, the UN General Assembly explicitly recognized that the Palestinian people were entitled to self-determination in accordance with the UN Charter, and to reaffirm their inalienable right of return in this context. From then on the Palestine question was no longer only a refugee problem, but a crucial political issue acknowledged by the assembly as lying at the heart of the Middle East problem. There is increasing recognition in world opinion that any settlement of the Middle East dispute will not be possible without the restoration to the Palestinian people of their inherent and inalienable rights."

In 1978, the General Assembly once again noted "with deep regret that repatriation or compensation of the refugees as provided for in paragraph 11 of General Assembly resolution 194(III) has not been effected . . . therefore, the situation of the refugees continues to be a matter of serious concern."[31]

It further reaffirmed "the inalienable right of all the displaced inhabitants to return to their homes or former places of residence in the territories occupied by Israel since 1967, and declared that any attempt to restrict, or to attach conditions to the free exercise of the right of return by any displaced person is inconsistent with that inalienable right and (is) inadmissible." It deplored "the continued refusal of the Israeli authorities to take steps for the return of the displaced inhabitants; and called once more upon Israel:

(a) to take immediate steps for the return of all the displaced inhabitants;

(b) to desist from all measures that obstruct the return of the displaced inhabitants, including measures affecting the physical and demographic structure of the occupied territories."[32]

The vote on Section A of the resolution was 136 in favor and two against (Israel and El Salvador); that on Section F was 115 in favor and four against (Israel, U.S.A., Australia and Canada).

What the General Assembly hoped to accomplish all these years by its annual abortive attempts for an equitable and just settlement, was dissipated by the continued policy of the U.S. government to block implementation by its negative vote in the General Assembly and the use of the veto in the Security Council.

XXI Palestine: Between War and Peace

President Sadat Visits Jerusalem

There was speculation as to the real purpose that prompted President Sadat to make his historic visit to Jerusalem on November 19, 1977, to talk with the enemy—was it a sincere desire on his part to end the state of war between the Arab states and Israel and his trust in Menachem Begin that the Israelis were now ready to respond positively? Or was he being pushed by the U.S. government to make the overtures in return for certain material benefits to his country? Or was it that Egypt's economic situation had reached such a stage that he had no alternative but to seek termination of the conflict and turn his attention to the development of his country and the feeding of his ever growing population even if that meant disaster for the Arab cause? Any of these three possibilities was probable, although President Sadat stated at the time that his heart was set on a just and comprehensive peace worth anything his critics might say or do.

The visit took the world by surprise, and the western countries hailed it as a step in the right direction. In the Arab world, however, the news was received with mixed feelings: A few Arab leaders believing in Sadat's good intentions supported him inwardly; many remained silent and pessimistic as to the outcome; and many others expressed anger and labelled Sadat as a traitor to the Arab cause.

In his speech to the Israeli Parliament, President Sadat was forthright and specific, and initially his approach was for a comprehensive peace that would end all wars in the Middle East, while his demands for a just peace were in conformity with what the Arabs had been demanding of the Israelis all along: Withdrawal from all occupied Arab territories, including East Jerusalem; and recognition of the right of the Palestinian people to regain their lost rights and to resolve their own destiny.

These two demands were in complete accord with the provisions of the UN Charter, which prohibits the acquisition by any country of the territory of another by force of arms; the Universal Declaration of Human Rights; and the numerous resolutions of the United Nations on the repatriation and compensation of the refugees, and their right to self-determination, sovereignty and independence.

The Israeli Position

Israeli Prime Minister Menachem Begin's reply speech, on the other hand, was vague and ambiguous. Without committing himself to anything, he repeatedly stated that "everything was negotiable"—a cliché that the Israelis have used since 1948. He suggested that talks now begun should continue indefinitely until peace is achieved. Later statements revealed, however, that Israeli policy would remain in what might be summed up as follows:

1. The security of the state of Israel and the safety of its citizens came first and will continue to guide the policy of his government;

2. Security Council Resolutions 242 of 1967 and 338 of 1973 do not require total Israeli withdrawal from the territories occupied in the War of June 1967: nor do they apply to the West Bank and the Gaza Strip;

3. The Jewish settlements already established will not be dismantled, and after peace is concluded, will remain under the jurisdiction of the Israeli government;

4. The status of Jerusalem was non-negotiable, and the Holy City will continue to be united and serve as the capital of Israel;

5. The establishment of a Palestinian state on the West Bank and the Gaza Strip was unacceptable because it poses a threat to the security of Israel. But the Israeli government was willing to give the inhabitants of what he described as Samaria, Judea and Gaza some form of self-rule or autonomy under Israel control for a period of five years, after which the matter would be reviewed without any commitment as to independence. Meanwhile, confiscation of Arab lands and the establishment of new Jewish settlements would continue unabated;

6. The Israeli government was not prepared, under any circumstances, to recognize the Palestine Liberation Organization as the representative of the Palestinian People, nor will it ever agree to deal with it.

Analysing the Arab-Israel Positions

To an objective observer, there is very little to criticize in the stated position of President Sadat of the time for demanding what legitimately belongs to the Arabs and which is covered by international instruments. Most Arab criticism focused on Egypt's agreement to sign a separate peace with Israel under terms that still denied Palestinians their basic national rights, and did not result in a return of all Israeli-occupied lands to their inhabitants.

As for the Israeli arguments, the following comments will disclose that territory rather than peace was the main target:

1. *Security*—Security of nations is normally based on trust, mutual

respect for each other's rights, and friendship. However, where a nation feels insecure, it is at liberty to take the precautions it deems necessary, but these measures are usually taken within the confines of its own boundaries, not in the territories of the neighbors. For example, the Maginot Line was built in France, and the Siegfried Line was constructed on German soil. So if Israel feels insecure, it should protect itself by measures taken within its own borders.

But then, the best remedy would be for the Israelis to mend their fences with their Arab neighbors, settle their differences with the Palestinian people, and build their future relations in the area on trust and friendship.

2. *Jewish Settlements*—It is difficult to see how the newly established settlements in occupied territories can give Israel the security it seeks. Neither the waters of the Suez Canal, nor the so-called formidable inpenetrable Bar-Lev Line were able to stem the Egyptian attack when it came in 1973. Besides, in this modern age with its highly sophisticated missiles, borders cannot determine security.

If Israeli logic were to be accepted, the new settlements will themselves, in time, be in need of security if there is no peace. Security is in the mind, and the term secure borders ceases to be an honest one when settlement is expanded up to newly acquired borders; and in order to make the new lines secure, additional land space is sought. In this way, the border line becomes an indefinite forward moving object to accord with the aggressive designs of the expanionist.

This is what actually happened before: In 1948, the Israelis occupied territory beyond that allotted to the Jewish State under the Partition Resolution on the pretext that the extra territory was required to make the new state more secure; in 1951, the Israelis occupied the demilitarized zones established under the Armistice Agreements on the grounds that the zones were needed to protect adjacent Jewish settlements; and after 1967, the Israelis argued that they could not relinquish the Golan Heights because they overlook Jewish settlements in the Hula Basin. The same argument is now being used in the case of the West Bank.

3. *A Palestinian State*—The state of Israel claims sovereignty on the basis of the UN Partition Resolution of 1947 which, it will be recalled, also recommended the creation of an Arab State. The terms of that resolution have never been altered or rescinded, and therefore the coming into existence of a Palestinian state on the West Bank and the Gaza Strip will be merely delayed action in a part of the territory originally reserved for the Arab State.

The right of people to self-determination, sovereignty and independence forms the cornerstone of democracy, and is provided for in the Charter of the United Nations. This right has been recognized and reaffirmed for the Palestinians in Resolution 3236 of November 22, 1974 and others that followed.

The allegation that a Palestinian state will pose a threat to Israeli security, does not conform to fact. Once a just settlement has been reached with the Palestinians, there should no longer be any cause of conflict between Arab and Jew. At any rate, the small Palestinian state will not have the means or capacity to constitute a danger to Israeli security protected, as it would be, by strong international guarantees. It is, however, a fact that Israel, the world's fourth strongest military power, is regarded as a super-power militarily, and has proved itself to be stronger than all the Arab states combined.

4. *The Palestine Liberation Organization*—It is not up to the Israelis, or anybody else, to decide who will and who will not represent the Palestinian people. It is for the Palestinians themselves to select their own representatives under the same principles of democracy; and, rightly or wrongly, they have made their choice. The wish of the Palestinian people has been endorsed by 105 nations of the world; and the United Nations has granted the Palestine Liberation Organization observer status as the sole representative of the Palestinian people.

A lesson should perhaps be learned from past precedents. For example, for ten years, the U.S. government refused to deal with the Viet Cong who were regarded by the Vietnamese as their legitimate representatives, but in the end the U.S. government was compelled to do so as the only way to extricate itself from its ordeal in Vietnam. The wisdom of that belated lesson was not lost sight of when it came to Rhodesia. The U.S. government did in the end advise the Smith regime to deal with the black guerilla leaders for the sake of peace; and it is only logical to predict that the same course of action will eventually be followed in the case of Palestine.* So why the delay?

If the Israelis are truly and sincerely interested in true peace, it should not mattter to them with whom they conduct the negotiations so long as the peace they say they seek becomes genuine and lasting. The Palestinians have made their position abundantly clear—"There can be no peace in the Middle East without the Palestinians, and there are no Palestinians without the PLO."

5. *Jerusalem*—The term "withdrawal from territories occupied" in the Security Council Resolution means withdrawal from East Jerusalem as well, and there can be no argument about it.

The Arabs, with the whole of the Islamic world behind them, are determined that East Jerusalem with its Holy Places must be freed from Israeli control. Thus, even if agreement were reached on all other issues,

---

*Despite the acceptance of the Palestine Liberation Organization as the sole representative of the Palestinian people by the majority of nations in the United Nations, the U.S. government for 14 years continued to support the Israeli position of non-recognition. But, Ambassador Andrew Young, Chief U.S. Delegate to the United Nations, declared in what might have been an early feeler toward a change in the U.S. position, that "the Palestine Liberation Organization must be viewed realistically because it has captured the imagination of the Palestinian people and has become a tremendous influence in Arab countries."

Young said of the PLO: "We may not like it; we don't recognize it." But U.S. dislike of the PLO will not make the organization's stature among Arab nations any "less true."

He then described the PLO's representatives at the United nations as "very skilled politicians and very intelligent, decent human beings." He concluded by noting that in its relationship to the United Nations, the PLO had acted as a "moderating influence."[1] Young later was fired as U.S. Ambassador to the UN as a result of an informal discussion with PLO diplomats.

After the Sadat-Begin peace agreement was signed on March 26, 1979, President Jimmy Carter was reported to have declared that the U.S. government would be prepared to recognize the PLO if it will recognize the state of Israel and Security Council Resolution 242. He did not call for equal recognition by Israel of the PLO as the sole representative of the Palestinian people and their inalienable rights in their homeland.

Jerusalem will continue to be a stumbling block to a permanent and lasting peace in the area.

The Camp David Conference

The negotiations that followed the Sadat visit to Jerusalem, continued with a return visit by Menachem Begin to Isma'ilia; then meetings were held between Moshe Dayan and Ezer Weizmann with their Egyptian counterparts; and finally ended with meetings between Israeli and Egyptian teams in Jerusalem and in Cairo.

The negotiations were abruptly called off by President Sadat because the Israelis showed no signs of flexibility, and he felt that no useful purpose would be served by continuing the dialogue. At this stage, the U.S. government stepped in, and President Jimmy Carter took over personally. A meeting between the three leaders, lasting for thirteen days, was held in Camp David, the proceedings of which were closed to the press and the outside world. In the end, the three leaders emerged with an accord consisting of two documents:

One document was entitled a Framework for an Egyptian-Israeli Peace Treaty whereby the Israelis would withdraw from the Sinai Peninsula in stages. The U.S. government undertook in return to bear the costs, said to be in the neighborhood of $1 billion, for the construction of two airfields in the Negev, to replace those which the Israelis would relinquish in Sinai. As regards the Jewish settlements, the Israelis demanded U.S. financial aid to the extent of about $4 billion to enable them to relocate the settlers in Israeli territory.

The other document entitled a Framework for a Comprehensive Settlement, outlined how the future of the West Bank and the Gaza Strip was to be determined. The agreement provided for the withdrawal of an unspecified part of the Israeli military forces from the West Bank and the Gaza Strip with the relocation of the remainder—also unspecified—in certain positions within the area.

The agreement also provided for the withdrawal of the Israeli military government and the civilian administration, and the establishment of an administrative council under Israeli control.

The agreement was silent on the question of the Jewish settlements that have been established in the West Bank and Gaza Strip in contravention of the provisions of the Fourth Geneva Convention. The Israelis have made it clear that these settlements will not be dismantled; on the contrary, new settlements were to be created, and all would be under the jurisdiction of the Israeli government. The result was a situation where Palestinians controlled only their most immediate municipal and social arrangements: garbage collection, some schooling arrangements, etc., but control of the land remained in Israeli hands, and Palestinian national rights were systematically denied.

Also, absent from the accord for a so-called comprehensive settlement, of course, is any reference to the right of the Palestinian people, living inside and outside Palestine territory, to self-determination, sovereignty and independence, and the restoration of their property rights, as so clearly expressed in General Assembly Resolution No. 3236 of November 25, 1974.

It should be noted that the Palestinians now outside their homes and scattered throughout the world represent three-fourths of the total Palestinian population. These poeple own homes and lands in which the Israelis now live and work, while most of them languish in refugee camps, subsisting on international charity. They have been treated in the accord as if they do not exist. Jerusalem also is not mentioned, giving the impression that it has been agreed between the parties that it will remain the eternal capital of Israel, as Menachem Begin repeatedly declared.

What is significant in the second document mentioned is the concept of self-determination. Throughout the agreement, the term "by agreement of all the parties" is used. By "all the parties" is apparently meant Egypt, Israel, the Palestinian Administrative Council and Jordan. All these must agree on the procedures for the establishment of the so-called self-governing authority on the West Bank and the Gaza Strip, but Israel will retain the right of veto over matters such as:

1. Which Palestinians, other than those from the West Bank and Gaza Strip, may be included in the Egyptian and Jordanian delegations;

2. The nature of the so-called self-governing authority to be exercised in the West Bank and the Gaza Strip;

3. Which refugees, displaced by the 1967 War, can return to the West Bank and the Gaza Strip;

4. Any decision made by the Palestinians must be on the grounds of security for Israel, which provision eliminates what little was left of the label of self-rule;

5. The final status, following the five-year interim period, of the West Bank and the Gaza Strip. Specifically—and this is the most important point—Israel can and will veto a Palestinian decision establishing an indepdendent Palestinian state. In this way, the Israelis have made sure that an independent Palestinian state will never come into existence, and that the territory of the West Bank and the Gaza Strip would continue to be administered by a sort of Quisling government under total Israeli control.

West Bank and Gaza Arabs Reject Camp David Accord

The response of the mayors and leaders of the West Bank and the Gaza Strip, whose destiny was being decided without their presence or acquiescence, issued a Declaration on October 1, 1978 indicating their strong opposition to the Camp David accord, in these words:

"We stand as one with all of our Palestinian people. We have reviewed the Camp David Agreements, and we wish to state that we reject them. We do so because they serve only to strengthen Sadat's policy of surrender and to defeat the political gains won by our Palestinian Arab people. Those political gains, it should be remembered, were achieved by our people only after great sacrifice, and they have been supported by the Algiers and Rabat Summit Conferences and the United Nations General Assembly . . .

"The so-called self-government proposals for the occupied West Bank and Gaza only legitimize and strengthen the Israeli occupation. We thus consider it a plot against our people's inalienable rights to self-determination and to national independence in an independent Palestinian state under the leadership of the Palestine Liberation Organization, the sole legitimate representative of the Palestinians . . .

" . . . the Palestinian people in the occupied territories affirm the following:

1. The Palestinian Arab people inside and outside occupied Paestine are one, united through history, destiny and struggle.

2. The self-government proposal is totally rejected in form and content because it strengthens Israeli occupation and perpetuates Israeli oppression of our people.

3. The Palestinian people affirm and insist that the Palestine Liberation Organization is its sole, legitimate representative and refuse any trusteeship or alternative, no matter in what form or shape.

4. We look forward to a just and lasting peace in the area, achieved only through our people's exercise of their right to self-determination and national independence, after total Israeli withdrawal from all the occupied territories and after establishing an independent Palestinian state.

5. Arab Palestinian sovereignty must return to Arab Jerusalem, which is an indivisible part of the West Bank. This is an historical and spiritual cause that cannot be compromised."

King Hussein Rejects Camp David Accord

Another rejection of the Camp David Accord came from King Hussein of Jordan. Hussein appears convinced that the then stalled peace talks between Egypt and Israel can never produce an honest and durable Middle East settlement, and he would like to see broader negotiations considered as rapidly as possible under the auspices of the United Nations Security Council.

Hussein contended in an interview with correspondent Christopher Wren that "it was up to President Anwar Sadat of Egypt to return to the ranks of the Arab majority on the issue of Israel so that the Arabs, including the Palestinian could negotiate from a position of solidarity. King Hussein said it was in the interests of Egypt as well as other nations to understand 'that the Arab world is a family, that it is not a situation where Egypt is a shepherd and the rest are a herd that can be moved in any direction without question.'"

The King made it clear that "Jordan had no interest in joining Sadat's efforts to arrange a transition to Palestinian self-rule in the Israeli-occupied West Bank of the Jordan River and the Gaza Strip. The role envisioned for Jordan at the Camp David summit meeting last September [1978], he said, amounted to protecting the Israelis from the Palestinian population under occupation."

Wren then remarked that "the interview left the impression that the King, who had long been considered a moderate, was siding squarely with the militant faction that gathered in Baghdad, the Iraqi capital, last October to denounce Sadat's dealings with Israel. The King's remarks seemed to close the door to any hopes in Cairo and Washington that Jordan might join the negotiations."

King Hussein was reported to have recalled previous efforts to reach "a meaningful solution" before Sadat went to Israel 14 months ago. "It is our feeling now," he said, "that events led us a different way and that there has been a concentration on an Israeli-Egyptian solution which, in the view of all of us in this area is not a solution to the Middle East problem, if it does not include a solution to the Palestinian problem."

The King side-stepped several questions, including whether Jordan would join other Arabs in imposing penalties on Egypt should Sadat sign a treaty with Israel. But the implication, Wren stated, was that Jordan would support the decision of the militant Arabs, "to protect the interests of the Arab states as a whole and to prevent Egypt being used as a doorway into the area for Israeli goods and interests."*

With regard to Jerusalem, which was not mentioned in the Camp David Accords, the King said that "Israel's annexation of the Arab eastern sector of the city has embittered the Arabs who revere the Islamic holy places there. If Arab sovereignty is restored, Jerusalem can be the symbol of peace."

The King then discussed a proposal he had raised the previous month in Europe that all parties go back to the Security Council "to seek guidance, to seek clarification" on Resolution 242, which it adopted after the 1967 Middle East war. This called on Israel to withdraw from captured Arab territory in return for its security.

The Camp David meeting accepted Resolution 242 as a basis for negotiation. But Hussein said that what had subsequently emerged "falls very much short of 242 as we understood it."

The Jordanian ruler concluded by suggesting that discussions at the United Nations could be patterned after the Geneva conference that was held briefly in late 1973, or could be "an enlarged gathering that might include some of our European friends." The King said he felt there was strong support for such a move among other Arabs.[2]

Egyptian-Israeli Agreement Signed

The Camp David Accords floundered because of the different interpretations placed upon their terms by the Israeli authorities, and there was fear in Washington that the negotiations would collapse completely.

Consequently, President Jimmy Carter decided to visit both President Sadat and Israeli Prime Minister Menachem Begin to salvage the situation with fresh proposals of mediation. He arrived in Cairo on March 8, 1979, and later went on to Jerusalem to meet with Menachem Begin and his cabinet.

On March 14, 1979, President Carter returned to Washington with broad smiles of satisfaction that his mission had accomplished what he went out to do, and he was hailed as a hero for having succeeded in

---

*Hussein did in fact participate in the Baghdad Conference, which decided to impose political, diplomatic and economic boycotts on Egypt should President Sadat sign a separate peace agreement with Israel, which he did on March 26, 1979.

getting President Sadat and Menachem Begin to accept his latest proposals of compromise.

On March 20, 1979, Menachem Begin commented on the peace proposals in the form of replies to statements made by Egyptian Prime Minister Mustapha Khalil which should have been sufficient for President Sadat to withdraw from the negotiations. Menachem Begin said:

"Dr. Khalil, Israel will never return to the pre-1967 lines, that is, the country's borders before the 1967 war with the Arabs.

"Secondly, Dr. Khalil, mark my words, united Jerusalem is the eternal capital of Israel. It will never be divided again.

"Thirdly, Dr. Khalil, in Judea, Samaria and Gaza, there will never be a Palestinian state."

Referring to the plan for Palestinian self-rule, Begin said: "We never agreed to autonomy for the territories, but only for the inhabitants," an innovation the like of which has never been heard of before. Opposition Leader Shimon Peres remarked in this respect: "Realistically, I cannot see how you can separate self-government of people and self-government of territory. Can you really distinguish between a man and his house, a farmer and his field? It's impossible."[3]

President Sadat and Menachem Begin were then summoned to Washington; and on March 26, 1979, a separate peace agreement was signed, the main points of which, in summary, were:

Withdrawal of Forces

Israeli forces and civilians will withdraw completely from the Israeli-occupied parts of the Sinai in phases, covering three years. Within nine months of signing of the treaty, Israeli forces will have moved east of a line from El Arish to Ras Muhammad in the south. Within that initial nine months, the Israelis will pull out in an agreed time period, starting with the northern coast near El Arish.[*]

Security

Agreed security arrangements will be established on both sides of the Egyptian and Israeli borders, including zones with limited armaments. United Nations personnel will be stationed in the Sinai to make it a buffer area. The security arrangements can be reviewed whenever either side asks but any change must be by mutual agreement.

A joint commission will facilitate the carrying out of the treaty's security provisions.

Normal Relations

A state of war will be ended and a state of peace established after the treaty is ratified on both sides. After the nine months initial period of withdrawal, normal and friendly relations will be established. These

---

[*]The town of El-Arish was handed back to the Egyptians on May 25, 1979. In return, the Suez Canal was opened to Israeli shipping, and two warships passed through on May 29, 1979. On June 5, 1979, it was agreed to open the borders between Egypt and Israel to civilian traffic by sea in the first instance.

EGYPTIAN-ISRAELI PEACE ACCORD
March 26, 1979

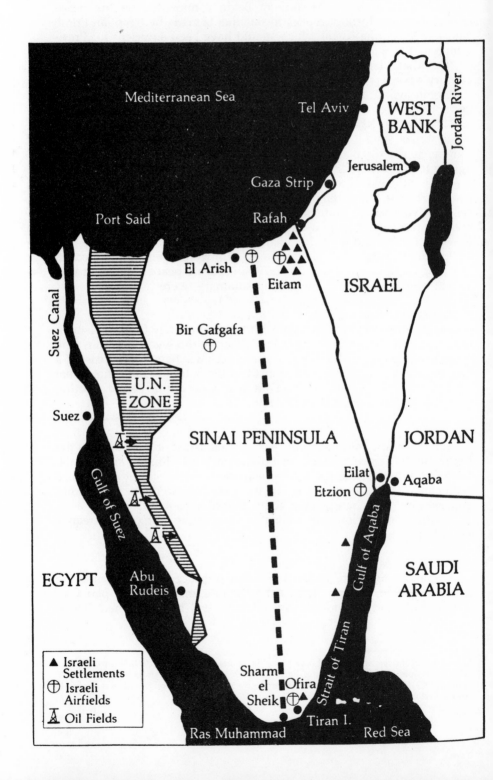

Mediterranean Sea

Tel Aviv

WEST
BANK

Jordan River

Jerusalem

Gaza Strip

Port Said

Rafah

El Arish

Eitam

ISRAEL

Suez Canal

Bir Gafgafa

U.N.
ZONE

Suez

SINAI PENINSULA

JORDAN

Gulf of Suez

Eilat

Etzion

Aqaba

EGYPT

Abu
Rudeis

Gulf of Aqaba

SAUDI
ARABIA

▲ Israeli
    Settlements
⊕ Israeli
    Airfields
⚒ Oil Fields

Sharm
el
Sheik

Ofira

Strait of Tiran

Ras Muhammad

Tiran I.

Red Sea

include an exchange of ambassadors 10 months after the treaty is signed, the removal of all trade and economic barriers and the lifting of boycotts. Normal cultural relations, including exchanges in all fields, are desired. Negotiations for such exchanges will begin no later than six months after completion of the interim withdrawal. There will be a free movement of people and vehicles between the two countries. Air travel will be implemented and Egypt agrees that the airfields to be turned over to it in the Sinai will be used for civilian purposes only. Normal communications will be established.

Free Passage
Ships of Israel and cargoes going or coming from Israel will enjoy the same right of free passage in the Suez Canal and its approaches as other countries. The Strait of Tiran and the Gulf of Aqaba will be regarded as international waterways.

Conflict of Obligations
If this treaty conflicts with other obligations assumed by Egypt, the treaty will nevertheless be binding and implemented. But it does not prevent Egypt from carrying out its obligations under the United Nations Charter to aid countries in self-defense.

Oil
Israel will be permitted to buy in normal commercial terms oil from the Sinai fields being returned to Egypt.

Linkage
Within a month after ratification, Egypt and Israel will begin negotiations for implementing the Camp David agreement on Palestinian self-rule. The two sides agree to make a good-faith effort to complete negotiations on the details of the self-rule within a year. The treaty is cited as "an important step" toward a comprehensive Middle East peace.[4]

Washington sources estimated that the cost of the agreement to the United States in terms of money will amount to about $5 billion per annum during the first three years. Some U.S. Senators remarked that, while the amount was substantial, peace was worth the price.

But the United States had not yet learned the hard lesson that buying influence with money, instead of applying principles of justice and equity and building its relations with other nations on the basis of reciprocal friendship, is not the best policy.

Studying the U.S. role in the Middle East in the light of the concluded peace agreement, the following brief notes should give the reader food for thought:

1. *The United States*—With the fall of the Shah of Iran, the United States was obliged to search for a replacement to the now dissolved U.S.-Iran-Israel axis. President Sadat's willingness to negotiate with the Israelis presented the U.S. government with the ideal opportunity of creating an U.S.-Egypt-Israel axis.

Like the first axis, the second was designed to provide a front against the Soviet Union and to protect the free flow of Arab oil to the western world. Given Egypt's instability, can the U.S. government be sure, under its present policies towards the Arabs, of its permanency? No matter how much military economic aid is pumped into the area, the effectiveness of the envisaged U.S.-Egypt-Israel axis cannot be assured so long as injustice, aggression and denial of Palestinian national rights continue to prevail in the area.

2. *Israel*—The strategic advantages accruing to Israel from a separate peace agreement with Egypt were many. Israeli policy all along has been:

(a) To disrupt, if not destroy, Arab unity to suit its aggressive-expansionist purposes;

(b) Israeli leaders had their eyes on achieving "Jewish leadership for the whole Middle East in the fields of economic development and control," as General Patrick Hurley reported to President Roosevelt in 1943; and

(c) The Israelis were anxious to regain their lost political, diplomatic and economic standing in the Afro-Asian countries following the latter's severance of diplomatic relations with the Jewish state after 1967.

An agreement with Egypt opened a window to Arab markets as well as to those Afro-Asian nations that so far supported the Arab position against Israel. Furthermore, the 40 million Egyptians might have provided the Israelis with a cheap labor force; paving the way towards the invasion of the country by Israeli technical, industrial and agricultural development projects from which the Israelis will benefit greatly.

In addition, the Israelis were promised by President Carter that the United States would continue its military and economic aid to the Jewish state. This alone enabled Israel to maintain its present military superiority over the Arabs and make the Israeli leaders less flexible toward any solution of the Palestine problem.

Other benefits to Israel lay in the implication that Jerusalem had been recognized by President Sadat as the capital of the Jewish state; that the West Bank and Gaza Strip would continue to be ruled by the Israelis under a so-called autonomy plan and that the position of the Palestinians now scattered throughout the world was to be discounted as something of the past.

3. *Egypt*—The advantages accruing to Egypt from the peace agreement included regaining possession of the entire Sinai Peninsula, but after the lapse of three years and under conditions degrading to the sovereignty of a nation. Egypt also received military and economic aid from the United States to replace the aid it now receives from certain Arab states making Egypt the leading Arab ally of the U.S.

The question may be asked: Which is better, to receive aid from an Arab state and be free to use it in the best interests of Egypt and the Arab cause, or receive it from the United States—which is known for its pro-Israeli policy—under conditions less favorable to those granted to the Israelis?

Furthermore, what guarantees did President Sadat have that the Israelis would not start to tamper with the interpretation of the agreement to suit their purposes?

Precedents of Israeli Disrespect for Their International Obligations

If the past is any guide to the future, the Israelis have a record of signing international documents and then violating their provisions to suit their purposes before the ink is dry. They use their signature to advance their interests step by step; pretend to the outside world that they are the good guys and the Arabs are the bad guys; and thereby win sympathy and financial support. The following are examples of how utterly the Israelis have disregarded international agreements in the past, and there is no evidence to show that any change has occurred:

1. In 1949, the Israelis signed Armistice Agreements with the Arab states as a first step toward permanent peace. The Syrian and Egyptian Agreements provided for demilitarized zones from which the military forces of both parties were to be excluded, while the Arab inhabitants were to be allowed to remain in their homes and be protected by locally recruited police.

No sooner where the agreements signed, when the Israelis occupied the demilitarized zones claiming that they were an integral part of Israel; expelled the Arab inhabitants; took possession of their lands; transferred their own farmers into the areas; and militarized the zones. All efforts by the UN Security Council failed to get the Israelis to respect their signature and to comply with the provisions of the agreements freely entered into.

2. The Armistice Agreement with Egypt was signed on February 24, 1949. On March 10,—only thirteen days later—the Israelis attacked and occupied the territory from their positions up to the Gulf of Aqaba coastline from which they were previously barred (See Annex II to the Agreement). Again the Security Council failed to get the Israelis to return to their original positions.

After the invasion of Egypt in 1956, David Ben Gurion declared: "The armistice with Egypt is dead, as are the armistice lines; and no wizard or magician can resurrect these lines."[5]

3. On May 12, 1949, the Israelis signed the Lausanne Protocol whereby they undertook to implement the 1947 resolution on territory and the 1948 resolution on the repatriation or compensation of the refugees. It later became evident that their signing was connected with their application for admission into membership of the United Nations, which was then before the Security Council for the second time. Having failed in the first application for admission made the previous December on the grounds that they had not fulfilled their obligations on the territory and refugee questions, the Israelis this time used their signature on the protocol as a ruse to make believe that they were now prepared to comply.

After their admission on May 11, 1949—almost to the hour with the signing of the protocol, if the time element between Switzerland and New York were taken into consideration—the Israelis reneged and began to apply different interpretations on the meaing of the wording of the protocol demanding that the international frontiers of Mandatory Palestine be considered the frontiers of Israel, with one provisional and temporary exception, namely, that the central area of Palestine, then under Jordanian military authority, in which the Israelis consented to "recognize the Hashemite Kingdom of Jordan as the *de facto* military power," without entering into the future status of the area for the time being.[6] This was not only a departure from their undertaking under the Lausanne Protocol, but also an innovation in flagrant disregard of the Partition Resolution of 1947 that created the Jewish State in the first instance, and the conditions specified in the resolution of admission.

4. The Israelis signed the Universal Declaration of Human Rights but resist to this day to comply with its provisions insofar as the Palestinian refugees are concerned. For example, Article 13(2) prescribes that "everyone has the right to leave any country, including his own, and to return to his country," and Article 17(2) stipulates that "No one shall be arbitrarily deprived of his property;" and yet the Israelis will not allow the refugees to return to their homes and have confiscated their property. On the other hand, the Israelis accuse the Soviet Union—which is not a signatory to the Declaration—of violating the provisions of Article 13(2) by not allowing Soviet Jews to emigrate to Israel.

5. Resolution 242 of November 22, 1967 was passed by the Security Council unanimously and accepted at the time by the Arab states and Israel. But when it came to implementation, the Israelis began to apply interpretations that are foreign to the spirit and intentions of the resolution. They claim that the resolution did not call for total withdrawal, otherwise it would have included the words of either "the" or "all" before the term "territories occupied." Later on, they came up with another novelty, that the resolution did not apply to the West Bank and the Gaza Strip.

Whether the words "the" or "all" were there or not, is immaterial; the UN Charter is the over-riding factor that prohibits "the acquisition by one nation of the territory of another by force of arms." Israel did just that; the Sinai Peninsula, and the Golan Heights, are territories belonging to other nations. The West Bank and the Gaza Strip should become an independent Palestine.

6. On December 6, 1961, the Israelis ratified the Fourth Geneva Convention Relative to the Protection of Civilian Persons in Times of War, but after the June 1967 War, they violated every provision despite the protests and directives of the United Nations. The violations of which the United Nations still complains, are:

Denying the right of return to the refugees and displaced persons;
Expelling and deporting some of the inhabitants of occupied areas;
Annexing East Jerusalem;
Establishing Jewish settlements in occupied territories and transferring some of their own population thereto;
Destroying whole Arab villages and houses, and confiscating Arab lands;
Ill-treating and torturing Arab prisoners and detainees;
Imposing collective punishments.

The Camp David Accord provides for implementation by stages. This was a very dangerous provision because it allowed the Israelis to utilize the time to place interpretations on the wording of the agreement to suit their purposes, as they did in the case of the Armistice Agreements and the Lausanne Protocol, both of which were supposed to lead to permanent peace, but which in fact had the opposite effect.

XXII After Camp David

1. Introductory Remarks

The publication of the second edition of this book coincided with the last year of Jimmy Carter as President of the United States and the beginning of the eight-year period of the Ronald Reagan Administration.

With the conclusion of the Camp David Accords in 1979, there was a general belief in Western countries that President Carter's efforts had helped to break the back of the Arab-Israeli conflict, and that all that needed to be done by the man who replaced him in the White House in 1980 was to follow up and enlarge the scope of the negotiations to gradually envelop the entire Middle East region in a final bid for an equitable and peaceful settlement. But the new Reagan Administration did nothing of the sort to further the cause of peace; and instead, by its unquestioning support of Israeli policies, caused the conflict to fester and grow.

In a nutshell, President Reagan expressed mild verbal opposition to the Israeli annexation of East Jerusalem; to the confiscation of Arab lands and water on the West Bank and the Gaza Strip; to the establishment of Jewish settlements on Arab lands; and the transfer of the new Jewish immigrants to the occupied territories. He increased military and economic aid to Israel, and allowed his then Secretary of State Alexander Haig to plan and implement with the Israelis the invasion of Lebanon in 1982 and provided them with the latest and most sophisticated and internationally prohibited weapons; he instructed the U.S. representative at the United Nations to veto any Security Council resolution condemning Israel or calling for Israeli troops to withdraw from Lebanon; and he allowed the Israelis to remain to this day in the south of

Lebanon holding on to what they describe as a security zone, without regard to the internationally recognized principle that nations establish security zones within their own borders and not in the territories of their neighbors.

Furthermore, Reagan consistently expressed his strong opposition to the violation of the principle of human rights, but confined this opposition to Soviet Jews and ignored the human rights of the Palestinians expelled from their ancestral homeland in 1948 and forced to live as refugees to this day in various parts of the globe and as residents of the occupied territories since 1967. He continued to ignore the reports of Israeli violations by the UN Commission of Human Rights, Amnesty International, and various other prominent international and church organizations, as well as the world press which drew attention to Israel's continued inhuman practices of oppression, persecution, torture of prisoners, imprisonment without trial, deportations, blowing up of buildings, confiscation of property.

This chapter and the next, revised in late 1990 for the book's fourth edition, update the record of the Palestine conflict during the years of the Reagan Administration. They are intended to provide a review of U.S. foreign policy regarding the Palestinians, a policy which claims to stand for human rights and democratic freedoms to be applied to all peoples without fear or favor. These chapters touch on the first years of the George Bush Administration as well, in the context of the U.S. response to the intifada and to the Palestinian peace initiative.

2. The Camp David Accords (1979)

Failure of the Second Camp David Accord, which relates to the West Bank and the Gaza Strip signed between Egypt and Israel in 1979 as a first step towards peace between Arabs and Jews, was foreseen as expressed in Chapter XXI, pp. 265–275. Anwar Sadat was free and within his rights and prerogatives to sign a peace treaty between Egypt and Israel as prescribed in the First Accord, but he was not at liberty to negotiate any settlement with Israel in regard to the West Bank and the Gaza Strip without the presence or the consent of the Palestinians. This failure is responsible for all the troubles and complications that have since followed. His apparent lack of interest in the Palestine problem was also shown in his failure to demand the return of the Gaza Strip to Egyptian administration as was the case before the war of 1967.

Had Anwar Sadat lived long enough to see the effect of his action, no doubt he would have shared in the statement made by Carter after he had left office: In reply to a question on the Canadian "Sunday Morning" radio program in December 1986, Carter said: "If I then knew [at the time of the Camp David conference] what I now know, I would have acted differently."

Instead of leading to a solution to the long-simmering Palestine-Israel dispute, the Camp David process rejected the international call for a UN-sponsored peace conference, proposing instead a series of separate treaties between Israel and various Arab countries, all designed to further U.S. influence in the region. Camp David denied any role for the

PLO, completely ignored the rights of those Palestinians who were expelled and dispossessed in 1948, and left the inhabitants of the West Bank and Gaza Strip looking forward only to long-term so-called "autonomy"—a result falling short of the historic and legitimate desire for independence and statehood.

I have no doubt that both Carter and Sadat were sincere in their desire for peace, but neither of them was sufficiently conversant with the aims and policies of political Zionism toward Palestine. The absence of Palestinian advisers in either camp was responsible for the pitfalls that subsequently developed.

In this respect, I can only blame the Arab states. Instead of cutting off diplomatic relations with Egypt and expelling it from the Arab League, those states should have used other means to show their opposition to the Camp David process. These means might have included demanding that Sadat take with him on his ill-advised mission Palestinian advisers whose rightful and legitimate suggestions would certainly have included the demand for statehood, and would therefore presumably have been rejected by the Israelis. This process, framed by the needs of the Palestinians themselves, might have halted the Camp David agreements altogether. Instead, alone and isolated, Anwar Sadat with Jimmy Carter was unable to challenge Menachem Begin, as subsequent events have shown.

The Palestinians and the Arab states were not alone in rejecting the Camp David Accords. In a resolution No. 34/65(B) of November 29, 1979, the UN General Assembly,

> "*Recalling and reaffirming* the declaration contained in paragraph 4 of its resolution 33/28A of December 7, 1978, that the validity of agreements purporting to solve the problem of Palestine requires that they be within the framework of the United Nations and its Charter and its resolutions on the basis of the full attainment and exercise of the inalienable rights of the Palestinian people, including the right of return and the right to national independence and sovereignty in Palestine, and with the participation of the Palestine Liberation Organization,
>
> 1. *Notes with concern* that the Camp David Accords have been concluded outside the framework of the United Nations and without the participation of the Palestine Liberation Organization, the representative of the Palestine people;
>
> 2. *Rejects* those provisions of the Accords which ignore, infringe upon, violate, or deny the inalienable rights of the Palestinian people, including the right of return, the right of self-determination, and the right to national independence and sovereignty in Palestine, in accordance with the Charter of the United Nations, and which envisage and condemn continued Israeli occupation of the Palestinian territories occupied by Israel since 1967;
>
> 3. *Strongly condemns* all partial agreements and separate treaties which constitute a flagrant violation of the rights of the Palestinian people, the principles of the Charter, and the resolutions adopted in the various international forums on the Palestine issue;
>
> 4. *Declares* that the Camp David Accords and other agreements

have no validity insofar as they purport to determining the future of the Palestinian people and of the Palestinian territories occupied by Israel since 1967."

In a second resolution No. 35/169D of December 15, 1980, the General Assembly, "Reaffirms rejection;" "Expresses strong opposition;" and

"3. *Declares* that no State has the right to undertake any actions, measures, or negotiations that could affect the future of the Palestinian people, its inalienable rights, and the occupied Palestinian territories without the participation of the Palestine Liberation Organization on an equal footing, in accordance with the relevant United Nations resolutions, and rejects all such actions, measures, and negotiations."

The objective of Menachem Begin in signing the Camp David Accords was certainly not peace, nor the beginning of a solution of the Arab-Israeli conflict as Carter had hoped. The exchange of the desert lands of the Sinai Peninsula for a peace treaty was used, among other things, to sow dissension in the Arab ranks, to reduce Arab military power against Israel, and to secure Israel's southern border when the renewal of planned military operations against Lebanon took place.

In 1982, when the Israelis finally invaded Lebanon, the editor of an Egyptian magazine who backed the Camp David Accords, told a group of Israeli journalists: "You turned peace into something hated for the Egyptians." The journalists discovered the truth of his statement from their own observations among officials, journalists, taxi drivers, salespeople, and others. Unlike those who were skeptical from the start, "the advocates of peace with Israel feel defeated, deceived, and scorned." The Egyptian editor stated: "I perceived the peace with Israel to be the cornerstone for a comprehensive peace in the Middle East. But for you peace was merely a trick to neutralize us so as to more easily strike at the Palestinian people."[1]

Anwar Sadat paid with his life for failing to pursue with equal passion in his search for peace the rights of the Palestinians, and the Arab states suffered years of discord and a major continuing tragedy in Lebanon.

3. The Israeli Invasion of Lebanon (1982)

This section is not intended to deal with the invasion of Lebanon except insofar as it affected the Palestine problem.*

The signing of the Camp David Accords in 1979 and the Iraq-Iran war that broke out in 1980 removed from the sphere of Arab defense against Israel the two principal Arab armies: those of Egypt and Iraq. Jordan as a result was neutralized; Syria found itself incompetent to deal with the Israeli army; while Lebanon was in the midst of an internal revolution. This left the Israelis free to pursue their objective of destroying the PLO whose headquarters were in Lebanon; scattering the Palestinian refugees whose camps were to the north and east of Israel; and establishing

---

*For a full study of the invasion of Lebanon and its aftermaths, see *The Fateful Triangle* by Noam Chomsky, pp. 181–328, 1983, South End Press, Boston.

a regime of the Christian Phalangists who were loyal to Israel while occupying much of South Lebanon directly.

But first, the Israelis needed the blessing and the military and financial support of the United States; then they needed an excuse to convince world public opinion that in their invasion of Lebanon they were acting in self-defense.

With regard to the first, in May 1982, General Ariel Sharon, who was then Israeli Defense Minister, visited Washington. During his visit he is purported to have disclosed to then U.S. Secretary of State Alexander Haig, Israel's plans to invade Lebanon, to destroy the PLO, and to establish a friendly Lebanese government with whom Israel could conclude a peace treaty on the lines of the Camp David Accords. Sharon later declared to the press that Alexander Haig had approved the plan—which the latter denied—but Carter confirmed that the United States had advance knowledge of Israel's intentions to invade Lebanon.

With approval of the invasion by the U.S. Administration secure, Sharon visited the then U.S. Secretary of Defense Caspar Weinberger, and he claimed to have informed him that "Israel must act in Lebanon." Pentagon figures "reveal a massive surge of military supplies from the United States to Israel in the first three months of (1982)—as Israel planned the invasion of Lebanon," plans that were perfectly evident, as already noted. Delivery of military goods was almost 50% greater than in the preceding year, including equipment effectively used in Lebanon. Pentagon spokesmen confirm that these deliveries continued through June at a very high level—though not subsequently, it is claimed— including "smart bombs," used with "devastating" effect in Beirut; one such bomb caused the instant destruction of an entire building, killling 100 people, in an apparent effort to finish off Yasser Arafat, who was thought to be there.[2]

With United States approval of the invasion of Lebanon in hand, the Israelis now sought to find an excuse to justify their action to world public opinion. They announced that the invasion was necessary to secure "Peace for Galilee" from attacks across the border by establishing a security zone 25 miles deep inside Lebanon territory from which the PLO guerillas would be driven out. But once the 25 mile limit was reached, the Israeli army pushed into the heart of Beirut.

It should be noted that all PLO guerrilla attacks against Israel had completely ceased after the cease-fire that was arranged by Philip Habib, the U.S. special envoy, between Israel and the PLO on July 24, 1981—eleven months before the invasion had started. The PLO had scrupulously respected the cease-fire agreement, and between July 1981 and June 1982 when the Israeli invasion was launched, there had not been a single incident from the Lebanese side of the border. The International Commission that investigated Israeli actions during the invasion of Lebanon, said that according to "the official reports of the Secretary-General of the United Nations, reviewing the work of UNIFIL in southern Lebanon and not contradicted by any party, there was virtually total observance of the Habib-negotiated ceasefire of July 1981. There were no serious breaches of the ceasefire from the Lebanese side throughout the period."

The United States supply of military equipment used in the invasion of Lebanon included internationally prohibited weapons, such as cluster and suction bombs, etc., that were used indiscriminately and without mercy against civilians without distinction between Palestinians and Lebanese. And when the matter was brought before the United Nations, the U.S. representative in the Security Council used the veto three times between June and August 1982 to prevent the adoption of any resolution against Israel.

Former Under-Secretary of State George Ball, in his testimony before the Senate Foreign Relations Committee in July 1982, condemned U.S. policy in Lebanon in no uncertain terms when he said:

"Our most valuable asset is our standing as a nation and a people committed to justice and humanity, and we diminish ourselves when we allow our weapons (including cluster bombs) to be used in Israel's sanguinary adventure without even a whimper of protest. We are made to appear as an accessory to Israel's brutal invasion—or at least as a nation too weak and irresolute to restrain our client state whose military strength largely derives from our gift of deadly arms and whose economic life depends on the constant blood transfusion of our economic aid."[3]

Australian journalist Tony Clifton and photographer Catherine Leroy were in Beirut when the Israeli invasion of Lebanon occurred. In their book *God Cried*, they give a graphic description of the devastation that occurred. Because of its importance, the relevant section is being reproduced as *Appendix D*.[4]

4. The Massacres at Sabra and Shatila Refugee Camps

Just as the massacre at Deir Yasin prompted the flight of the Palestinians in 1948, so did the massacres at the refugee camps of Sabra and Shatila in Lebanon bring about the planned further displacement of the Palestinian civilians.

That this was the main purpose of the joint Israeli-Lebanese-Phalangist strategy was confirmed by the military correspondent of *Haaretz* Hebrew newspaper on September 28, 1982, who stated that it was "an operation planned and aimed at effecting a mass exodus by the Palestinians from Beirut and Lebanon."

The story of the massacre is too gruesome and too lengthy to repeat. Attention of the reader is drawn to the book by A. Weisfeld, *Sabra and Shatila: A New Auschwitz* published by the Jerusalem International Publishing House, Inc., 1983, Ottawa. Suffice it to point out here that the victims were not fighting men but consisted mostly of women and children. According to International Red Cross sources, the number of the dead by September 1982 had reached the figure of 2,750.[5] But author Amnon Kapeliouk places the number between 3,000 and 3,500 to include:

(1) those buried in mass graves whose number cannot be ascertained;
(2) those who were buried under the ruins of houses;
(3) those who were taken alive to an unknown destination but never

returned. The bodies of some of them were found by the side of roads leading to the south.[6]

While the actual operation was carried out by the Lebanese Phalange, responsibility for the massacre rests on the shoulders of the Israelis who armed and paid them, and lit the skies above the camps with flares as the killing went on through the night, and who had planned the massacre. It also rests on the United States, which undertook to guarantee the safety of the inmates of the two camps after the PLO had departed from Lebanon. Former Under-Secretary of State George Ball commented on the subject as follows:

"In America our nation's responsibility for the whole tragic incident has gone largely unnoticed, yet the facts are clear enough. We put our own good faith behind Israel's word of honor, otherwise the PLO would never have agreed to leave. The PLO leaders trusted America's promise that Palestinians left behind would be safe-guarded. When America promised 'to do its utmost' to ensure that Israel kept its commitments, they took that commitment at face value. They would never have trusted an Israeli promise, but they trusted us. We betrayed them."[7]

5. The Status of the West Bank and the Gaza Strip

The legal status of the West Bank and the Gaza Strip is governed, until revoked or amended by the United Nations, by three international instruments, namely:

(a) By the Partition Resolution of 1947 whereby both occupied territories fall within the area reserved for the "Arab State" under the Plan of Partition;

(b) By the provisions of the General Armistice Agreements concluded in 1949 between Israel and the governments of Jordan and Egypt respectively; and

(c) By the provisions of UN Security Council resolutions No. 242 of November 22, 1967 and No. 338 of October 22, 1973.

Since the war of 1967, the instruments under (a) and (b) above have been ignored by the supporters of the state of Israel, but they will no doubt be resurrected as a basis for discussion if and when the problem reaches the negotiating table for final settlement. What is now mentioned are the two resolutions of the Security Council referred to in (c) above. For the sake of clarity, they are being reproduced below:

1. Resolution 242 *emphasized* "the inadmissibility of the acquisition of territory by war and the need to work for a just and lasting peace in which every State in the area can live in security," and that "all Member States in their acceptance of the Charter of the United Nations have undertaken a commitment to act in accordance with Article 2 of the Charter."

The Resolution then *affirmed* "that the fulfillment of Charter principles requires the establishment of a just and lasting peace in the Middle East which should include the application of both the following principles:

> (i) Withdrawal of Israeli armed forces from territories occupied in the recent conflict;
> (ii) Termination of all claims or states of belligerency and respect for and acknowledgement of the sovereignty, territorial integrity, and political independence of every State in the area and their right to live in peace within secure and recognized boundaries free of threats or acts of force."

Lord Hugh Caradon, the British Chief Delegate to the United Nations and the prinicipal author of the resolution, made it clear in a subsequent statement that "the overriding principle" of the Resolution was "the inadmissibility of the acquisition of territory by war."

2. Resolution 338 called for:

> "2. The start immediately after the cease-fire of the implementation of Security Council Resolution 242;
> "3. The start immediately and concurrently with the cease-fire, of negotiations aimed at establishing a just and durable peace;
> "4. A just settlement of the Palestine Problem."

6. Establishment of Jewish Settlements in the Occupied Territories

The situation has been further complicated by the establishment of Jewish settlements on confiscated Arab lands in the occupied territories and the transfer of Jews to become permanent residents. By its action, Israel stands in violation of the Hague Convention on the Laws and Customs of War on Land of October 18, 1907 and the Fourth Geneva Convention Relative to the Protection of Civilian Persons in Time of War of August 12, 1949. Both forbid a military occupier to appropriate, confiscate, or expropriate private or public property in occupied territories.

The establishment of Jewish settlements in the occupied territories involves two elements, namely, the appropriation of land and the establishment of settlers on such land, both of which are forbidden by Articles 49 and 147 of the Geneva Convention of August 12, 1949. The latter Article considers as "grave violations" of the Convention "the appropriation of property which is not justified by military necessity" and "illegal transfers" of persons; while Article 49 provides that the occupying power cannot "transfer a part of its own civilian population to the occupied territory." Israel is guilty on all counts.

The position of the United Nations was clearly defined by Ambassador Khawaja Wasiuddin, Permanent Representative of Bangladesh to the United Nations. Speaking as the Special Representative of the President of the 39th Session of the UN General Assembly before the International Symposium on Israeli Settlements that was held in Washington D.C. in April 1985, the Ambassador made the following statements:

> "Israeli settlements in the Palestinian and other Arab occupied territories are illegal and are definite impediments to the achievement of a comprehensive solution to the Middle East problem. Both the Security Council and the General Assembly have repeatedly affirmed that the Geneva Convention Relative to the Protection of Civilian

Persons in Time of War of August 12, 1949, is applicable to the occupied territories. The Security Council by its resolution 465(1980) of March 1, 1980, *inter alia*, has confirmed the applicability of the Convention to the occupied territories. The General Assembly has expressed similar views on a number of occasions and as recently as its 1984 session, it reaffirmed this position by adopting the Resolution 39/95B of December 14, 1984, by recorded affirmative votes of 140 to 1 against and three abstentions. But what is more significant is that when a separate vote was taken on the operative paragraph 1 of this resolution, which reads 'Reaffirms that the Geneva Convention Relative to the Protection of Civilian Persons in Time of War of August 12, 1949, is applicable to the Palestinian and other Arab territories occupied by Israel since 1967, including Jerusalem' was adopted by 143 votes in favour, 1 against, and no abstentions. The only negative vote was cast by Israel, which clearly asserts that all Member States, except Israel, are unanimous about the applicabilility of the Geneva Convention of 1949 to the occupied territories.

"At its last session, the UN General Assembly, in its Resolution 39/95C of December 14, 1984, expressing grave anxiety and concern at the present serious situation in the occupied Palestinian and other Arab territories, including Jerusalem, as a result of the continued Israeli occupation and the measures and actions taken by Israel, the Occupying Power, designed to change the legal status, geographical nature, and demographic composition of those territories, stated 'strongly deplores the persistence of Israel in carrying out such measures, in particular the establishment of settlements in the Palestinian and other occupied territories, including Jerusalem.' The Assembly again in operative paragraph 7(d) of its resolution 39/95D of December 14, 1984, strongly condemned 'establishment of new Israeli settlements and expansion of the existing settlements on private and public Arab lands, and transfer of an alien population thereto.' Then on the question of violation of the provisions of the Geneva Convention of 1949, the General Assembly by the operative paragraph 6 of the same resolution stated 'declares once more that Israel's grave breaches of that Convention are war crimes and an affront to humanity.'

"Israel's unrelenting policy of establishing new settlements in the occupied territories in arrogant defiance of the resolutions of the Security Council as well as those of the General Assembly, creates major impediments toward a comprehensive settlement of the Middle East problem. It places in jeopardy even the Security Council Resolution 242, which the supporters of Israel contend, spells out the basic elements of a peaceful solution of the problem. It is most unfortunate that some sections of public opinion, particularly in this country [the United States], fail to appreciate this fact."[8]

The consensus of world opinion is that the only power that can compel the Israelis to comply with the United Nations directions is the United States. While rhetorically the U.S. government opposes the Israeli actions in the occupied territories as morally and legally wrong, in practice it finances the establishment of the Jewish settlements with military and economic aid. This double-standard policy has encouraged the Israelis to defy the rulings of the United Nations and create a situation that may be disastrous for the area and world peace.

The number of Jewish settlements established between 1967 and 1987 on the West Bank and the Gaza Strip, and the number of their Jewish residents, are shown on the maps that follow (pp. 286–289).

7. The Crisis Facing World Jewry

The invasion of Lebanon in 1982, the Sabra-Shatila massacres, and the Intifada (uprising) in the occupied territories have created a crisis of conscience for many Jews and Israelis and a rethinking of the state of Israel's role in the region.

More than forty years have passed since the establishment of the Jewish state and, instead of its leaders finding ways and means to incorporate into the peaceful life of the Middle East, they alienated themselves by relying on brute force to expel and disposses the indigenous inhabitants of the country, and by oppressing and persecuting the Palestinian population of the occupied territories, believing that might not right, and a constant reminder of the tragedies of the Holocaust from which Jews suffered, will preserve their state's integrity and existence. Time has begun to prove them wrong.

The late Nahum Goldmann, an ardent Zionist for fifty years and one-time president of the World Jewish Congress, reminded his co-religionists in 1979 that "Since the Second World War, Jews have been treated with silk gloves. Without Auschwitz," he pointed out, "there would be no Israel." In October 1981, he issued the following statement:

> "We will have to understand that the Jewish suffering during the Holocaust no longer will serve as a protection, and we certainly must refrain from using the argument of the holocaust to justify whatever we do. To use the holocaust as an excuse for the bombing of Lebanon, for instance, as Menachem Begin does, is a kind of 'Hillul Hashem' [sacrilege], a banalization of the sacred tragedy of the 'Shoah' [holocaust], which must not be misused to justify politically doubtful and morally indefensible politics."

Following the Israeli invasion of Lebanon in 1982, Goldmann, together with Pierre Mendes France, one-time Prime Minister of France, and Philip M. Klutznick, one time U.S. Secretary of Commerce and President of B'nai B'rith, issued the following joint statement:

> "Peace need not be made between friends, but between enemies who have struggled and suffered. Our senses of Jewish history and the moral imperatives of this moment require us to insist that the time is urgent for mutual recognition between Israel and the Palestinian people. There must be a stop to the sterile debate whereby the Arab world challenges the existence of Israel and Jews challenge the political legitimacy of the Palestinian fight for independence. The real issue is not whether the Palestinians are entitled to their rights, but how to bring this about while ensuring Israel's security and regional stability.
>
> Ambiguous concepts, such as 'autonomy,' are no longer sufficient.

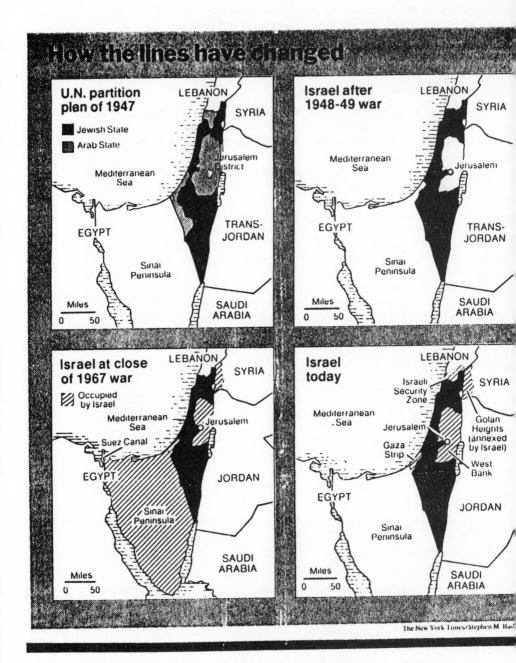

How the lines have changed

U.N. partition plan of 1947
- Jewish State
- Arab State

LEBANON
SYRIA
Jerusalem District
Mediterranean Sea
EGYPT
TRANS-JORDAN
Sinai Peninsula
Miles 0 50
SAUDI ARABIA

Israel after 1948-49 war

LEBANON
SYRIA
Mediterranean Sea
Jerusalem
EGYPT
TRANS-JORDAN
Sinai Peninsula
Miles 0 50
SAUDI ARABIA

Israel at close of 1967 war
- Occupied by Israel

LEBANON
SYRIA
Mediterranean Sea
Jerusalem
Suez Canal
EGYPT
JORDAN
Sinai Peninsula
Miles 0 50
SAUDI ARABIA

Israel today

LEBANON
Israeli Security Zone
SYRIA
Mediterranean Sea
Jerusalem
Golan Heights (annexed by Israel)
Gaza Strip
West Bank
EGYPT
JORDAN
Sinai Peninsula
Miles 0 50
SAUDI ARABIA

The New York Times/Stephen M Had

(*The New York Times*, Feb. 28, 1988)

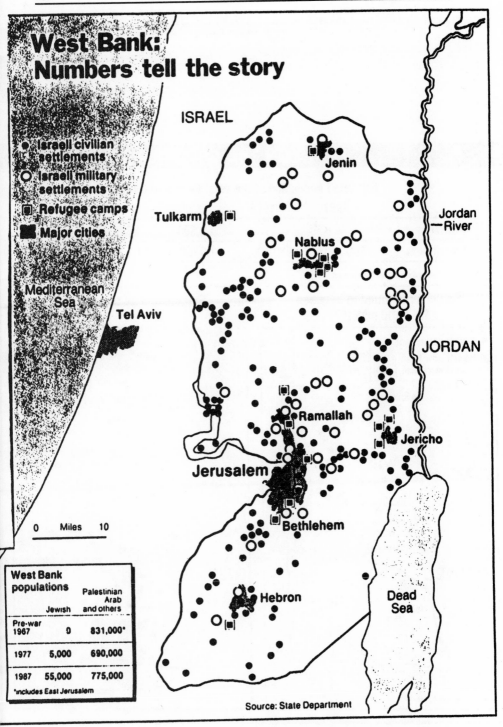

West Bank:
Numbers tell the story

● Israeli civilian settlements
○ Israeli military settlements
▣ Refugee camps
◼ Major cities

ISRAEL

Mediterranean Sea

Tel Aviv

Jenin

Tulkarm

Nablus

Jordan River

JORDAN

0   Miles   10

Ramallah

Jericho

Jerusalem

Bethlehem

Dead Sea

West Bank populations	Jewish	Palestinian Arab and others
Pre-war 1967	0	831,000*
1977	5,000	690,000
1987	55,000	775,000

*includes East Jerusalem

Hebron

Source: State Department

(*The New York Times*, Feb. 28, 1988)

ISRAELI OCCUPATION OF THE WEST BANK
(Source: *U.S. News & World Report*, Feb. 22, 1988, page 53)

FACTS ON THE GROUND

Estimated population of the West Bank and Gaza

	1967	1968	1972	1983	1987
Jewish	-	-	1,500	23,800	53,300
Palestinian	966,700	939,900	1.0 mil.	1.1 mil.	1.2 mil.

USN&WR—Basic data: Israeli government

Settlements founded between 1967 and mid-1977

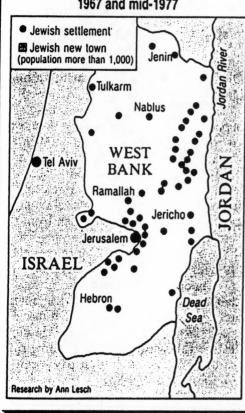

● Jewish settlement
▦ Jewish new town (population more than 1,000)

Research by Ann Lesch

Settlements as of April, 1987

Scale of miles
0   20

Forbes in the *Christian Science Monitor* © 1988 TCSPS

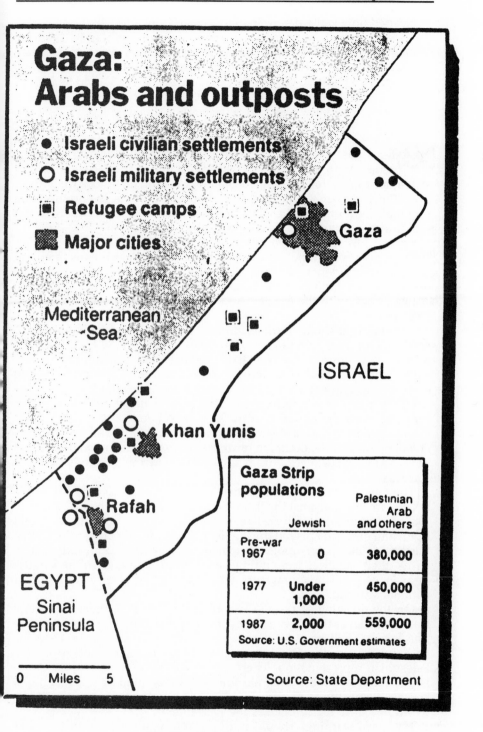

(The New York Times, Feb. 28, 1988)

Needed now is the determination to reach a political accommodation between Israeli and Palestinian nationalism. The war in Lebanon must stop. Israel must lift its siege of Beirut in order to facilitate negotiations with the PLO, leading to a political settlement. Mutual recognition must be vigorously pursued, and there should be negotiations with the aim of achieving co-existence between the Israeli and Palestinian peoples based on self-determination."[9]

The record of Israel since its establishment towards the Palestinian inhabitants has become the source of crisis for the Jewish community worldwide. A group of distinguished American Jews issued a joint statement calling for the United States government to dissociate itself from the repressive policies of Israel. Because of its importance, the statement is reproduced in full in its original text with names of the signatories as *Appendix G*.

Certain Jewish elements living outside Israel are not alone in their concern over Israel's policy and treatment of the Palestinians; many of the Jewish residents of Israel disapprove and have expressed their disapproval in various ways. Even some hawkish Israelis have recently drawn attention to the dangers and futility of Israeli policy toward the Palestinians.

General Yehoshofat Harkabi, former head of Israeli military intelligence, exhorts his compatriots in his book *Israel's Fateful Hour* to recognize the PLO, give up the West Bank and the Gaza Strip, and relinquish sole ownership claims to Jerusalem. He writes: "The path [Israel] chooses will not just affect the tenor of the nation's life but determine whether it can continue to exist . . . Many of the disasters of recent years, such as the Lebanon War, Israel's economic crisis, the increasingly degenerate stands of Israeli civic and political life, and above all the attempt to annex the occupied territories of the West Bank and the Gaza Strip, stem," he believes, "from a failure to view the country's situation correctly."

The General then seriously questions the iron fist policy which the Israelis are using against the Intifada (uprising) that started in December 1987, and points out: "Those Israelis who trumpet the great bravery that Irgun and others displayed during their comparatively brief fight against the British mandate should remember that in numerical and relative terms, their sacrifices were infinitesimal when compared to the lengthy caravan of Palestinian martyrs who have given their lives in their national struggle."

On the question of the PLO representing the Palestinians, General Harkabi believes that "Even if they [the Israelis] don't like the PLO, they [the Israelis] will have to negotiate with the PLO simply because the Palestinians say the PLO represents them. Israel cannot appoint a Palestinian representation. There is no possibility of settling the Arab-Israeli conflict without the Palestinians," he pointed out. So, he says, "criminalizing the PLO and describing it as a terrorist organization is wrong, because it criminalizes the Palestinians."[10]

Harkabi's warnings should not be taken lightly. He is an Israeli of wide knowledge who experienced for himself during the past forty years the futility of the Israeli policy and the determination of the Palestinians to regain what rightfully belongs to them. The Intifada (uprising) should convince the Israelis that time is not on their side and that it is in their interest to recognize the PLO as the representative of the Palestinian people; to start negotiations to exchange land for peace, and to admit that Jerusalem is not "the eternal capital of Israel" but the holy city of the members of the three monotheistic faiths.

8. The United States and the Zionist Lobby

The Palestine conflict, if it has lasted for more than forty years with no signs of a solution, is only due to the one-sided policy of the United States and the influence of the pressure groups that place Israeli interests over those of the United States. The U.S. representative at the United Nations either voted against or vetoed resolutions affecting the following:

(a) To permit the Palestinian refugees of 1948 to return to their homes and to compensate those who did not wish to return and for damages and losses sustained;

(b) Israeli withdrawal from territories occupied in the 1967 war and from the south of Lebanon following the invasion of that country in 1982;

(c) To respect the inalienable rights of the Palestinians in their own homeland;

(d) To respect the right of the Palestinians to self-determination and independence; and

(e) To condemn Israel for terrorist attacks against refugee camps in Lebanon.

Such policy satisfied the Zionist lobby and the Israelis, but certainly had an adverse effect on conditions in the Middle East and Arab-American relations, not to mention the dangers that a policy of support for aggression poses to world peace.

The latest example of American favoritism toward Israel was in the stand of the United States at the 77th Conference of the Interparliamentary Union that was held from April 27 to May 2, 1987. The participants comprised 957 delegates from 69 countries, including the United States. The conference approved by a large majority (832 for, 46 against, and 79 abstentions) a resolution calling for the convening of an international peace conference in which all parties to the Arab-Israeli conflict, including the PLO, should participate. Only the delegations of Israel and the United States voted in toto against the resolution that:

1. *Calls on* the parliaments and governments of all countries to do everything they can to make possible the speedy convening of an international peace conference on the Middle East under the auspices of the United Nations, involving all the parties concerned, including Israel, Jordan, Syria, Egypt, the Palestine Liberation Organization, the USSR, and the United States of America, as well as the other permanent members of the UN Security Council;

2. *Supports the call* by the UN General Assembly in Resolution 41/43D for the immediate convening of an international peace conference

on the Middle East, and endorses the call for the establishment of a preparatory committee under the Security Council's auspices, with the participation of all permanent UN Security Council members, to take steps necessary for its convening;

3. *Reaffirms* its belief that a just and comprehensive settlement of the conflict in the Middle East should envisage Israel's full and unconditional withdrawal from all the Arab territories occupied since 1967; the ensuring of the inalienable rights of the Arab people of Palestine, including their rights to self-determination and the establishment of their own state, and the guaranteeing of a peaceful and secure existence and independent development for all states and peoples of this area, including Israel;

4. *Calls on* parliamentarians and governments effectively to help in defusing the conflict in the Middle East by promoting the early establishment of the preparatory committee, since this would allow progress to be made toward undoing the dangerous knot of tension in the Middle East;

5. *Requests* the Interparliamentary Council to establish a parliamentary support committee actively to contribute to the world campaign for the successful holding of the international peace conference on the Middle East.[11]

Those who were anxious for peace between Arab and Jew were disappointed by the negative stand of the United States, which regards itself as the preserver of peace and security in the world and is expected to go to any length to achieve that objective.

Author Cheryl Rubenberg, in her latest book *Israel and the American National Interest* explains in her conclusion that "the power of the Israeli lobby over the formation and execution of U.S. Middle East policy has become a virtual strangle-hold. It no longer matters whether elected officials subscribe to the perception of Israel as a strategic asset to American interests or not. What matters is that the Israeli lobby is able to maintain the dominance of that perception as virtually unquestionable political truth and to assure that regardless of how severely American interests in the Middle East are compromised by Israel's policies, the U.S. government will continue to provide Israel with complete support. The lobby's effectiveness in impacting on the electoral process and its ability to shape public opinion and affect political culture are major factors in fostering the perception."[12]

Dr. Nahum Goldmann blamed the Israeli lobby for United States failures to bring about a comprehensive settlement in the Middle East. "It was," he said, "to a very large degree because of electoral considerations, fear of the pro-Israel lobby, and of the Jewish vote." He warned of trouble ahead if the lobby continued its present course. "It is now slowly becoming something of a negative factor. Not only does it distort the expectations and political calculations of Israel, but the time may not be far off when the American public opinion will be sick and tired of the demands of Israel and the aggressiveness of American Jewry."

Former U.S. Congressman Paul Findley commented: "In 1978, two years before (Goldmann) wrote his alarmed evaluation of the Israeli lobby, *New York* magazine reported that Goldmann had privately urged officials of the Carter Administration 'to break the back' of the [Zionist] lobby. Goldmann pleaded with the Administration to stand firm and not back off from confrontation with the organized Jewish community as other administrations had done. Unless this was done, he argued, 'President Carter's plans for a Middle East settlement would die in still-birth.' His words were prophetic. The comprehensive settlement Carter sought was frustrated by the intransigence of Israel and its U.S. lobby."[13]

Jewish pressure is not confined to the United States; attempts have been made to influence the Vatican and Pope John Paul. On September 6, 1987, a group of American Zionists visited the Vatican and had an audience with the Pope. They demanded, among other things, that the Vatican should recognize the state of Israel and establish diplomatic relations with the Jewish state. On September 11, 1987, a second meeting with the pontiff was held in Miami, during the Pope's visit to the United States. The Jewish delegation repeated the demand made during the visit to the Vatican.

This time the Pope is reported to have replied that "he supported the due tranquility that is the prerogative of every nation and conditions of life and of progress for every society, the right to a homeland also applies to the Palestinian people, so many of whom remain homeless and refugees." He advised his visitors that "it is time to forge those solutions which lead to a just, complete, and lasting peace in that area," and he promised that "for this peace he would earnestly pray."

9. Peace Proposals

A number of plans and proposals for an equitable settlement and peace in the Middle East have been presented from time to time, but none has been accepted by the parties concerned as fulfilling their demands and aspirations.

They are being reproduced as appendices to give an opportunity to readers to decide which is the best approach toward a just and equitable peace.

1. The Arab Fez Peace Plan (1982)—*Appendix I*
2. The Ronald Reagan Plan (1982)—*Appendix J*
3. The Jerome M. Segal Proposals (1988)—*Appendix K*
4. The U.S. Presbyterian Church Proposals (1988)—*Appendix L*
5. Proposals by a Group of Distinguished Individuals (1988)—*Appendix M*

XXIII   The Uprising and Beyond

1. The Palestinian Intifada (Uprising)—1987

With the passage of time, the occupation of the West Bank and the Gaza Strip in 1967 came to be treated by the Israelis as an accomplished fact and accepted as such in silence by world public opinion. The territory of the West Bank was given the names of "Judea and Samaria" and there was much discussion about annexation to the state of Israel. The Haram Ash-Sharif and Al-Aqsa Mosque area, the third holy place in Islam, is referred to by the Israelis as the "Temple Mount," with the clear intention of obliterating its Muslim character and replacing it with a Jewish historical name. On the other hand, any violence as a result of dissatisfaction by the local inhabitants was described as terrorism and dealt with by the harshest of methods.

Abba Eban, writing in *The New York Times* of November 9, 1986, described the conditions under which the Palestinian inhabitants lived. He said:

"The Palestinians live without a right to vote or to be elected, without any control over the government that determines the conditions of their lives, exposed to restraints and punishments that could not be applied against them if they were Jews, permitted to cross into Israel to work, but without permission to sleep overnight. It is a bleak, tense, disgruntled, repressed existence, with spurts of violence always ready to explode. There is no precedent for believing that this condition can long endure without explosion.

"Israel lives in a state of structural incoherence. If we were to hear that the Netherlands was imposing an unwanted jurisdiction on four million Germans, or that America proposed to incorporate 80 million Russians into the United States against their will, we would assume that they had taken leave of their senses. Yet, some people still talk of Israel ruling a foreign population that accounts for 33% of its own inhabitants as though it were a serious option."

In December 1987, the young Palestinians, who were born during the occupation and knew no better life, decided that enough was enough, that they could not stand any longer the oppression, persecution, and deprivation of human rights. They rose in protest, not with arms but with stones, knowing full well that they could not compete with Israeli bullets and the other sophisticated weapons from the United States.

The uprising began in the Gaza Strip in response to an incident in which four Palestinian workers were run over by an Israeli truck. While the intention of the Israeli driver remains in dispute, for Palestinians the incident recalled the killing of seven members of an Arab family in Lebanon when their car was crushed by an Israeli tank on September 18, 1972. This time, the protests began in the Jabaliya refugee camp where the men had lived, and at the funeral a young Gazan teenager was shot and killed by Israeli soldiers. The demonstrations spread to other refugee camps and towns in Gaza, and very quickly to the West Bank as well, beginning in the Balata camp near Nablus. As the resistance spread, stone-throwing against the occupying soldiers became more organized, and soon emerged as a leitmotif among young Palestinians.

At first, the uprising was blamed on outside influences and described as terrorism. Even President Ronald Reagan joined in this chorus despite the most sophisticated intelligence service at his disposal.

On February 25, 1988, the President held a press conference at the White House, and the first question came from correspondent Helen Thomas who asked: "Through the years, Mr. President, you've been very eloquent on the subject of human rights in the Soviet Union and Nicaragua. Why have you never condemned the treatment of the Palestinians in the occupied areas: shooting unarmed protesters, beating people to death—children—trying to bury some alive?"

The President's reply was timid and unconvincing. He said: "Helen, we have spoken to the government there, and we've also spoken to Palestinian leadership, because there's every evidence that these riots are not just spontaneous and home-grown. They have been stirred up by outsiders;" and he added: "American intelligence has proof of it," but, he claimed, that for security reasons, he was unable to disclose more. Ironically, it was the same tactic he used to justify the bombing of Libya in so-called retaliation for the Berlin disco-restaurant bombing for which it was later proven that Muammar Qaddafi was not responsible.

An editorial in the *Arab News* of Saudi Arabia (February 26, 1988) expressed the reaction of public opinion in the Arab world to the President's strange statement. The paper stated: "One's reaction [to Reagan's reply] is to laugh at the naivity of the man, then to feel sorry for the Americans for having such an absurdly incompetent intelligence service, and, lastly, to wonder who is writing the President's speeches—a member of the White House staff or Yitzhaq Shamir?"

The brutality of Israel's efforts to crush the Intifada kept the occupation on the front pages of the world's newspapers for months. But Ronald Reagan was not alone in his indifference to the atrocities that are being committed by the Israelis against the unarmed inhabitants of the West Bank and the Gaza Strip. Columnist Mary McGrory, writing under the title of "Israel's Shameful Iron Fist," stated: "You could comb the pages of the Congressional Record for the last 10 days of the session and not find a single reference to the shameful events unfolding in Israel and the occupied territories.

"On the West Bank, Israeli soldiers have been clubbing unarmed teenage Arab demonstrators into the ground. The week before Christmas, having terrorized relatives of patients who were waiting in the courtyard, Israeli troops stormed into an Arab hospital in Gaza and beat up doctors and nurses.

"If the 21 killed and scores wounded had been Israelis, you can imagine the outcry. But the casualties were Palestinians, who are voiceless here, and the silence on Capitol Hill was awful."[1]

The number of Palestinian men, women, and children killed by Israeli soldiers and settlers just in the uprising's first three years was 892, while the number of wounded is estimated to be over 106,000, and those arrested runs into scores of thousands.[2] The number of people who had their limbs deliberately broken is unknown. The demolition of Palestinian homes by explosives continues to be employed as a punitive measure and as a means of displacing the inhabitants of an Arab village to make way for new Jewish settlements.

Despite the repression, the Intifada grew and matured. For the first weeks, it was largely spontaneous, focusing on the immediate and direct challenge to the soldiers in the camps, towns and villages. But very soon, the uprising broadened to encompass many different forms of direct resistance, as well as the creation of the nascent institutions of a state apparatus.

The existing sectoral organizations, most linked to the main factions of the PLO's consensus bloc, expanded their popular base and took on new areas of responsibility. The medical committees, for example, took on the task of providing emergency care to the numerous victims of Israeli repression, organized first-aid training courses, and coordinated new blood-typing registers to assure sufficient supplies of blood in emergency situations. But at the same time the committees continued and even expanded their work of providing primary health care to the camps and isolated villages with no resident medical facilities.

The women's organizations still carried out their child care, literacy courses, economic self-help projects and consciousness raising work, but as the Intifada developed they also played the central role in creating popular education projects; coordinating food storage and distribution during curfews and sieges; as well as initiating independent women's demonstrations against the occupation, attempting (with some notable successes) to rescue young people under arrest by Israeli soldiers, and participating with the men in stone-throwing clashes. The trade unions renegotiated contracts with Palestinian factory owners, designed to increase production and employ larger numbers of Palestinian workers during the uprising; they have also forced concessions from the owners regarding payment of workers kept home by strikes or curfews.

In addition to the new areas of responsibility for existing grassroots organizations, new institutions sprang up to answer needs posed by the new conditions of resistance. Merchants' committees, for example, convened to determine the breadth of the boycott of Israeli goods, fix the hours of commercial strikes, decide which of their number would be exempt from the 21-hours-a-day closure (usually medical and legal offices, pharmacies, bakeries and taxis), and discuss broadening product lines to make the boycott of Israeli goods more complete. Guarding committees, based among the "shabab" (the guys, or young people of the village or camp) function to warn of impending attack by soldiers or settlers. Popular committees, at the neighborhood, village, town, camp, and regional level, took on the look of a de facto Palestinian government structure with responsibility for internal decision-making and conflict resolution within society.

The organizations created for direct resistance joined the newer alternative social, economic and political institutions to construct the beginnings of what would come to look very much like a state apparatus. At the national level, the Unified National Leadership of the Uprising (UNLU) emerged, composed of representatives of the constituent organizations of the PLO's consensus bloc, as well as of the grassroots bodies, to become the day-to-day leadership of the Intifada. All the organizations reflected the PLO's vision of an independent state, and the already-popular notion of the Palestinians living under occupation being defined as the "internal wing" of the PLO began to take on new meaning.

By the end of the first few months, state construction had emerged as the primary characteristic of the Intifada. But because that process went on quietly, within Palestinian society rather than under the glare of international television lights, it remained mostly invisible to the outside world.

Notwithstanding the efforts used to suppress it, the uprising against the occupation continues unabated and could escalate from stone-throwing against bullets into bullet for bullet if the occupation is not ended. A similar situation occurred against the British Mandatory in the 1930s. Palestinian dissatisfaction began with a peaceful general strike and lasted for six months after which it developed into an armed open rebellion that necessitated the employment of over 100,000 British troops for two years. The rebellion was called off only because of the outbreak of World War II in 1939.

The seriousness of the uprising attracted international attention, and many were those who visited the occupied territories to see for themselves what was going on. I have selected two eye-witness reports that I shall include in their entirety. The first is by Reverend Don Wagner, National Director of the Palestine Human Rights Campaign in Chicago, who toured the occupied territories in February 1988, whose report is reproduced as *Appendix E*. The second is by Dr. James Graff, Chairman of the Toronto Universities Middle East Group (TUMEG) who visited the occupied territories in March 1988. His report is reproduced as *Appendix F*.

The position of the Palestinian inhabitants of the occupied territories has been made abundantly clear in Proclamation No. 18 made public in May 1988. The Unified National Leadership of the Uprising declared that the only way the Intifada will be terminated is:

1. By sending international observers to offer protection for the Palestinians;
2. By the withdrawal of the Israeli army from the cities, villages, and refugee camps;
3. By releasing the Palestinian prisoners and lifting the state of siege;
4. By allowing the return of the expelled Palestinians;
5. By canceling all special military orders and new civil regulations as a result of the uprising;
6. By allowing democratic and free elections to be held;
7. By removing the restrictions placed on the national economy, allowing the development of the industrial, agricultural, and service sectors.

The proclamation then called for these steps to be monitored by international observers "to provide the necessary protection for our people." It also called on the Arab states to work for the Palestinian cause "not by statements of denunciation and condemnation" of Israel, but by advocacy of Palestinian concerns. The leadership envisioned these steps as leading to implementation of "the right to return, to self-determination, and the right to establish our own independent state."

The message of the Intifada is a clear and simple one: Palestinians assert their presence in the West Bank and the Gaza Strip and their determination not only to stay, but to claim their right to self-determination and to the establishment of an independent Palestinian state against all the daunting odds posed by the greater configuration of powers. The humiliations and oppression of the past have engendered a level of defiance of the odds, above all among the "occupation generation." It is this past which makes the young Palestinians ready to confront the occupier with stones—and their claim for a future—in their own hands.[3] One thing is so far certain: The stone-throwing youths against Israeli bullets have already made enough dents in Israel's claimed invincibility to start the Israelis worrying.

Early in the Intifada, Palestinian mothers in the occupied territories addressed an open letter to their American counterparts appealing for their help. They wrote: "Our hurt is very deep. Today all the world is celebrating Children's Day with joy and hope; while we are commemorating the deaths of about 300 of our children. It grieves us to listen to your official representatives preaching about human rights while your government does not question the morality of its unconditional support to Israel which not only violates our human rights, but uses all forms of terror and brute force in an attempt to make us acquiesce to their aggression and to legitimize the consequences of that aggression. We often wonder if you, as women, will not be instrumental in effecting basic changes in the attitude of your government which, we feel, acts within the short-sighted framework of vested interests, ignoring the humanitarian basis of actions. This humanitarian basis generally guides our behavior as women and makes us more qualified to build a better world for all. It seems preposterous that we, the givers of life, should not be consulted when lethal arms are being developed and used to destroy our children, to quell their spirits aspiring to justice, peace, equality, and freedom. We as mothers have taken great pains to mold that spirit.

"Dear sisters . . . we address you today with the hope that you will spare us a little of your time to learn the truth. For we know that the truth is the shortest means to achieve solutions . . . We are also confident that you will realize that no solution to our problem can be achieved unless we are recognized as a people with political rights and not as a group of displaced refugees asking for charity. Foremost among these rights is our right to self-determination, to establish our independent state in our homeland under our legitimate leadership, the PLO."[4]

2. Declaration of Palestinian Independence

Just before the Intifada's first anniversary, the Palestine National Council, the Palestinians' parliament-in-exile, was called into special session. Convening in Algiers on November 15, 1988, the "Intifada Session" of the PNC announced Palestine to be a free and independent state.

The Declaration of Independence, written by Palestinian poet Mahmoud Darwish and read by PLO leader Yasser Arafat, "proclaims the establishment of the State of Palestine on our Palestinian territory with its capital Jerusalem (Al-Quds Ash-Sharif)."

The Declaration marked a new stage in Palestine's difficult march towards statehood. It reflected a new level of unity inside the PLO and among the major factions, allowing the organization to speak with one voice on the world's stage. Convening the PNC in the midst of the Intifada placed the power and prestige of the uprising behind the new initiatives.

The content of the Declaration of Independence itself reflects the changes the uprising had wrought in Palestinian society. Questions of democracy, long deemed irrelevant or perhaps at best of secondary importance within the national struggle, now emerged at center stage as the PNC shaped the future contours of an independent Palestine.

It includes the following: "The State of Palestine is the state of Palestinians wherever they may be. The state is for them to enjoy in it their collective national and cultural identity, theirs to pursue in it a complete equality of rights. In it will be safeguarded their political and religious convictions and their human dignity by means of a parliamentary democratic system of governance, itself based on freedom of expression and the freedom to form parties. The rights of minorities will duly be respected by the majority . . . Governance will be based on principles of social justice, equality and non-discrimination in public rights of men or of women on grounds of race, religion, color or sex, under the aegis of a constitution which ensures the rule of law and an independent judiciary. Thus shall these principles allow no departure from Palestine's age-old spiritual and civilizational heritage of tolerance and religious coexistence."

It is especially noteworthy that the Declaration of Independence, now the overarching articulation of Palestinian nationalism, makes such strong assertions regarding democracy. In a region characterized by profound inequity and oppression of women, the commitment to gender equality at the very foundation of national identity is of particular significance.

The PNC vote endorsing the Declaration of Independence was unanimous and unequivocal. The discussion and debate about the accompanying report of the Political Commission, however, was somewhat more complex. The statement called for an international peace conference with the PLO on an equal footing with all other participants, to resolve the crises in the Middle East. Most significantly, it spelled out that the conference should be based on "UN Security Council Resolutions 242 and 338 and the assurance of the legitimate national rights of the Palestinian people and, first and foremost, their right to self-determination . . . and in accordance with the resolutions of the UN regarding the Palestinian cause."

The vote was decisive, but not unanimous. The final count was 253 to 46 with 10 abstentions. But the Intifada's influence on the PNC remained dominant, and all major opposing forces agreed that PLO unity remained the primary consideration.

Taken together, the Declaration of Independence and the political statement provided a broad framework for Palestinian strategy, a framework that would lead a month later to the articulation of a fully developed Palestinian peace initiative. The creation of an independent state was rooted in changes going on within Palestinian society; Palestinians living under occupation were to play the determinative role, rather than those in the widespread diaspora.

The Declaration of Independence reflected an autonomous assertion of political direction, a refusal to wait for the occupier itself, or any other external actor, to respond to Palestinian pleas or demands. The Intifada had provided a new, internal dynamic in the search for statehood; no longer would Palestinians be content to wait for unreliable allies to speak in their name, or for Israel to agree voluntarily to recognize an independent Palestine. The Intifada's political expression cohered in the Declaration of Independence, and gave a newly strengthened Palestinian voice to the world.

3. The Palestinian Peace Initiative

The Palestine struggle, it should be noted, is, first and foremost, between the Palestinians and the Israelis before it can be considered an Arab states-Israeli conflict. The position of the Arab states in the whole affair is one of support of the Palestinian position, as well as self-defense against Israeli ambitions for territorial expansion and political power games in the region. The occupation and subsequent annexation of the Golan Heights of Syria, which were never a part of Palestine and Israel's continued occupation of part of the south of Lebanon, under the fiction of a security zone, confirm Arab fears.

At any rate, which Israel does the United States want the PLO to recognize? Is it:

The Israel of the Partition Resolution of 1947?
or
The Israel of the Armistice Agreements of 1949?
or
The Israel following the war of 1967?
or
The Israel that annexed East Jerusalem and
declares the city as its "eternal capital?"
or
The Israel that annexed the Golan Heights of
Syria and occupies the southern part of Lebanon?
or
The Israel that describes the West Bank as
Judea and Samaria as a first step toward
annexation?
or
The Israel that rejects the exchange of territory for peace?

It should be noted that the state of Israel has neither a Constitution nor defined boundaries, although the United Nations Partition Resolution of 1947 set such boundaries. This is not accidental but deliberate, in order to absorb gradual expansion into adjacent Arab territories as opportunities arise to reach the dream of an Israel "from the Nile to the Euphrates."

Israel and the United States are relying on time and brute force to settle the Palestine conflict; but after the lapse of more than forty years, they are still waiting.

The PLO has been chosen by the Palestinian people inside and outside the Israeli occupied territories as its sole representative and has been recognized as such by the League of Arab States, by the United Nations and all its organs, which granted it observer status, and by over 100 foreign governments, some of which have elevated its office to the ambassadorial level.

Despite all this, and despite opening a short-lived "dialogue" with the PLO, the U.S. government continues to withhold official recognition of the PLO. This refusal is tantamount to ignoring the natural preroga-tives of the Palestinians who are directly concerned to decide who does and does not represent them. No outside force is entitled to object or question their choice. They and only they bear full responsibility for their actions.

Ironically, recognition of Israel by the PLO is being insisted upon by the United States, but nothing is being said about the recognition by the Israelis of the Palestinians and their indubitable rights to their properties and ancestral homeland. To break the deadlock, suggestions have been made by neutral sources for simultaneous reciprocal recognition by the PLO and Israel in order to get the peace process moving. But the proposal was turned down by both the Israelis and the U.S. government.

The continuation of a no-war no-peace situation is clearly Israel's policy to use the element of time to tighten its hold on the occupied territories and render the return to the 1967 boundaries effectively impossible. In fact, Menachem Begin is quoted by Harold H. Saunders to have said that "Israel is creating facts that will be irreversible in a negotiation."[5] The Israeli policy under Yitzhaq Shamir remains the same, and there will be no change unless the U.S. Government intervenes.

The promise made by Henry Kissinger to Israel when he was U.S. Secretary of State to deny recognition of the PLO unless the latter accepts the provisions of UN resolutions 242 and 338 and recognizes the existence of the state of Israel is not valid since in neither resolution (see Section 5 of Chapter XXII) is the name of the PLO mentioned or referred to; nor has it been called upon by the UN Security Council to do anything.

The resolutions emphasize Israeli withdrawal from the territories occupied in the war of 1967 and on the fulfillment of certain conditions by all *states* in the region—a category not yet considered applicable to the Palestinians or the PLO. Furthermore, there is no mention in the resolutions that the PLO must recognize the existence of the state of Israel as a precondition to Israeli withdrawal from the occupied territories. The UN Charter is explicit on this point that "it is inadmissible for any nation to occupy the territory of another nation by force of arms," and this is exactly what the Israelis have done with impunity and what the Security Council has demanded be ended. So whether the PLO recognizes the state of Israel or not is irrelevant and is a matter to be discussed at the negotiating table.

On December 13, 1988, Yasser Arafat appeared before the General Assembly of the United Nations meeting in Geneva and delivered a historic speech in which he outlined Palestinian proposals for a permanent solution to the Palestine conflict.

The highlights of the Palestinian peace initiative were:

(1) The convening of an international peace conference under the auspices of the United Nations;

(2) The United Nations to assume, temporarily, the administration of the West Bank and the Gaza Strip pending final settlement;

(3) The PLO condemns all forms of terrorist activities, including state-terrorism;

(4) The PLO accepts Security Council resolutions 242 and 338 and more specifically the provision that prescribes "respect for and acknowledgement of the sovereignty, territorial integrity, and political independence of every state in the area, and their right to live in peace within secure and recognized boundaries free of threats or acts of force," as the basis of negotiations, along with recognition of the Palestinians' rights to self-determination and an independent state.

Resolution 242 called for an Israeli withdrawal from the territories it occupied in 1967. But it contained no reference to the PLO, national rights, or statehood, and so was widely interpreted to mean de facto PLO recognition of Israel and acquiescence to a two-state solution, abandoning once and for all the long-nurtured dream of a democratic and secular state in all of Palestine.

Arafat's Geneva statement led to an erroneous impression that the Palestine conflict consisted solely of the West Bank and Gaza Strip controversy. This is not so. The Palestine conflict started in 1948 with the expulsion and dispossession of the Moslem and Christian inhabitants of the country, and the West Bank and Gaza Strip conflict of 1967 is a subsequent part of it. The United Nations has been seized with the entire problem ever since, and the resolutions adopted remain legal and binding until abrogated or amended by the world body.

Except for the United States and Israel, the immediate response to the speech was unanimously favorable. The spokesman of the Reagan Administration, while admitting that the speech contained certain positive aspects, stated that it did not go far enough to meet the objections of the United States. The following day, Arafat clarified the position of the PLO at a press conference in order to meet those objections. In the evening, Secretary of State George Shultz announced at a press conference that the United States was now ready to start a dialogue for peace with the PLO and had, in fact, issued instructions to the U.S. Ambassador in Tunis—the present headquarters of the PLO—to begin talks with representatives of the PLO.

Israeli Prime Minister Yitzhaq Shamir's reaction to the speech was outright rejection; he declared that Israel will not deal now or ever with the PLO, which he regards as a terrorist organization. At the same time he said Israel will not give up one inch of the occupied territories. The altered position of the United States was received with shock and anger.

On December 15, 1988, the General Assembly ended its special session by adopting another resolution in which it voted overwhelmingly to convene an international Middle East peace conference and to place the Israeli occupied territories under United Nations supervision. This resolution was passed by a vote of 138–2 with Israel and the United States voting against, while Canada abstained.

In addition, the General Assembly decided that the PLO, which retains its observer status, will be referred to in future as Palestine. This resolution was passed by 104–2 with the United States and Israel again opposing.

While the United Nations action may be regarded as a victory for the PLO and the Palestinian people, there is much skepticism over the success of the peace process unless the Bush Administration alters United States policy toward the Palestine conflict to one of absolute neutrality.

Throughout much of 1989, the U.S.-PLO talks in Tunis stalled. The United States Ambassador refused to enter into substantive discussion, focusing instead on pressuring the PLO to accept Israel's plans for elections in the occupied territories in which the PLO would be excluded, and the end result would be only a form of autonomy (see below, Section 5). Self-determination and an independent Palestinian state were precluded from the outset. For many Palestinians, the proposal remained insufficient.

In the spring of 1990, the U.S. government called off the talks. Using the excuse that the PLO's disavowal of a failed guerrilla raid was "insufficient," Washington announced an end to the already-sputtering dialogue in Tunis. Palestine was off the U.S. agenda once again.

Arafat went to great length and pain to finally convince all factions within the PLO to support his peace efforts, which enabled him to meet the demands of the U.S. government. Now, it is the duty of the United States to pressure the Israelis to comply equally with their obligations under Security Council resolutions 242 and 338, which call for the "withdrawal of Israeli forces from the occupied territories" and the "start of negotiations at establishing a just and durable peace."

4. U.S. Responses to the Intifada and Palestinian Peace Initiatives

In 1987 it became known that the PLO was in the process of formulating plans for a negotiating position that would meet certain objections of the United States. To bar any such improvement in relations, pressure was brought to bear to remove the presence of the PLO from the United States. The government took action to have the Palestine Information Office in Washington closed down by the end of the year, while Congress passed a law to close the Observer Mission accredited to the United Nations in New York by March 21, 1988. The UN General Assembly held two meetings and in each case adopted resolutions against any such decision and decided to refer the matter to the World Court of Justice at The Hague. In the first instance, Israel voted against while the United States abstained; but on the second resolution, both countries voted against. The U.S. courts subsequently rejected the U.S. government request to oust the PLO Mission from the United States.

In November 1988, the United States refused to grant a visa to Chairman Yasser Arafat to come to New York to address the UN General Assembly on the latest PLO peace plan. This refusal was in violation of the accord concluded between the United States and the United Nations entered into in 1947 concerning the granting of visas and the obligations of the United States as host country to persons connected with the world body. The accord provides:

Article IV—Communications and Transit
Section 11: The federal state or local authorities of the United States shall not impose any impediments to transit to or from the headquarters district of representatives of members or officials of the United Nations, or of specialized agencies or representatives of non-governmental organizations recognized by the United Nations for the purpose of consultation. . . .
Section 12: The provisions of Section 11 shall be applicable irrespective of the relations existing between the governments of the persons referred to in that section and the government of the United States.
Section 13: (A) Laws and regulations in force in the United States regarding the entry of aliens shall not be applied in such manner as to interfere with the privileges referred to in Section 11. When visas are required for persons referred to in that section, they shall be granted without charge and as promptly as possible.
(B) Laws and regulations in force in the United States regarding the residence of aliens shall not be applied

in such manner as to interfere with the privileges referred to in Section 11.

With Israel casting a negative vote and the United Kingdom abstaining, the General Assembly condemned the U.S. action and declared it to be in violation of its international obligations. The General Assembly then decided to move the debate to Geneva to give Arafat the opportunity to address the world body on the peace proposals of the PLO for a solution of the Palestine problem.

Arguably the greatest expression of support the Israelis received from the United States came from Henry Kissinger when he was Secretary of State. In 1975, he promised Israel that the United States would not recognize the PLO as the representative of the Palestinians and would not negotiate with it until the organization recognized the existence of the state of Israel and accepted UN resolutions 242 and 338. Since that time, his promise has become United States policy.

Kissinger's attitude towards the Palestine conflict was reflected more recently in a confidential memorandum of a February 3, 1988 meeting he held with the leaders of the most influential Zionist organizations in the United States (see Appendix H). Kissinger's advice, given during the third month of the Intifada, included the following:

"1. Now is not the time for Jewish community leaders to publicly attack Israel or its policies with respect to the Palestinians;
2. Israel should bar the media from entry into the territories involved in the present demonstrations, accept the short-term criticism involved in the present demonstrations, accept the short-term criticism of the world press for such conduct, and put down the insurrection as rapidly as possible—overwhelmingly, brutally, and rapidly;
3. The proposed international peace conference, as presently conceived by Foreign Minister Peres, may lead to a 'disaster' for Israel."

Kissinger ends up by stating that "Israel should retain *all* the territory that it took from the 1967 war, [and that] Israel should announce the specific territories within 'Judea or Samaria' that it is willing to relinquish, provided that there be no military forces situated there and that there be no PLO controlled government in that area."[6]

5. Israel vs. the Intifada

Throughout the first three years of the Intifada, the Israeli government scrupulously followed Kissinger's advice. Despite several changes in government, the "Three No's" of Israeli rejectionism continued to frame policy towards the Palestinians: no to negotiations with the PLO, no to a withdrawal from all the territories occupied in 1967, and no to an independent Palestinian state.

The diplomatic accomplishments of the PLO in gaining new international credibility during the course of the uprising, and especially following the Declaration of Independence, did not change the Israeli position. Tel Aviv became only more isolated from the emerging world consensus favoring an international peace conference and the possibility of an independent state. Only the U.S. stood by Israel, in the United Nations and other forums, to defend its ally.

The year 1989 saw the announcement of the Shamir Plan for ending the Intifada and settling the Palestinian issue on Israeli terms. He called for elections to be held in the occupied territories, to choose representatives who would participate in preliminary talks in Cairo aimed at future negotiations—which themselves would lead only to a Camp David-style autonomy; independence and statehood were explicitly not on the table. Additionally, those running for office would have to be Palestinians accepting the Israeli restrictions, and with no connection to or support for the PLO; Israeli officials indicated they would arrest any candidate who supported the PLO in a campaign speech. Further, the entire plan would not be implemented until the Intifada had been halted. It surprised no one that the "plan" did not get off the ground.

In the spring of 1990, new elections were held in Israel. The paralysis caused by several years of shared power between the centrist Labor and right-wing Likud blocks was over. The new government, headed by Likud chief Yitzhaq Shamir, brought together only the Likud and its far-right allies: the religious fundamentalists and the secular nationalists intent on establishing "Greater Israel" including the occupied territories, and with a growing commitment to "transfer" as an acceptable political option. Transfer is the euphemistic term for large-scale forced expulsion of Palestinians from their land, replacing them with Jewish settlers.

The settlement question took on new urgency from 1989 on, as events in Eastern Europe and the Soviet Union opened the way for a flood of Soviet Jewish emigrants. Most of them would have preferred settling in the U.S., but Washington imposed new immigration quotas, limiting Soviet immigrants for the first time, and those Jews wishing to leave the Soviet Union found entry rights only in Israel. In 1990 alone, over 200,000 Soviet Jews emigrated to Israel, sorely taxing Israel's economic and political infrastructure.

Those who paid the cost, of course, were the Palestinians. While U.S. Congressional regulations forbade the Israelis from spending U.S. aid money to settle the new immigrants inside the occupied territories, a new $400 million loan guarantee from the U.S. was answered with the announcement (only two days later) of new housing construction plans for over 20,000 units to be built for Soviet Jews in Arab East Jerusalem and its environs. A small-scale scandal broke in the spring of 1990, when it was revealed that Likud cabinet ministers had been involved in financing a new Jewish settlement within the Christian Quarter of Jerusalem's Old City, leading to daily clashes at the height of the Easter celebrations in the Holy City.

Throughout the period of the Intifada, Israeli repression continued, regardless of new initiatives or efforts to present the occupation as "benign." In May 1990, an Israeli soldier, dismissed as "crazed" by officials, rounded up Palestinian workers in a suburb of Tel Aviv and fired into the crowd, killing seven and wounding many more. In response, fierce clashes erupted throughout the West Bank and Gaza. More than a dozen Palestinian academic and political leaders launched a hunger strike in Jerusalem that brought the eyes of the world back to the occupation and the resistance.

When the crisis in the Persian Gulf broke out that summer, it was the U.S. commitment to Israel that proved its greatest tactical annoyance. With new strategic links between Washington and a number of Arab countries arrayed against Saddam Hussein's Iraq, the U.S. feared that touting its Israeli connections too publicly might jeopardize the newly formed unity with its Arab allies. But at the same time, the commitments to Israel precluded U.S. support for some of the initiatives its Arab allies vigorously endorsed—especially the convening of an international peace conference to resolve the issue of Palestine along with other crises in the region.

At the United Nations, U.S. diplomats delayed the vote on protecting Palestinians living under occupation, until after their carefully orchestrated Security Council vote to approve war against Iraq after January 15, 1991 if Iraq did not withdraw from Kuwait. It escaped no one's notice that the "use of force" resolution was approved by the Security Council on November 29, the date first set in 1974 by the United Nations as the International Day of Solidarity with the Palestinian People.

And in the midst of the crisis, Israeli Prime Minister Shamir added more fuel to the fire when he declared in November 1990 that he was dedicated to an Israel "from the Jordan to the sea," thus denying any possible land for peace exchange. This statement raises special fears in the light of the longstanding Israeli aspirations towards Jordan.

Israel needs space for the hundreds of thousands of Soviet Jews coming into the country. Israel alone lacks sufficient space to absorb the newcomers. So Jordan is viewed as a venue to which the Palestinians of the West Bank and Gaza could be forcibly "transferred," leaving the occupied territories to be annexed and settled by the new Soviet-Israelis.

Months before the Gulf crisis, the Israelis were telling the world that "Jordan is Palestine," and that the British established Palestine as a separate mandate territory only in 1923. This is not true. The territory east of the Jordan River was never a part of Palestine. It was a *Wilayet* (province) of Damascus, and comprised the Sanjaks (districts) of Huran and Maan (see map on page 308). Palestine was governed completely separately. During the Ottoman period it was actually governed in two sections: a *Wilayet* from Nablus north to Lebanon was administered by the Mutasarref (governor) in Beirut; while the Sanjak of Jerusalem, south to the Egyptian border, was administered directly by the Central Government in Istanbul. Throughout the 400 years of Ottoman rule and the decades of British Mandate, Palestine and Jordan were separate entities.

Through it all, clashes continued, although in ebbs and flows, and Palestinians continued to die. One of the most horrifying massacres took place October 8, 1990, in the Haram Ash-Sharif and Al-Aqsa Mosque area of Jerusalem's Old City. Thousands of Palestinians were in the area to protest a march by Jewish fundamentalists planning to "lay a cornerstone" for a new Jewish temple they want to establish on Judaism's Wailing Wall, the site of the third holiest shrine of Islam. Israeli soldiers and border police opened fire, killing 21 Palestinians. Hundreds more

OTTOMAN ADMINISTRATIVE DISTRICTS
(1914)

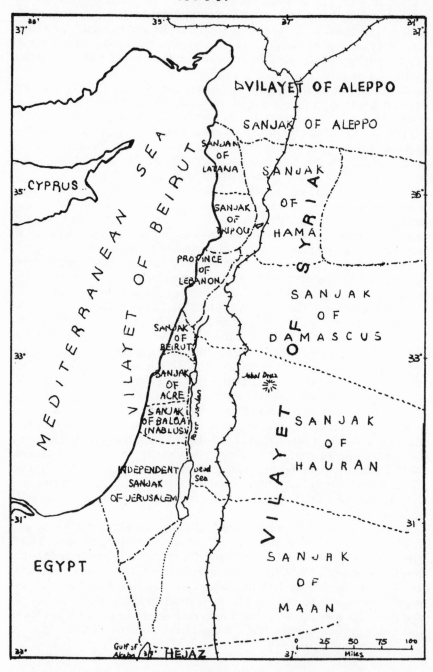

were seriously injured. Ambulance crews were shot trying to provide aid to the wounded. Tear gas was fired at lines of people waiting to donate blood and into the maternity ward of Al-Makassad Hospital, where many of the injured were taken. Israeli brutality and the nature of its occupation could once again no longer be hidden.

The clash between the fanatical Jewish settlers and the Moslem defenders of the Haram brings to mind a similar clash between Moslems and Jews that occurred in September 1928. Then, as now, a group of fanatical Zionists, bent on laying physical claim of possession to the Wailing Wall, marched to the site in an aggressive manner that resulted, as now, in riots breaking out between Arabs and Jews.

Following those clashes, the British Mandatory Power approached the League of Nations, and a Committee was formed in January 1930 composed of Eliel Lofgren, former Swedish Minister of Foreign Affairs (Chair), Charles Barde, Vice-President of the Court of Justice at Geneva, and C.J. Van Kempen, former Governor of the East Coast of Sumatra, to decide on the rights and claims of Moslems and Jews in the Western Wall area of the Al-Aqsa Mosque. It is known by Jews as the "Wailing Wall," and by Moslems as the "Buraq," after the name of the horse which carried the Prophet Muhammad on his nocturnal trip to Heaven.

The Committee heard the claims of both parties, and in December 1930 arrived at the following verdict (Cmd. 58–9096):

"To the Moslems belongs the sole ownership of, and the sole proprietary right to, the Western Wall, seeing that it forms an integral part of the Haram Ash-Sharif area, which is a *Waqf* [pious foundation] property.
"To the Moslems also belongs the ownership of the pavement in front of the Wall and of the adjacent so-called Moghrabi (Moroccan) Quarter opposite the Wall, inasmuch as the last-mentioned property was made *Waqf* under Moslem Sharia Law, it being dedicated to charitable purposes."

The "Verdict" gave the Jews certain privileges which they were to enjoy unhindered. These were: "The right to place near the Wall the Cabinet or Ark containing the Scroll or Scrolls of the Law and the Table on which the Ark stands and the Table on which the Scroll is laid when being read from," but only on certain specified occasions. "No objection or obstacle was to be raised to the Jews, in their individual capacity, carrying with them to the Wall hand-books or other articles customarily used at their devotions, either as a general thing or upon special occasions, nor to their wearing such garments as were of old used at their devotions."

6. UN Secretary-General Calls for Protection of the Palestinians in the Occupied Territories

The United Nations secretary-general suggested on November 1, 1990 an unprecedented meeting of the 164 nations signatory to the Fourth Geneva Convention to discuss means of protecting the Palestinians under Israeli occupation.

The call came in an 11-page report to the Security Council ordered after the October 8, 1990 massacre of 21 Palestinian stone-throwing youths by the Israeli forces in the Haram Ash-Sharif and Al-Aqsa Mosque area in the Old City of Jerusalem.

The secretary-general emphasized that the international community rejected Israel's claim that the convention did not apply to the occupied West Bank and Gaza Strip. He stressed that "under the convention, the civilian population in the occupied territories is entitled to safety and protection as clearly stated in its article 27," the first paragraph of which he quoted:

"Protected persons are entitled, *in all circumstances* (emphasis added), to respect for their persons, their honor, their family rights, their religious convictions and practices, and their manners and customs. They shall *at all times* (emphasis added) be humanely treated, and shall be protected especially against all acts of violence or threats thereof and against insults and public curiosity."

The secretary-general also cited article 29, which states the responsibility of the occupying power:

"The Party to the conflict in whose hands protected persons may be, is responsible for the treatment accorded to them by its agents, irrespective of any individual responsibility which may be incurred."

The secretary-general pointed out the "important responsibility" of the international community under the convention's article 1, which states:

"The High Contracting Parties undertake to respect and to ensure respect for the present convention in all circumstances."

The secretary-general observed that "the message that is repeatedly conveyed to me by the Palestinians—whether in meetings with the leadership of the Palestine Liberation Organization (PLO) or personalities from the occupied territories, in numerous communications and appeals sent to me from groups and individuals in the area, or in conversations that members of staff have had with individuals from all walks of life in the territories—is that far more is required on the part of the international community to ensure the safety and protection of the Palestinian civilian population in the occupied territories.

"While it would not be possible for me to summarize in a few paragraphs the intensity of the feeling that has consistently been conveyed to me both in conversations with and in appeals by Palestinians, I would like to comment on several recurring themes that emerge from them. Palestinians have expressed a profound feeling of vulnerability at all times, whether in the workplace, at school, in places of worship or simply walking down the street. This fear was compounded by their view that there was no recourse to any authority, other than the security forces who were so often responsible for the measures inflicted upon them. They have stated that they felt unsafe even inside their homes, which were frequently subjected to midnight searches, and during which entire households, including children, were beaten. It was said that arrests during such operations were common. A wide range of collective punishments had, they said, become routine during the past three years, such as curfews, the demolition of homes, administrative detention and the uprooting of trees. A system of arbitrary and heavy taxation had been imposed, which, if not complied with, might lead to the confiscation of personal property and even arrest. Furthermore, the Palestinians have complained bitterly about a number of longstanding Israeli practices: the taking of land, especially for Israeli settlements and the privileged access that these settlements were given to water supplies; the closure for prolonged periods of the universities, and the periodic closure of elementary and high schools, which, in the Palestinian view, amounted to a denial of their right to education; and the overall economic exploitation of the territories.

"Palestinians emphasized that their distrust of the Israeli occupation authorities—be they the security forces charged with maintaining law and order or officials of the civil administration whose role affected most aspects of their daily lives—had grown so deep that they felt that only an impartial presence, properly mandated by the United Nations, would be able to provide them with a credible sense of protection . . .

"The issue before us today is what practical steps can, in fact be taken by the international community to ensure the safety and protection of the Palestinian civilians living under Israeli occupation. Clearly, the numerous appeals—whether by the Security Council, by myself as secretary-general, by individual member states or by the International Committee of the Red Cross, which is the custodian of the Geneva Conventions—to the Israeli authorities to abide by their obligations under the Fourth Geneva Convention have been ineffective . . . given the special responsibility of the High Contracting Parties for ensuring respect for the convention, the Security Council might wish to call for a meeting of the High Contracting Parties to discuss possible measures that might be taken by them under the convention . . .

"It would be misleading to conclude this report—which has focused essentially on the need to ensure the safety and protection of the Palestinian civilians living under Israeli occupation—without underlining that it is a political conflict that lies at the heart of the tragic events that led to adoption of Security Council resolutions 672 (1990) and 673 (1990.) The determination of the Palestinians to persevere with the *intifada*, is evidence of their rejection of the occupation and their commitment to exercise their legitimate political rights, including self-determination.

"It is essential in these circumstances that progress be made, and soon, to ensure an effective negotiating process, acceptable to all, that can secure the interest of both Israelis and Palestinians, and enable them to live in peace with each other. For my part, I will do whatever I can to be of help."

The Palestinian reaction to the secretary-general's report was favorable, although reservations were voiced that further steps were necessary to protect the Palestinians under occupation. "Our position is positive," President Yasser Arafat said, "and we will deal with this initiative positively even though we consider it incomplete."

Israel's response to the report, on the other hand, was contemptuously dismissive. The foreign ministry rejected the call for a meeting of the parties of the Fourth Geneva Convention, calling it "one-sided" and "a grave attack on the effectiveness of this important humanitarian instrument."

7. The Gulf Crisis: Inequities of Double-Standard Policies

Little did the world imagine that the year 1990 would see the dramatic changes which have taken place: The end of the "cold war" between East and West; a distinct change in the political system of the East European countries; greater freedoms for the peoples of the Soviet Union; the destruction of the Berlin Wall; the re-unification of East and West Germany; and the leader of the Soviet Union—a country once described by former President Ronald Reagan as an "evil empire"— receiving the Nobel Peace Prize.

At the same time another change appears to be building up in South Africa: Black leader Nelson Mandela was released after spending 27 years in prison; the "apartheid" laws are being relaxed in certain respects; and there are hopeful signs of their complete abolition.

Even Korea appears to be on the verge of change for the better. The leaders of both North and South divisions have met for the first time and there are indications that they will agree in the not too distant future to unification.

But in the Middle East, where the key to peace remains in U.S. hands, the situation remains explosive.

What should surprise no one is the swiftness with which the United States reacted to the Iraqi invasion of Kuwait in comparison with the indifference with which it continues to treat the Israeli invasions of Arab lands in 1967 and 1982. Both Israel and Iraq violated the provisions of the United Nations Charter which make it inadmissable for any nation to invade the territory of another; both sets of Security Council resolutions call on the invaders for "immediate and unconditional withdrawal"; both arrogantly refuse to comply; yet United States reaction treats Israel with kid gloves and the Iraqi invasion of Kuwait with an iron fist.

With regard to Iraq, the United States used its influence to get the UN Security Council to apply sanctions and had this enforced by its navy. It augmented its action by sending to the area about 500,000 troops and an armada of tanks, planes, and ships—equal if not larger than at the height of the Vietnam War—and then demanded that Saddam Hussein immediately withdraw from Kuwait or else face a horrifying war. But in the case of the West Bank and the Gaza Strip, the United States continues to oppose Security Council resolutions condemning any aggressive actions in the occupied territories by using its veto against a majority vote. Resolution 242 of 1967 is just as explicit on withdrawal as the resolution adopted in the case of Kuwait; and when this apparent discrepancy was pointed out to President Bush, he merely remarked that there was "no linkage" between the two cases.

The United States takes pride in describing itself as the champion of democratic freedoms and defender of human rights for all peoples without exception. In fact, when Secretary of State James Baker visited the American troops in the Saudi Arabian desert in November 1990, he told them that "whenever a principle is affected in any part of the world, you will find American troops there to defend it." Palestine is a dismal exception to this claim, and exposes American declarations and prestige to international ridicule. The Israeli invasions and occupations of 1967 and 1982 are flagrant examples of American hypocrisy and double dealing.

The Gulf crisis has given Israel's U.S. supporters the opportunity to flex their muscles at a time when the American people were just beginning to understand the real character of Israel and the dangers it poses to U.S. interests in the Middle East. In an essay published in *Time* magazine on September 10, 1990, Otto Friedrich wrote:

"It is hard to remember a time when such influential American opinion molders were so frantically demanding that the U.S. go to war, and the sooner the better. 'The ultimate goal now,' writes A.M. Rosenthal, columnist and former executive editor of the *New York Times*, 'has to be the elimination of the incurably murderous Baghdad dictatorship by Western . . . economic and military reprisals.' His fellow columnist at the *Times*, William Safire, even offers a game plan: 'Our declared-war strategy should be to (1) suppress Iraqi air defenses; (2) take out war production at the 26 key targets; (3) launch a three-front land war at the Turkish, Syrian and Kuwaiti borders . . . Our great danger is delay.' A *Wall Street Journal* editorial writer day-dreams: 'If we take Baghdad and install a MacArthur regency, that is the optimum.'"

The Senate and House of Representatives took up the question of support for President Bush's war against Iraq if Saddam Hussein did not comply with Security Council resolutions calling for withdrawal from Kuwait by January 15, 1991. On January 13, 1991, the Senate voted 52 to 47, and the House 250 to 183, to give the President the support he needed.

How the votes were orchestrated was commented on by Rowland Evans and Robert Novak in the *Washington Post* of January 14, 1991:

"Dole's heart was not where his shoulder was because of misgivings, widely felt within the Senate minority, about where Bush is leading the nation. Senator William Cohen, a liberal Republican, is defying public opinion in Maine to support the president . . . Other Republicans were made uncomfortable by the central backstage role of the American-Israel Public Affairs Committee, the pro-Israel lobby, in lining up enough Democratic votes to pass the war authorization. It is bitter for GOP leaders to rely on the organization that has created so much mischief over the past generations for U.S. governments seeking an even-handed policy in the Middle East."

U.S. missile attacks against Iraq began on January 16, 1991. Writing in the *Toronto Star* on January 27, 1991, Tom Harpur described the war against Iraq as "insane and unjust," and added that "morality and war are obviously and mutually contradictory . . . Justice, like truth is among the first casualties of any war . . . This insane Gulf war is not just by any standards."

He then quotes a professor at Berea Christian College whose students spent a semester researching the reasons behind the Gulf conflict. Their research focused on "what the crisis is not about:"

". . . it is not about stopping 'another Hitler.' Saddam Hussein is not a world-class threat. He's a regional dictator of a medium-sized Third World country. He is no more or less evil today than when he was the recipient of massive U.S. support against Iran in that eight-year war . . .

"It's not about defending democracy. Neither Kuwait nor Saudi Arabia is a democracy; both are feudal oligarchies where enormous wealth has been monopolized for the benefit of the few at the top. They want to keep it that way.

"Clearly it's not about upholding the principle that larger countries must not invade smaller ones . . . 'History shows the U.S. has virtually written the book on shaping the destinies of weaker neighbors,' one student wrote.

"Nor is the war about maintaining 'the international rule of law,' they found. Indeed, the U.S. has a very uneven track record in this area. 'It supports UN and World Court decisions only when those coincide with U.S. self-interest.' The most glaring example of this is the way the U.S., along with Israel, has simply ignored UN resolutions demanding the withdrawal of Israeli troops from their 23-year occupation of the West Bank and Gaza. . . .

"This conflict is not even about protecting innocent people from atrocities carried out by brutal military dictators or others. The students quickly realized that the U.S. has never backed away from supporting leaders with the most abysmal of human rights records—Marcos in the Philippines, Somoza in Nicaragua, or Pinochet in Chile . . ."

The Author's Closing Remarks

Whatever the outcome of the Gulf crisis, the situation in the Middle East will remain explosive until the Palestine problem is equitably and justly resolved. Part of the fault lies in the ineffectiveness of the United Nations and its manipulation by the U.S.. This has been proven by the difference in the manner in which the Palestine problem and the Gulf crisis have been handled.

In the case of Palestine, Security Council resolutions not serving the interests of Israel are routinely vetoed by the United States representative, and this has been going on since the Israeli invasion of the West Bank and the Gaza Strip in 1967.

In the case of Iraq, the resolutions for sanctions and ultimately for war were promptly approved and implemented. It is not difficult to explain this odd difference. The Iraqi government has no Great Power to back its aggression against Kuwait; the Israelis, on the other hand, have the full, unqualified support of the United States.

In such circumstances, the veto power has proved to be an impediment to a proper and just world order. It is therefore in the interest of world peace that the veto power should be removed from the Charter of the United Nations.

The question may be asked why the United States is so inconsistent in its foreign policies in regard to the Middle East. The answer is reflected in a conversation I had with a member of the U.S. Mission to the United Nations in New York in 1968. I was trying to impress upon him the justice of the Palestinian cause. In the end he said before rising to leave: "Off the record. When we get our freedom we will give you yours." I did not then grasp the meaning of his words. But with the power of the pro-Israeli lobby in the United States growing stronger from day to day, I realize what he was talking about.* That power has now reached its zenith and is creating a dangerous situation for United States interests in the Middle East.

There was a time when Americans were able to move about freely in the Arab world and be treated as friends. Today, even those who realize the injustices inflicted on the Palestinian people and support their cause are kidnapped and held, not for ransom, but in revenge for the United States pro-Israel policy; while American embassy staffs are compelled to work in fortified premises. The war with Iraq will only worsen this situation in the Middle East.

Unless a serious and determined effort is made by the American people as a whole to arrest the influence of the pro-Israeli lobby the situation in the Middle East will continue to deteriorate. The dangers which face the United States because of its pro-Israel policy, are adequately described by a group of Jewish intellectuals in Appendix G, to which attention is drawn.

It is time for the United States to re-assess its position towards the Palestine issue, replacing it with one based on the principles of human justice and equity which the American people cherish and uphold. At the same time the Israelis should be advised to re-evaluate their policy towards their Palestinian victims. It is foolish to expect that an aggressive Israel, comprising no more than five million souls in the future will be able to exist without challenge among 200 million Arabs with Palestinian blood, expulsion, and confiscation of property on their record. Today the United States serves as a protector and supplier of political, military, and economic aid to the Jewish state, but a day may come when the Israelis will have to rely on their own limited resources.

In the circumstances, the Israelis cannot continue to exist as a nation and as a people surrounded by antagonism and hatred of their own making. History has it on record that there is an end to everything, and the Palestine tragedy is no exception. Israel's supporters inside and outside the country should be reminded of the biblical saying: "The sins of the fathers shall be visited upon the children," and try to be merciful to their future generations.

---

* See *They Dare to Speak Out* by Paul Findley (Westport, Conn: Lawrence Hill & Co., 1985)

Appendices

Appendix

A - Photostat copy of letter (in Arabic with English translation) submitted by the Arab Higher Committee for Palestine to the Prime Minister of Egypt on March 8, 1948 demanding that Palestinians who left their homes should be required to return and that none others should be given entry visas

B - Focus on Restitution in Germany, dated May 1985 on the payment of reparations to Jews for Nazi crimes committed during World War II

C - Palestinian National Covenant of 1968

D - A graphic description of the devastation that occurred in Beirut as a result of the Israeli invasion of Lebanon in 1982 by Tony Clifton & Cathering Leroy

E - Report by Reverend Don Wagner, National Director of the Palestine Human Rights Campaign in Chicago on Israeli treatment of the Palestinian inhabitants of the occupied territories

F - Report by Dr. James Graff, Chairman of the Toronto Universities Middle East Group (TUMEG) on the treatment of the Palestinian inhabitants of the occupied territories.

G - Statement by a group of distinguished Jewish personalities on Time to Dissociate from Israel.

H - Memo of Henry Kissinger's advice to Zionist leaders

I - The Arab Fez Peace Plan (1982)

J - The Ronald Reagan Plan (1982)

K - The Jerome M. Segal Proposals (1988)

L - The U.S. Presbyterian Church Proposals (1988)

M - Proposals by a group of distinguished personalities (1988)

N - Declaration of Palestinian Independence

Appendix A

(*Note:* This Document appeared as Appendix B (Document 17) on pages 383–384 of *The Palestine Diary 1945–1948* by Robert John and Sami Hadawi, published in 1970)

Photostatic copy of letter (in Arabic) submitted by the Arab Higher Committee for Palestine to the Prime Minister of Egypt on March 8, 1948.

ديوان الرسائل

الهيئة العربية العليا
لفلسطين
القاهــــرة

الرقم : ٨٠٨
الدائرة :

التاريخ ٢٧ ربيع الاخر ١٣٦٧ (٨ مارس ١٩٤٨)
رقم الملف س/ ١٣٢

حضرة صاحب الدولة رئيس الوزارة المصرية الافخم
القاهـــرة

السلام عليكم ورحمة الله وبركاته ٠ وبعد فان الهيئة العربية العليا لفلسطين تتشرف
برفع ما يلي الى حكومتكم الموقرة ٠

لمناسبة الاحوال الحاضرة التي تسود فلسطين ، واخذ عدد من ابنائها ينادرون البلاد
للاقامة بالاقطار العربية التجاورة ، ولا يخفى على دولتكم ان مثل هذا العمل يشوه جـــلال
حركة النضال العربية الشريفة ، ويسيء الى سمعة الشعب العربي في فلسطين ، ويخلق احتــالا
لاضعاف معنويات الشعوب العربية ، التي يرى هؤلاء الفلسطينيين بلادها للاقامة بها ، نحـــو
جهاد فلسطين ٠ وقد كان سلوك بعض هؤلاء سببا للانتقاد والشكوى في الاقطار العربية ٠

وقد درست الهيئة العربية العليا لفلسطين هذا الوضع الخطير ، فنظرت ان من مصلحة
القضية الفلسطينية ان لا ينادر فلسطين احد من ابنائها الا في الحالات الاضطرارية والضروريـة
كالمهام السياسية او التجارية او الضرورات الصحية ٠ وهذه الحالات تقررها الهيئة العربية العليا
لفلسطين ، باستشارة اللجان القومية في مختلف البلاد الفلسطينية ، وتقدم بها توصية كتابية الـى
مثل حكومتكم الموقرة في فلسطين للتفضل باعطاء التأشيرة اللازمة ٠ وان الهيئة العربية العليـا
ترجو من حكومتكم المحترمة اصدار التعليمات اللازمة لقناصلكم في فلسطين ، ليتكرموا بمساعدتنــا
في هذا الموضوع ٠

وبنهم الان في الاقطار الشقيقة عدد من الفلسطينيين قادر على البلاد على اثر قيام حركـــة
الجهاد ٠ وهؤلاء الاشخاص تحتم المصلحة القومية ان يعودوا الى فلسطين للقيام بواجباتهــم
نيها على النحو المستطاع ، وكل في ناحية عمله ٠ وقد تكرمت حكومتكم الموقرة باعطاء اذن للاقامـة
لهؤلاء الفلسطينيين ، والهيئة العربية العليا التي تقدر لحكومتكم هذا العطف وتشكركم عليـــه
جزيل الشكر ، ترجو ان لا تجدد حكومتكم اذن الاقامة المعطى للفلسطينيين الا بعد موافقة الهيئة
العربية العليا بمصر او القنصران تأمر بإعادتهم الى بلاد هم ، بعد التثبت من عدم وجود اى
اضطرار صحي ، او سبب معقول لبقائهم في القطر الشقيق ٠ وان الهيئة العربية العليا مستعـدة
لمعاونة الدوائر المختصة في حكومتكم للتثبت من حالات الفلسطينيين المقيمين ببلادكم العزيزة ٠

وتفضلوا يا صاحب الدولة بقبول اخلص التحية واوفر الاحترام ، والسلام عليكم ورحمـــة
الله وبركاته ٠

رئيس الهيئة العربية العليا

(English translation overleaf)

No. 808 (File S/132)   Arab Higher Committee for Palestine
                                              Correspondence Division, Cairo
                                              27 Rabi' El-Akher, 1367
                                              (Equivalent to March 8, 1918)
His Excellency
The Prime Minister of Egypt, Cairo.

With compliments. The Arab Higher Committee for Palestine has the honor to submit to your government the following:

In view of the events that are now taking place in Palestine, certain of the Arab inhabitants have begun to leave the country for the neighboring Arab states. This exodus will adversely affect the national movement, reflect badly on the Palestine Arabs, and create conditions that will weaken Arab morale in adjacent Arab territories in their defence of Palestine. Furthermore, the behaviour of some of these people has been the subject of criticism and complaint in the adjoining countries.

The Arab Higher Committee has studies this serious question and has resolved that it is in the interests of Palestine that no Palestinian should be permitted to leave the country except under special circumstances, such as for political, commercial or extreme health reasons. Such reasons will be decided upon by the Arab Higher Committee in consultation with the Local Committees of the various Palestine towns and will be presented to your Government's consular officers in Palestine before visas are issued. The Arab Higher Committee requests from your Government the issue of the necessary instructions to your consulates in Palestine to assist us in this respect.

There are at present resident in the adjacent Arab countries a number of Palestinians who left Palestine as soon as Arab defence operations commenced. The national interest demands that these persons should return to Palestine to carry out their obligations according to their abilities and each in his own sphere. Your government has graciously permitted these persons to stay in the country, and while it appreciates and thanks the Government for its consideration toward them, the Arab Higher Committee requests that their residence permits should not be renewed and that they should be returned to Palestine, except in cases where it is found that there are health or other extenuating circumstances for them to stay, in which event the approval of the Arab Higher Committee in Cairo or Jerusalem must first be sought. The Arab Higher Committee is prepared to assist the responsible departments of your government in investigating the conditions of Palestinians resident in your country.

With respects, etc.   Mohammad Amin El-Husseini
                                              Chairman
                                              Arab Higher Committee

(*Note:* Similar letters were sent to the governments of adjacent Arab countries).

Appendix B

Focus On

Restitution in Germany

The German word for restitution, *Wiedergutmachung*, means literally: to make something good again. For more than thirty years, the Government of the Federal Republic of Germany and the individual German states have been striving to "make good again" the history of injustice inherited from the National Socialist regime. Three decades of effort have been directed at making amends to those who suffered, within and outside of Germany, either because they were considered politically opposed to the Nazis, or simply because they were Jews.

The Beginnings

After the war, the occupation powers enacted laws in their individual zones that restored property confiscated by the Nazis to the original owners. These laws were restricted to property. They did not encompass personal damage to the victims of Nazi persecution—physical and psychological suffering, or unjust deprivation of freedom, or injury to a perons's professional or economic potential. Nor did these laws provide for assistance to the widows and orphans of those who had died as a result of Hitler's policies. The occupation forces placed the responsibility for the reparation of such damages on the newly constituted German states (the Federal Republic did not come into existence until 1949).

The Moral Obligation

Both Houses of Parliament in the Federal Republic of Germany, as well as the Federal Government, have often restated the policy that restitution for the crimes of the National Socialists in one of the most important and urgent obligations of the German people.

In the fall of 1949, the late Dr. Kurt Schumacher, then chairman of the Social Democratic Party of Germany, called for appropriate legislation. Dr. Schumacher had himself spent several years in Nazi concentration camps. Similarly, another internee during the Hitler regime, Dr. Konrad Adenauer, the first Chancellor of the Federal Republic of Germany, made the following historic statement before the Bundestag (Parliament) on September 27, 1951:

"The Federal Government and the great majority of the German people are deeply aware of the immeasurable suffering endured by the Jews of Germany and by the Jews of the occupied territories during the period of National Socialism. The great majority of the German people did not participate in the crimes committed against the Jews, and wish constantly to express their abhorrence of these crimes. While the Nazis were in power, there were many among the German people who attempted to aid their Jewish fellow-citizens in spite of the personal danger involved. They were motivated by religious conviction, the urgings of conscience and shame at the base acts perpetrated in the name of the whole German people. In our name, unspeakable crimes have been committed and they demand restitution, both moral and material, for the persons and properties of the Jews who have been so seriously harmed . . ."

Transitional Stage: The Luxembourg Agreement and the Israeli-German Treaty

One of the first acts of the Federal Republic of Germany was an official expression of intent to make restitution. A major provision of the treaty with the three Western occupying powers of May 26, 1952, which was to effect the transition of the Federal Republic of Germany from occupied territory to sovereign state, obligated the new state to make restitution. The Luxembourg Agreement between the Government of the Federal Republic of Germany and the

State of Israel and various Jewish organizations defined further the eventual shape of the legislation that was to regulate this restitution.

The Jewish organizations were represented by the Conference on Jewish Material Claims against Germany, or simply, the Claims Conference. Negotiations took place in Luxembourg and at the Hague and the agreement was signed in Luxembourg on September 10, 1952. Among its provisions: the requirement that the Government of the Federal Republic of Germany pay DM 3 billion ($714,300,000*) to the State of Israel and DM 450 million to various Jewish organizations. Payments to Israel, particularly in the form of goods, recognized the fact that the young nation had assumed a tremendous financial burden in accepting so many victims of Nazi persecution in Europe. Monetary payments to the Claims Conference were designed to aid Jewish organizations throughout the world in resettling Jews who lived outside Israel.

Legislation

Legislation was enacted subsequently to guarantee the compensation promised in the Transitional Treaty and in the Luxembourg Agreement.

The "Supplementary Federal Law for the Compensation of the Victims of National Socialist Persecution" of October 1, 1953, was followed on June 29, 1956 by the "Federal Law for the Compensation of the Victims of National Socialist Persecution" (Bundesentschädigungsgesetz, or BEG), which substantially expanded the effectiveness of the 1953 law in favor of those receiving compensation. A "Final Federal Compensation Law" was enacted on September 14, 1965, to increase the number of persons eligible for compensation and to improve the assistance offered.

Indemnification for Persecution of Persons

The BEG laws compensate those persecuted for political, racial, religious, or ideological reasons—people who suffered physical injury or loss of freedom, property, income, professional and financial advancement as a result of that persecution. In addition to racial and political victims of the Third Reich, the law includes compensation for artists and scholars whose works disagreed with Nazi tenets. It also provides compensation for people who were persecuted merely because they were related to or friendly with victims of the Nazis. Finally, it guarantees assistance to the survivors of the deceased victims.

The BEG legislation extends far beyond the responsibilities assumed by the Government of the Federal Republic of Germany in the Transitional Treaty and in the Luxembourg Agreement. Of 4,393,365 claims submitted under this legislation, between October 1, 1953 and December 31, 1983, 4,390,049 or 99.9% had been settled by January 1, 1984. Up to this date, payments equaling DM 56.2 billion had been made. Approximately 40% of those receiving compensation live in Israel, 20% reside in the Federal Republic of Germany and 40% live in other countries.

An additional DM 400 million in compensation was appropriated by the Bundestag (Parliament) in December 1970. This appropriation is earmarked for Jews whose health was damaged by the Nazi regime but who, because they were unable to comply with the deadline for filing or to qualify because of the residency requirements in the legislation, had not been able to obtain restitution previously.

In 1981, the Bundestag decided to grant a further amount up to DM 100 million for payments to non-Jewish victims of the Nazi regime in cases similar to the ones mentioned above.

Restitution for Lost Property

Claims for property lost as a result of National Socialist persecution are handled according to the provisions of the Federal Restitution Law (Bundesrückerstattungsgesetz, or BRüG) of July 19, 1957.

---

*The amounts agreed upon were almost exclusively expressed in German Mark. The dollar figures are in accordance with the rate of exchange accepted at the respective dates. The totals given in dollars express an average of the different rates in effect over the last thirty years.

As mentioned before, the original restitution statues were issued by the occupation forces of the three Western zones and Berlin to expedite the return of still-existing property and to settle related legal questions. Difficulties in handling claims for objects that had ceased to exist arose under these statutes; their extent was limited and enforced variously in the different zones. The BRüG recognized the obligation of the Federal Republic of Germany to pay compensation for all objects confiscated by the Third Reich that were no longer existent and which, therefore, could not be returned in their natural state.

This legislation was further developed in four supplementary laws, the last of which was approved on September 3, 1969. Compensation for lost property is made according to the estimated replacement value as of April 1, 1956.

The BRüG legislation is also applicable to property confiscated outside the territory of the Federal Republic of Germany, provided that, at the time of confiscation, it was brought into or kept in territory covered by BRüG legislation.

As of January 1, 1984, 734,952 claims had been made on the basis of the BRüG, 734,786 of which were settled. In addition, claimants who missed the 1959 deadline were able to make hardship applications for lost household goods, precious metals and jewelry in areas outside the Federal Republic of Germany up to 1966. The responsible government office in West Berlin reports that approximately 300,000 claims have been processed on the basis of this provision.

Initially, international agreements had limited the Federal Republic's financial obligations under the BRüG to DM 1.5 billion. The amount actually paid exceeds DM 3.9 billion. It is estimated that when all claims for losses of property will have been settled, the Federal Republic of Germany will have paid DM 4.25 billion as restitution in this category alone.

In addition to this basic legal complex, several other compensatory laws have been enacted to aid those who suffered as a result of the discrimination practiced by the Nazi regime.

On August 22, 1949, a law was passed restoring the rights and privileges of those who had been discriminated against in Nazi social legislation. This law has been steadily improved. On the same day, another law was approved extending the benefits of assistance to war victims ruled ineligible by Nazi law. This laws was also considerably improved by new legislation on June 25, 1958. A further law of May 11, 1951, provided for restitution to members of the civil service who had suffered injustice at the hands of the Nazis. Their condition had also been steadily improved by new legislation.

Mention must be made of the lump sum payments made to former concentration camp internees who were the objects of "medical experimentation" by the Nazis. Lump sum payments were also made to Palestinian prisoners of war who, due to their Jewish background, did not receive the humane treatment guaranteed to all prisoners of war by the provisions of international law. While the BEG legislation attempts to aid persecuted Jews, a special fund was set to assist those persecuted by the Nazis for having Jewish ancestry although they themselves were not Jews.

Table 1.: Payments made by the Federal Republic of Germany as a result of global agreements with eleven European nations

Country	Date of Agreement	million DM
Luxembourg	July 11, 1959	18
Norway	August 7, 1959	60
Denmark	August 24, 1959	16
Greece	March 18, 1960	115
Holland	April 8, 1960	125
France	July 15, 1960	400
Belgium	September 28, 1960	80
Italy	June 2, 1961	40
Switzerland	June 29, 1961	10
United Kingdom	June 9, 1964	11
Sweden	August 3, 1964	1
	Total:	876

Table 2.: Public expenditures in restitution for Nazi damages (as of January 1, 1984)

	in billion DM
I. Expenditure thus far:	
Compensation of Victims (BEG)	56.200
Restitution for Lost Property (BRüG)	3.912
Israel Agreement	3.450
Global agreements with 12 nations including Austria	1.000
Other (Civil Service etc.)	5.200
Final Restitution in Special Cases	0.356
	70.118

	in billion DM
II. Anticipated future expenditures:	
Compensation of Victims (BEG)	13.800
Restitution for Lost Property (BRüG)	0.338
Other (Civil Service etc.)	1.400
Final Restitution in Special Cases	0.184
	15.722

III. Total (in round figures):	
Compensation of Victims (BEG)	70.000
Restitution for Lost Property (BRüG)	4.250
Israeli Agreement	3.450
Global agreements with 12 nations including Austria	1.000
Other (Civil Service etc.)	6.600
Final Restitution in special Cases	0.540
	85.840

Global Agreements

Between 1959 and 1964, the Federal Republic of Germany worked out "global agreements" with the eleven European nations listed below. As a result of these agreements, the Federal Republic of Germany assumed an obligation of almost DM 900 million to these countries, thus enabling them to compensate citizens not eligible under the BEG for damages incurred as victims of Nazi policies. Their survivors also became eligible for compensation.

Austria

At the time when the discriminatory policies of the National Socialists took effect, Austria was an integral part of the German Reich and thus, according to international law, was itself responsible for injustices committed within its territory. The Federal Republic of Germany, nevertheless, made available to the Austrian government DM 102 million for compensatory payments. Of this amount, DM 96 million were used for the establishment of two funds: to compensate for loss of income to the victims of political persecution in Austria, and to aid such victims in other countries. The remaining DM 6 million were set aside to pay claims for lost property.

Summary

By December 31, 1983, the Federal Republic of Germany and the individual German states had paid more than DM 70 billion in restitution to victims of the National Socialist regime. Table 2 itemizes the individual amounts.

It is estimated that another DM 15.7 billion will be spent for the same purpose, bringing the total to DM 85.84 billion.

No matter how large the sum, no amount of money will ever suffice to compensate for National Socialist persecution. On this, the Federal Republic of Germany, its Western allies and responsible independent organizations have always concurred.

But in dealing with the legacy of the Hitler regime, the Federal Republic of Germany has established a precedent; namely that of making restitution for injustice.

Appendix C

The Palestinian National Covenant

JUNE 1968
1. This Charter shall be known as "the Palestine National Charter."
Articles of the Charter:
Article 1. Palestine, the homeland of the Palestinian Arab people, is an inseparable part of the greater Arab homeland, and the Palestinian people are a part of the Arab Nation.
Article 2. Palestine, within the frontiers that existed under the British Mandate, is an indivisible territorial unit.
Article 3. The Palestinian Arab people alone have legitimate rights to their homeland, and shall exercise the right of self-determination after the liberation of their homeland, in keeping with their wishes and entirely of their own accord.
Article 4. The Palestinian identity is an authentic, intrinsic and indissoluble quality that is transmitted from father to son. Neither the Zionist occupation nor the dispersal of the Palestinian Arab people as a result of the afflictions they have suffered can efface this Palestinian identity.
Article 5. Palestinians are Arab citizens who were normally resident in Palestine until 1947. This includes both those who were forced to leave or who stayed in Palestine. Anyone born to a Palestinian father after that date, whether inside or outside Palestine, is a Palestinian.
Article 6. Jews who were normally resident in Palestine up to the beginning of the Zionist invasion are Palestinians.
Article 7. Palestinian identity, and material, spiritual and historical links with Palestine are immutable realities. It is a national obligation to provide every Palestinian with a revolutionary Arab upbringing, and to instil in him a profound spiritual and material familiarity with his homeland and a readiness both for armed struggle and for the sacrifice of his material possessions and his life, for the recovery of his homeland. All available educational means and means of guidance must be enlisted to that end, until liberation is achieved.
Article 8. The Palestinian people is at the stage of national struggle for the liberation of its homeland. For that reason, differences between Palestinian national forces must give way to the fundamental difference that exists between Zionism and imperialism on the one hand and the Palestinian Arab people on the other. On that basis, the Palestinian masses, both as organizations and as individuals, whether in the homeland or in such places as they now live as refugees, constitute a single national front working for the recovery and liberation of Palestine through armed struggle.
Article 9. Armed struggle is the only way of liberating Palestine, and is thus strategic, not tactical. The Palestinian Arab people hereby affirm their unwavering determination to carry on the armed struggle and to press on toward popular revolution for the liberation of and return to their homeland. They also affirm their right to a normal life in their homeland, to the exercise of their right of self-determination therein and to sovereignty over it.
Article 10. Commando action constitutes the nucleus of the Palestinian popular war of liberation. This requires that commando action should be escalated, expanded and protected and that all the resources of the Palestinian masses and all scientific potentials available to them should be mobilized and organized to play their part in the armed Palestinian revolution. It also requires solidarity in national struggle among the different groups within the Palestinian people and between that people and the Arab masses, to ensure the continuity of the escalation and victory of the revolution.
Article 11. Palestinians shall have three slogans: national unity, national mobilization and liberation.
Article 12. The Palestinian Arab people believe in Arab unity. To fulfil their role in the achievement of that objective, they must, at the present stage in their national struggle, retain their Palestinian identity and all that it involves, work for increased awareness of it and oppose all measures liable to weaken or dissolve it.
Article 13. Arab unity and the liberation of Palestine are complementary objectives; each leads to the achievement of the other. Arab unity will lead to the liberation of Palestine, and the liberation of Palestine will lead to Arab unity. To work for one is to work for both.
Article 14. The destiny of the Arab nation, indeed the continued existence of the Arabs, depends on the fate of the Palestinian cause. This interrelationship is the point of departure of the Arab endeavour to liberate Palestine. The Palestinian people are the vanguard of the movement to achieve this sacred national objective.

Article 15. The liberation of Palestine is a national obligation for the Arabs. It is their duty to repel the Zionist and imperialist invasion of the greater Arab homeland and to liquidate the Zionist presence in Palestine. The full responsibility for this belongs to the peoples and governments of the Arab nation and to the Palestinian people first and foremost.

For this reason, the task of the Arab nation is to enlist all the military, human, moral and material resources at its command to play an effective part, along with the Palestinian people, in the liberation of Palestine. Moreover, it is the task of the Arab nation, particularly at the present stage of the Palestinian armed revolution, to offer the Palestinian people all possible aid, material and manpower support, and to place at their disposal all the means and opportunities that will enable them to continue to perform their role as the vanguard of their armed revolution until the liberation of their homeland is achieved.

Article 16. On the spiritual place, the liberation of Palestine will establish in the Holy Land an atmosphere of peace and tranquility in which all religious institutions will be safeguarded and freedom of worship and the right of visit guaranteed to all without discrimination or distinction of race, color, language or creed. For this reason, the people of Palestine look to all spiritual forces in the world for support.

Article 17. On the human plane, the liberation of Palestine will restore to the Palestinians their dignity, integrity and freedom. For this reason, the Palestinian Arab people look to all those who believe in the dignity and freedom of man for support.

Article 18. On the international plane, the liberation of Palestine is a defensive measure dictated by the requirements of self-defence. This is why the Palestinian people, who seek to win the friendship of all peoples, look for the support of all freedom, justice and peace-loving countries in restoring the legitimate state of affairs in Palestine, establishing security and peace in it and enabling its people to exercise national sovereignty and freedom.

Article 19. The partition of Palestine, which took place in 1947, and the establishment of Israel, are fundamentally invalid, however long they last, for they contravene the will of the people of Palestine and their natural right to their homeland and contradict the principles of the United Nations Charter, foremost among which is the right of self-determination.

Article 20. The Balfour Declaration, the Mandate Instrument, and all their consequences, are hereby declared null and void. The claim of historical or spiritual links between the Jews and Palestine is neither in conformity with historical fact nor does it satisfy the requirements for statehood. Judaism is a revealed religion; it is not a separate nationality, nor are the Jews a single people with a separate identity; they are citizens of their respective countries.

Article 21. The Palestinian Arab people, expressing themselves through the Palestinian armed revolution, reject all alternatives to the total liberation of Palestine. They also reject all proposals for the liquidation or internationalizaton of the Palestine problem.

Article 22. Zionism is a political movement that is organically linked with world imperialism and is opposed to all liberation movements or movements for progress in the world. The Zionist movement is essentially fanatical and racialist; its objectives involve aggression, expansion and the establishment of colonial settlements, and its methods are those of the Fascists and the Nazis. Israel acts as cat's paw for the Zionist movement, a geographic and manpower base for world imperialism and a springboard for its thrust into the Arab homeland to frustrate the aspirations of the Arab nation to liberation, unity and progress. Israel is a constant threat to peace in the Middle East and the whole world. Inasmuch as the liberation of Palestine will eliminate the Zionist and imperialist presence in that country and bring peace to the Middle East, the Palestinian people look for support to all liberals and to all forces of good, peace and progress in the world, and call on them, whatever their political convictions, for all possible aid and support in their just and legitimate struggle to liberate their homeland.

Article 23. The demands of peace and security and the exigencies of right and justice require that all nations should regard Zionism as an illegal movement and outlaw it and its activities, out of consideration for the ties of friendship between peoples and for the loyalty of citizens to their homelands.

Article 24. The Palestinian Arab people believe in justice, freedom, sovereignty, self-determination, human dignity and the right of peoples to enjoy them.

Article 25. In pursuance of the objectives set out in this charter, the Palestine Liberation Organization shall perform its proper role in the liberation of Palestine to the full.

Article 26. The Palestine Liberation Organization, as the representative of the forces of the Palestinian revolution, is responsible for the struggle of the Palestinian Arab people to regain, liberate and return to their homeland and to exercise the right of self-determination in that homeland, in the military, political and financial fields, and for all else that the Palestinian cause may demand, both at Arab and international levels.

Article 27. The Palestinian Liberation Organization shall cooperate with all Arab countries, each according to its means, maintaining a neutral attitude vis-à-vis these countries in accordance with the requirements of the battle of liberation, and on the basis of that factor. The Organization shall not interfere in the internal affairs of any Arab country.

Article 28. The Palestinian Arab people hereby affirm the authenticity and independence of their national revolution and reject all forms of interference, tutelage or dependency.

Article 29. The Palestinian Arab people have the legitimate and prior right to liberate and recover their homeland, and shall define their attitude to all countries and forces in accordance with the attitude adopted by such countries and forces to the cause of the Palestinian people and with the extent of their support for that people in their revolution to achieve their objectives.

Article 30. Those who fight or bear arms in the battle of liberation form the nucleus of the popular army which will shield the achievements of the Palestinian Arab people.

Article 31. The Organization shall have a flag, an oath of allegiance and an anthem, to be decided in accordance with appropriate regulations.

Article 32. Regulations, to be known as Basic Regulations for the Palestine Liberation Organization, shall be appended to this Charter. These regulations shall define the structure of the Organization, its bodies and institutions, and the powers, duties and obligations of each of them, in accordance with this Charter.

Article 33. This Charter may only be amended with a majority of two thirds of the total number of members of the National Assembly of the Palestine Liberation Organization at a special meeting called for that purpose.

Appendix D

A Graphic Description of Devastation that Occurred in Beirut Following
Invasion by the Israelis

In one of the bloodiest bombings of the war the Israelis totally destroyed a building in the Rue
Assi—the eight-storey apartment block near the Sanayeh Gardens that comes to mind again and
again as I write. It was hit by a sortie of two planes and collapsed totally. This was the bombing
which was so accurate that nothing else in the area was touched, and rumor had it that Arafat
had been seen going into it less than an hour before the planes hit it. It would be no surprise to
learn that he had been in the area, because both the nearby Sanayeh Gardens and buildings in
the area, including this one, were filled with refugees; the disintegrated building was ironically,
populated by Christian Arabs who had fled early in the civil war from the Christian Palestinian
camp of Jisr al Basha, which was overrun and destroyed a few months before Tal Zaatar. The
Rue Assi building was wrecked so utterly that hardly anybody got out of the wreckage alive and
its pulverization led to rumors that the Israelis had some terrifying new vacuum bomb that
somehow imploded rather than exploded and therefore sucked in the walls of buildings, causing
them to collapse. Nobody knows exactly how many people were killed there, but the Palestinians claimed around 260, and it is certain that more than 100 people died. The rescuers
scrabbled desperately in the wreckage for days, looking for bodies and for still-living people. As
with all the many collapsed buildings in west Beirut, it was a nearly impossible job because there
were so few heavy earth-moving machines and so many buildings to dig out. To save many of
the people who were alive under the wreckage of these buildings, the sites should have been
dug out immediately with bulldozers, earth-movers and heavey cranes. As it was, you rarely
saw more than one machine laboring away, while all but the heaviest work was done by main
force: hundreds of people sometimes, manhandling great lumps of shattered concrete with their
bare hands and listening all the time for the planes to come back.

Catherine grew obsessed by the destruction of the building in Rue Assi; it seemed to her (as it
did to me) that the Israelis, on the off chance of hitting Yasser Arafat, has wantonly killed 100
civilians . . . or maybe 200 or 300. She was on the scene before the dust of the bombing had
cleared; and she would go back day after day to take pictures and watch the volunteers
desperately trying to move away the great slabs of concrete in their search for the living and the
dead. The work would start about 5:30 each day—as soon as there was light enough to see.
There was an earth-mover working, and a crowd of thirty or forty people gathered on the edge
of the site. The earth-mover would grind in and scoop up a great load of earth and rubble and
carry it out to the edge of the site, and dump its load on the ground. The crowd would rush
forward to pick through the wreckage for the bodies of their relatives and friends. Most times,
there would be nothing, but every third or fourth time there would be a body. They were hardly
recognizable as human bodies, just blackened mashed-up bundles—and of course, none had
any recognizable features. The people would have to search for things they could recognize: a
medallion around a neck, a ring on a hand, maybe a dress or a jacket. The workers on the site
had masks and gloves on to protect them from the smell and infection from the rotting flesh, but
the people waiting would have to search through this mess with their bare hands.

"I photographed this drama every day, for a week or more. You would see people rush
forward and suddenly someone would find something they recognized, a ring or an I.D. card or
something like that; and women would start crying. After a while, I began to recognize faces in .
the crowd, and I became aware of a teenage boy, maybe about eighteen, in green military
fatigues, who was always there and always with a much smaller boy who would hold his hand
or sit very close to him. I couldn't be sure if they were brothers, or if the older boy was just
looking after the younger one. I still don't know why they were there, but I suppose it was
because one of them had a friend or some of his family in the ruins. After about four days, the
elder one came to me and asked me, not angrily, but very calmly: 'Why are you taking all these
pictures, you are here every day taking photographs?' And I thought for a minute and then I
said: 'I'm taking these pictures so that things like this won't be forgotten.'"

As she said, she still remembers every word of his reply: "Why shouldn't it be forgotten? Who
cares? Nobody cares about us. They'll keep doing this to us, again and again and again. You're
wasting your time here."

You start to ask yourself questions when people say things like that to you. Were we all
wasting our time in Beirut in 1982; do reporters actually ever do anything that moves world
opinion enough to stop suffering of the magnitude that was inflicted on Beirut? We weren't
wasting our time journalistically, of course: we were reporting the biggest story of the year; we

got big play in our newspapers and magazines and on television around the world; we got bonuses and plaudits when we got back and, looking back on it, I am proud to have been in Beirut with a group of brave reporters who cared very deeply about what was being inflicted on the city and its people.

But did we change anything; could we look back and say that what we wrote saved a single life?. . . Six months later, it's hard to find much evidence that we did. We wrote that the Israelis were using cluster-bombs . . . we wrote that they were using white phosphorus . . . we wrote that their shelling and bombing was almost always indiscriminate . . . we wrote how hospitals seemed to have become major targets . . . we wrote about the way cluster-bombs were blanketing the city and how at least 80% of those killed and wounded were civilian. We told the world that we believed that the Israelis were cutting off power and water and food, and that the first sufferers were going to be the children.

So what? No country protested by breaking off relations with Israel . . . no country declared that it would sell no more arms to Begin . . . certainly nobody had the guts to make a stupendous gesture like sending in an unarmed hospital ship to Beirut Harbor to take out civilian casualties. These would have been gestures—but they would have shown that somewhere out there, someone had absorbed the message we were all writing from Beirut. More than anyone, the Americans should have known, because most of the journalists working in Beirut were American, and most of the ordnance being dumped on us was American-made and brought to us via American planes and through American gun barrels. If Ronald Reagan watches television news, he must mentally edit out the nasty bits. I saw most of the film that was shot, and I can still cry over some of it, six months later. When he finally got mad, after Horrendous Thursday, August 12 when the Israeli air force bombed Beirut from morning to night, it was far too late. The shelling and bombing on that Thursday was an act of simple murderous vandalism and it finally irritated even Ronald Reagan into ringing up Begin.

"Mr. Prime Minister," he said, "we have been very patient, and this country has been very patient. But these bombings are getting to the point where they could seriously affect our long-term relationship," and he ended by saying, "I want it stopped, and I want it stopped now." Begin then stopped—but not because of Reagan, because his troops had done their job. Reagan had been impotent to stop Begin before all the damage and death were inflicted.

I believe that Israel's only hope for the long-term future lies in the creation of a Palestinian state, on the West Bank and in Gaza to begin with. The Israelis say they can't have this because it would be a threat; 'a dagger at the heart of Israel' seems to be the popular way to describe it. Of course the opposite is exactly true, because it would be a weak little infant, entirely at the mercy of the people next door; a Palestine Liberation Organization whose offices were literally within cannon shot of Israel would be far more vulnerable and far less aggressive than one in Beirut or Tunis. If it comes to that, the thousands of fighters who have nothing to do now but plot vengeance would be too busy putting together their new world to have time to think of vengeance and—to be practical—they're going to be a lot more careful about risking their own state than they are about someone else's. I don't know if the plan would work, but proximity might give each side a chance to get to know the other as neighbors and give the Israelis a chance to integrate into the Middle East.

The alternative is yet more war, more Israeli preemptive strikes, more graves in martyrs' cemeteries from Beirut to Baghdad; and in the end, the state of Israel will be overrun. The Arabs have much more money, their numbers are increasing at a far greater rate and more importantly, even now the Israeli population is declining because nobody wants to go there. The Russian Jews who should be their main source of new blood, have heard all the stories already, so they head straight for American when they can escape from the *gulags*. It's not Arab will and skill that's going to overcome Israel if it doesn't change, but Arab money and numbers. The question has absolutely nothing to do with right or wrong: Israel will go because it has chosen to use the diplomacy of the gun to deal with its neighbors, and therefore they have no reason at all to want it to survive. I think this will happen in my lifetime—if I manage three score and ten—but if the Americans suddenly couldn't afford to pay for all their playthings, the whole thing could go in under five years.

Appendix E

Israeli Violence Against Palestinians Report by Reverend Don Wagner

Rev. Don Wagner, National Director of Palestine Human Rights Campaign, toured the occupied territories in February 1988. He visited the family of Khader Tarazi, a 19-year-old Palestinian beaten to death by Israeli soldiers in Gaza on February 8. The head of the Chicago-based human rights organization related the family's account of the incident:

Witnesses claim that Khader did not participate in the stone throwing but ran as soon as the scene turned ugly. Four soldiers from the tough Golani Brigade saw Khader run and followed him to the home of a former neighbor, Um-Issam, a friend of the family. Khader ran inside and hid under a bed. The soldiers smashed down the door and searched the house, finding the frightened boy in a bedroom. They dragged him out into the living room and began to beat him with clubs and the butts of their guns. The elderly Um-Issam (approximately 65–66 years) screamed and tried to interfere but was clubbed and pushed aside. Khader had collapsed from the initial beating and was lying on the floor. One of the Golani [soldiers], crazed with rage, lifted Khader over his head and slammed his body to the cement floor. Um-Issam, who witnessed everything, later said blood flowed from his mouth and eyes. Another soldier kicked him in the genitals. Khader did not react. His limp body lay motionless in a pool of blood.

Within a few minutes two officers entered the house. By this time neighbors had heard the screams and noises and had gathered at a safe distance in adjacent houses in the alley. One neighbor who understood Hebrew heard an officer use his "walkie talkie" to contact another IDF unit to report their capture and the beating. The officer then asked what they should do next. The reply came back loud and clear, "Finish him off."

Khader was then dragged out of the house and thrown on the hood of the jeep, with his head hanging over the front and his feet straight back toward the windshield. His arms were stretched outward and tied down in a crucifixion position. Then the Golanis began to beat him again, clubbing him on the head, back, arms and legs. Scores of people witnessed the scene. Blood spurted out of his mouth and nose, running down the front of the jeep. Many feel that Khader was dead at this point. The jeep drove away with the boy still tied to the front.

Family members told us that on receipt of the body, one of Khader's cousins who is chief surgeon at Gaza's Shifa Hospital examined the body and photographed it prior to the funeral. He noted that the back was broken, the right front skull was fractured, bones in each arm and the right hand were broken, multiple lacerations appeared on the back, stomach, face, legs and arms. Internal injuries could not be measured. Khader was mutilated.

(Source: Palestine Perspectives No. 34, March/April 1988)

Appendix F

The following statement was made by Dr. James Graff, Chairman of the Toronto Universities Middle East Group (TUMEG) following his visit to the Israeli-occupied territories of the West Bank and the Gaza Strip in March 1988:

We were struck by the unity and high degree of organization among the Palestinians, by the unprecedented levels of co-operation among Palestinian organizations of differing ideological positions, and by the high morale and determination, the courage and sense of mission among Palestinians of all classes. In our view, the Israeli "Iron Fist" will not succeed in smashing the leadership or suppressing the rebellion because much of that leadership comes from the grass roots. We also found that people who are better-off are sharing with the neediest, sometimes risking life, limb, beatings, imprisonment in getting foodstuffs and medical supplies to camps and villages under strict curfew. The National Committee's circulars are being heeded in the Territories.

The demand is for the withdrawal of Israeli troops from the Occupied Territories, for negotiations with the PLO and the establishment of an independent Palestinian state on the West Bank and in Gaza alongside Israel. We believe that the uprising will continue until either these demands are met or a mad Israeli government "transfers" hundreds of thousands of Palestinians to S. Lebanon, Jordan or Syria. The last two "transfers" could occur only within the context of a war. The human costs of such "transfers" would be staggering. Israeli public opinion is becoming increasingly polarized, with more shifting to the extreme Right (which favors "transfers") but many shifting to the Peace Camp. More and more reservists are refusing to serve in the Territories, peace committees are springing up spontaneously throughout Israel and some efforts are now underway to try to network among them. The divisions are deepening and becoming increasingly bitter.

There are daily demonstrations (stone-throwing, displaying the Palestinian flag, etc.) throughout the Occupied Territories. The death toll among Palestinians from shootings by the IDF or "settlers" averages now two to three per day. Most of the victims are youths. More and more, Israeli troops are rounding up youths at night, beating them savagely and dumping them unconscious or semi-conscious, with broken limbs and concussions miles from home. They are breaking arms, smashing hands, elbows and kneecaps. They also focus on boys' genitals and girls' abdomens in many of the beatings. They are increasingly cutting deep wounds in fractured limbs to enhance the risks of gangrene. They continue to fire the new U.S. tear gas into homes. This gas is manufactured in Salzburg, PA, much of it stamped "1988" and all the cigar-shaped cannisters saying "not for use in confined spaces" since "death or serious injury can result". The day the PLO killed three workers on a bus going to Dimona, three Palestinian infants suffocated to death from tear gas shot into their homes. Israeli troops are also firing rubber bullets into homes at close range. This can and does result in very serious injuries. There are few journalists or foreigners visiting Gaza—it is dangerous from both sides. But this means that the Gazans have less protection from IDF brutality than do those on the West Bank. In our view, a massacre by "settlers" with IDF collusion is a very distinct possibility. But also in our view, unlike '47-'48, Palestinians will not flee because of massacres.

Appendix G

Time to Dissociate from Israel

We are Americans and Jews and we come together at this time publicly to express our strong desire to see the United States take meaningful steps to dissociate our country from the policies of Israel.

For some years we have witnessed Israel increasingly deviating from political policies that we find acceptable and from moral values that we hold dear. These developments are not the responsibility of any particular political party in Israel but rather stem, in our judgment, from a tragically misguided approach toward the Arab world in which Israel is located, a racialist ideology and a growing militancy. We can no longer condone or be associated with such Israeli behavior, nor, do we believe, should our country.

In recent years Israel has twisted away from basic commitments made at Camp David in 1978; annexed further territories, including East Jerusalem and the Golan Heights, while continuing to expand settlements in all the occupied territories; and grotesquely invaded Lebanon, resulting in the death of tens of thousands of Lebanese and Palestinians as well as hundreds of Israelis and Americans, and the taking as hostages of many others.

Furthermore, Israeli policies and attitudes toward the Palestinian people have made it evident that only major changes in Israel's basic posture will allow for a peaceful political settlement with the Palestinians.

Israeli complicity in Irangate and Contragate coupled with Israel's employment of American Jews as spies against our country further underscore the growing dangers inherent in the current U.S.-Israeli relationship. The close identification in the public mind between Israel and Jews—an equation vigorously fostered by both the Zionist movement and the American Jewish lobby, which has come under its control—threatens to stigmatize Jews everywhere.

The recent acts of killings, beatings, curfews, expulsions and house arrests—all against unarmed Palestinians living in areas Israel has occupied for 20 years—further demonstrate that Israel has become a badly divided country with many unfortunate similarities to the situation that prevails in South Africa.

Our ancestors came to the United States because, as a result of their Jewishness, they were discriminated against and abused. The European experience culminated in the horrors of the Nazi Holocaust. How tragic that in our own time the very state established by Jews in the aftermath of this evil has become a place where racialism, religious discrimination, militarism and injustice prevail; and that Israel itself has become a pariah state within the world community. Events taking place today are all too reminiscent of the pogroms from which our own forefathers fled two and three generations ago—but this time those in authority are Jews and the victims are Moslem and Christian Palestinians.

We believe that Israel's course could not be maintained but for the continuing financial, political, military and covert support of the U.S. government. And we fear that unless firm steps of disengagement from Israel are taken now our country might get dragged into a major war for which preparations are under way.

In addition, we believe that unless the United States takes serious steps to distance itself from Israel the Israelis will mistakenly continue to think that the course they are on is one acceptable to the American people.

For all these reasons we believe the time has come to *normalize* the U.S. relationship with Israel. A complete re-evaluation of what has become since 1967 the American sponsorship of Israel is required. The unprecedented amounts of economic aid should be cut back over the next two to three years to much smaller levels. Furthermore, the considerable military and intelligence assistance should also be radically reduced.

Unfortunately, during the years of the Reagan Administration much the opposite course has been followed, and Israel has practically become a ward of the United States. In this election year we urge an open debate about the serious problems and dangers which have resulted from the current structure of U.S.-Israeli relations. Few foreign policy issues are of such importance to our country. Consequently we urge our leading politicians to resist the widespread inhibitions from speaking up about Israel, inhibitions which result from the severe financial, political and ideological pressures often brought to bear against those who do.

We further believe that the time is overdue for negotiations between the Israeli government and the PLO, which is quite clearly the chosen representative for the great majority of Palestinians—negotiations that should quickly lead to a Palestinian state in the occupied territories and reasonable security guarantees for all parties. In the security guarantees we think our country should participate; but no longer in the financing and supporting of the kinds of policies Israel has been pursuing. The continual oppression and denial of the Palestinians of their right to self-determination is an injustice which has become intolerable not only to those demonstrating for their freedom in Jerusalem, the West Bank, Gaza and throughout Israel itself.

The citizens of Israel, of course, will ultimately choose their own country's destiny. But at the very least the citizens of the United States should stop financing and supporting policies that are contrary to the principles and values we hold precious as Americans and as Jews.

Professor Yigal Arens
Computer Science Department, USC.
Santa Monica, CA

Mark Bruzonsky
Former Washington Associate,
  World Jewish Congress
Washington, DC

Noam Chomsky
Institute Professor, MIT
Cambridge, MA

Rabbi Susan Einbinder
Colgate University
Hamilton, NY

Professor Herbert Hill
University of Wisconsin—Madison
Former Labor Director, NAACP
Madison, WI

Jane Hunter
Publisher, *Israeli Foreign Affairs*
Berkeley, CA

Jeremy Levin
Former CNN Bureau Chief & Former
  Hostage in Lebanon
Washington, DC

Professor John Mack
Professor of Psychiatry, Howard Medical School
Cambridge, MA

Professor Seymour Melman
Professor Emeritus of Industrial Engineering,
  Columbia University
New York, NY

Eileen Newmark
Ph.D., Intercultural Communications
Boston, MA

Professor Don Peretz
Professor of Political Science, SUNY
Binghamton, NY

Henry Schwarzschild
American Civil Liberties Union
New York, NY

Professor Steven Schwarzschild
Professor of Philosophy and Judaic Studies,
  Washington University
St. Louis, MO

Saul Wechter
Retired, General Motors
San Jose, CA

Gertrude M. Welch
Interfaith Peace Coalition
San Jose, CA

Richard Walden
President, Operation California
Los Angeles, CA

Danielle Yariv
Computer Analyst
Pasedena, CA

Solomon Zeltzer
Attorney
San Jose, CA

[Affiliations noted only for identification]

Appendix H

Confidential Memo on Henry Kissinger's Advice to Israel, New York,
3 February 1988.*

Re: Breakfast Meeting with Dr. Henry Kissinger

Dear Friend:
I attended a private "off-the-record" breakfast meeting with Henry Kissinger early this week to
discuss the current situation in the Mideast and I believe you will find of interest the following
report on the discussion that took place.
In sum, as I will amplify below, Dr. Kissinger conveyed three major points, as follows:
1. Now is not the time for Jewish community leaders to publicly attack Israel or its policies
   with respect to the Palestinians.
2. Israel should bar the media from entry into the territories involved in the present demonstrations, accept the short-term criticism of the world press for such conduct, and put down
   the insurrection as quickly as possible—overwhelmingly, brutally and rapidly;
3. The proposed international peace conference, as presently conceived by Foreign Minister
   Peres, may lead to a "disaster" for Israel.
I now will elucidate somewhat on the development by Dr. Kissinger of these points.
He started out by making it clear that he wants to be perceived by the public as an American
[sic] leader and not as a representative of the Jewish community, but that we should realize that
he would never participate in anything that would negatively affect the security of Israel.
The real "tragedy" facing Israel is obvious: it cannot give up all of the territories and end up
like Czechoslovakia at the beginning of World War II, yet it cannot maintain dominion over all of
the Arabs that are located in the territories.
Focusing on the situation in the last few weeks in Israel, Kissinger appropriately noted that
Israel's public relations were horrible. In his opinion, it made two major mistakes. First, it did
not throw all of the media out of the relevant territories. Second, it announced that it would
"beat" the participants in the violence (and not shoot them). Israel may have felt that that
approach was more humanitarian, but they overlooked the fact that when you "beat" someone
it means you already have control of that person and can no longer claim self-defense.
Kissinger repeatedly emphasized that, under no circumstances, should Israel make any
concessions during the present insurrection. If one learns anything from the history of revolutions, such as the Russian or French Revolution, it is that concessions during an insurrection
merely accelerate the revolution rather than hastening its end. Therefore, what is critical at this
time is to put down the insurrection as quickly as possible. It was at that point that Kissinger
added that he "really thinks that Jewish leaders should not yell at Israel now and make them
even more paranoid. We must close ranks and not let the enemy utilize quotations from Jewish
leaders as evidence to support their position about Israel in general."
Kissinger then turned to the international peace conference which has been proposed by
Foreign Minister (Shimon) Peres. He said that he was fully apprised of all the procedural
conditions that Peres has placed on the conference and the respective roles of the parties
involved, but he still feels Peres overlooked one major problem. What is going to happen during
the second week of the conference? All the deals that Peres has made with the various
prospective participants in the conference reflect, in his opinion, naiveté and read a bit childish.
After all is said and done, Israel does not have a government at present that could formulate a
substantive policy for the proposed conference and, on the other side of the coin, there is no
Arab leader that is able to make peace right now. Israel must always be aware of the fact that the
American [sic] government is not against the return by Israel to the 1967 borders (except for,
possibly, Jerusalem). In his opinion, the State Department has never given up on the Rogers
Plan.
Kissinger recently had a conversation with Assistant Secretary of State Richard Murphy in
which the latter explained to him in excruciating detail all the procedural protections for the
beginning of the conference. He noted, however, that no one was focusing on what happens in
the course of the conference itself. He feels that if the United States and Israel do not have any

---

*This memo was written on the letterhead of the firm Kaye, Scholer, Fierman, Hays & Handler,
425 Park Avenue, New York, NY 10022, dated 3 February and marked "CONFIDENTIAL." A
copy was obtained and published by *The Saudi Gazette* (Jeddah), 19 March 1988—*Ed.*

prearranged agreement as to what positions will be taken at the conference itself, it may lead to a disaster. It is totally naive to believe that the five permanent members of the United Nations will come to the conference and be prevented from taking substantive positions. For example, assuming that after the opening there will be subcommittees for bilateral negotiations, there is no question that they will come to an immediate deadlock. What happens then? According to the Peres formula, Israel will have the right to say that nobody could talk from that point on. That simply cannot be done. For that matter, the idea of Israel just walking out of the conference and meeting . . . the whole thing is ridiculous.

Kissinger noted that other than Israel, there is no state attending the conference that does not favor return by Israel to the 1967 borders and, in his opinion, Israel could not survive that type of withdrawal.

In general, Kissinger feels that the issue of a peace treaty is overblown. It is not the be all and end all of peace in the Mideast. Mutual recognition did not stop Iran and Iraq from its [sic] war; not has it stopped India and Pakistan from continuing to fight with each other.

Focusing on the conference itself, Kissinger said that there is no question in his mind that China will adamantly support an "extreme" Arab position. This is necessary to outdo the Russian "romancing" of the Arabs. Syria, in his opinion, must also take a radical position on the Palestinian claims so that it will not end up being isolated on the Golan Heights issue. Israel on the other hand can never give up the Golan. He recalls having a discussion with the Russian ambassador in which the latter delineated to Kissinger the distinction between bilateral issues which will be dealt with at the international peace conference directly between Israel and the individual Arab nation involved and multilateral issues which will be dealt with by all of the participants at the international conference. The Russian ambassador then went on to offer examples of multilateral issues. He said that, of course, Jerusalem is a multilateral issue. In addition, the establishment of borders for Israel is also a multilateral issue—especially since they will eventually be guaranteed by the international community.

Returning to the current situation in Israel, he repeated his prior point that the insurrection must be quelled immediately, and the first step should be to throw out television *à la* South Africa. To be sure, there will be international criticism of the step, but it will dissipate in short order. As he put it, ". . . there are no awards for losing with moderation."

He feels that international guarantees are not worth a damn. They can only be used to stop Israel from appropriately defending itself from "terrorist" activities; they are no help against "guerrilla' infiltration.

In terms of an ultimate solution to the issue, Kissinger feels that Israel should negotiate with [the United States of] America and work out a unified position, if at all possible, and then unilaterally announce that it was prepared to transfer control of Gaza to Jordan—not Egypt; he does not want Egyptian troops on Israel's borders. Moreover, he feels that Egypt would allow the PLO to take over the Gaza [Strip].

As noted above, he does not believe that Israel should retain *all* the territory that it took from the 1967 war. Consequently, at the same time Israel is making its unilateral announcement on Gaza, Israel should announce the specific territories within "Judea or Samaria" that it is willing to relinguish, provided that there be no military forces situated there and that there be no PLO controlled government in that area.

The announcement would then conclude with an offer to have an international conference convened for [the] purpose of implementing the proposal.

(Signed)
Julius Berman

Note: This document was published in *Without Prejudice*, an EAFORD International Review of Racial Discrimination publication, Volume II, No. 1 of 1988, pages 147–149.

Appendix I

The Arab Fez Peace Plan (1982)

The final draft of the Fez Peace Plan approved by the Arab states provided for:
1. Israeli evacuation of the West Bank, including East Jerusalem, the Gaza Strip, and the Golan Heights of Syria;
2. Dismantling of all Jewish settlements established in the occupied territories since 1967;
3. Guarantee of access and worship for all religions to the Holy places;
4. Exercise of the inalienable rights and of self-determination by the Palestinian people under the leadership of the Palestine Liberation Organization;
5. Placing the West Bank and the Gaza Strip under UN trusteeship for a transitional period of time;
6. Establishment of an independent Palestine State with (East) Jerusalem as its capital;
7. The Security Council to guarantee the security and peace of all states in the area;
8. The Security Council to guarantee respect of these principles.

The Plan was rejected outright by the Israelis; the United States withheld its reaction; while the European powers approved certain parts of it. The Palestine National Council issued a statement of policy on February 22, 1983 declaring that the plan was "the minimum level for a political initiative by the Arab states" to which it will agree.

Appendix J

The Ronald Reagan Plan (1982)

President Reagan made his peace plan known on September 3, 1982, following the Israeli invasion of Lebanon. He is reported to have declared that "Israel's military successes alone could not bring about a just and lasting peace" and that "the question now is how to reconcile Israel's legitimate security concerns with the legitimate rights of the Palestinians." The answer, he added, could only come through negotiations "on the basis of the Camp David Agreement." If he really believed that, the question may be asked why he did not follow up when he took over the presidency from Jimmy Carter in 1980 instead of allowing the situation to deteriorate to the extent it did that first it led to the invasion of Lebanon in order to destroy the PLO and then to the present uprising five years later?

The Reagan Peace Plan was no plan at all, but merely proposals serving one side of the conflict. Summarized, they are as follows:

(1) He proposed full autonomy for the Palestinians in the West Bank and the Gaza Strip during a transitional period of five years that would begin to run after the election of a self-governing authority; but he made no reference to the majority of the Palestinians scattered throughout the world and what their fate would be;

(2) He suggested a freeze on Israeli settlements during the transitional period but did not call for their dismantlement or whether the freeze means no new settlement would be established thereafter;

(3) He stated that the United States would not support the establishment of an independent Palestine state in the West Bank and the Gaza Strip, ignoring the fact that both territories fall within the boundaries of the Arab state provided for under the United Nations Resolution of Partition of 1947, which was neither rescinded nor amended and consequently remains the legal instrument under which a Palestine state could come into existence;

(4) He does not require Israel, in return for peace, to withdraw from all the territory of the West Bank and the Gaza Strip as required by Security Council Resolution 242 but suggests that it retain "such parts as would be required to assure its security;"

(5) In regard to Jerusalem, Reagan calls for it to remain "undivided" and that its final status should be decided by negotiations.

The Israelis rejected the Reagan plan outright and announced their determination to continue to establish more settlements, which they did; the Arab states and the Palestinians saw in it full support for the Israeli position and nothing in it to suggest an equitable settlement; while the rest of the world realized its futility and gave it no support.

The American-Israel Council for Israeli-Palestinian Peace, which has recently come into existence, asked the question in its 1984 newsletter: "What kind of a friend of Israel is the United States?" It then proceeded to say:

"In our definition of friend, a friend is someone who helps you to end a bitter quarrel, to make peace. By our standards, the American response to both the Fahd and Fez Plans has not been genuinely helpful to Israel, nor has it promoted American interests in the Middle East. Instead of warmly welcoming the Fez Plan as a clear indication that the Arab world, including the PLO, is now ready to make peace with Israel, provided only that Israel will make some accommodation to Palestinian rights, the United States continued, and continues, to insist on Palestinian recognition of Israel without any reciprocity at all. Our country also continues to announce that as far as the head of the free world is concerned, for some reason the Palestinian are less equal than others and are not entitled to their freedoms."

The Council concluded by stating: "We in AICIPP believe that if more Americans fully understood their government's policy on Arab-Israeli peace, they would share our conviction that our own country at the present time remains an obstacle to comprehensive Middle East peace."

Appendix K

The Jerome M. Segal Proposals (1988)

Professor Jerome M. Segal, research scholar at the Center for Philosophy and Public Policy at the University of Maryland and a founder of the Jewish Committee for Israeli-Palestinian Peace, has a formula for the coming into being of a Palestinian state that has merit; and it is not clear why the Palestinians have not thought of it before.

Professor Segal begins by pointing out that "The uprising in the occupied territories is the most important event in the last 20 years of Palestinian history. The most fundamental meaning of the uprising consists in the transformation it is bringing to virtually the entire Palestinian population of the territories. For the first time they have fully entered history as agents of their own destiny."

He believes that "it is time to rethink some of the basic premises;" and he points out that "up till now, Palestinians have placed tremendous import on an international conference, negotiations, and PLO representation at such negotiations. Not much is heard about what happens if such negotiations begin and then deadlock. Perhaps it is believed that the price of failure would be so great that once started, it would necessitate a comprehensive solution. Yet this is wishful thinking. It is perfectly likely that negotiations will simply be unable to generate a solution acceptable to Israelis and Palestinians, and it is also likely that the super-powers will lack the will to impose a solution."

This comment by Professor Segal brings to mind the history of the Palestine conflict since 1948 and the failures of the United Nations in implementing its own resolutions. Professor Segal is not far from the truth that any negotiations—international or otherwise—which are not entirely in Israel's favor, are not likely to succeed.

The writer then draws attention how the state of Israel came into being. He said: "If we probe a bit deeper, we see that the present strategy for attaining an independent Palestinian state embodies a model that needs to be challenged. That model is that statehood emerges from negotiations and agreements. In short, it assumes that no Palestinian state can come into existence unless there is prior Israeli approval. Yet," he said, "consider how Israel itself came into existence. Following the UN partition resolution of 1947, the Israelis simply declared the existence of the state of Israel. Indeed, they made that declaration contrary to the urging of the U.S. State Department. They did not get Arab or Palestinian advance approval. They did not negotiate with the Palestinians. They proceeded unilaterally, and gradually secured international recognition, admission to the United Nations, and effective control of territory."

Professor Segal then points out that "There are important analogies in history for the Palestinians. Today's military and political realities preclude achieving statehood through force of arms. But, on the other hand, today's political, moral, economic, and psychological realities offer new alternatives within the same basic concept: The Palestinians do not need advance Israeli approval to bring a state into existence, and there is no reason why they should cede such power to Israel. Indeed, to do so is inconsistent with the underlying spirit of the uprising. An alternative strategy is possible—one that overnight will transform the political agenda, and place the two-state solution (Palestine and Israel) in center stage as the only peace option."

Professor Segal concludes by making certain elaborate proposals how the PLO should proceed, which include the following:

* The PLO should issue a declaration of independence and statehood, announcing the existence of the state of Palestine in the West Bank and the Gaza Strip. Simultaneously, the declaration should be announced throughout the occupied territories;
* The PLO should proclaim, as its final act, its transformation into the provisional government of the state of Palestine. The Palestine National Council (PNC) should be transformed into the legislative body of the provisional government. All governmen: positions should be declared provisional pending the possibility of free elections by the Palestinian people;
* A worldwide diplomatic offensive should be declared seeking recognition of the new state and its admission to the United Nations;
* Israeli withdrawal from the West Bank and the Gaza Strip should become the central demand, internationally and within the territories, and all the energies currently expanded on peripheral matters should be concentrated on the single demand. *Whereas, previously Israel was occupying a territory, it is now occupying a foreign country that has declared itself to be at peace;*
* The povisional government and the new constitution should proclaim to the world that Palestine shall be a democracy with an independent judiciary and a bill of rights to protect

individual liberties. The United Nations should be asked to supervise the first national elections.

In his final paragraph Professor Segal states that "The great merit of his approach is that the two-state solution, which continues to be viewed as a 'non-starter' in Israel and the United States, will simply start itself. In doing so, it will follow the spirit of the uprising: That the Palestinian people on the ground will decide their own destiny." He ends up by stating his conviction that "the struggle for an independent Palestinian state is also the struggle for a humane and safe Israel, and that there can be no Judaism without a commitment to justice." (Source: The *Arab News* (Saudi Arabia), May 22, 1988)

Appendix L

Proposals for Middle East Peace Made by the General Assembly of Presbyterian Church of the United States (1988)

The Presbyterian Church of the United States has shown deep concern over the existing situation in the Middle East, and has met on a number of occasions to find ways and means to resolve the dispute between Palestinians and Israelis. On June 2, 1988, representatives of the church met with Zuhdi Terzi, representative of the PLO at the United Nations; and in July 1988, met with Uri Gordon, Adviser to the Israeli Foreign Minister at the Israeli Consulate in New York.

Following these meetings, the General Assembly of the Church adopted at its 200th meeting the following resolutions: 31.117

1. *Calls upon the Palestinian leadership* to renew its commitment to the resolutions of conflict with Israel through an international peace conference under United Nations sponsorship in conformity with existing UN General Assembly and Security Council resolutions.

2. *Calls upon the Palestinian people and leadership* to exert sustained efforts to control acts of violence in order to facilitate the peace process.

31.118–129—*Calls upon Israel to:*

1. Cease the systematic violations of the human rights of Palestinians in the occupied territories. Specifically, we call for an end to the policies and (or) practices of administrative detention, collective punishment, the torture of prisoners and suspects, and the deportation of dissidents.

2. End the policies and (or) practices of beatings and of food embargoes in the attempt to subjugate and break the will of the Palestinian population, thus ending resistance to Israeli control of the occupied territories.

3. End the settlements policy and the acquisition of land within the occupied territories, since these simply provoke the Arab peoples and reduce the opportunity for a peaceful resolution of the conflicting claims of Israelis and Palestinians.

4. End its occupation of the West Bank and Gaza as part of a larger peace process.

5. Participate in an international peace conference under the auspices of the United Nations in order to meet with the Palestinian people through representatives of their own choosing and to resolve the outstanding differences that confront the two peoples.

31.124–128—*Calls upon the Government of the United States* to:

1. Discourage retaliation as a counter-terror strategy in the Middle East and to address the injustices that are among the root causes of terrorism.

2. Insist that weapons supplied by the United States for Israel's defence not be used against civilian populations in the occupied territories or in aggressive attacks or disproportionate retaliation upon other countries, and that further military and security assistance to Israel be contingent upon the honoring of these principles and upon the cessation of repression against Palestinians in the occupied territories.

3. Condemn the excessive use of force and human rights abuses by the government of Israel in the occupied territories.

4. Stop all aid to Israel that subsidizes new Israeli settlements in the occupied territories and to use U.S. aid resources to encourage an optional compromise for all inhabitants of the region.

5. Resist efforts to move the United States Embassy from Tel Aviv to Jerusalem or its environs, except as part of a total peace settlement. The U.S. government should support efforts to establish Jerusalem as an open city with access for all religious groups.

6. Give public support to the concept of an international peace conference under the auspices of the United Nations as the most appropriate arena for seeking a settlement of the claims and conflicts of Israel and the Palestinian people, and to call upon Israel to take part in such a conference.

7. Permit the continued operation of the PLO Mission to the United Nations in New York in conformity with international law and treaty obligations.

8. *Calls upon all parties* to recognize that retaliatory vengeance will not lead to justice, peace, or security.

31.129–133—*Calls upon the members and agencies of the Church* to:

1. Pray for an end to the suffering and oppression of the people in the occupied territories and to communicate concern for these people to Palestinians in the United States and in the Middle East.

2. Advocate with the U.S. government to achieve the policies indicated above. Toward that end, church members are urged to join Presbyterian Advocates for the Middle East.
3. Make contributions for emergency relief and development assistance for use among Palestinians of the occupied territories.
4. Work with the Israeli Jews and Jews in the United States and elsewhere in the world who, both in recognition of the requirements of justice and self-determination for Palestinian for Palestinians and in anguish regarding the moral integrity of Israel, are seeking to end Israel's repressive and expansionist policies and practices affecting the Palestinians.
31.134—*Calls upon the Stated Clerk* to:

Communicate the above actions and concerns to appropriate officials of the government of Israel, to the Palestinian people through the PLO Mission at the United Nations, as well as to the United Nations and the congregations of the Church.

In submitting its recommendations to the 200th (1988) session of the General Assembly of the Presbyterian Church in the United States, the Committee on Social Witness Policy drew attention to the following most pertinent point on which the hard-minded Zionists and Israelis would do well to ponder:

"31.111—Many Israelis have come to realize that demographic realities pose a serious dilemma. Because of their more rapid population growth rate, within a generation there will be more Arabs than Jews in the combined area of Israel and the occupied territories. If Israel annexes the West Bank and Gaza and makes all residents citizens, Israel will cease to be a Jewish state. If Israel chooses instead simply to annex the territories without granting citizenship, it will have effectively institutionalized the apartheid system in the Middle East. That is an unhappy choice for a country that perceives itself as both Jewish and democratic. The inability or unwillingness to make such a hard choice is a principal factor in continuing the occupation status. The recent uprising of Palestinians and the heavy-handed crackdown by the Israeli military portends what lies ahead unless a political settlement is reached."

Appendix M

A Declaration of Peace Proposals for the Middle East by a Group of
Distinguished Personalities from the United States and Abroad (1988)

"We the undersigned urge immediate international attention at the highest level to foster
negotiations between the state of Israel and the Palestinians based on mutual recognition of
national legitimacy and the exchange of territory for peace. The bloody violence and the loss
of life in the disputed territory underscores the urgency of constructive negotiations. Now is
the time for a Declaration of Peace for the Middle East.

"We support the continued independence and security of the state of Israel. We equally
affirm the right of self-determination and security for the Palestinian people. We believe that
mutual recognition and good-faith negotiations between Israelis and Palestinians can achieve
a just settlement and that such a settlement should be guaranteed by appropriate international peace-keeping arrangements. We further believe that such a political settlement can
result in a reduction of the military burden for the people of the Middle East and open the
way for constructive economic, social, and cultural development in the region.

"Negotiations must involve not only the Palestinians but also the Arab states in conflict
with Israel over substantive issues.

"An international peace conference including active roles by the United States and the
Soviet Union can facilitate bringing the various parties together, establishing assurances of
fairness, and opening the way for substantive bilateral negotiations."

George Ball,
Former U.S. Under-Secretary
of State.

Barry Goldwater,
Republican Presidential Nominee

George McGovern,
Democratic Presidential Nominee

Philip Klutznick,
Former U.S. Secretary of Commerce
and also former President of the
World Jewish Congress and International
President of B'nai B'rith

Garret Fitzgerald,
Former Head of Government of
Ireland

Anker Jorgensen,
Former Head of Government of
Denmark

Bruno Kreisky,
Former Head of Government of
Austria.

(Source: Palestine Perspectives, July/August 1988)

Appendix N

Declaration of Independence

Palestine, the land of the three monotheistic, is where the Palestinian Arab people was born, on which it grew, developed and excelled. The Palestinian people was never separated from or diminished in its integral bond with Palestine. Thus the Palestinian Arab people ensured for itself an everlasting union between itself, its land and its history.

Resolute throughout that history, the Palestinian Arab people forged its national identity, rising even to unimagined levels in its defence, as invasion, the design of others, and the appeal special to Palestine's ancient and luminous place on that eminence where powers and civilizations are joined . . . All this intervened thereby to deprive the people of its political independence. Yet the undying connection between Palestine and its people secured for the land its character, and for the people its national genius.

Nourished by an unfolding series of civilizations and cultures, inspired by a heritage rich in variety and kind, the Palestinian Arab people added to its stature by consolidating a union between itself and its patrimonial Land. The call went out from the Temple, Church and Mosque that to praise the Creator, to celebrate compassion and peace was indeed the message of Palestine. And in generation after generation, the Palestine Arab people gave of itself unsparingly in the valiant battle for liberation and homeland. For what has been the unbroken chain of our people's rebellions but the heroic embodiment of our will for national independence? And so the people was sustained in the struggle to stay and to prevail.

When in the course of modern times a new order of values was declared with norms and values fair for all, it was the Palestinian Arab people that had been excluded from the destiny of all other peoples by a hostile array of local and foreign powers. Yet again had unaided justice been revealed as insufficient to drive the world's history along its preferred course.

And it was the Palestinian people, already wounded in its body, that was submitted to yet another type of occupation over which floated the falsehood that "Palestine was a land without people." This notion was foisted upon some in the world, whereas in Article 22 of the Covenant of the League of Nations (1919) and in the Treaty of Lausanne (1923), the community of nations had recognized that all the Arabs territories, including Palestine, of the formerly Ottoman provinces, were to have granted to them their freedom as provisionally independent nations.

Despite the historical injustice inflicted on the Palestinian Arab people resulting in their dispersion and depriving them of their right to self-determination, following upon UN General Assembly Resolution 181 (1947), which partitioned Palestine into two states, one Arab, one Jewish, yet it is this Resolution that still provides those conditions of international legitimacy that ensure the right of the Palestinian Arab people to sovereignty.

By stages, the occupation of Palestine and parts of other Arab territories by Israeli forces, the willed dispossession and expulsion from their ancestral homes of the majority of Palestine's civilian inhabitants, was achieved by organized terror; those Palestinians who remained, as a vestige subjugated in its homeland, were persecuted and forced to endure the destruction of their national life.

In Palestine and on its perimeters, in exile distant and near, the Palestine Arab people never faltered and never abandoned its conviction in its rights of Return and Independence. Occupation, massacres and dispersion achieved no gain in the unabated Palestinian consciousness of self and political identity, as Palestinians went forward with their destiny, undeterred and unbowed. And from out of the long years of trial in evermounting struggle, the Palestinian political identity emerged further consolidated and confirmed. And the collective Palestinian national will forge for itself a political embodiment, the Palestine Liberation Organization, its sole, legitimate representative recognized by the world community as a whole, as well as by related regional and international institutions. Standing on the very rock of conviction in the Palestinian people's inalienable rights, and on the ground of Arab national consensus and of international legitimacy, the PLO led the campaigns of its great people, molded into unity and powerful resolve, one and indivisible in its triumphs, even as it suffered massacres and confinement within and without its home. And so Palestinian resistance was clarified and raised into the forefront of Arab and world awareness, as the struggle of the Palestinian Arab people achieved unique prominence among the world's liberation movements in the modern era.

The massive national uprising, the *intifada*, now intensifying in cumulative scope and power on occupied Palestinian territories, as well as the unflinching resistance of the refugee camps outside the homeland, have elevated awareness of the Palestinian truth and right into still higher realms of comprehension and actuality. Now at last the curtain has been dropped around a whole epoch of prevarication and negation. The *intifada* has set siege to the mind of official Israel, which has for too long relied exclusively upon myth and terror to deny Palestinian existence altogether. Because of the *intifada* and its revolutionary irreversible impulse, the history of Palestine has therefore arrived at a decisive juncture.

Whereas the Palestinian people reaffirm most definitively its inalienable rights in the land of its patrimony:

> Now by virtue of natural, historical and legal rights, and the sacrifices of successive generations who gave of themselves in defense of the freedom and independence of their homeland
>
> In pursuance of Resolutions adopted by Arab Summit Conferences and relying on the authority bestowed by international legitimacy as embodied in the Resolutions of the United Nations Organization since 1947.
>
> And in exercise by the Palestinian Arab people of its rights to self-determination, political independence and sovereignty over its territory.
>
> The Palestine National Council, in the name of God, and in the name of the Palestinian Arab people, hereby proclaims the establishment of the State of Palestine on our Palestinian territory with its capital Jerusalem (Al-Quds Ash-Sharif).

The State of Palestine is the state of Palestinians wherever they may be. The state is for them to enjoy in it their collective national and cultural identity, theirs to pursue in it a complete equality of rights. In it will be safeguarded their political and religious convictions and their human dignity by means of parliamentary democratic system of governance, itself based on freedom of expression and the freedom to form parties. The rights of minorities will duly be respected by the majority, as minorities must abide by decisions of the majority. Governance will be based on principles of social justice, equality and non-discrimination in public rights of men of or women, on grounds of race, religion, color or sex, under the aegis of a constitution which ensures the rule of law and an independent judiciary. Thus shall these principles allow no departure from Palestine's age-old spiritual and civilizational heritage of tolerance and religious coexistence.

The State of Palestine is an Arab state, an integral and indivisible part of the Arab nation, at one with that nation in heritage and civilization, with it also in its aspiration for liberation, progress, democracy and unity. The State of Palestine affirms its obligation to abide by the Charter of the League of Arab States, whereby the coordination of the Arab states with each other shall be strengthened. It calls upon Arab compatriots to consolidate and enhance the emergence in reality of our state, to mobilize potential, and to intensify efforts whose goal is to end Israeli occupation.

The State of Palestine proclaims its commitment to the principles and purposes of the United Nations, and to the Universal Declaration of Human Rights. It proclaims this commitment as well to the principles and policies of the Non-Aligned Movement. It further announces itself to be a peace-loving State, in adherence to the principles of peaceful co-existence. It will join with all states and peoples in order to assure a permanent peace based upon justice and the respect of rights so that humanity's potential for well-being may be assured, an earnest competition for excellence may be maintained, and in which confidence in the future will eliminate fear for those who are just and for whom justice is the only recourse.

In the contest of its struggle for peace in the land of Love and Peace, the State of Palestine calls upon the United Nations to bear special responsibility for the Palestinian Arab people and its homeland. It calls upon all peace and freedom-loving peoples and states to assist it in the attainment of its objectives, to provide it with security, to alleviate the tragedy of its people, and to help it terminate Israel's occupation of the Palestinian territories.

The State of Palestine herewith declares delares that it believes in the settlement of regional and international disputes by peaceful means, in accordance with the UN Charter and resolutions. Without prejudice to its natural right to defend its territorial integrity and independence, it therefore rejects the threat or use of force, violence and terrorism against its territorial integrity or political independence, as it also rejects their use against the territorial integrity of other states.

Therefore, on this day unlike all others, November 15, 1988, as we stand at the threshold of a new dawn, in all honor and modesty we humbly bow to the sacred spirits of our fallen ones, Palestinian and Arab, by the purity of whose sacrifice for the homeland our sky has been illuminated and our Land given life. Our hearts· are lifted up and irradiated by the light emanating from the much blessed *intifada*, from those who have endured and have fought the fight of the camps, of dispersion, of exile, from those who have borne the standard for freedom, our children, our aged, our youth, our prisoners, detainees and wounded, all those whose ties to our sacred soil are confirmed in camp, village and town. We render special tribute to that brave Palestinian Woman, guardian of sustenance and Life, keeper of our people's perennial flame. To the souls of our sainted martyrs, to the whole of our Palestinian Arab people, to all free and honorable peoples everywhere, we pledge that our struggle shall be continued until the occupation ends, and the foundation of our sovereignty and independence shall be fortified accordingly.

Therefore, we call upon our great people to rally to the banner of Palestine, to cherish and defend it, so that it may forever be the symbol of our freedom and dignity in that homeland, which is a homeland for the free, now and always.

In the name of God, the Compassionate, the Merciful:
"Say: 'O God, Master of the Kingdom,
    Thou givest the Kingdom to whom Thow wilt,
    and seizest the Kingdom from whom Thow wilt,
    Thou exaltest whom Thou wilt, and Thou
    abasest whom Thou wilt; in Thy hand
    is the good; Thou art powerful over
    everything."

    Sadaqa Allahu Al-Azim

BIBLIOGRAPHY
(List of Principal Documents Used)

A. *British Mandatory Government Documents*
1. *Cmd.5957* – The Hussein-McMahon Correspondence, July 1915 to March 1916.
2. *Cmd.1785* – The Mandate for Palestine
3. *Cmd.1540* – Report of the Haycraft Commission of Enquiry on the Disturbance in Palestine in May 1921
4. *Cmd.1760* – The British Statement of Policy (known as the Churchill Memorandum), June 3, 1922
5. *Cmd.58–9096* – Report of the Commission appointed to determine the rights and claims of Moslems and Jews in connection with the Western or Wailing Wall of Jerusalem, December 1930
6. *Cmd.3530* – Report of the Shaw Commission on the Palestine disturbance of August 1929 dated March 30, 1930
7. *Cmd.3686* – The Hope-Simpson Report, October 20, 1930
8. *Cmd.3692* – Statement of Policy (known as the Passfield White Paper), October 1930
9. Letter from British Prime Minister J. Ramsey MacDonald to Chaim Weizmann dated February 13, 1931 and published in the London *Times*, February 14, 1931
10. *Cmd.5479* – Report of the Royal (Peel) Commission, June 22, 1937
11. *Cmd.5513* – Statement of Policy, July 7, 1937
12. *Cmd.5854* – Report of the Partition (Woodhead) Commission, October 1938
13. *Cmd.5893* – Statement of Policy, November 9, 1938
14. *Cmd.5974* – Report of the Maugham Commission on the Hussein-McMahon Correspondence, March 16, 1939
15. *Cmd.6019* – Statement of Policy (known as the MacDonald White Paper), May 17, 1939
16. *Cmd.6808* – Report of the Anglo-American Committee of Inquiry regarding the Problems of European Jewry and Palestine, April 20, 1946
17. *Cmd.6873* – Palestine Statement Relating to (Jewish) Acts of Violence, July 24, 1946
18. The Palestine Government, the *Village Statistics 1945*

B – *Books*
1. J.M.N. Jeffries, *Palestine: The Reality*, (London: Longmans, Green & Co., 1939)
2. Palestine Government, *A Survey of Palestine 1945–1946* Presented to the Anglo-American Committee of Inquiry on the Administration of Palestine.
3. George Antonius, *The Arab Awakening*, (London: Hamish Hamilton, 1955)
4. Charles Luke & Edward Keith-Roach *Handbook of Palestine* (London: Macmillan, 1930)
5. James Malcolm, *Origins of the Balfour Declaration* (Zionist Archives)

6. Theodor Herzl, *The Jewish State*, (New York: American Zionist Emergency Council, 1946)
7. E.L. Woodworth and R. Butler *Documents on British Foreign Policy 1919–1939*
8. Harry N. Howard, *The King-Crane Commission*, (Beirut: Khayyat Press, 1963)
9. Arhtur Koestler, *Promise and Fulfillment* (London: Macmillan & Co., 1949)
10. John Bagot Glubb, *A Soldier with the Arabs*, (London: Hodder & Stoughton, 1957)
11. Jon Kimche, *The Seven Fallen Pillars*, (New York: F.A. Praeger, 1953)
12. Dov Joseph, *The Faithful City: The Siege of Jerusalem 1948*, (New York: Simon & Schuster, 1960)
13. Arnold Toynbee, *A Study of History*, (London: Oxford University Press, 1953–1954)
14. Edgar O'Ballance, *The Arab-Israeli War 1948*, (New York: F.A. Praeger, 1957)
15. Chaim Weizmann, *Trial and Error*, (London: East and West Library 1950)
16. James MacDonald, *My Mission to Israel*, (New York: Simon & Schuster, 1951)
17. L. Oppenheim, *International Law* (London: Longmans, Green & Co., 1963)
18. E.H. Hutchison, *Violent Truce*, (New York: Devin-Adair, 1956)
19. George E. Kirk, *A Short History of the Middle East*, (London: Methusen Press, 1948)
20. Carl Von Horn, *Soldiering for Peace*, (London: Cassel & Co., 1966)
21. E.L.M. Burns, *Between Arabs and Israelis*, (New York: Ivan Obolensky, 1963)
22. A.W. Kayyali, *Palestine: A Modern History*, (London: Croom Helm Ltd. 1979)
23. Sami Hadawi, *Palestine: Loss of a Heritage*, (San Antonio: The Naylor Press:; 1963)
24. Moshe Menuhim, *The Decadence of Judaism in Our Time*, (New York: Exposition Press, 1965)
25. William Zukerman, *The Voice of Dissent*, (New York: Bookman Associates, Inc., 1964)
26. Alfred Lilienthal, *What Price Israel?* (Chicago: Henry Regnery, 1953)
27. Robert John and Sami Hadawi *The Palestine Diary 1914–1945 and 1945–1948*, (New York: The New World Press, 1970)
28. Sami Hadawi, *Palestinian Rights and Losses in 1948*, (London: Saqi Books Publishers, 1988)
29. *The Israeli Settlements in the Occupied Territories: A Collection of Paper Studies Presented to the International Symposium on Israeli Settlements in the Occupied Arab Territories*, Published and distributed by Dar Al-Afaq Al-Jadidah on behalf of the Secretariat of the League of Arab states, 1988.
30. Noem Chomsky, *The Fateful Triangle*, (Boston: South End Press, 1983)
31. Paul Findley, *They Dare to Speak Out*, (Lawrence Hill & Co., 1985)
32. Tony Clifton and Catherine Leroy, *God Cried*, (London: Quartet Books, 1983)

C – Miscellaneous

The following sources were also consulted where relevant material for the study was found to be available:
1. The local and foreign press
2. The Jewish Newsletter published in New York by William Zukerman until his death
3. *Issues* magazine put out by the American Council for Judaism in New York
4. Material put out by Zionist and Jewish organizations
5. Israeli publications
6. UN documents relating to Palestine including resolutions adopted
7. Reports on the activities of the UN Palestine Conciliation Commission relating to the classification and valuation of the properties of the Palestine refugees.

References

Chapter I—Introduction

1. UN Documents S/888.
2. Ben Gurion, David, *Rebirth and Destiny of Israel*, (New York: The Philosophical Library, 1954), p. 419.
3. *Israeli Yearbook 1952*, pp. 63, 65.
4. Statement by Menachem Begin in the Israeli Parliament on October 12, 1955.
5. Quoted from the Hope-Simpson Report–Cmd. 3686, pp. 53–54.
6. *New York Times*, December 6, 1953.
7. Translated from the Israeli Hebrew-language Magazine *Ner*, January-February 1961 issue and published in the American Council for Judaism Magazine *Issues*, Fall 1961, p. 19.

Chapter II—Historical Background

1. Luke, Charles & Keith-Roach, Edward, *Handbook of Palestine and Transjordan*, (London: Macmillan, 1930), pp. 233–234.
2. For further deatails, see Population and Land in Chapter V–Palestine under Mandate.
3. *Jewish Life*, A bi-monthly magazine of the Union of Orthodox Jewish Congregations of America, October 1960, pp. 21–31.
4. Jeffries, Joseph M.N., *Palestine: The Reality*, (New York: Longmans, Green & Co., 1939), pp. 237–238.
5. Howard, Harry N., *The King-Crane Commission*, (Beirut: Khayats, 1963), p. 5.
6. Cmd. 5957–*Hussein-McMahon Correspondence 1915–1916*, Letter No. 1 dated July 14, 1915.
7. See *Cmd. 5974*, Annex C, pp. 30–38.
8. Woodward, E.L., Butler, R. *Documents on British Foreign Policy, 1919–1939*, 1st Ser., Vol. 4, pp. 241–251.
9. Antonius, George, *The Arab Awakening*, (London: Hamish Hamilton, 1938), p. 248.
10. Lloyd George, David, *Memoirs of the Peace Conference*, (New Haven: Yale University Press, 1939), pp. 664–665.
11. *Ibid.*
12. Herzl, Theodor, *The Jewish State*, (New York: American Zionist Emergency Council, 1946), p. 92.
13. Malcolm, James, *Origins of the Balfour Declaration*, (Zionist Archives), pp. 2–3.
14. Wise, Stephen and De Haas, Jacob, *The Great Betrayal*, (New York: Brentano's, 1930), p. 288.
15. Lloyd George, *op. cit.*, Vol. II, p. 738.
16. *Cmd. 5479*–Palestine Royal (Peel) Commission Report, p. 17.
17. *A Survey of Palestine 1945–1946*, Vol. I, p. 1.

18. Antonius, *op. cit.*, p. 268.
19. Jeffries, *op. cit.*, pp. 216–217.
20. Antonius, *op. cit.*, pp. 433–434.
21. Jeffries, *op. cit.*, pp. 237–238.
22. *Ibid.*, pp. 234–235.
23. Hoover, Herbert, *Ordeal of Woodrow Wilson*, (New York: McGraw-Hill Book Co., 1958), pp. 23, 25.
24. Miller, David Hunter, *My Diary at the Conference of Paris*, New York: 1924), Vol. III.
25. U.S. Dept. of State, *Papers Relating to the Foreign Relations of the U.S.*–The Paris Peace Conference 1919, pp. 785–786.
    (Quoted in the *King-Crane Commission*, by Harry Howard, p. 20).
26. Jeffries, *op. cit*, pp. 237–238.
27. Howard, *op. cit.*, pp. 349–352.

Chapter III—Palestine and the Jews

1. *Israel According to Holy Scriptures*, (Cedar Rapids: Ingram Press), pp. 11–15.
2. *Ibid.*, pp. 6–9.
3. *Ibid.*, pp. 29–31.
4. *Ibid.*, p. 28.
5. *Ibid.*, pp. 35, 45.
6. *Ibid.*, pp. 19–25.
7. For a full and revealing study of the Khazar problem in relation to present-day Jews see *The 13th Tribe*, by Arthur Koestler (Random House, 1976–Paperback: Popular Library, #0–445–04242–7 (1978).
8. From the secret documents released by the British government: Paper No. CAB. 24/24–*The Anti-Semitism of the Present Government*, by Sir Edwin S. Montagu, Secretary of State for India, dated August 23, 1917.
9. Shapiro, Harry L., *The Jewish People: A Biographical History*, (UNESCO, 1960), pp. 74–75.
10. American Council for Judaism, *Issues* magazine, (New York: Winter 1965–1966), pp. 21–23.
11. Litvin, Baruch, *The Jewish Identity*, Edited by Sidney Hoenig, Feldheim. (Quoted in the *Jerusalem Post*, September 14, 1966.)
12. From a review of the book "The Jewish Identity" in an article published in *Jerusalem Post*, September 14, 1966.

ChapterIV—The Zionist Movement

1. Stein, Leonard, *Zionism*, (London: Kegan Paul, Trench, Trubner and Co., Ltd., 1932), p. 62.
2. Hocking, William E., Alford Professor Emeritus of Philosophy, Harvard University, Letter published in *The New York Times*, March 23, 1944.
3. American Council for Judaism, *Issues* magazine, Fall 1961, pp. 91–92.
4. For methods and extent of Zionist pressure groups on U.S. government, see statement by Senator William Fulbright before the Senate (U.S. Congressional Record, 86th Congress, 2nd Session, Vol. 106, No. 78, April 29, 1960.)
5. For investigation of the Foreign Relations Committee into the Activities of the Zionist Organization of America, see Hearings before Committee on Foreign Relations (U.S. Senate, 88th Congress, 1st Session, Part 9, May 23, 1963).
6. The Jewish Chronicle (London), April 8, 1960.
7. Israeli Yearbook 1959–1960, January 1960, p. 94.
8. *Issues* magazine, Spring 1966, p. 54.
9. Ben Gurion, op. cit., p. 489.
10. *Jewish Newsletter*, January 9, 1961.
11. *New York Times*, May 18, 1961.
12. *Israeli Yearbook 1953–1954*, p. 35.
13. *Issues* magazine, Spring 1962, p. 7.
14. *The Jewish Chronicle* (London), March 24, 1961.
15. Mallison Jr., W.T. *The Zionist-Israel Juridical Claims to Constitute the Jewish People Nationality and to Confer Membership on It: Appraisal in Public International Law*, (Washington DC: 1964) Vol 32, No. 5, Appendix B, p. 1075.
16. Menuhin, Moshe, *The Decadence of Judaism in Our Time*, (New York: Exposition Press, 1965), p. 324.
17. *Ibid.*, p. 317.
18. *Ibid.*, p. 308.
19. *Ibid.*, p. 359.
20. For a full study of Zionism how it developed from a spiritual to a political movement, and

the extent of Arab opposition thereto as voiced in the press and Turkish Parliament before World War I, as well as what transpired between 1920 and 1939, see *Palestine: A Modern History*, by A.W. Kayali (London: Croom Helm, Ltd., 210 St. John's Road, London, S.W.11).
21. Quoted by Ian Gilmour in *The Spectator Magazine*, June 24, 1960.
22. *The New York Times*, May 7, 1961.
23. From a letter by Richard J. Marquardt, published in *Holiday* magazine of March 1963.
24. Jewish Newsletter, January 9, 1961.
25. Menuhin, op. cit., pp. 400–401.
26. *Jerusalem Post*, January 14, 1966, p. 8.
27. Lilienthal, Alfred, *What Price Israel?* (Chicago: Henry Regnery, 1953), p. 207.
28. Kimche, Jon and David, *Both Sides of the Hill*, (London: Secker & Warburg, 1960), pp. 20, 31.
29. *The Spectator* (London) magazine, July 22, 1960.
30. Ernst, Morris L., *So Far So Good*, (New York: Harper & Bros. 1952), pp. 176–177.
31. American Council for Judaism, *Council News*, May 1950, p. 2.
32. *The Spectator* magazine, July 22, 1960.
33. Cross, Richard, *Palestine Mission: A Personal Record*, (New York: Harper and Brothers, 1947), p. 47.
34. *Jewish Newletter*, May 18, 1959.
35. *The Spectator* magazine, June 24, 1960.

Chapter V—Palestine Under Mandate

1. League of Nations, *Responsibilities of the League arising out of Article 22 (Mandates)*, No. 20/48/161, Annex I, p. 5.
2. Cmd. 1785–Text in *A Survey of Palestine 1945–1946* pp. 5–6.
3. Jeffries, op. cit. p. 314.
4. Barbour, Neville, *Nisi Dominus*, (London: George Harrap & Co., 1946), p. 97.
5. Palestine Government: *A Survey of Palestine 1945–1946*, Vol. I, p. 141.
6. *Ibid.*, p. 143.
7. UNSCOP Report, Vol. I, Supplement 11, paras. 12–13 & footnote.
8. Estimated by author on the basis of the method used by the Palestine government in respect of the previous estimation.
9. *A Survey of Palestine 1945–1946*, p. 242.
10. Calculated from the *Village Statistics 1945*, published by the Palestine government. To convert to dunums, multiply by four.
11. Palestine government memorandum submitted to UNSCOP, dated July 12, 1947.
12. Cmd. 3686–The Hope-Simpson Report 1930, pp. 53–54 and 78–79.
13. *Ibid.*
14. The Palin Commission of 1920 (Report not published, but mentioned in *A Survey of Palestine 1945–1946*, p. 17.)
    The Haycraft Commission of 1921 (Cmd. 1540–See Survey of Palestine, p. 18).
    The Shaw Commission of 1930 (Cmd. 3530–*Ibid.*, pp. 24–25).
    The Royal Peel Commission of 1937 (Cmd. 5479–*Ibid.*, p. 38).
15. Ziff, William, *The Rape of Palestine*, (New York: Longmans, Green & Co., 1938), p. 171.
16. Cmd. 1700–The Churchill Memorandum dated June 3, 1922.
17. Cmd. 3692–The Passfield White Paper dated October 1930.
18. Cmd. 6019–Known as The MacDonald White Paper dated May 17, 1939.
19. A Survey of Palestine 1945–1946, p. 54.
20. *Ibid.*, p. 57.
21. Royal Institute of International Affairs, *Great Britain and Palestine 1915–1945* (New York and London: Oxford University Press, 1946), p. 128.
22. R.I.I.A., *The Middle East* (2nd Edition), p. 36.
23. *Jewish Newsletter* (New York), November 3, 1958.
24. ESCO Foundation for Palestine, Inc., *A Study of Jewish, Arab and British Policies*, (New Haven: Yale University Press, 1947), Vol. II p. 1085.
25. R.I.I.A., *Great Britain and Palestine 1915–1945*, pp. 139–140.
26. Cmd. 6873–Statement of Information Relating to Acts of Violence, July 24, 1946.
27. A Survey of Palestine 1945–1946, p. 33.
28. *Ibid.*, p. 58.
29. *Ibid.*, pp. 67–68.
30. *Ibid.*, p. 73.
31. Marlowe, S.H., *The Seat of Pilate*, (London: Cresset Press, 1959), p. 183.
32. Zaar, Isaac, *Rescue and Liberation: America's Part in the Birth of Israel*, (New York: Bloch Publishing Co., 1954), p. 115.
33. A Survey of Palestine 1945–1946, p. 73.

34. Palestine: *Supplementary Memorandum to UNSCOP*, p. 14.
35. Koestler, Arthur, *Promise and Fulfilment*, (London: Macmillan & Co. 1949), p. 88.
36. *Supplementary Memorandum to UNSCOP*, p. 24.
37. *New York Times*, August 1, 1947, i:8.
38. *Cmd. 6873*.
39. *Supplementary Memorandum to UNSCOP*, p. 58.
40. Begin, Menachem, *The Revolt*, (London: W.H. Allen, 1951), p. 185.
41. *Supplementary Memorandum to UNSCOP*, p. 57.
42. *Ibid.*, p. 56.
43. Zaar, *op. cit.*, pp. 241–242.
44. *Cmd. 7088*–Proposals for the Future of Palestine.
45. *Supplementary Memorandum to UNSCOP*, p. 27.

Chapter VI—Palestine Problem before the UN

1. UN Document A/364, Add. 1: Supplement No. 11, Annex 1, p. 1.
2. *Ibid.*, Annex II (pp. 1–2): Documents A/287, A/288, A/290, and A/291.
3. Official Records of First Special Session, Vol. II, p. 12.
4. *Ibid.*, p. 81.
5. *Ibid.*, p. 23.
6. *Ibid.*, pp. 59–60.
7. Resolution 104(S–1): Document A/310.
8. Resolution 105(S–1): *Ibid.*.
9. Records of First Special Session, Vol. III, pp. 183–184.
10. *Ibid.*, pp. 345ff.
11. *Ibid.*, Vol. I, pp. 122–177, See also Document A/310: Resolution 106(S–1) of May 15, 1947.
12. UN Document A/364. Add 1, Vol. II, Annex 5, p. 5.
13. *Ibid.*, Annex 18, p. 16.
14. *Ibid.*, Vol. I.
15. UN Document A/516: Report of *Ad Hoc* Committee, pp. 2–19.
16. UN Document A/AC/14/34 of November 19, 1947.
17. UN Document A/AC/14/32 of November 11, 1947.
18. Official Records of Second Session, Vol. II, p. 1632.
19. *Ibid.*: Summary Records of meetings of *Ad Hoc* of September 25 to November 25, 1947, pp. 150, 199–201.
20. *Ibid.*, Vol. II, Annex 33, p. 1633.
21. *Ibid.*, p. 1634.
22. Ibid.
23. *Ibid.*, p. 1637.
24. UN Document A/516.
25. UN Document A/364.
26. Official Records of Second Session, Vol. II, pp. 1313–1314.
27. Official Records of Second Session, Vol. II, p. 1312.
28. *Ibid.*, p. 1319
29. *Ibid.*, p. 1357.
30. *Ibid.*, p. 1365.
31. *Ibid.*, pp. 1367–1369.
32. *Ibid.*, p. 1314.
33. UN Resolution 181(II) of November 29, 1947.
34. 128th Meeting of General Assembly: Official Records, Vol II, p. 1426.
35. Lilienthal, *op. cit.*, pp. 72–73.
36. Bethmann, Erich W., *Decisive Years in Palestine* 1918–1948, (Washington DC: American Friends of the Middle East, 1959), p. 35.
37. Millis, Walter (Ed.), *The Forrestal Diaries*, (New York: The Viking Press, 1951), p. 344.
38. *Ibid.*, p. 345.
39. Lilienthal, *op. cit.*, p. 64.
40. *Ibid.*, p. 124.
41. Neuman, Emanuel, in *American Zionist*, February 5, 1953.
42. U.S. Congressional Record, December 18, 1947, p. 1176.
43. *Chicago Tribune*, February 9, 1948, Part 2, 8:1.
44. Welles, Sumner, *We Need Not Fail*, (Boston: Houghton Mifflin, 1948) p. 63.
45. Millis, *op. cit.*, p. 363.
46. Menuhin, op. cit., from the statement about the author.
47. *Ibid.*, p. 114.
48. *Ibid.*, p. 115.
49. UN Resolution of Partition No. 181(II) of November 29, 1947.

Chapter VII—Strife, War, Truce
1. UN Resolution 181(II) of November 29, 1947.
2. UN Official Records of General Assembly, Plenary Session, May 14, 1948.
3. Bethmann, *op. cit.*, p. 41.
4. Glubb, *op. cit.*, p. 302.
5. *Jewish Telegraphic Agency, Daily News Bulletin*, April 26, 1963.
6. Glubb, *op. cit.*, p. 81.
7. From an Article by Nathan Chofshi in *Jewish Newsletter*, February 9, 1959.
8. Glubb, *op. cit.*, p. 251.
9. Kimche, Jon, *The Seven Fallen Pillars*, (New York: F.A. Praeger, 1953), p. 228.
10. Joseph, Dov, *The Faithful City: The Seige of Jerusalem 1948* (New York: Simon and Schuster, 1960), p. 71.
11. Toynbee, Arnold, *A Study of History*, (London: Oxford University Press, 1953–54), Vol. VIII, p. 290.
12. *Jewish Newsletter*, October 3, 1960.
13. Glubb, *op. cit.*, p. 99.
14. O'Ballance, Edgar, *The Arab-Israeli War 1948*, (New York: F.A. Praeger, 1957), p. 209.
15. *Jewish Newsletter*, October 3, 1960.
16. The Yediot Aharonot articles were reproduced in the *journal of Palestine Studies* (published in Beirut), Vol. I, No. 4, Summer 1972, pp. 142–146.
17. *The Journal of Palestine Studies*, Vol. I, No. 4, Summer 1972, pp. 142–146.
18. R. Barkan in *Al-Hamishmar* Hebrew newspaper. '(Quoted from *Journal of Palestine Studies*, Vol. VIII, No. 4, Summer 1978, Issue 28, pp. 143–144.
19. *Ibid.*, p. 143.
20. Shahak, Professor Israel, *Begin and Co. As They Really Are*, An Anthology, Edited and Prepared by Professor Shahak, September 1977, 2 Bartenura Street, Jerusalem, Israel.
21. Begin, *op. cit.*, p. 162 and 348.
22. O'Ballance, *op. cit.*, p. 64.
23. Ben Gurion, *op. cit.*, p. 296.
24. *Ibid.*, pp. 291–292.
25. Weizmann, Chaim, *Trial and Error* (London: East and West Library, 1950), p. 556.
26. McDonald, James, *My Mission to Israel*, (New York: Simon and Schuster, 1951), p. 176.
27. UN Library Document UNX/956.9–A/658.
28. Glubb, *op. cit.*, p. 302.
29. UN Resolution No. 49 of 22 May 1948.
30. UN Resolution 50 of 29 May 1948.
31. Kimche, *op. cit.*, pp. 249–250.
32. Ben Gurion, *op. cit.*, p. 247.
33. Glubb, *op. cit.*, p. 81.
34. *Jewish Newsletter*, February 9, 1959.
35. *Ibid.*, May 19, 1958.
36. Glubb, *op. cit.*, p. 251.
37. From an article by Erskine Childers, entitled *The Other Exodus*, published in *The Spectator* (London) magazine, May 12, 1961.

Chapter VIII—The Armistice
1. UN Document S/773–Resolution 49 of May 22 1948.
2. UN Document S/801–Resolution 50 of May 29, 1948.
3. Resolution No. 53 of July 7, 1948.
4. Resolution 54 of July 15, 1948.
5. Resolution 59 of October 19, 1948.
6. Resolution 61 of November 4, 1948.
7. UN Resolution 62 of November 16, 1948.
8. UN Documents: S/1264/Rev. 1; S/1296/Rev. 1; S/1302/Rev. 1; and S/1353/Rev. 1 respectively.
9. UN Document A/1264/Rev. 1–Armistice Agreement with Egypt–p. 11.
10. Oppenheim, L., *International Law*, (London: Longmans, Green & Co., 1963), Lauterpacht Editions, Vol. II, pp. 546–547.
11. Security Council Resolution 44 of April 1, 1948.
12. Oppenheim, *op. cit.*, p. 244 (n.1).
13. UN Document S/1353/Rev. 1–Israeli-Syrian Armistice Agreement.
14. Following the Israeli invasion of Egypt in 1956, *The New York Times* of November 8, 1956, reported that David Ben Gurion declared: "The Armistice with Egypt is dead, as are the armistice lines, and no wizard or magician can resurrect these lines."
15. UN Document S/PV.635, pp. 27–28.

16. UN Document S/2049, Section IV, para. 3.
17. Cited by the Chief of Staff at 542nd meeting of Security Council on April 25, 1951, as being from summary record of Syria-Israel Armistice Conference of July 3, 1949, at which Acting Mediator Ralph Bunche was present, which culminated in signing of Israel-Syrian Armistice Agreement on July 20, 1949. Text was embodied in Council Resolution 93 of May 18, 1951.
18. UN Resolution 93 of May 18, 1951.
19. UN Document S/3343, para. 18.
20. UN Document S/3596, Annex VII, para. 1.
21. Horn, Carl Von, *Soldiering for Peace*, (London: Cassel & Co. Ltd., 1966), p. 75.
22. *Ibid.*, p. 123.
23. *Ibid.*, p. 85.
24. *Ibid.*, p. 263.
25. See UN Document A/1873, pp. 55, 57, 60.
26. UN Document S/1797.
27. UN Document S/PV.635, p. 36.
28. UN Document S/3596, Annex VIII.
29. UN Document S/3638, para. 10.
30. UN Document S/3659, Annex, Section II, paras. 1,9–10.
31. Hutchison, E.H. *Violent Truce*, (New York: Devin-Adair, 1956), pp. 20–29.
32. *Ibid.*, pp. 40–41.
33. *Ibid.*, pp. 87–88.
34. Burns, E.L.M., *Between Arabs and Israelis*, (New York: Ivan Obolensky, 1963), p. 158.
35. UN Resolution No. 127 (1958).
36. Articles II(2) and V(3) of Agreement with Egypt, and Articles III(2) and IV(2) of agreements with Lebanon, Jordan and Syria.
37. *Forward*, New York newspaper, December 27, 1952.
38. *The New York Times*, January 2, 1953.
39. Zukerman, William, *Voice of Dissent*, (New York: Bookman Associates, Inc., 1964), pp. 33–34.
40. UN Document S/902–Resolution No. 54.
41. UN Document S/3538–Resolution No. 111.
42. UN Document S/PV.1003 of April 5, 1962, pp. 16,21.
43. UN Document S/PV.999 of March 28, p. 42.
44. UN Document S/PV.1001 of April 4, 1962, p. 1.
45. UN Document S/PV.1320 of November 16, 1966.
46. *Ibid*.
47. UN Document S/PV.1321 of November 16, 1966.
48. *Ibid*.
49. Security Council Resolution S/228 of November 25, 1966.
50. UN Document S/PV.630, p. 14, para. 59.
51. Hutchison, *op. cit.*, p. 102.
52. UN Document S/PV.1320 & S/PV.1321 of November 16, 1966.
53. UN Document S/PV.635, p. 41.
54. *Ibid.*, pp. 41–42.
55. Hutchison, *op. cit.*, pp. 173–174.
56. Burns, *op. cit.*, pp. 173–174.
57. Horn, *op. cit.*, p. 96.
58. UN Document S/2157–Resolution 93 of May 18, 1951.
59. UN Document S/PV.630, para. 13.
60. *Ibid.*, para. 17.
61. *Ibid.*, para. 48.
62. *Ibid.*, para. 25; also UN Document S/3139/Rev. 2–Resolution No. 101 of November 24, 1953.
63. UN Document S/3251, para. 11.
64. UN Document S/3290, para. 8.
65. *Ibid.*, paras. 1–7 and Annex.
66. UN Document S/3516, Appendix I.
67. See UN Document S/3373 and A/2935, paras. 33–43; also UN Document S/3378–Resolution 106 of March 29, 1955.
68. UN Document S/3430, para. 2.
69. *Ibid*, para. 16.
70. UN Document S/3516, Appendix II.
71. *Ibid.*.
72. *Ibid.*, See also report in *The New York Times*, November 4, 1955.
73. UN Document S/3516, paras. 1–10; also UN Document S/3538–Resolution 111 of January 19, 1956.

74. UN Document S/3638, paras. 6–10.
75. UN Document S/3660, para. 6.
76. *Ibid.*
77. *Ibid.*, para. 2.
78. *Ibid.*, para. 7.
79. UN Document S/3685 & Corr. 1, paras. 1–21.
80. See General Assembly Resolutions Nos. 997(ES.I) to 1003(ES.I) and Nos. 1120(XI), 1123(XI) to 1125(XI).
81. UN Document S/5111–Resolution 171 of April 9, 1962.
82. UN Document S/5102, p. 40, para. 32.
83. UN Document S/6248 of March 19, 1965.
84. See UN Document S/6390 of May 28, 1965.
85. See UN Document S/6898 of November 11, 1965.
86. See UN Document S/7412 of July 18, 1968.
87. Security Council Resolution S/228 of November 25, 1966.
88. See UN Document S/7843 of April 7, 1967.
89. From an *Editorial* in *Sign* magazine, December 1953.
90. Excerpts from Diary of Moshe Sharett, published in *Ma'ariv* (Hebrew) newspaper and reproduced in *Jerusalem Post* (Israel), October 31, 1965.
91. Von Horn, *op. cit.*, pp. 282–283.

Chapter IX—UN Efforts for Settlement.

1. UN Document A/648–Report of Mediator, paras. 5–6.
2. Menuhin, *op. cit.*, 129–130.
3. UN Document A/648, p. 14.
4. UN Resolution 194(III) of December 11, 1948.
5. UN Document A/SPC/SR.433 of October 19, 1965.
6. UN Resolution 394(V) of December 14, 1950.
7. UN Document A/927 of June 21, 1949.
8. *Ibid.*, para. 10 and annex.
9. *Ibid.*, paras. 24–29.
10. *Ibid.*, paras. 32–33.
11. UN Official Records of First Committee of Third Session, November 23 and 29, 1948.
12. See Nineteenth Progress Report of the Palestine Conciliation Commission No. A/4921 of October 13, 1961.
13. Israeli Government Yearbook 1950, pp. 140–142.
14. UN Resolution 273(III) of May 11, 1949.
15. Israeli Government Yearbook 1950, pp. 43–45.
16. Trusteeship Council Resolution No. 114(II) of December 9, 1949.
17. Ben Gurion, *op. cit.*, p. 362.
18. Ben Gurion, *op. cit.*, pp. 227, 232.
19. As quoted in the *Jewish Observer and Middle East Review*, Vol. IV, No. 18, May 6, 1955, p. 3.
20. Ben Gurion, *op. cit.*, p. 247.

Chapter X—The Arab Refugee Problem

1. UN Document A/4121.
2. UN Document A/3686.
3. UN Document A/SPC/PV.199, p. 26.
4. UN Document A/5813–UNRWA Report 1963–1964, pp. 1–4.
5. UN Document A/6013–UNRWA Report 1964–1965, pp. 4–5.
6. UN Document A/6313–UNRWA Report 1965–1966, p. 3, para. 5.
7. For further information, see Chapter XVI.
8. UN Document A/5813, p. 5, para. 21.
9. UN Document Supplement No. 13 (A/33/13)–UNRWA Report 1977–1978, p. 1.
10. See Hadawi, Sami, *Palestinian Rights and Losses in 1948* (London: Saqi Books Publishers, 1988).
11. UN Document A/SPC/SR.437 of October 26, 1965, pp. 3–4.
12. UN Document 442 of November 2, 1965, p. 5.
13. UN Document A/SPC/L.116.
14. UN Document A/SPC/SR.456 of November 18, 1965, p. 2.
15. For details of laws on indemnification, reparation and restitution, enacted by the Allied Nations after the surrender of Nazi Germany, see Appendix.
16. UN Document A/SPC/SR.457 of November 19, 1965, pp. 6–7.
17. UN Document GA/AH/356 of November 22, 1955.

18. UN Press Release PAL/861; UNRWA Newsletter, February 1961.
19. *Israeli Yearbook 1950*, pp. 44–45.
20. UN Document A/3931, para. 4.
21. Toynbee, *op. cit.*, Vol. VIII, p. 290.
22. From a lecture and subsequent debate between Professor Toynbee and Israeli ambassador at McGill University, Montreal, January 1961.
23. *Jewish Newsletter*, December 1, 1958.
24. Ibid., December 1, 1958 and December 14, 1959.
25. See Halim Barakat and Peter Dodd, *Refugees: Uprootedness and Exile*, A sociological field study on the June Refugees, Institute for Palestine Studies, Beirut, 1968.
26. Security Council Resolution 237 of June 14, 1967 and General Assembly Resolution 2252(ES–V) of July 4, 1967.
27. UN Resolution 2252(ES–V) of July 4, 1967.
28. *The Times*, London, July 27, 1967.
29. UN Resolution 3236(XXIX) of November 22, 1974.

Chapter XI—The Minority

1. Jewish Agency for Palestine, *Statements and Memoranda*, 71–72.
2. Israeli government, *Laws of State of Israel*, (English Edition) Vol. I. Ordinances, 1948, p. 5.
3. *Statistical Abstract of Israel 1967*, p. 19.
4. Zogby, James J. (Ed.), *Perspectives on Palestinian Arabs and Israeli Jews*, an A.A.U.G. Publication Series No. 7 (1977). See article on *The Arabs of Israel*, by Tawfiq Zayyad, pp. 46–58.
5. Schwarz, *op. cit.*, p. 119. Emphasis in the original.
6. *Statements and Memoranda* (Jerusalem 1947), p. 43.
7. Laws of state of Israel 1948, p. 5.
8. Israel government, *Collection of Regulations 1949*, pp. 169–170.
9. Peretz, *op. cit.*, pp. 95–96.
10. *State of Israel Laws*, Vol. II, pp. 70–77.
11. Text published in *Middle East Journal* (Washington D.C.), Vol. VIII, No. 3, Summer 1953, pp. 358–360.
12. From an article entitled *How Israel Treats Her Arabs*, published in *American Mercury* magazine, August 1957.
13. Quoted by Peretz, *op. cit.*, p. 172.
14. From an article entitled *We Accuse*; published in the Hebrew paper Haaretz, January 14, 1955.
15. From an article entitled *The Arabs Among Us*, published in the Hebrew Newspaper, *Haaretz*, January 14, 1955.
16. *Israeli Government Yearbook 1952*, pp. 207–210.
17. UN Resolution 181(II) of November 29, 1947, Chapter 3, Para. 1.
18. Peretz, *op. cit.*, p. 125.
19. *Haaretz*, April 3, 1953.
20. *American Mercury* magazine, August 1957.
21. *Ner* magazine, September/October 1953.
22. *Jewish Newsletter*, April 15, 1957.
23. *Haaretz*, April 11, 1957. For a detailed description of the trial on court records, see Jiryes, *op. cit.*, pp. 9–61.
24. *Jewish Newsletter*, July 8, 1958.
25. *New York Herald Tribune*, February 27, 1959.
26. See Tawfiq Zayyat, *op. cit.*, pp. 51–58.
27. *The Christian Century* magazine, January 13, 1954.
28. From a speech delivered at Mishkan Israel Synagogue, New Haven, on November 27, 1959 (See *Jewish Newsletter*, November 30, 1959).

Chapter XII—Repatriation and Compensation

1. UN Document A/1775 (Supplement No. 20), p. 24.
2. UN Document A/AC.25/W.81./Rev. 2, Annex II.
3. UN Document A/AC.25/W.81./Rev. 2, Annex I.
4. See UN Document No. A/1985, pp. 11–13.
5. UN Document A/1985, p. 5.
6. Peretz, *op. cit.*, pp. 250–251.
7. *Ibid.*, p. 180.
8. *Ibid.*, p. 181.
9. UN Resolution 181(II) of November 29, 1947, Part I, Chapter 2, Article 8, Section C and Chapter 4(1).

10. Universal Declaration of Human Rights, Article 17(2). Adopted by the General Assembly on December 10, 1948.
11. UN Document A/AC.25/W.84 of April 28, 1964.
12. UN Document A/2699.

Chapter XIII—Violation of Human Rights

1. *The Shahak Report,* by Israel Shahak, Chairman of the Israeli League for Human and Civil Rights in Tel-Aviv, February 15, 1973. Published by the Free Palestine, P.O. Box 21096, Washington, D.C..
2. Resolution adopted at its 22nd International Convention of November 10, 1973.
3. Resolution 3092-A(XXVIII) of December 7, 1973.
4. Resolution 2252(ES-V) of July 4, 1967.
5. Resolution 2431B(XXII) of December 19, 1967.
6. Resolution 2443(XXIII) of December 19, 1968.
7. UN Document E/CN.4/SR.10/2 of February 28, 1969.
8. First Report—UN Document A/8389 of September 17, 1971; Second Report—UN Document A/8828 of October 9, 1972.
9. Resolution 2546(XXIV) of December 11, 1969.
10. See Resolutions Nos. 2546(XXIV) of December 11, 1969; 2675(XXV) of December 9, 1970; 2727(XXV) of December 15, 1970; 2792C(XXVI) of December 6, 1971; 2851(XXVI) of December 20, 1971; 2963C(XXVIII) of December 13, 1972; 3005(XXVIII) of December 15, 1972; 3092B(XXVIII) of December 7, 1973; 3240A-C(XXIX) of November 29, 1974; 3525A-D(XXX) of December 15, 1975; and 33/113A-C of December 18, 1978.
11. See Resolutions Nos. 6(XXIV) of February 27, 1968; 6(XXV) of March 4, 1969; 10(XXVI) of March 23, 1970; 9(XXVII) of March 15, 1971; 3(XXVIII) of March 22, 1972; 4(XXIX) of March 14, 1973; and Resolution of February 11, 1974.
12. Resolution No. 3(XXVIII) of March 23, 1972.
13. UN Press Release No. UNESCO/NYO/74–12B of December 2, 1974.
14. Resolution No. WHA/24/33 of May 18, 1971.
15. *The Globe and Mail* (Toronto), September 23, 1977.
16. See Article by Israeli Lawyer Felicia Langer, published in booklet *Perspectives on Palestinian Arabs and Israeli Jews,* (Illinois; Wilmette Medina Press, 1977), p. 62.
17. *Ibid.,* pp. 61–62.
18. *Ibid.,* p. 63.
19. *Ibid.,* pp. 64–65.

Chapter XIV—Racism and Racial Discrimination

1. UN Resolution No. 1904(XVIII) of November 20, 1963.
2. UN Resolution No. 2106(XX) of December 21, 1965.
3. UN Document A/PV.2400 of November 10, 1975, p. 117.
4. *Ibid.,* p. 27.
5. UN Resolution No. 3379(XXX) of November 10, 1975.
6. See Article by Donald Will—*The UN, Zionism and Racism,* published in *The Link,* Vol. 8, No. 5, Winter 1975–1976, pp. 4–9.
7. UN Document A/PV.2400, p. 42.
8. *The Toronto Star,* November 11, 1975.
9. UN Document A/PV.2400, pp. 152 and 153–155.
10. *The Toronto Star,* June 5, 1976.
11. Peretz, *op. cit.,* p. 125.
12. Rackman, and Emmanuel, *Israel's Emerging Constitution,* p. 155.
13. *Jewish Newletter,* May 12, 1952.
14. Ghilan, Maxim, *How Israel Lost its Soul,* p. 178. All quoted from *The Land of Promise,* by Abdelwahab M. Elmessiri, (New Brunswick, N.J.: North American, Inc., 1977), p. 148.

Chapter XV—Terrorism

1. See Cmd.6873—*White Paper Relating to Acts of Violence* dated July 24, 1946; also section titled Jewish Agency Directs Violence in Chapter V.
2. See *A Survey of Palestine 1945–1946,* vol. I, pp. 58–83; also *Crime and No Punishment,* by Sami Hadawi (Beirut: Palestine Research Center, 1972). For a comprehensive record of The Roots of Violence in the Middle East, see *The Gun and the Olive Branch,* by David Hirst (London: Faber and Faber, 1977).
3. The incident came to light in 1960, and became known as "The Lavon Affair." See article by Rev. Humphrey Walz, published in the *Jewish Newsletter* March 6, 1961.
4. *The Daily Star* (Beirut), October 13, 1972.

5. *Evening Star* (Auckland, New Zealand), July 2, 1975.
6. Koestler, *op. cit.*, p. 139.
7. Article by Correspondent Juan de Onis in the *International Herald Tribune*, September 12, 1972.
8. *Ibid.*

Chapter XVI—The Palestine Resistance Movement

1. *Sunday Times* (London), June 15, 1969.
2. *Fateh*, Beirut, January 1, 1970. (Quoted from Lehn, *op. cit.*, p. 19).
3. See *The Link* (Published by Americans for Middle East Understanding), Vol. II, Number 1, Spring 1978.
4. U.N. Resolution No. A/RES/3210(XXIX) of October 14, 1974.
5. General Assembly Records of XXIX Session, November 13, 1974.
6. UN Resolution 3237(XXIX) of November 22, 1974.
7. Taken from documents and statements of the Palestine National Council, published by the PLO Palestine Information Office, 1326 18th Street, N.W., Washington D.C., 20036.
8. The material in this section was taken from a study by Rashid Hamid, published under the title *What is the PLO?* in the Journal of Palestine Studies, Vol. IV, No. 4, Summer 1975, Issue 16, pp. 90–105.
9. See Tibawi, Visions of the Return: The Palestine Arab Refugees in Arabic Poetry, *Middle East Journal*, Vol. XVII, 1963, p. 523.

Chapter XVII—The Arab Boycott Of Israel

1. *The Middle East Economic Digest*, January 16, 1976, p. 4.
2. For a comprehensive discussion of the Arab Boycott of Israel, see booklet by Sami Hadawi, published by the Arab Information Center in Ottawa, Canada.
3. From article entitled The Arab Boycott: An Instrument of Peaceful Self-Defence—*Arab Report*, January 15, 1976.
4. *Cmd. 3686*—Sir John Hope-Simpson Report dated October 20, 1930.
5. *The New York Times*, August 7, 1933, 4:3.
6. *The Toronto Star*, February 4, 1977.

Chapter XVIII—Israel Policy of Expansion

1. Kirk, George E., *A Short History of the Middle East*, (London: Methuen Press, 1948), pp. 156–157.
2. Ionides, Michael, *Divide and Lose: The Arab Revolt*, (London: Geoffrey Bles, 1960), p. 43.
3. Lowenthal, Marvin, (Trans.) *The Diaries of Theodor Herzl*, (New York: Dial Press, 1956), p. 124.
4. Patai, Raphael (Ed.), *The Complete Diaries of Theodor Herzl*, (New York: Herzl Press, 1960), Vol. 2, p. 711.
5. Rabinowicz, Oskar K., *A Jewish Cyprus Project*, (New York: Herzl Press, 1962), p. 17.
6. Halpern, Ben, *The Idea of the Jewish State*, (Cambridge: Harvard University Press, 1961), pp. 303–304.
7. *Ibid.*,
8. ESCO Foundation for Palestine, Inc., *Palestine: A Study of Jewish, Arab and British Policies*, (New Haven: Yale University Press, 1947), Vol. II, p. 268.
9. *Cmd. 6019*: Statement of Policy (MacDonald White Paper, 1939).
10. ESCO Foundation, *op. cit.*, pp. 1084–1085.
11. *Ibid.*, p. 1087.
12. Taylor, Alan, *Prelude to Israel*, (New York: The Philosophical Library, 1959), pp. 60–61.
13. United States, *Foreign Relations of the U.S.: Near East & Africa*, (Washington, D.C., 1964), Vol. IV, pp. 776–777.
14. Morton, Geoffrey J., *Just the Job*, (London: Hodder and Stoughton, 1957), p. 156.
15. Kirk, *op. cit.*, pp. 186–187.
16. *Ibid.*
17. Israeli government *Yearbook 1951–1952*, p. 64; and *Yearbook 1952*, pp. 63 & 65. (Emphasis added).
18. From a speech delivered at a meeting of *Mapai* Party in Beersheba in 1952.
19. From a statement broadcast on the Arabic program, Israeli Radio, February 12, 1952.
20. From a statement made in the Israeli Parliament on October 12, 1955. (Emphasis added).
21. *The New York Times*, January 25, 1956.
22. Joseph, Dov, *op. cit.*, pp. 322–323.
23. For text of communique, see U.S. Policy in the Middle East Documents, (Washington D.C.: Department of State, 1957), pp. 135–136.

24. *Jewish Observer*, November 9, 1956.
25. Burns, E.L.M., *op. cit.*, p. 180.
26. *The New York Times*, November 8, 1956. (Emphasis added).
27. *Ibid.*
28. UN Document A/3354—Resolution No. 997(ES–1).
29. Radio and Television Statement of February 20, 1957, DSP.6505, pp. 301–307.
30. Burns, *op. cit.*, p. 243.
31. UN Document S/1044—Decision adopted at 367th meeting.
32. UN Document S/1070—Resolution No. 61 of November 4, 1948.
33. UN Document A/1264/Rev. 1, p. 11.
34. See Article by Eric Rouleau, J.F. Held and S. Lacoutre, on *Israel et les Arabes: Le 3eme Combat*, (Paris: Editions de Seuil), pp. 73, 176. Also, John S. Badeau, The Arabs 1967, in *Atlantic Monthly*, December 1967, p. 108.
35. Dept. of State Bulletin, June 12, 1967, pp. 870–871.
36. See Fisher-Bassioume, *Storm Over the Arab World*, pp. 350–351.
37. UN Document A/SPC/PV.505 of November 8, 1966.
38. *The Washington Post*, May 23, 1967.
39. From an Israeli Radio Broadcast on June 5, 1967.
40. *The New York Times*, June 5, 1967.
41. Statement made before the Security Council on June 5, 1967.
42. From an Israeli Radio broadcast from Jerusalem on June 5, 1967.
43. UPI Despatch, June 17, 1967.
44. From an interview with *Der Spiegel*. Reported in *Jerusalem Post*, July 10, 1967.
45. UPI Despatch, June 17, 1967.
46. From an interview on West German television, July 5, 1967.
47. *The New York Times*, June 19, 1967.
48. *Reuter* dispatch, August 14, 1967.
49. *The Daily Star* (Beirut), September 19, 1967.
50. *UPI* dispatch, June 10, 1967.
51. From a statement made on June 12, 1967.
52. *UPI* dispatch, June 19, 1967.
53. *The Christian Science Monitor*, July 7, 1967.
54. *The Guardian* (London), August 11, 1967.
55. From statements on CBS Face the Nation.
56. *UPI* dispatch, August 9, 1967.
57. Quoted in *The Daily Star* (Beirut), February 22, 1968.
58. For contraventions against the 1949 Geneva Conventions, see *Israel and the Geneva Conventions*, published by the Institute for Palestine Studies, Beirut, 1968.
59. *Penthouse*, May 1976, pp. 54, 56, 58, 137, and 141–147.
60. *Penthouse*, June 1976, pp. 60, 62, 64, 147–148, and 150–151.
61. Pearson, Anthony, *Conspiracy in Silence: Attack on the USS Liberty*, (London: Quartet Books, 1978).
62. See book review by Peter Mansfield in Middle East International, September 1978, (A CAABU—London—Publication).

Chapter XIX—Israel And The United States

1. U.S. Resolution No. 31, 86th Congress, 1st Session, June 15, 1959, p. 57.
2. *Holiday* magazine, March 1963.
3. From an article by Fred V. Winnett entitled *Why the West should stop supporting Israel*, published in *McGill Magazine* (Montreal), January 18, 1958.
4. Statement made in a commentary on CBS News on March 7, 1973 and reported in the *Christian Science Monitor*, March 9, 1973. See also Chapter XV on Terrorism, particularly the part dealing with Western attitudes.
5. Letter by Hasan Abdullah, of Chicago, published in *The New York Times*, December 13, 1973.
6. Statement issued as a press release from the White House on May 23, 1967—Dept. of State Bulletin dated June 12, 1967, p. 871.
7. U.S./UN Press Release dated May 24, 1967—Dept. of State Bulletin dated June 12, 1967, pp. 872–873.
8. Resolutions: No. 2253(ES-V) of July 4, 1967, and No. 2254(ES-V) of July 14, 1967—UN Document A/6798, p. 4.
9. From an article entitled *Profit from U.S. Relief Funds* published in *Brief*—A publication of the American Council of Judaism, October 1965.
10. *Jerusalem Post* (Israel), September 13, 1965.
11. *Jewish Newsletter*, November 30, 1959.

12. Menuhin, *op. cit.*, p. 367.
13. U.S. Congressional Record, 85th Congress, 2nd Session, July 18, 1958.

Chapter XX—United Nations Peace Efforts And Failures
1. Resolution 2799(XXVI) of December 13, 1970.
2. Resolution 2535B(XXIV) of December 10, 1969.
3. Resolution 2672C(XXV) of December 8, 1970.
4. Resolution 3070(XXVIII) of November 30, 1973.
5. Resolution 2949(XXVII) of December 8, 1972. See also Resolutions 3005(XXVII) and 2963(XXVII) of 1972.
6. Security Council Records, S/PV. 1717 of June 6, 1973, p. 27.
7. *Ibid.*, pp. 31–32.
8. Israeli Newspaper *Maariv*, January 6, 1973.
9. Security Council Records, S/PV. 1717, p. 36.
10. Security Council Records, S/PV. 1718 of June 7, 1973.
11. Security Council Records, S/PV. 1718 pp. 33–35, 36–37.
12. *Ibid.*, S/PV. 1719, p. 17.
13. *Ibid.*, pp. 60–61.
14. Security Council draft Resolution No. S/10974 of July 24, 1973.
15. Resolution 3375(XXX) of November 10, 1975.
16. Resolution 3376(XXX) of November 10, 1975.
17. Official Records of the General Assembly, Thirty-First Session, Supplement No. 35, Document A/31/35.
18. See UN Document ST/SG/SER.F/2, pp. 37–38.
19. Official Records of the General Assembly, Thirty-First Session, Plenary Meetings, Vol. II, 66th meeting, paras. 2, 4, 6, 13, 27, 33.
20. Document S/PV.1924, p. 26.
21. Official Records of Security Council, 31st Session, Supplement for April, May and June 1976. Document S/12119.
22. Document S/PV.1938, p. 62.
23. Document S/PV.2041, p. 8.
24. *Ibid.*, p. 11.
25. Resolution 31/20 of November 24, 1976.
26. Resolution 32/40 of December 15, 1977.
27. Resolution 32/40B of December 2, 1977.
28. UN Document ST/SG/SER.F/1 (1978). See Chapter V.
29. UN Document ST/SG/SER.F/1 Part II (1978). Dealt with at some length in preceding pages of this Chapter.
30. See UN Document ST/SG/SER.F/2 (1978).
31. Resolution No. 33/112 of December 18, 1978, Section A, para. 1.
32. *Ibid.*, Section F, paras. 1–3.

Chapter XXI—Palestine Between War and Peace
1. *International Herald Tribune*, January 18, 1979.
2. *The New York Times*, January 12, 1979.
3. *International Herald Tribune*, March 21, 1979.
4. *Ibid.*, March 17–18, 1979.
5. *The New York Times*, November 8, 1956.
6. UN Document A/927 of June 21, 1949.

Chapter XXII—After Camp David
1. Amnon Kapeliouk, *The New Outlook*, August/September 1982. (Quoted from *The Fateful Triangle* by Noam Chomsky, p. 202).
2. Claudia Wright, *New Statesman*, August 20, 1982: *In These Times*, September 8, 1982. (Quoted from *The Fateful Triangle* by Noam Chomsky).
3. *Middle East International*, August 20, 1982, p. 12.
4. Tony Clifton & Catherine Leroy, *God Cried*, (London & New York: Quartet Books, Ltd., 1983, pp. 45–47.
5. Report of the *International Red Cross*, p. 176.
6. Amon Kapeliouk, *Sabra and Chatila*, pp. 93–94.
7. George Ball, *Error and Betrayal in Lebanon*, (Foundation for Middle East Peace, Washington D.C., 1984), p. 57.
8. Secretariat of the League of Arab States, *Israeli Settlements*, (Published by Dar Al-Afaq Al-Jadidah, 1988), pp. 48–49.

9. *Le Monde*, July 3, 1982.
10. Yehoshafat Harkabi, *Israel's Fateful Decisions*, (London: I.B. Tauris, 1988).
11. Arab News (Saudi Arabia), *The Other Wall*, January 29, 1986.
12. Cheryl Rubenberg, *Israel and the American National Interest*. (Quoted from Report No. 52 of the American Jewish Alternatives to Zionism, p. 22).
13. Paul Findley, *They Dare to Speak Out*, (Westport, Conn.: Lawrence Hill & Co., 1985), p. 274.

Chapter XXIII—The Uprising and Beyond
1. *The Washington Post*, December 27, 1987.
2. DataBase Project on Palestinian Human Rights, Chicago, Illinois.
3. From translation in Joel Brinkley's "Ex-Israeli Officers Ask Deal on Peace: Former Military Figures Say the Occupation Is Hurting the Nation's Security." *The New York Times*, May 31, 1988. (Quoted from "Without Prejudice: The International Review of Racial Discrimination," by EAFORD, Vol. I, No. 2, pp. 93–94.
4. *Palestine Perspectives* (Washington), No. 36, July/August 1988, p. 7.
5. Paul Findley, *They Dare to Speak Out*, (Westport, Conn.: Lawrence Hill & Co., 1985), p. 274.
6. Memo by Julius Berman, published in *Without Prejudice*, an EAFORD International Review of Racial Discrimination publication, Vol. II, No. 1, 1988, pp. 147–149.

Appendix
1. Robinson, Nehemiah, *Idemnification and Reparations (Jewish Aspects)*, (New York: Institute of Jewish Affairs of the American-Jewish Congress and World Jewish Congress, 1944).
2. Reference is made to these agreements in a letter to the UN Palestine Conciliation Commission of November 22, 1949, from the Chairman of the UN Economic Survey Commission. Also, a discussion of these agreements may be found in *Idemnification and Reparations*, by Nehemiah Robinson, Annex 2, 1946, pp. 157–162.
3. This law was published in German and English in *Rückerstatungsgesetz*, by H.G. van Koblenz, 1949.
4. This law was published in English by the IRA Documentation Branch, IRO/LEG/LS/5 of November 3, 1949.

Index

ABOUT THE AUTHOR

Sami Hadawi is a Palestinian scholar who was born in Jerusalem in 1904. He was official land valuer and in charge of land taxation under the British mandate over Palestine. In 1943, he was awarded the M.B.E. for "Outstanding Service". After termination of the mandate, he served in the Jordan government, as Chief of Inland Land Revenue, then as Land Specialist to the UN Palestine Conciliation Commission in New York, and was entrusted with the task of identifying and evaluating Arab property in the Israeli occupied part of Palestine. In 1956, he established with a fellow Palestinian a Palestine Arab Refugee office in New York and served as Advisor on Palestine Affairs to the Iraq Mission to the United Nations; in 1969 he joined the staff of the Information Center of the League of Arab States in New York and served as Advisor on Palestine Affairs to the Yemen Mission to the United Nations; in 1960 he established an Arab Information Center in Dallas, Texas, and in 1965 transferred as Director of the newly established Institute of Palestine Studies in Beirut. He retired from active service in 1968. His many books and pamphlets include *Palestine: Loss of a Heritage* (1963), *Bitter Harvest* (1967, 1979 and 1989), co-author of the *Palestine Diary 1914–1948* (1970), *Village Statistics Indicating a Classification and Ownership of Land in 1945* (1970); and *Palestinian Rights and Losses in 1948* (1988).